VOLUNTEER MANAGEMENT

Mobilizing All the Resources Of the Community

SECOND EDITION

Written by
Steve McCurley & Rick Lynch

Volunteer Management *is a proven invaluable tool that should be on the bookshelf of every Volunteer Program Manager*

Published by INTERPUB GROUP
Knowledge Dissemination, Publishing, Consulting

VOLUNTEER MANAGEMENT
Mobilizing All the Resources of the Community

Second Edition

Published by INTERPUB GROUP CORPORATION
1080 MILITARY TURNPIKE, SUITE 3
PLATTSBURGH NY 12901
www.interpubgroup.com
info@interpubgroup.com
1-800-501-6431

PRINTED SIMULTANEOUSLY IN THE U.S. AND CANADA

10 9 8 7 6 5 4

All INTERPUB GROUP titles are available at special discounts for bulk quantity purchases. Please contact us for details and to order.

Introduction to the 2nd Edition

This is the 2nd edition of *Volunteer Management* published in North America. Since its original publication in 1996 *Volunteer Management* has been the most widely utilized text on managing a volunteer program in the world, with companion editions published in the United Kingdom (Directory for Social Change, 1998), the Ukraine (Gurt Resource Center, 1999) and Taiwan (Living Psychology Publishers, 2000). Over 50,000 volunteer program managers have benefited from the original work.

This 2nd edition has been updated and expanded while still retaining much of the core information contained in the first edition.

Volunteer Management discusses the theory and practice of involving volunteers effectively within a structured organizational setting, primarily either a charitable or governmental agency or program. While the theory and methods discussed also apply to other types of volunteer settings (membership groups, small neighborhood associations, employee volunteer programs, etc.) the focus is on making volunteers operate effectively within an organization that delivers services to clients or the community.

Despite its size *Volunteer Management* is an overview of an extremely complex subject. Those wishing more information on particular aspects of working with volunteers should review the Bibliography provided in Appendix One that lists a small number of the thousands of recent works on volunteerism.

Volunteers can be an effective resource for program operation, both supplementing and extending the work of program staff. This, however, requires the application of management principles different from those utilized in managing paid employees. Volunteer Management is not a book about managing a program; instead it focuses on the element of connecting volunteers with an organization, concentrating on those unique aspects of working effectively with staff that do not receive a monetary salary. In many ways the managerial expertise required to involve these unpaid employees is far more sophisticated than that required to work with paid ones.

It can also be far more creative, and *Volunteer Management* is designed to provide the new and the experienced volunteer program manager with both basic knowledge and state of the art information, based on the more than 50 years of experience the authors have acquired in their work with thousands of volunteer programs.

Table of Contents

Chapter One
An Introduction To Volunteer Involvement

An Overview of Volunteer Activity

Volunteering has a long and pervasive tradition in North American history. Since the days of Alexis de Tocqueville, commentators have noted our penchant for forming voluntary groups of citizens to work on mutual problems and interests.

Currently, volunteering is one of the most commonplace activities in society. A 2005 study in the US by the Bureau of Labor Statistics found:

1. 65.4 million people volunteered for an organization between September 2004 and September 2005, 28.8% of the population. One-fourth of men and about one-third of women did volunteer work.

2. Persons age 35 to 44 were the most likely to volunteer (34.5%), closely followed by 45- to 54-year olds (32.7%). Teenagers had a high volunteer rate – 30.4%. Volunteer rates were lowest among persons in their early twenties (19.5%) and among those 65 and over (24.8%).

3. Whites volunteered at a higher rate (30.4%) than did blacks (22.1%) and Asians (20.7%). Among Hispanics or Latinos, 15.4% volunteered.

4. Married persons volunteered at a higher rate (34.1 percent) than never-married persons (23.0 percent) and persons of other marital statuses (23.1 percent).

5. Parents with children under age 18 were more likely to volunteer than persons without children, 37.0 percent compared with 25.5 percent.

6. Among employed persons, 31.3 percent had volunteered during the year ended in September 2005. The volunteer rates of persons who were unemployed (26.4 percent) or not in the labor force (24.4 percent) were lower. Among the employed, part-time workers were more likely than full-time workers to have participated in volunteer activities--38.2 versus 29.8 percent.

7. Volunteers spent a median of 50 hours on volunteer activities. This was down slightly from the level in three previous surveys. Men spent 52 hours volunteering and women spent 50 hours. Median annual hours spent on volunteer activities ranged from a high of 96 hours for volunteers age 65 and over to a low of 36 hours for those 16 to 19 and 25 to 34 years old.

8. Most volunteers were involved with one or two organizations--69.6 and 18.9 percent, respectively. Individuals with higher educational attainment were more likely to volunteer for multiple organizations than were individuals with less education. Parents also were more likely to volunteer for more than one organization than persons with no own children under age 18.

9. Older volunteers were more likely to work for religious organizations than were their younger counterparts. For example, 45.0 percent of volunteers age 65 and over performed volunteer activities mainly through or for a religious organization, compared with 27.5 percent of volunteers age 16 to 24 years. Younger individuals were more likely to volunteer through or for educational or youth service organizations.

10. Among volunteers with children under 18 years old, 45.2 percent of mothers and 36.1 percent of fathers volunteered mainly for an educational/ youth service-related organization, such as a school or sports team. Parents were more than twice as likely to volunteer for such organizations as persons with no children of that age--51.5 and 21.6 percent, respectively.

11. Conversely, volunteers with no children under 18 were considerably more likely to volunteer for some other types of organizations, such as hospitals or other health organizations and social or community service organizations.

12. Volunteers were able to report more than one activity that they had performed for their main organization. Fundraising was the most commonly reported activity (29.7 percent), followed by collecting, preparing, distributing, or serving food (26.3 percent), engaging in general labor or supplying transportation to people (22.5 percent), and tutoring or teaching (21.3 percent).

13. Two in five volunteers became involved with the main organization for which they did

volunteer work on their own initiative; that is, they approached the organization. A slightly larger proportion, almost 43 percent, was asked to volunteer, most often by someone in the organization.

14. Among those who had volunteered at some point in the past, the most common reason given for not volunteering in the year ended September 2005 was lack of time (45.6 percent), followed by health or medical problems (15.2 percent), and family responsibilities or childcare problems (9.3 percent). Lack of time was the most common reason for persons in all age groups except for those aged 65 and over, who reported health or medical problems as the primary reason.

Volunteering is also prevalent in other countries. The 2003 Home Office Citizenship Survey in the UK found that around 20.3 million people were engaged in active community participation, about 28% of the population. The 2000 Scottish Household Survey found a 27% volunteering rate. The 2000 NSGVP survey in Canada determined a 27% rate of volunteering and a survey by the Australian Bureau of Statistics in 2002 determined a 34% rate of volunteering. In each of these countries the patterns of volunteering are quite similar to those shown in the BLS survey above.

Most nonprofit organizations involve volunteers, but they involve them in very different ways. A survey by the Urban Institute in 2003 found:

" In 2000, approximately 215,000 charities filed Form 990 or 990EZ with the IRS, the form required of those charities with more than $25,000 in annual gross receipts. We learned that 81 percent of these charities – or an estimated 174,000 organizations – use volunteers in one way or another."

The ways in which volunteers were involved included:

56% Direct service, such as tutors or mentors
23% External administration (such as fundraising)
10% Indirect service (planting trees)
11% Internal Administration, such as filing and copying

Volunteer involvement is also common among religious institutions:

"...an estimated 83 percent of the nation's 380,000 congregations have some kind of social service, community development, or neighborhood organizing project. Although most congregations have social service outreach programs, most are involved as partners or sponsors and therefore do not manage volunteers themselves. However, one in three congregations – an estimated 129,000 such organizations – have responsibility for managing volunteers in social service outreach activities."

Reasons for Volunteering

Volunteers get involved for a variety of reasons. Among the most often cited are:

- "Wanted to help others."
- "Felt obligated to give back what I got."
- "Sense of civic duty."
- "Religious convictions."
- "Want to make a difference in the world."
- "Believed in the cause."

These altruistic reasons are also accompanied by some self-interest motivations:

- "Wanted to gain work experience and learn new skills."
- "Like meeting new friends and being involved."
- "Felt I could impress my employer and show leadership."
- "It made me feel needed."
- "Let me experience new life-styles and cultures."
- "Do it because my job is boring and this lets me have fun."

Many volunteers get involved for reasons having to do with their families:

- "Good way to spend time with my family."
- "Wanted to set an example for my children."
- "Had to get involved so that my children would have the benefit of the program."
- "Wanted to pay back help that members of my family received."

A typical volunteer will experience a variety of motivations, ranging from the purely altruistic to the highly self-interested, and these motivations may change through the volunteering "career." Volunteers will see their motivation vary considerably from organization to organization and even over time within a single organization.

Volunteers also seem to derive some direct personal benefits from volunteering. A 2004 survey of volunteers in the UK's Make a Difference Day events found:

- nearly half of all volunteers say volunteering has improved their physical health and fitness
- 25% of people who volunteer more than five time a year say volunteering has helped them lose weight
- 22% of 18 to 24-year olds say volunteering help them cut down on alcohol use
- 9% of men and 8% of women say that volunteering has improved their sex life
- 65% of 25 to 34-year olds say volunteering helps them feel less stressed

The pattern of a volunteer's connection with an organization or cause will also vary. The "typical" volunteer in the United States is involved with two organizations at any one time, which tend to change over the years. Some volunteers, however, are dedicated to or involved with a single cause and might spend hundreds of hours a year working on that effort.

Volunteers also vary in the length of time they stay with an organization. Some volunteers prefer to work with many organizations, changing from group to group within the course of a single year. Others are committed to a specific cause, remaining with that group for years or even decades.

A well-run volunteer program attempts to develop opportunities for all of these styles of involvement.

Understanding Volunteer Motivations

Willie Mosconi, perhaps the greatest pool player of all time, was once asked how he was able to shoot pool so well, moving balls to precise positions on the table. His answer was, "it's easy; it's all done with little circles."

Oddly enough, the same might be said about understanding volunteer motivations, and about seeing some of the opportunities and dangers in volunteer involvement.

Understanding volunteer motivations is a key skill for good Volunteer Program Managers. Knowing why people do what they do is a necessity in helping them fulfill those motivations as well as predicting some places where the motivations might cause difficulties.

It All Starts with Three Little Circles...

The three circles illustrated in the diagram show you the primary motivational circles with which a volunteer program is concerned.

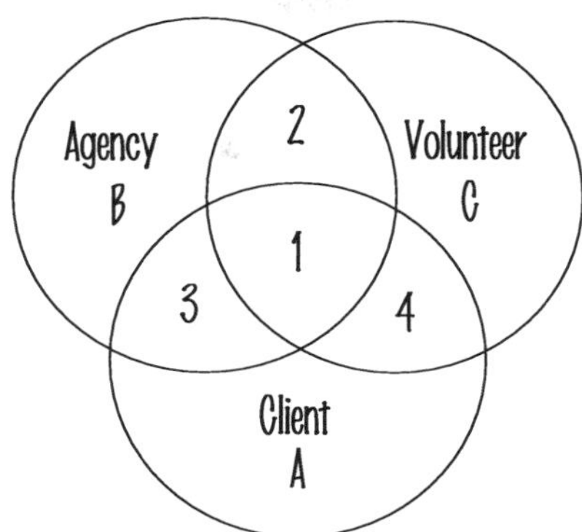

These circles represent the following:

- *Circle A: The Client*

This circle represents the needs and wishes of the client whom the agency wishes to serve. The client might be an individual, another agency, or the community at large, but within the circles are all the various requirements that the client needs filled, all the problems for which the client needs a solution, and all the difficulties for which the client needs help. These may range from immediate survival needs to long-range developmental needs. Some of these needs may even be unknown to the client, such as opportunities for improvement that the client has never considered.

- *Circle B: The Agency*

This circle represents the range of services that the agency is engaged with. It also represents the operations of the agency as it maintains itself, including such items as fundraising and public relations. Within this circle are activities the agency needs done in order to maintain its existence and to do its work.

- *Circle C: The Volunteer*

This circle represents the individual motivational needs and aspirations of a potential volunteer. This may include anything from a basic desire to help others to a highly specific need such as learning computer skills in order to get a paid job.

These three circles together represent the basic motivational universe with which the Volunteer Program Manager has to contend. Success lies in putting the circles together so as to maximize the ability of each participant to achieve as many of their motivational needs as is safely possible. To understand this, we have to look at the areas of possible overlap of the circles.

...And The Places They Overlap

The circles may overlap in various combinations including overlap of all three parties, or overlap of any two. Each of the four numbered sub-areas of overlap on the diagram represents something different to the smart Volunteer Program Manager.

- *Overlap #1: The Perfect Match*

The area of overlapped labeled #1 represents an opportunity for a perfect volunteer job. It shows that the client has an area of need which falls within the type of services offered by the agency and which also falls within the motivational range of a particular volunteer (i.e., is a job which the volunteer would want to do because it in turn satisfies some of the volunteer's motivational needs). Common examples of positions of this type are tutoring and mentoring, delivery of meals to clients, and other types of jobs in which volunteer personally deliver core agency services directly to clients.

If you are just beginning a volunteer program, this is an excellent area in which to start developing volunteer positions, since it allows volunteers to easily satisfy their own needs while directly contributing to the central mission of the agency.

- *Overlap #2: Still a Good Match*

The area of overlap labeled #2 also represents a fruitful area for volunteer involvement, although of a different sort. As you will notice, area #2 does not directly overlap with the client's needs, but does show an overlap between the needs of the agency and that of a potential volunteer. Since two of the parties involved can be satisfied, this still represents a good area for volunteer jobs. Examples are those in which the volunteer actually views the agency as a "client," such as helping in the office, assisting staff with research projects, etc. These jobs in turn enable the agency to assist clients, but only in an indirect way.

While these jobs are productive, they usually require the Volunteer Program Manager to work a bit harder in order to demonstrate to a volunteer that they are really contributing to meeting needs. This can be done either by making sure that the volunteer continually sees the eventual impact of their work within the agency on outside clients, or in making the staff with whom the volunteer works show their own gratitude for the assistance they are receiving.

- *Overlap #3, A Slice of Potential*

Overlap #3 shows the conjunction of an agency need and the client's need, but no overlap with the potential volunteer. This is an area which indicates possible expansion of the volunteer program, probably first by exploring with staff the creation of new volunteer jobs in this area and then by recruiting volunteers with additional skills or interests who could fill these new jobs.

- *Overlap #4, The Danger Zone*

Area of overlap #4 is a very interesting motivational area, one that explains why some "good" volunteers do the wrong things.

Look at it this way: area #4 shows that the volunteer has a motivational need focused on the client, who also has a motivational need, but whose need is outside the range of agency services/needs.

A common example of the danger represented by these slightly overlapping motivational areas would be the client of a Meals on Wheels program who also needs some home repair work done. Home repair is not done by the Meals on Wheels agency, i.e., it is outside its motivational circle. It is, however, clearly needed by the client and this is noted by the volunteer that delivers food for the Meals on Wheels agency. Since the volunteer's motivational needs encompass the home repair function (the volunteer is motivated to give *whatever* help is necessary to meet the needs of the client and has the skill to meet them in this case), the volunteer may want to expand the volunteer job to include home repair services, despite the fact that it is clearly outside the scope of the Meals on Wheels program. In this case the motivational need of the volunteer to help "my" clients outweighs the interest of the Meals on Wheels program in the mind of the volunteer.

The only way to stop this impromptu job expansion is to assure the volunteer that some method for meeting the need of the client will be devised (such as referral to another agency that does home repair). The fascinating thing about this is that the stronger the volunteers are motivated to help the client the more likely they are to go outside the boundaries of agency restraints, since their primary focus will be on meeting the needs of the client, not of the agency. In some cases volunteers will be so highly motivated that no attempt to restrain them to activities within the purview of agency operations can be successful, and the only alternative is to separate the volunteer from the agency. You can read more about this phenomenon in Chapter Ten.

Changing Styles of Volunteer Involvement

Volunteering now appears to be going through some changes related to the "style" in which people choose to participate. In some ways we seem to be moving toward a system in which there are at least two distinct types of volunteers:

The Long-Term Volunteer

The first type might be called the long-term volunteer. This type of volunteer is probably the traditional model that most of us think of when we hear the word "volunteer."

The long-term volunteer matches the common notion of the volunteer who is dedicated to a cause or a group. Among the characteristics of the long-term volunteer are the following:

- Dedication to a cause or an organization. The long-term volunteer has a strong sense of affiliation with the volunteer effort and is connected to it in an "institutional" sense, i.e., considering him/herself an "owner" of the effort. Long-term volunteers often have a strong personal and psychological investment in their volunteer role and in the sense of personal worth and identity they gain from their participation.

- A long-term volunteer is commonly recruited in one of three ways: By "self-recruitment" (finding the organization on their own because of an already existing personal commitment to the cause), by growth from within (becoming increasingly connected over time), or by "cloning," that is, being brought to the organization because of a close connection to the existing circle of volunteers.

- Long-term volunteers will tend to shape their own job and determine the duration of their work, adapting their time and energies to whatever is necessary to make the cause succeed. Long-term volunteers tend to be "generalists," willing to do whatever type of work is required and willing to do work that is necessary to make the effort function but which is not always exciting or rewarding in itself.

- Motivation for the long-term volunteer is a matter of both "achievement" and "affiliation," and often recognition is best expressed as a greater opportunity for involvement or advancement in the cause or the organization.

Many established organizations have relied for years on long-term volunteers, designing jobs that require a steady donation of time over a prolonged period. In many cases these long-term volunteers were the actual "creators" of the organization for whom they continued volunteering, helping found a structure that they later "joined."

The primary supply for this type of volunteer has traditionally been middle and upper income housewives, who have had the free time to donate, who have been able to offer steady hours, and who have often utilized volunteering to give more meaning and significance to their lives, making it their equivalent of a successful career.

Of course, long-term volunteers are not drawn solely from this category. There are also many unemployed, retired, and lower income volunteers who contribute their time on a long-term basis.

The Short-Term Volunteer

During the past ten years, a different style of volunteering has begun to develop. For purposes of comparison, this style might be called that of the short-term volunteer. Among the characteristics of the short-term volunteer are:

- A general interest in an organization or cause, but usually not of extreme depth. Short-term volunteers are not "true believers" even though they support they cause. They do not usually view the organization or their involvement as a central part of their lives.

- Short-term volunteers are usually actively recruited to join the organization. This recruitment commonly happens through one of three methods:

They may connect with an organization because of a particular volunteer job in which they are interested, and it is the actual type of work that attracts them, not necessarily what the organization will try to accomplish through that work.

They may be recruited through participation in a specific event, such as a weekend sports program or race. It will usually be the type of event that attracts them, or the social activity that it allows, and not the organization or cause for whom the event is being conducted.

Or they may be recruited by "forced choice," being "asked" by a friend or employer to volunteer. Commonly they are volunteering for and because of their personal connection with the requester, not from any knowledge of or commitment to the organization or cause.

- Short-term volunteers want a well-defined job of limited duration. They want to know at the beginning of their volunteering what exactly they are being asked to do and for how long they are committing to do it. Many short-term volunteers can be considered "specialists," because they are only with the organization long enough to learn one job or are only willing to perform one kind of work. Usually the more limited the expected time commitment and the better delineated the scope of work, the easier it will be to recruit the short-term volunteer. Short-term volunteers may well volunteer throughout their lives, but they will tend not to remain too long with any single organization. Or they will only work on tasks that will allow them to closely control the extent of time that they donate to any one organization.

- Motivation for short-term volunteers is a matter of recognizing their personal achievement, not of recognizing their status within the group. Recognition is a matter of thanking them for their contribution and allowing them to move on.

Oddly enough, individuals may be a short-term volunteer with one group and a long-term volunteer with another group. And over the entire term of a relationship with a particular organization, volunteers will often shift styles periodically, based on other commitments in their lives or their relationship with the organization.

On balance, it seems there is a clear shift occurring toward a preference for being a short-term volunteer. In attempting to cope with competing demands from work, home, leisure activities, and other possibilities for involvement, potential volunteers are more often choosing to limit their participation by changing the way in which they to become involved.

There may well be a variety of styles of volunteer involvement or a variety of ways to describe how people go about volunteering.

Gaskin suggests the following stages of involvement:

- The *doubter* is outside volunteering, and may have attitudes, characteristics or circumstances that keep them a non-volunteer.

- The *starter* has entered volunteering by making an enquiry or application.

- The *doer* has committed to being a volunteer and begun volunteering.

- The *stayer* persists as a long-term volunteer.

Hustinx in a study of volunteers with the Flemish Red Cross, discovered the following patterns of styles of volunteering:

1. *Episodic Contributors:* those who volunteered only one or two times during the year, but who often continued volunteering over the course of several years in a recurrent basis (23% had been involved for more than ten years). These volunteers typically were involved in providing project or program assistance.

2. *Established Administrators:* those who volunteered on a regular basis, usually in a formal office with specialized job responsibilities.

3. *Reliable Co-Workers:* those involved on a fairly stable, regular and time-consuming basis, usually in assisting staff with activities.

4. *Service-Oriented Core Volunteers:* who participate on a regular basis, spending a significant amount of time, and are typically involved both in service provision and administrative tasks. Many of these volunteers were relatively new, with 65% having been involved for less than five years.

5. *Critical Key Figures:* those involved on an intense basis with critical leadership tasks and fundraising. Over 80% of them had been Red Cross volunteers for more than five years.

Within this pattern of styles, some volunteers tended to remain within a single style and others changed style over the years, typically by moving to higher levels of responsibility.

Implications of Changing Styles and Types of Volunteers

These changes have had an impact on volunteer

management in several ways:

They have necessitated major changes in job design and recruitment techniques. Organizations seeking volunteers have been forced to make jobs "smaller" and more manageable and to cater more to the requirements of the volunteer related to availability and duration. Jobs have in some cases had to become "simpler" to meet the abilities of relatively unskilled or inexperienced volunteers, and in some cases have become more complex to match the abilities of very skilled professionals donating their time. A study by Statistics Canada found:

"In 1997, more Canadians volunteered than ten years earlier, but they did so for shorter periods of time. This suggests that voluntary groups may want to consider restructuring their volunteer opportunities differently. This could mean shorter, more task-oriented assignments, or, perhaps, changing the nature of the placements so as to include other family members. Family volunteering can stretch the precious time of volunteers if tasks are designed so that the entire family can take part."

In a similar report the Institute for Volunteering Research in the UK noted:

"Flexibility is given top priority by young people, especially in respect of flexible work and working times for volunteering. The young have many pressures and demands on them and find it hard to make the time and commitment. They have a sizable number of other outlets for their free time and volunteering has to compete with this. Much of their lives are controlled by others and it is important to them to have an element of choice and spontaneity in volunteering."

Some organizations have encountered difficulties in adjusting to new types of volunteers, particularly when several types have been mixed together. As an example, long-term volunteers may well view short-term volunteers as "uncaring" or uncommitted to the organization. The lack of willingness of short-term volunteers to sacrifice their own lives to the interests of the cause can be met with a lack of understanding or even outright hostility by the long-term volunteer. Organizations have also encountered difficulties because their staff members have equally difficult times adjusting to populations with whom they are not accustomed.

To get enough long-term volunteers, who are easier to manage and highly necessary for some leadership volunteer functions, organizations have to rely more on "promotion from within," grooming volunteers to assume more responsibilities and slowly convincing volunteers to commit to greater donation of time. Much more effort has to be invested in volunteers to develop them to their full potential.

Organizations are facing greater competition for all types of volunteers. Increasingly, volunteers are in a favorable bargaining position, sought by several organizations, and able to pick among the organizations for the situation that best meets their own needs and interests.

Some Trends in Volunteer Involvement

Some trends that have occurred during the last decade will also exert strong influence during the next ten years. These include:

Workplace Volunteering

The workplace is where the vast majority of American adults spend the preponderance of their time. It is the place where most people hear about opportunities for volunteering. And it is the locus around which many formal volunteer activities will be oriented, thanks to the strong growth in employee volunteer programs. For many, the workplace has become the primary social unit, taking the place of the old service groups and clubs as a mechanism for both companionship and community involvement.

According to the 1999 Gallup Survey, 12% of those who volunteered were asked by someone at work, and 24% learned about their volunteer activity through their workplace or employer. A 1998 study by Charities@Work found that 72% of large businesses surveyed have programs to help employees find volunteer opportunities. A recent survey by the Points of Light Foundation indicates that 20% of companies with a workplace volunteer program report that more than half of their employees participate in the program.

According to a 1999 survey by the Points of Light Foundation, many corporations provide formal opportunities for community agencies to recruit their employees:

- 57% offer volunteer events on company premises
- 32% provide a directory of community volunteer opportunities
- 21% provide release time for volunteering
- 21% operate a retiree volunteer program

The NSGVP in Canada found:

- *"65% of all volunteers were employed and many of these volunteers reported they received support from their employers for their volunteer activities. This support most frequently took the form of allowing employees to use the facilities and equipment of the business for the volunteer activities (reported by 27% of employed volunteers). In addition, almost one-quarter (24%) of employed volunteers stated that they received authorization to take leave or time off from their hours of work in order to engage in volunteer activities."*

- *"Slightly less than one-quarter of respondents (22%) said they had received approval to modify their hours of work in order to take part in volunteer activities. Such approval was granted to a larger percentage of young people under 25 (27%) than to those aged 25 to 44 (23%) or 45 to 64 (17%), and to a larger percentage of young men (31%) than young women (24%)."*

- *"Another form of employer support is recognition of the value of employee involvement in various volunteer activities. Among workers who volunteered, 14% said that they had received recognition from their employer. Here again, a larger proportion of young people under 25 said that they had received this type of support (16%)."*

While workplace volunteering began in large companies, it is rapidly spreading throughout the for-profit community. It is also starting to permeate governmental employers. The federal government recently released the first report on measures taken by federal agencies to comply with an executive order to expand opportunities for volunteer involvement.

Oddly enough, the non-profit sector has lagged the most in organized efforts to encourage workplace volunteering.

Episodic Volunteering

The day of the always-there long-term volunteer has clearly begun to pass. Today's volunteers are interested in smaller and more manageable commitments, and also want to test an organization before they become involved in significant tasks or projects. The 1999 Gallup Survey sums it up: 41% of those who volunteered did so for a sporadic or one-time activity, as opposed to 39% who wanted an on-going scheduled commitment. The average hours per week volunteered has decreased, to 3.5 in 1998, versus an average of 4.2 hours per week in 1995, the same as in 1993 and 1991. Similar results were found by Handy and Srinvasan - among directors of volunteer programs in hospitals in Canada, 81% reported an increase in short-term volunteers, and 63% reported an increase in volunteers requesting assignments of less than three months.

A survey by the National Volunteer and Philanthropy Centre of Singapore in 2002 found that *"for the non-volunteers who are very likely/likely/may volunteer in the future, 29% prefer commitments of less than 3 months and another 20% prefer commitments of between 3 to 6 months."*

In a study of volunteers over age 45, AARP (2003) found that 48% of them only volunteer from time to time, for a specific project or activity. A similar study of AARP members in Delaware (AARP, 2001) found that 33% of them volunteer occasionally during the year for special projects, 28% volunteer a regular time each month and, in addition, volunteer extra hours for special projects, and 19% usually spend about the same amount of time volunteering each month. Younger members (age 50-59) are more likely than older volunteers to volunteer occasionally during the year.

A 2002 study of young adults by Lake Snell Perry & Associates found that episodic volunteering was popular among young adults with children – with 30% volunteering every month and 10% volunteering every week. Lopez (2004), analyzing a US survey of 16-25 year-olds, found that while 40.3% reported volunteering, *"just over half, 22.2 percent, volunteered regularly, suggesting that they engage in episodic volunteering more often than their older counterparts."*

Agencies will clearly need to concentrate on developing events or projects that will attract volunteers and then develop a system for cultivating the most interested and encouraging their continued involvement. This will require a greater variety of volunteer assignments with shorter time commitments and the development of a "career ladder" which can progressively lead volunteers into greater involvement. The name of the game will be retention and promotion, not recruitment. This subject is investigated more completely in our book *Keeping Volunteers: A Guide to Retention.*

Youth and Senior Involvement

Youth once was an uninvolved segment of the volunteer community, but that has changed dramatically in the past ten years. According to a survey by Public Allies, 72% of young people volunteer with an organized group in their community. In the three years prior to the study:

- 6% volunteered just once
- 39% several times a year
- 16% once a month
- 16% several times a month
- 22% once a week or more

According to the National Association of Secretaries of State, most youth volunteer activities take the form of social service in a one-on-one setting, such as soup kitchens, hospitals and schools. Their study suggests *"this type of volunteer work is motivated by a young person's desire to help others in a personal way."*

And, according to the Close Up Foundation, *"The only form of community and government involvement that students value more than voting entails service to others - 63% of high school students say that they have a great deal or a fair amount of interest in 'volunteering for charitable causes.' This is the preferred form of involvement for young women (72%)."*

Interestingly enough, we are seeing strong growth at both of the extreme ends of the age segments. Youth volunteer programs are moving into elementary schools, while at the same time older seniors are increasing their involvement. According to the 1999 Gallup Survey, 43% of those 75 and older volunteered, an increase of eight percentage points since 1995. According to a study by Civic Ventures about volunteering by upcoming retirees, 33% listed volunteering as a "very important" part of their retirement, 17% said it will be fairly important, and 25% said it will be "somewhat important." Volunteering ranks only slightly behind travel in importance.

Minority Involvement

Volunteering is continuing to move away from a traditional, white middle-class activity.

According to the 1999 Gallup Survey, 46% of Hispanics volunteered during 1998 (an increase of six percentage points since 1995), and 47% of African-Americans volunteered (a 12% increase).

Kamilat, an organization working on issues of Muslim women, found in a survey that 44% of Muslims are willing to volunteer to effect community change.

And, in perhaps the most comprehensive survey of a population sub-sector ever conducted, the Institute for Gay and Lesbian Studies determined the following about volunteering among Gays, Lesbians, Bisexuals and Transsexuals:

- Average volunteer hours per month was 29, compared with an average of 18 for the typical US volunteer. The highest rate of volunteering was among African-Americans and Asian-Americans.

- Overall distribution of volunteer time was approximately 45% per month to GLBT organizations, 15% to HIV/AIDS organizations and 40% to non-GLBT organizations.

- When comparing men and women with the same income and other characteristics, men volunteer almost two hours more per month and donate $245 more than women to GLBT organizations.

- People with lower incomes volunteer more hours than people with higher incomes.

Volunteering has moved out of the mainstream and become the entire river and its tributaries.

Computerized Volunteering

The computer is affecting everything else, so there is no wonder that it will increasingly impact volunteer involvement. This will happen in two major ways:

First, more and more people will use the Internet as their way to find volunteer opportunities. Some of this will occur simply through visiting Web sites and examining programs and volunteer recruitment information, but more and more it will involve using the on-line brokers who have been set up to fulfill the functions that Volunteer Centers have traditionally performed at the local level. See Appendix Two for a listing of websites offering volunteer matching services.

According to the 1999 Gallup Survey, 1% of those who volunteered in 1998 learned about volunteering via the Internet. You can expect that number to grow significantly in the next five years. You will find a partial list of websites listing volunteer opportunities in Appendix Two.

Second, more and more volunteering will happen on-line, as opposed to in-person. This "virtual volunteering" provides a convenient answer for some problems that have plagued volunteer management for some time:

- individuals with limited time availability (i.e., most people, and especially those who work)
- individuals with heavy travel schedules
- individuals in rural areas, particularly those with large geographic territories
- individuals who are home-bound through age or disability or inclination

Currently about 3% of those volunteering report performing volunteer work via computer (Independent Sector, 2001), but this percentage is expected to grow. It has particular application to rural communities, where transportation is an issue, and to efforts to involve those with disabilities, particularly the home-bound, for whom transportation may pose an absolute barrier.

The demographics of computer users make them an ideal volunteer recruitment target, which may explain a recent finding by AARP that those who have used a computer at work, school, or at home during the past year are more likely to volunteer.

Recreational Volunteering

One explanation for volunteering is that it is "serious leisure." In the coming decade, we'll see more people take that definition very seriously indeed. Note these two approaches to volunteering:

- *Vacation volunteering*

Want to see the world and do good at the same time? Simple - take your vacation while working for a cause. You can help build homes in Central America, harvest turtle eggs in the Caribbean, excavate archeological digs in the Middle East or just about anything you want. There are even magazines devoted to advertising for these projects.

- *Migratory volunteering*

Retired and want to see the country in a leisurely fashion? Simple - drive your RV from national wildlife refuge to national wildlife refuge and park for a few months on one of their trailer-pads while donating time. You can even set up a "migratory" pathway and follow the migrating bird or animal of your choice. And you can come back year after year after year...

While seemingly strange, these tactics simply conform to the needs and interests of the would-be volunteers, and are a novel way of dealing with time constraints and the desire to move around. With the impending population of healthy, active and wealthy baby-boomer retirees, both of these types of volunteering will blossom.

Affinity Group Volunteering

People used to volunteer through affinity groups such as service clubs, religious congregations and neighborhood groups. We're about to go way beyond that.

There has been a huge explosion of volunteering by fan clubs of every celebrity you can think of. One of my favorites is Sword and Staff, the Xena fan club (www.swordandstaff.com). As they explain it: *"Obviously our primary goal is to help others by channeling our Xena-inspired obsessiveness to charities and causes that need our talents. There very obviously is a vast desire by many fans to give something back. Sharing that experience with our fellow Xena nutballs seems like a natural progression for our maturing fandom and evolving friendships."*

And, of course, there are the Goths, who, disturbed by the bad publicity they were getting after Columbine, decided to pitch in and help out the Red Cross - on a blood drive, naturally.

Add to that the X-Files fans, the Trekkies, the Elvis fans and a host of others and you've got a real movement.

Volunteering has always happened among those who felt themselves members of a group, but it is also increasing among those who would like to be a member of a group (or of something). Note the success of Single Volunteers of DC, which describes itself as "a volunteer group...with a twist." You can catch the drift from reading this paragraph from their volunteer agreement, which you must read before signing up for any volunteer project: *"I also agree that SVDC holds no responsibility for the outcome of any relationship that may or may not form between myself and another person that I might meet through SVDC. In accepting a date or otherwise agreeing to meet with another member either within an SVDC-sponsored volunteer project or social, or on my own time, I take sole responsibility for any actions that might occur during that date or meeting, and agree to hold SVDC free from any liability."*

Family Volunteering

At some point, nonprofit organizations decided that the right way to involve volunteers was one at a time. No one is sure why this happened; some people are now trying to change the process. The most natural "unit" for volunteering may be the family.

According to a survey by AAL, half of American adults (51.4%) do volunteer work with family members "several times a year" or more frequently. Nearly one-fifth of Americans (19.5%) volunteer as a family "weekly or more often." All told, a majority of Americans (61.9%) report volunteering with family members at least occasionally. Among families with children under 12 who have never volunteered before, 65.9% said family volunteering was a good idea or were planning to do it.

A Lutheran Brotherhood survey also looked at people who volunteer together with others on projects:

- 34% had volunteered with a spouse during the last year
- 30% had volunteered with a friend
- 24% had volunteered with their children

Those most likely to volunteer with a spouse are ages 35-49, while Gen X's are more likely to volunteer with a friend or with their children. Parents overwhelmingly want their children to volunteer, with 78% saying they encourage their children to volunteer. A study for the Points of Light Foundation found that of participants in National Family Volunteer Day 93% wanted to be part of more activities where they can volunteer with their family.

Encouraging children to volunteer with their parents is one of the surest ways to create a lifelong value of volunteering. The 1999 Gallup survey found that among those who reported that one or both of their parents had set an example and volunteered while they were young, 69% reported volunteering as adults and 75% reported having made a charitable contribution. Statistics Canada reports that: *"Early life experiences bear some relationship to the likelihood of volunteering in adult years. Compared with the volunteer rate for all Canadians (31.4%), the volunteer rate was substantially higher among people with specific life experiences during their youth: 43% for those whose parents were volunteers and 40% for those who did some kind of volunteer work. These findings demonstrate how, for many, the roots of volunteering are put down early in life and how an interest in contributing as a youth is likely to be maintained in adulthood."*

Besides instilling good habits into a future generation of volunteers, family volunteering also offers the surest and quickest method for changing the demographic patterns of a volunteer organization. It could offer the best method for revitalizing organizations whose volunteer cadre is facing significant aging. More information about many of the groups mentioned above is provided in Chapter Ten.

Styles of Volunteer Program Management

Volunteer programs also vary in style of operation. One might picture a continuum of programs, ranging from those that are very structured, with a high degree of paid staff supervision of volunteers (such as a volunteer program to aid those who are in prison) to those that are operated primarily by volunteers themselves (such as a Neighborhood Watch program).

While the principles of volunteer management remain the same in both styles of program, the exact methods used will vary from the more institutional to the more personal orientation. The operational style of the volunteer program has to fit the culture of the organization.

Effective involvement of volunteers requires a planned and organized process similar to that required by any organizational project or effort. The process of volunteer management involves the following operations:

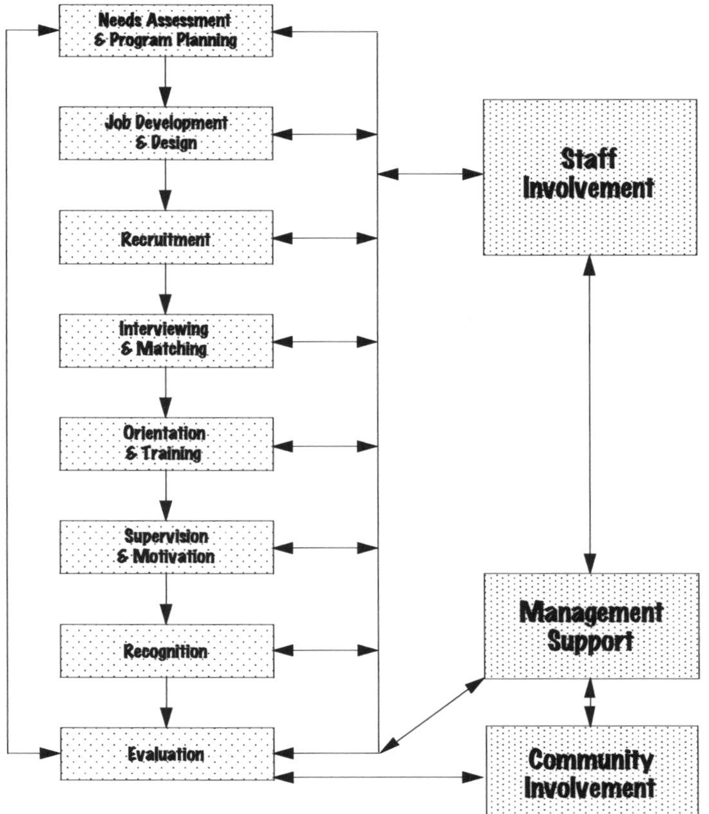

The descending steps on the left side of the diagram represent the major elements involved in determining the needs for volunteers within the organization, identifying suitable volunteers, and then creating a motivational structure to support those volunteers. They are roughly analogous to the personnel and supervisory procedures for paid staff. The elements on the right side of the figure represent the other universes that interact with and must support volunteer personnel (the community at large, upper management of the organization, and staff with whom volunteers will be in contact) and which therefore must be involved in the process of volunteer utilization.

All of these elements are interactive, and as in most creative management processes, rarely proceed in a totally linear fashion. During the existence of the overall volunteer program elements within this process will tend to recur with the addition of each new area of volunteer utilization (as new projects or areas of usage are created) and with the addition of each new volunteer (as the process is customized to the requirements of the individual). The process will also be re-enacted as new staff that interact with volunteers are taken on.

The Role of the Volunteer Program Manager

The functions of volunteer management are sometimes delivered haphazardly by individual members of staff.

A 2003 study by the Urban Institute determined that *"Three out of five charities and only one out of three congregations with social service outreach activities reported having a paid staff person who worked on volunteer coordination. However, among these paid volunteer coordinators, one in three have not received any training in volunteer management, and half spend less than 30 percent of their time on volunteer coordination."*

Organizations that involve volunteers most effectively, however, do so as part of a coordinated volunteer program. This systematic approach to volunteer involvement requires a manager, someone to find people who want to help and to match them with the needs of the organization. This person plans and coordinates all the activities of the volunteer management process. The Urban Institute study cited above went on to conclude:

" The percentage of time a paid staff volunteer coordinator devotes to volunteer management is positively related to the capacity of organizations to take on additional volunteers. The best prepared and most effective volunteer programs are those with paid staff members who dedicate a substantial portion of their time to management of volunteers. This study demonstrated that, as staff time spent on volunteer management increased, adoption of volunteer management practices increased as well. Moreover, investments in volunteer management and benefits derived from volunteers feed on each other, with investments bringing benefits and these benefits justify greater investments."

This does not mean that the Volunteer Program Manager—sometimes called the Volunteer Coordinator or Director of Volunteers—supervises all the volunteers directly, although she or he may do so in a small agency where volunteers work in a "stand alone" program. If all the volunteers work in a thrift shop, for example, they may work directly under the supervision of the Volunteer Program Manager.

Many volunteer programs start out this way. As volunteers start to become involved in other aspects of the agency, however, the Volunteer Program Manager quickly reaches the limits of her ability to supervise volunteers directly. At this point, volunteers start to work under the direct supervision of other paid staff. An accounting student, for example, might volunteer in the administrative office, supervised by the chief accountant.

In a large, sophisticated operation, the effective Volunteer Program Manager plays a critical role in the success of the entire organization. When new projects or new directions arise, the role of volunteers is planned into them from the beginning. The Volunteer Program Manager helps top management identify needed expertise that will help the project succeed and works with paid staff to design volunteer jobs to meet those needs. She or he plans and coordinates a recruitment effort to identify people who will find such work fulfilling enough to devote their leisure time to doing it, assists in the screening, interviewing, and selection processes, provides an overall orientation to the organization, evaluates the success of the volunteer program, and plans recognition events.

The major role of the modern Volunteer Program Manager is thus not working directly with volunteers, save those she or he recruits to help in these processes. Rather, effective Volunteer Program Managers focus their attentions on paid staff, securing top management support for volunteer efforts and helping individual staff do a good job of managing and retaining their volunteer helpers.

Nonprofit agencies that excel in serving their clients realize they cannot ever hire enough expertise to achieve their missions fully. To succeed, they must encourage concerned people to donate their expertise just as they encourage people to provide financial support. In this, staff should value the Volunteer Program Manager as much as they do the (usually much higher paid) fund-raiser.

The importance of volunteering in relation to fundraising is clear for those organizations where the value of the volunteer time is far in excess of the cash they raise and spend each year. The lack of importance given to volunteering is shown by the unfulfilled potential of this resource, whether it is being used directly to further the agency's work or just to raise money for it.

Unfortunately, in too many organizations, the volunteer program is regarded as an optional extra to benefit bored housewives. The role of the Volunteer Program Manager is undervalued in such organizations, and volunteers are confined largely to menial or clerical functions that are not directly related to the agency's mission. Such organizations are overwhelmed by the problems they exist to solve, spending more and more resources chasing elusive grants and donations.

Effective organizations involve volunteers in ever more significant roles. Volunteers, drawn from all walks of life and with all manner of skills, will be involved as equal partners with staff in pursuing the agency's goals. When staff members plan new efforts, they will identify needs for expertise and plan to involve volunteers to meet them. In order to accomplish this, top management must give more status, support, and resources to the Volunteer Program Manager.

Little research has been done about Volunteer Program Managers, but one of the better surveys was done in Canada in 2003. Among its findings:

- *"The managers of volunteer resources surveyed report holding a wide variety of job titles within their organizations. About two in ten each hold the title of volunteer co-ordinator (17%) and co-ordinator (16%). Other titles held by those who have responsibility for co-ordination, supervision or management of volunteers are: executive director (12%), manager (11%), director or assistant director (11%), assistant/administrator or secretary (10%) and president, principal, chairman or CEO (6%)."*

- *"The percentage of time devoted to volunteer management varies considerably. One-third of respondents (34%) spend ten percent or less of their time in volunteer management activities. About two in ten each devote between 11 and 25 percent of their time (21%), between 26 and 50 percent of their time (21%), or more than 50 percent of their time (22%) to volunteer management."*

- *"There is a considerable range in tenure of volunteer managers. About one-half of respondents (53%) have been in their current position for three years or less, including 28 percent who have one year or less in their current position. Fourteen percent of respondents have held their current positions for four to five years, 17 percent for six to ten years, and 14 percent for 11 to 20 years."*

It seems common for Volunteer Program Managers to hold other responsibilities within their organizations. Brudney found in a study of volunteer managers in government programs that the average percentage of time actually spent on managing the volunteer effort was 32.2%.

Despite this, when posed with the statement "In general, I am satisfied with my role in volunteer administration," 63% agreed strongly and 31% agreed somewhat. Only 6% disagreed strongly.

The Geometry of Volunteer Involvement

Another way of looking at the process of volunteer management can be represented through the use of simple geometric figures. These figures illustrate what and how the interacting processes of volunteer management work. Throughout this book we will be referring to these figures as a way of demonstrating what actually ought to be happening throughout the process of managing a volunteer program. We will be working with three simple shapes:

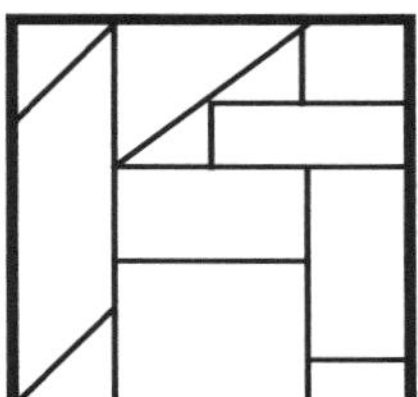

The Puzzle Square representing the work that the organization needs done.

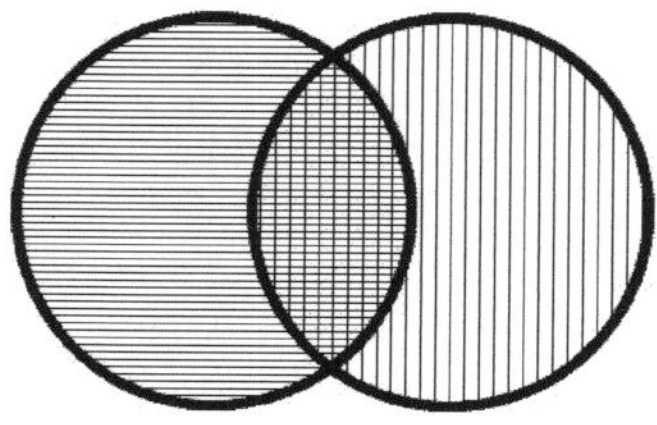

The Overlapping Circles representing the commonly met needs of the organization and the volunteers.

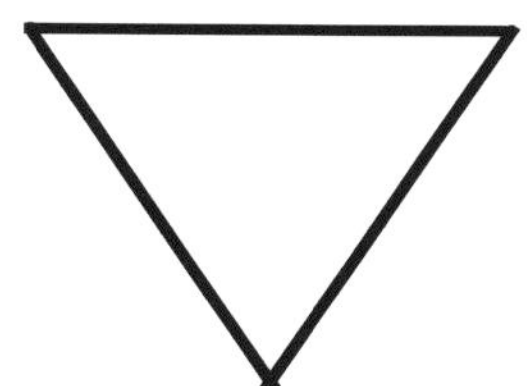

The Triangle representing the web of relationships among the Volunteer Program Manager, the volunteers, and staff.

Taken together, these three shapes illustrate the major tasks that must be accomplished in order for volunteer management to be effective, as well as some of the concepts we have presented in this introductory chapter. We will be discussing all of them extensively throughout this book.

Chapter Two Planning a High-Impact Volunteer Program

Most nonprofit organizations have barely scratched the surface of the potential of their volunteer programs, regarding the volunteer component as one that provides useful, ancillary services. An effective volunteer program, by contrast, is one that makes a significant contribution to achieving the agency's mission. In planning the volunteer program, the Volunteer Program Manager should begin with this concept.

When agencies plan their work, they usually allow themselves to be constrained by the extent of their financial resources. They plan to do only what they can do with the staff they can afford to hire and the things they can afford to buy. An effective volunteer program frees agencies from these constraints. An effective volunteer program provides all the resources of the community necessary to help the agency accomplish its mission.

Nonprofit agencies exist to solve problems or meet needs in communities. These problems are usually far greater in magnitude than the resources of the agency. No nonprofit will ever have enough money to hire all the people with all the skills necessary to make a serious difference in solving the problems they address in their communities. A few people in a storefront office working at low pay can make a difference in the lives of a few others. But the problem the agency exists to solve usually remains or gets worse.

The only way agencies will ever make serious differences in their communities is through the involvement of a significant number of skilled volunteers who work on the problem or need in significant ways. When volunteers are involved in this way, staff will regard the volunteer program as one that gives them access to all the skills they need to make a difference. The Volunteer Program Manager becomes the one who has "the keys to the kingdom." She is the one who brings the necessary skills together to make significant progress toward the achievement of the agency's mission.

This does not happen easily, however. It often involves a change in the way the agency looks at itself as well as how it looks at volunteers. It requires a new vision of how the agency plans and operates.

Creating a Mission

Effective planning begins with the mission of the agency. In an exhaustive study of sixteen agencies in four cities, the Points of Light Foundation found that one of the hallmarks of an effective volunteer program is the way in which the mission is defined. If the volunteer program is to be a means of solving a community problem or meeting a community need, the mission of the organization must be phrased in terms of that problem. Thus, the first step in planning an effective volunteer program is to define the mission of the organization in such terms.

The mission is a statement of the purpose of the agency, a statement of its ultimate goal. When this goal is achieved, the organization will no longer need to exist.

We could contrast such mission statements with the more common sort which describe what the organization does, rather than what it intends to accomplish. A literacy program, for example, might talk about providing tutoring services to functionally illiterate adults rather than about putting an end to illiteracy in the community. A statement such as "We exist to provide hot meals to senior citizens" is not an effective mission statement. One that says "Our mission is to put an end to senior malnutrition" is.

Mission statements that are phrased in terms what the organization does do not galvanize followers as readily as mission statements that talk about meeting a need or solving a problem. It may be tedious or boring to prepare and serve hot meals, but it is rewarding to help put an end to senior malnutrition. Missions that describe what a group does also tend to limit the organization to that activity and to lock people into doing things because "we've always done it that way." They tend to promote the status quo and so make effective change unlikely.

The need the group proposes to meet should ordinarily be one that exists outside of the organization. "We have a problem recruiting volunteers" is not the sort of external need we're referring to. In the case of nonprofit organizations involved in direct service activities, the need will be the need of the clients they serve.

Some examples of this are:

- Youth organization

"Many young people grow up without the skills and self-confidence to become competent, successful adults. Our mission is to equip youth to have a fulfilling, successful life, however they may define it."

- Mental Health Center

"Many people are in doubt, fear, and pain in our community. Our mission is to help them cope with this condition so as to prevent their doing harm to themselves and others and to help them return to independent living as productive members of the community."

- Community Action Agency

"Our mission is to help people overcome their poverty and become self-sufficient."

- Volunteer Center

"Many people in our community are concerned about community problems but either feel powerless to do anything about them or don't know how to get involved in the solution. At the same time, many agencies in our community are unable to meet fully the needs of their clients due to lack of personpower. Our mission is to solve both of these problems by enabling people to get involved in meaningful volunteer work."

So far the examples have been mission statements for an entire agency. Individual units of an agency can also have mission statements based on an external need. For example, a State Department of Wildlife Habitat Division might have a unit whose mission reads:

"Essential wildlife habitat is being lost. Our mission is to insure the survival of native wildlife by protecting its habitat against the encroachments of developers."

The achievement of this unit's mission will make a direct, logical contribution to the overall agency purpose of protecting populations of all species of native wildlife in the state.

The mission statement should be developed with the involvement of the people who will be attempting to carry it out. This insures that they will feel a sense of ownership in the mission. The leader should facilitate this process by asking questions such as "What is our purpose? What is the need in the outside world that we are trying to meet? Under what circumstances could we happily go out of business?"

Sometimes a discussion of the mission will uncover a deep conflict between some segments of the group. Where the mission is assumed rather than explicit, these conflicts tend to play themselves out in petty politics, their roots obscured by the issues of the day. At an art museum, for example, the discussion of the mission uncovered a conflict between most of the curators, who thought that the mission was to preserve valuable works of art, and others who thought the mission should be to provide the public with the works of art they wanted to see. Others were adamant that the purpose of the museum was to expand the taste of the public for all forms of art. Until this discussion, there had been many conflicts about the types of exhibitions and programs the museum should sponsor, conflicts that had turned into nasty, personal infighting. As the group discussed the mission, they suddenly understood the source of the conflict and came to understand each other's behavior.

The mission statement should not be some dusty paragraph that is locked away in a drawer, liberated only to preface grant proposals. It should be a statement that galvanizes the volunteers and staff, a statement from which their daily activities draw meaning. It should be a living declaration of what the group is trying to accomplish. It should be a statement of the difference the group intends to make in the world.

Strategic Involvement of Volunteers

The mission statement is the foundation of strategic planning. This involves three basic steps:

1. Identifying obstacles to accomplishing the mission;
2. Developing a strategy to overcome each obstacle;
3. Setting goals to implement the strategy.

An example of this process comes from an agency whose mission was to solve the problem of teen drug abuse in a large city. Paid staff and volunteers identified peer pressure at school as one of several major obstacles to accomplishing this mission. This obstacle was a particular problem when youth left treatment programs and returned to their high schools and the old peer group encouraged them to return to their old ways. The strategy they chose to overcome that obstacle was to create an environment where youth who had been through treatment would experience positive peer pressure. This led to the decision to set a strategic goal of overcoming that obstacle by starting an alternative high school for recovering, chemically dependent teens.

An effective plan should also take into consideration the resources in the world outside the group that could help to meet the need. Mobilizing those resources that would not be engaged as part of overcoming the obstacles would become additional strategic objectives. In the above case, for example, the group identified the major newspapers of the city as a resource. Use of the media had not been identified as a means of overcoming any of the obstacles. The group asked what purpose the newspaper could serve in achieving the mission of overcoming teen drug abuse. The group decided the papers were already doing an adequate job of spreading the news of the negative consequences of drug abuse but were not letting teens know about the successes former drug users were making of their lives. Thus the goal was to change teens' attitudes toward former drug users through increased newspaper coverage of such cases.

When a nonprofit agency uses this method for strategic planning, it will invariably find that it lacks the financial resources to hire enough people to accomplish all its strategic goals. The drug abuse agency described above, for example, did not have any paid staff that could work on setting up the new school. The common reaction to this problem is to prioritize those goals and pursue the most important or the most feasible. A more effective approach is to look at how volunteers could help accomplish the strategic goals of the organization.

It is at this point that the volunteer program becomes a critical and integral part of the agency's success. Instead of being limited to pursuing a few objectives in a partial way, the agency can pursue all its strategic objectives with total commitment. If pursuing the mission involves improving the public image of the organization, for example, a volunteer from a public relations firm could be recruited to pursue that strategic goal.

For many organizations, this is not the sort of volunteer or volunteer position that staff associate with the volunteer program. To create such a strategic role for volunteers thus often involves creating a new vision of the role of volunteers in the agency.

Creating a Vision for Volunteer Involvement

The Points of Light Foundation study also found that in agencies where volunteers were most effective there was a broadly understood, widely articulated vision of the role of volunteers. This vision should be an integral part of the vision of the organization.

A vision is a detailed sense of the future the agency is trying to create. A vision produces a commonality of purpose and a sense of excitement. Part of this vision is the sense of change that will be wrought in the world through the accomplishment of the organization's strategic goals. The other part is more internally focused. It is a vivid sense of what the organization will look like, how it will operate, and how it will be regarded in the future. And it should provide a positive role for volunteers to play in mission-critical activities.

Sometimes people get mission and vision confused. The mission statement should be a one paragraph or one sentence statement of purpose. It is a statement of why the group exists. It is the skeleton upon which the flesh of the organization's vision statement is hung. The vision is a more detailed description of a desired future.

A good vision statement should be mission focused, and it should include the broad elements of the strategic plan. Creating an effective vision involves answering these questions:

- *Who do we need to influence in order to implement our strategies?*
- *What do we want them to do?*

A systematic way to do this is to list the obstacles the group faces in accomplishing its mission and the resources (both actual and potential) that could help in moving toward the mission. The groups and individuals that show up on this list are people the organization should try to influence.

The board and staff of one historical museum, for example, identified the following groups:

- the county commissioners
- the local newspaper
- tourists
- people who use the museum for research
- the chamber of commerce
- the city manager
- local businesses
- a local developer
- the schools

After identifying such groups, the next task is to ask "What do we want these people to do for us?" In the case of the museum, the answers were as follows:

County Commissioners:

- give us regular funding
- give us a one time grant to help purchase a new building

The Local Newspaper:

- give us coverage of museum events
- recognize our value to the community

Researchers:

- letters of support to funding sources
- materials to enhance our collection

Tourists:

- visit the museum (and pay admission fees)
- spread positive word about the museum back home
- buy things at the gift shop
- buy food in the restaurant

The Chamber of Commerce:

- provide information to members about museum events
- encourage members to support the museum financially

The City Manager:

- provide regular funding

Local Businesses:

- contribute to the building fund
- endow chairs

A Local Developer:

- donate a plot of land downtown that will be an historic preservation district and on which the museum will be built as a replica of an old hotel

The Schools:

- make our educational offerings part of the curriculum
- give students credit for volunteering at the museum
- support our funding requests

These answers create a sense of an ideal climate for the organization. They create a powerful vision of what the organization can strive to become. A vision statement for the museum, for example, might contain the following language:

In the year 2010, the XYZ Historical Museum has moved into a new building, a replica of a turn-of-the-century hotel that was destroyed by fire in 1928. The site was donated by a local developer and features a view of the harbor. The building was built partly from private donations and partly from a grant from county government. Funding for four staff is secure through an endowment fund and the regular budget contributions of local government and the public schools. In addition, grants are received from state sources for special projects and exhibits. The chamber of commerce is active in helping the museum acquire new objects of historical interest. Each year, high school students compete for the fifteen volunteer slots where they serve in a variety of exciting capacities.

The museum is a popular tourist destination, with people coming to see the exhibits, buy gifts, and relax at the cafe. Local residents show off the museum to their visitors. The deck behind the cafe is a popular spot for people to wait for the ferry. Scholars travel from across the region to work in the research room. Their letters of thanks assist in securing funding for special projects. The high school uses museum resources to assist in teaching local history. The museum has been such a popular attraction that it has encouraged local businesses to spring up on the same block, increasing the vitality of the neighborhood.

Such a statement sets an ambitious and stretching set of goals for the museum. And at first, it may seem daunting. But as volunteers and paid staff make small steps toward the realization of the vision, the sense of purpose and excitement grows. They can clearly picture the type of institution they are creating, and that picture provides meaning to their daily actions.

In addition to this systematic approach, the leader can further formulate the vision by having small groups of people answer this question:

If we were going to go across the street and start a competing organization, what would we do over there to make our present organization obsolete?

This question helps people escape the bonds of what is, so they can think about what ought to be. It therefore helps the organization escape the trap of its own past so it can renew itself.

An example of this process comes from a community organization in Canada. The mission of the organization was meeting the recreation needs of the community. It raised money through Bingo and other special events, and received technical assistance from the city parks department. It had built a hall and a skating rink and equipped hockey, soccer, and softball teams that played in a city league. The group considered the task of deciding what they would do if they were to start a competing organization across the street. They were to create an organization that would be more appealing to both citizens and volunteers than their present organization. The following is a list of some of their ideas:

- Offer 24-hour childcare
- Have a party room with a hot tub and Jacuzzi
- Offer aerobics classes
- Have large and small rooms for community activities
- Own a bus to take residents to the hall
- Have fashion shows
- Have an island kitchen with microwave ovens
- Have a well-trained executive board skilled in volunteer management
- Have a welcome wagon
- Encourage a neighborhood pub to open next door
- Sponsor neighborhood picnics and block parties
- Begin an adopt-a-neighbor program
- Have plush carpets
- Have a pool table and Ping-Pong table
- Have a carpentry shop that could be rented out to community residents
- Have board meetings in luxurious locations
- Have good toys for kids
- Have a good sound system
- Hold dances
- Install skateboard ramps
- Operate a sports equipment store at the hall

In the case of the historical museum, such an exercise led them to add this paragraph to their vision statement:

"The museum attracts top staff because of its training program, location, and public support. Staff and volunteer workspaces are furnished with a combination of modern equipment and antique furniture. Volunteers who started in high school often continue their volunteer work as adults. A self-supporting, on-site, childcare service is free for staff and volunteers and also serves the community. An atmosphere of mutual support and camaraderie exists among staff and volunteers."

Another example of a vision statement comes from Missouri CASA, a professional association of directors of Court Appointed Special Advocates. The mission of this group is "to improve the lives of abused and neglected children in Missouri by directing an integrated approach to program development, education, training, advocacy, agency coordination and public relations in support of Court Appointed Special Advocate Programs statewide." The vision that they have created reads:

Vision:
A state where all children have a safe, permanent home free of abuse and neglect, where a CASA program exists in every judicial circuit, where a CASA is provided for every child who needs one, and where the needs of children are a priority on the legislative and judicial agendas;

An association of CASA programs statewide, which is a strong, positive advocate for the children of Missouri, where services are integrated, technical assistance is provided, innovative ideas are encouraged, quality is monitored and enhanced, volunteers are motivated, and dialogue is facilitated, and which is a national model for how to speak up for children effectively;

An environment which encourages the development of new possibilities for abused and neglected children, in which warmth and nurturing replace hurt and fear, and in which children receive the attention and support they need to realize their potential and build self-esteem, free from the continuum of violence that plagues their world today.

After groups come up with a vision such as this, some group members may say "But we could never do that. It would take too much money. It isn't realistic." The truth of the matter is, however, that with enough desire, we can create anything we can imagine. And if we refuse to imagine a better situation, we are unlikely to get one. If we can be stopped by a thought in our heads, what will we do when we encounter a real obstacle?

More importantly, this negative sentiment ignores the possibility of involving high-impact volunteers in the realization of the vision. If the agency believes "We can never do that," it is usually only focusing on its own limited resources. It needs to think bigger. It needs to realize it has access to all the resources in the community through its volunteer program. This means that the vision should also incorporate a vision of how volunteers should work in the agency. The "Changing the Paradigm" project of the Points of Light Foundation suggests some aspects of that vision:

- Staff and volunteers work together as equals
- Staff are empowered to identify and create any volunteer job
- The organization learns from the experience of volunteers
- There is a recognition of the value of volunteers

in mission-critical activities
- There is a central point for volunteer management in the agency
- However, all staff play a role in developing jobs for and supervising volunteers.

These factors interact to create a perception among staff that volunteers have a significant purpose to play in contributing to the agency.

A Case Study of Creating a Vision for Volunteers

Volunteers can enable an agency to achieve much more of its vision than it currently does. To look at how all this ties together, imagine an agency whose mission is to enable frail and handicapped elderly people to stay in their homes instead of having to go to a nursing facility. Historically, it has done this by providing housekeeping services to its clients. The organization had four paid staff. Volunteers provided all direct service to clients. They performed no other role.

The program gets some support from United Way and a local foundation. This, however, is not enough to fully support the staff, rent the facilities, provide for volunteer reimbursement, and purchase cleaning supplies. As a consequence, all staff and board members spend vast amounts of time in developing local fund-raising events, such as the sale of pre-decorated Christmas trees, trout fishing festivals, and bake sales at street fairs.

Because so much time is spent in fund-raising, the agency does not devote adequate time to screening, training and supporting its volunteers. As a consequence, there is high turnover, and the Volunteer Program Manager also spends a lot of time recruiting new volunteers. This becomes increasingly difficult as volunteers quit and word of their disaffection spreads.

The easiest way to recruit volunteers in this state is through the welfare office, which has a requirement that all able-bodied welfare recipients volunteer or lose their benefits. The second easiest way to recruit is through a "Volunteers are Needed" ad in the local newspaper. Some of the volunteers recruited by these two methods have had no prior work experience and need basic training in things like showing up on time. They also lack an appreciation of the plight of the frail elderly, seeing their job as one of simply doing housework. They also have no knowledge of gerontology and as a result frequently find the clients boring, racist, and irritating. There is no time to train the volunteers in any of these areas, however.

To improve the agency, the board, staff, and some volunteers and clients of the agency meet for a strategic planning session one weekend. One of the board member's friends is a vice president for strategic planning for a local marketing company. She volunteers to help them with the process. She has the group begin by clarifying the mission, which they agree is to enable seniors to maintain themselves in their own homes for as long as possible. They agree that this mission should become part of the volunteer training and be prominently displayed in the lobby of the agency.

The group identifies many obstacles to achieving the mission. Participants vote on the most important ones, with each person having three votes. They find that six obstacles receive almost all the votes:

- The inability of clients to do household chores
- The inability to pay for minor home repairs
- Lack of ability to get out and socialize with others
- Rodent and pest infestation;
- Inability to cook for themselves
- Inability to shop for themselves

The obvious strategy in each of these cases is to get someone to provide these services to the client. But the agency can't afford to do any more than it does now. In order to address the last five of these issues, the agency had to consider a new vision of the involvement of volunteers that goes far beyond simply doing chores for the frail elderly. The vision is one of recruiting volunteers who have the skills necessary to keep clients from going to the nursing home before there were serious medical reasons to do so. This led to the development of many new roles for volunteers. A year later, this vision has transformed the agency:

- A new corps of volunteers now provides clients with basic home repairs. The Deputy Director recruited a retired union official as a volunteer whose job is to recruit volunteers from the trades. The retired official is a neighbor of many of the clients. He has been very successful at recruiting unemployed and underemployed members of the trades to provide these services.

- Exterminators have been recruited as volunteers. The agency reimburses them for the cost of insecticides and other materials.

- The agency organizes block parties among elderly clients to meet their socialization needs. The agency supplies food for these events, cooked by volunteer chefs.

- The agency does shopping for clients, using volunteer shoppers who meet with clients to identify their needs. Many of these are youth from the local high school.

Additionally, the agency has involved volunteers in other ways.

- As part of their training, chores service volunteers get trained in gerontology by two members of the gerontology department of the local university. These faculty members volunteer to do this once per quarter.

- The agency has new brochures developed by a volunteer graphic designer. These have increased the number of clients and of volunteers from the general population.

- The numbers further increased when the agency developed a 15-second TV spot which is shown as a public service announcement. The TV spot was developed by student volunteers in the telecommunications department of a university. It opens with an elderly man saying a tearful good-bye to his neighbors, then shows agency volunteers fixing up his house, and shows him returning to a warm welcome from his neighbors.

- The agency has also involved volunteers in fund-raising efforts. Additional funding is gained by a yearly raffle run by a volunteer who has retired as a fund-raising consultant. He lives in the same neighborhood as many of the clients.

- Because of the new vision of volunteer involvement, volunteers are now invited to regular agency staff meetings where progress toward the plan is discussed. Initially, some staff didn't think that volunteers would come to such meetings, but there has been an increasing number who do come. To accommodate volunteers who work, these meetings are now held on Saturday.

- Staff members see their jobs as supporting the volunteers who make the work of the agency possible. In addition to the annual recognition event, the staff frequently praise volunteers for their contributions.

- Volunteers have contributed several ideas that have shaped the agency's strategic plan. For example, the idea for block parties came from a volunteer chore worker after attending a gerontology session.

- Volunteers represent diverse sections of the community, from welfare recipients to university professors, to retirees, to students, to members of the building trades.

As demonstrated by this example, the volunteer program should not be seen as an add-on to the essential work of the agency but as an integral part of its efforts to achieve its mission. The effective volunteer program gives an agency access to all the skills in the community. The vision for the volunteer program both leads the efforts of those involved and encourages them to contribute their utmost to achieve that vision. As a Volunteer Program Manager, you will be responsible for helping those in the agency develop that vision.

Making a Vision About Volunteer Involvement a Reality

Many charities would, if asked, espouse support for the organizational value of involving volunteers. The British Red Cross, for example, says:

"We have a long history of volunteering which we are commitment to maintaining because:

- *service participants place special value on the care which skilled and trained volunteers can give – care given willingly, in their own time, with expectation of material reward*

- *volunteers enable us to draw on a very wide pool of skill, derived from professional and personal experience, which enriches the services we offer*

- *volunteers provide an invaluable insight to the needs of the communities in which they live, thus better informing our work."*

Making this value a reality, however, is a far different proposition.

Consider the value statement of Community Service Volunteers, one of the largest volunteer-involving organizations in the UK:

We believe:

- *Everyone has something significant to offer the community. We therefore actively encourage diversity and reject no one.*

- *Public and non-profit organisations and the community thrive on the contribution of volunteers.*

- *Access to training and lifelong learning is essential to personal development and community strength.*

Note the phrase "reject no one" in the first value statement. CSV takes this statement seriously, and expends considerable effort and ingenuity in volunteer interviews making the ability of everyone to volunteer with a CSV program a reality. It requires creativity in design of volunteer positions and, occasionally, the willingness to provide additional management resources. But, as an organization which truly believes that volunteering is something which should be encourage and enabled, both for the good of organizations and of the larger community, CSV fosters the extra effort to make its value a matter of practice.

One way to connect the organizational value to what the organization should do in actually supporting volunteers is to develop a statement of commitment giving further guidance. The following is an example of such a statement, developed by the Alberta Children's Hospital.

Statement of Commitment to the Volunteer

The Alberta Children's Hospital recognizes the contribution of volunteers in assisting staff fulfill the mission of the hospital.

Towards the continued pursuit of excellence in volunteerism and in support of volunteers as valued members of the ACH team, the hospital's administration makes the following commitment to the volunteer community at ACH.

1. The hospital will support a Volunteer Resources Department providing appropriate staffing to manage the volunteer program.

2. Hospital staff, both professional and support, who are directing volunteers will be oriented to the needs of volunteers. In specific terms, all new staff, as part of their orientation, will receive instruction from Volunteer Resources. All staff working with volunteers will receive ongoing education from Volunteer Resources as required.

3. Hospital staff will play a role in the orientation, directing, evaluation and recognition on volunteers working in their areas.

4. Staff will facilitate a positive environment for volunteers working in their areas. This will involve welcoming them, assisting them, mentoring them when necessary and thanking them regularly for their contributions.

5. Staff working with volunteers will be recognized for this contribution.

Signed in March 1998 by the Administrative Leaders of the Alberta Children's Hospital and the Regional Senior Operating Officers responsible for the hospital and its volunteer program.

This statement, if implemented, makes it much more likely that the vision of the volunteer program will receive the true support of the organization.

Chapter Three Organizing a Volunteer Program

Some volunteer efforts have suffered from the problems generated by "spontaneous creation." This phenomenon occurs when an over-enthusiastic administrator learns of the potential of volunteer involvement and pronounces at a staff meeting: "Let there be volunteers!"

The assumption behind this pronouncement is that instituting a volunteer effort is simple and can be done instantaneously. The pronouncement is usually followed by the designation of some unsuspecting staff person as "in charge of volunteers," with the immediate assignment of "going out and rounding up a small herd of them."

This simple-minded approach might, in fact, work if all that is being considered is an ad hoc usage of volunteers, bringing in a few volunteers specifically to work on a single project, with no expectation that they will stay beyond that project or attempt to work in other areas. The approach will not work at all when considered on an institutional basis: enabling volunteers and staff to work on an on-going basis in a variety of programs and tasks throughout the organization.

Getting Things Started

Effective volunteer management is simple in theory but subtle in operation. It has all the complexities of basic personnel management—job development, interviewing, supervision, evaluation of performance, recognition and reward, and so on. And it also has complexities all its own. An interesting example, not seen as often in the environment of paid staff, is that of the over-enthusiastic worker. Quite often, a Volunteer Program Manager will have to deal with a volunteer who causes difficulties for the program not from a lack of motivation but from a surplus of it. This volunteer will be so dedicated to the cause that they will expect and work for instant solutions to any problem that arises, and will not understand why the system sometimes operates so slowly. The volunteer may become impatient and infuriated with anyone, paid staff or volunteer, who doesn't give total dedication to making the system work perfectly, and immediately.

Volunteer involvement depends upon the creation of a good system for working with volunteers. A program that has insufficient infrastructure, inadequate staff and leadership support, insufficient budgeting, or other defects in management will fail to attract and keep volunteers. A 2003 study in Australia found that volunteers with the Australian Threatened Bird Network preferred projects where organizers set clear goals, provided feedback and supervised in a friendly and helpful manner, all basic elements of competent management. These are the same elements cherished by paid staff.

Fitting Together the Puzzle

In a way, one might think about volunteer management within an organization as the construction of a puzzle.

The overall square shape of the puzzle represents the total universe of work that the organization desires to be accomplished through the work of volunteers.

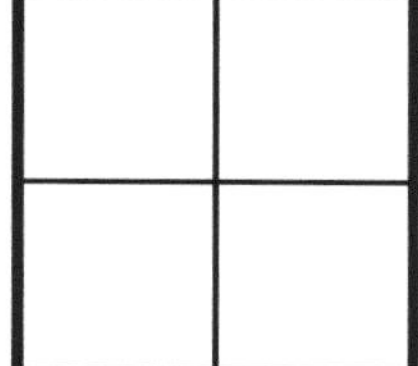

Within that square are the individual pieces of jobs that are to be done by specific volunteers, with each piece representing a volunteer.

Over recent years, the configurations of this puzzle have become increasingly complicated. The size of the square has increased, as agencies have developed broader uses for volunteers, involving volunteers in tasks previously reserved for paid staff. And the complexity of the job mix has changed, as organizations have developed more short-term volunteer jobs, jobs that require a briefer time commitment and greater flexibility to meet the needs and interests of the short-term volunteer. As the stable base of long-term generalist volunteers has eroded, organizations have had to be more creative, and more opportunistic, about developing more volunteer roles and finding a wider variety of ways to "fit" volunteers within the organization.

As this has intensified the puzzle has become more complicated:

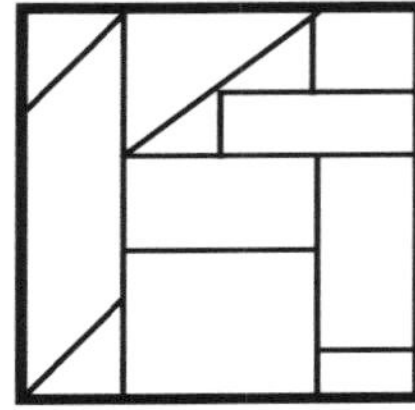

For the typical organization today, the puzzle more closely resembles a jigsaw puzzle, one that changes shape every week.

The Volunteer Program Manager is usually responsible for designing the overall puzzle shape and for fitting together the individual pieces that complete the puzzle. This has to be done in concert with both the staff that help design the parameters, and the volunteers, who help determine the design of individual jobs.

Determining the Rationale behind Your Program

The first step in constructing the design of an agency's volunteer program requires determining why the organization wishes to involve volunteers. This decision will influence the following:

- It will determine the types of positions and responsibilities that the organization will create for volunteers.
- It will enable the organization to explain to volunteers how and why they are contributing to the work of the organization.
- It will enable the organization to explain to staff why volunteers are being sought.
- It will enable the organization to evaluate whether the involvement of volunteers has been effective.

Potential Rationales

There are many potential rationales for involving volunteers. These include:

- Providing an outreach to the community.
- Supplementing staff resources and experiences, adding value to the organization and its work.
- Engaging needed skills when the resources are simply not there to make a staff appointment.
- Allowing a channel for community input.
- Giving a more personal touch in services to clients.
- Building linkages to other groups.
- Assisting in fund-raising efforts.
- Increasing cost-effectiveness in service delivery.
- Allowing quick reaction to changing needs or crisis situations.
- Responding to a request by someone to do something useful for the cause.

The Duval County Public School System in Jacksonville, FL offers the following rationales (phrased as goals) for their involvement of volunteers:

1. *Provide opportunities for community members to become directly involved with Duval County Public Schools*

2. *Strengthen school-community relations through direct volunteer participation*

3. *Enrich students' curriculum, broadening their awareness and experiences*

4. *Provide individual educational assistance to students*

5. *Reinforce lessons taught by schools*

6. *Assist school personnel with instructional tasks and duties*

7. *Enhance all aspects of the educational process*

Reaching Agreement on a Rationale

It is highly desirable that agreement among organization leadership and line staff is reached on this rationale. In a sense, the rationale will represent part of the "mission" of the volunteer program. It will provide a quick and clear understanding of what benefit the organization thinks will be derived from engagement of volunteers, and provide a sense of purpose for the volunteer program. In essence, it should answer the question, "Why are we doing this?"

This is important. But it is particularly important where there is or appears to be a substitution of paid work.

The consensus agreement should then be written down and provided to volunteers and staff. Here is a sample statement regarding volunteers involved by the Juvenile Court in Spokane, Washington State:

The Spokane County Juvenile Court is committed to providing the best and most appropriate services possible. To realize this goal, our Department shall make every effort to enlist the cooperation of all available resources. The Department is committed to the development of a public/private partnership which includes volunteers as an important and necessary ingredient in the development and delivery of services.

In addition to the above, our Department plans to actively implement and maintain a responsible program of citizen involvement because:

1. *Our Department will never have sufficient resources to meet all service needs. Even if such resources were available (professional staff, finances, facilities, etc.), the Department would still believe it necessary for the community to become involved in juvenile issues.*

2. *It has been demonstrated repeatedly that volunteers can significantly enhance, expand, and upgrade services. With appropriate recruitment, screening, training, and supervision, volunteers can perform almost any task effectively and responsibly.*

3. *The Department feels it necessary to involve the community in the problems we are trying to alleviate or solve. Efforts to involve the community in organization affairs will help to educate the public about these problems and will create a more enlightened and active citizenry. Because volunteers are regarded as key members of the Juvenile Court team, their increased involvement in our Department will be pursued.*

To insure effective implementation and maintenance of citizen involvement efforts within this organization, the following principles shall be followed:

1. *Volunteers shall be involved in the organization's service delivery system in every unit of operation which is feasible under the laws of this State and within the scope of this Department's policies and procedures.*

2. *The Volunteer Program shall have representation at the organization's general management and administration level. A professional staff member will be designated a Volunteer Coordinator to direct volunteer recruitment, screening, orientation, and training.*

3. *Volunteers will be used in both direct and indirect services, and staff will be encouraged to utilize this valuable resource in planning programmatic activities.*

4. *Professional staff and volunteers shall be involved collectively in the planning and implementation of the Volunteer Program.*

5. *The organization shall take steps to insure that professional staff are prepared and actively participate in implementing the Volunteer Program. Consequently, general orientation sessions for new employees shall include information about the organization's citizen involvement efforts, and staff shall be trained in working with and supervising volunteers. Such training shall be incorporated into the on-going organization staff development program.*

6. *All aspects of the Volunteer Program and its implementation will be monitored and evaluated on an on-going basis. The need to develop services that are effective, efficiently delivered, and cost-effective make this a necessity.*

7. *Volunteers within the organization are not intended to replace existing professional staff. Volunteers are regarded as non-paid staff working in conjunction with professional staff to:*

- *Lend their skills and abilities from a unique perspective*
- *Amplify many areas of our Department's service to the community*
- *Make direct contributions to staff effectiveness*
- *Benefit the community at large through their added awareness of juvenile issues.*

The mere existence of a rationale forvolunteer program does not, however, guarantee that equal rationality will occur in making it happen. The Points of Light Foundation discovered in a survey of national health agencies in 1996:

"Volunteer satisfaction with the agency was identified as the most important current issue for Voluntary Health Agencies. All of the agencies reported that this issue was at least somewhat important, with over 90% indicating that this was a very or extremely important issue...when asked about the types of data collected by VHAs, only 31% reported that they collected data on volunteer satisfaction."

Brudney and Gazley found a similar incongruity among state coordinators of the USA Freedom Corps, who generally indicated that effective volunteer involvement would be essential to their programmatic success – meanwhile, 62% had not established any guidelines regarding volunteer management.

Staff Involvement in Program Design

Throughout the volunteer program design process it is essential to involve all levels of staff. If volunteers are going to be working in conjunction with paid staff, whether for them, alongside them or in support of them, it is vital that staff be in agreement about the purpose and worth of the volunteer job and the volunteer program as a whole.

Staff that do not want to work with volunteers can

destroy a volunteer effort, either through direct opposition or through indifference. If staff are not willing to cooperate in developing realistic jobs for volunteers; if they ignore volunteers or give them second-class status in the agency; if they indicate by word or by action or inaction that volunteers are a hindrance, not a help, then volunteers will quickly become disillusioned and de-motivated, and they will quickly find other causes and other organizations with which to volunteer, or they may stop volunteering altogether.

Surveying Staff Attitudes

One method of assessing staff attitudes is to conduct a survey. The survey, which can be done either through in-person interviewing or through a printed questionnaire, should ascertain:

1. The level of *experience* of paid staff in working with volunteers:

- Have they supervised volunteers before?
- Have they ever worked in an agency that involved volunteers?
- Do they volunteer themselves at an agency?

2. The level of *comfort* of staff in regard to volunteers:

- Are there jobs that staff feel that volunteers should not be doing? And why?
- Are there program elements, such as additional staff training, which should be instituted before volunteers are brought in?

3. Any *fears* that staff might have about volunteer utilization:

- Are there potential difficulties, such as organizational liability or quality control questions that should be addressed?
- Are there worries about loss of staff jobs?

A sample survey is provided in Appendix Three.

The responses to the survey should tell the Volunteer Program Manager how staff will react to the inclusion of volunteers, a topic we discuss in greater depth in Chapter Thirteen.

The key item to assess in talking to staff is to learn what they are trying to accomplish in their work and where they are having problems reaching their goals. This will allow you to develop meaningful roles for volunteers, which we will discuss in Chapter Four.

Top Management Support

The volunteer program will be more effective if it has the support of the top management of the agency. This support might be represented by the official adoption by the board, management committee, or executive committee of the agency of a policy supporting the use of volunteers, or by a position statement on volunteers approved by the chief staff of the agency.

One essential element of this support is that the top management and senior staff should have a clear vision of how the volunteer program will contribute to the achievement of the agency's mission. Some key questions that top management should consider when contemplating the creation of the volunteer program include:

- How would you describe the mission of the organization and how do you see volunteers aiding in the fulfillment of that mission?
- What is it at this specific time that leads the organization to consider starting a volunteer program?
- What specific goals are envisioned for the volunteer program during its first year of operation?
- What kind of resources is the agency willing to invest in involving volunteers?
- What type of return value does the agency see itself getting from the involvement of volunteers?

It is important to note, however, that while it is desirable to have top management support for utilization of volunteers, it is not desirable to have that support become coercive in nature. It is not possible for management to compel staff to involve volunteers. Opposing staff can too easily drive volunteers away or can too easily make it impossible for volunteers to be successful. What is desirable is an attitude by top management that encourages and rewards effective utilization by staff of volunteer resources, an approach using the "carrot" and not the "stick."

Getting support from management is discussed more fully in Chapters Thirteen and Sixteen.

Organizational Climate

Overall organizational climate will also influence how volunteers can be involved. Volunteers will quickly become aware of overall attitudes within the agency – whether about how well the agency is doing, how things are done, or who and what is important to the agency. These subtle cues regarding organizational style will influence the determination by volunteers of whether the organization is worth the donation of their time. It is actually possible to simply walk through an organization, sense the general climate, and make a very good guess about how it will welcome volunteers. Since the organization will become a work site for the volunteers, they are more likely to appreciate and stay at an agency that has a positive environment. What is needed is a sense of common mission and purpose, and an understanding that productive steps are being taken toward accomplishment of that mission and purpose.

Some indicators of good organizational climate include:

- Clear sense of individual roles, with respect for roles of others
- Willingness to sacrifice for a goal
- Trust
- Tolerance and acceptance
- Open and honest communication
- Group identity: "we're in this together"
- Inclusion, not exclusion
- Mutual support and interdependence

An organizational climate that is favorable toward volunteers will communicate two feelings or attitudes to the volunteers:

- *Acceptance*: The volunteers are welcomed by and connected with the overall purpose and operations of the agency

- *Appreciation*: Each volunteer has a unique, recognized contribution to make to the purpose and operations in the agency

Policies and Procedures

Volunteer program management also requires the creation of some formal rules and procedures. After the determination of why volunteers are to be involved, the organization will need to develop its own set of policies and procedures governing the engagement of volunteers. Sample volunteer management policies are provided in Appendix Four.

The policies will allow the Volunteer Program Manager to develop a consistent pattern of volunteer involvement, and will provide assistance in dealing with problem situations. Both the policies and the procedures by which they will be implemented should be developed in conjunction with staff, particularly if the agency is involving volunteers in a variety of different types of projects or activities.
If you have a question about the content of a policy or procedure, refer to the policies and procedures that the agency uses for paid staff. The rules should be as similar as possible: *"When in doubt, copy."*

The volunteer program will also need to develop some basic personnel-related systems. Volunteer programs operate with the essential forms required for any operation involving people:

- intake forms
- position descriptions
- personnel records
- evaluation instruments

Individual records need to be maintained for each volunteer, giving:

- biographical and contact information
- records of positions and training
- hours contributed and tasks accomplished
- expenses claimed and reimbursed
- dates of connection with the agency

The systems and files developed should match those of paid staff, and can often use the same forms. We have included examples of many of these forms in Appendix Three.

Records such as those above are not only important to the current Volunteer Program Manager, they are essential to their successor. These records provide a history both of the program and of individual volunteers than can be invaluable in creating an understanding of what is going on.

Investigate the utilization of computer software packages to assist in these personnel functions. Software packages are now available (or can be custom developed for your program) that will greatly aid you in keeping track of the names, skills, interests, and availability of your volunteers. They can greatly assist you in performing the paperwork functions of volunteer management, conserving your time to deal with those parts of the job that require human contact.

Contact information for some of the volunteer management software providers is provided in Appendix Two.

Program Evaluation

The plan for the volunteer program should also

consider the process by which the volunteers' contribution is to be evaluated. The design of program operations should include the management information systems that will enable staff, management, volunteers, and the Volunteer Program Manager to determine how things are going and whether things can be improved on a regular basis.

The intent of evaluation is to uncover problems (low rates of volunteer retention; need for additional training) and to reward accomplishment. Much like individuals, organizations and programs need to know when they are successful; without measurements of what success is and when it has been accomplished, it is impossible to know when you have "won."

In developing the evaluation plan, consider the following questions:

1. What would volunteers like to know about themselves, about the program?
Hours contributed, benefits to clients, etc.

2. What would staff who work with volunteers like to know?
Numbers of volunteers in their area, number of clients served, etc.

3. What would top management like to know?
Who is utilizing volunteers, value of volunteer time donated, etc.

4. What would the Volunteer Program Manager like to know?
Where volunteers are coming from, rate of volunteer turnover, etc.

This topic is covered much more extensively in Chapter Fourteen.

Possible Elements within a Volunteer Program

The elements of a volunteer program will naturally depend upon the shape, size, structure, and purpose of that program. Here are some "parts" that you might wish to consider for their applicability to your program:

- Overall written agency policy on volunteers
- Separate budget for volunteer program coordination
- Budgeted funds at individual department level for volunteers
- Formal staff training in volunteer management
- Mention of volunteers in union contract
- Written job descriptions for volunteers
- Minimum time commitment for volunteers
- Use of mass media recruitment techniques (TV, radio ads)
- Website space for the volunteer program
- Organized outreach efforts to diversify volunteer recruitment
- Formal interview process for potential volunteers
- Criminal record checks of potential volunteers
- Reference checks of potential volunteers
- Health screening of potential volunteers
- Probationary or trial period for new volunteers
- Written agency/volunteer agreement
- Formal volunteer orientation & training session
- Scheduled evaluation sessions with all volunteers
- Volunteer involvement in evaluating staff
- System for tracking volunteer hours
- Annual volunteer recognition event
- Reimbursement of volunteer expenses
- Insurance coverage for volunteers
- Formal volunteer exit interview
- Preferential hiring of staff with volunteer experience
- Use of volunteers to assist the volunteer manager
- Use of volunteer management computer software

Assessing Your Plan

Assess your plan for volunteer involvement by reviewing the following checklist. If you have not completed the items on the list, then you still have preparations to finish before you and your agency can effectively involve volunteers:

- ❑ Does the organization have a clearly defined mission with long-range goals which relate to the community?

- ❑ Have staff and volunteers been involved in developing the plan to accomplish these goals and have they considered and discussed the involvement of volunteers in accomplishing the mission of the agency?

- ❑ Is the volunteer work to be done meaningful? Is it useful and significant to the agency, program, and clients?

- ❑ Can the need for the job be adequately explained to a potential volunteer? Can we describe how this job contributes to the mission of the agency?

- ❑ Can the work be done by a volunteer? Can it be reasonably split into tasks that can be done on evenings or weekends? Is it amenable to a part-time situation? Are the needed skills likely to be available from volunteers, or can people be easily trained in the knowledge and background needed?

- ❑ Is it cost effective to have the work done by volunteers? Will we spend more time, energy and money to recruit, orient, and train volunteers that we would if we utilized staff? Are we looking at volunteer involvement on a long-term or short-term basis?

- ❑ Is a support framework for the volunteer program in existence? Do we have a person ready to act as volunteer manager, volunteer policies and procedures, and inclusion of the volunteer program in the agency plan and budget?

- ❑ Are staff willing to have the work done by volunteers? Do all staff understand their roles in relation to the utilization of volunteers? Can we explain to volunteers what their roles will be in working with staff?

- ❑ Can we identify volunteers with skills to do the job? Are they likely to be available in our community?

- ❑ Will people want to do this volunteer job? Is it a rewarding and interesting job or have we simply tried to get rid of work that no one would really wants to do, paid or unpaid?

- ❑ Do we know what we will do with the volunteers after we get them? Do we have adequate space for them? Do we know who is in charge of them? Does that person know what they are doing?

- ❑ Do we know how we will evaluate success and how and to whom feedback will be given?

- ❑ Is, in the end, the agency committed to the involvement of volunteers or is someone just looking for a "quick fix" solution to their problem?

Resist the impulse to quickly initiate a volunteer effort. The time spent in planning and preparation will greatly reduce both confusion and problems that arise later. Operate by these rules:

Think first, and get volunteers later. They'll appreciate your consideration.

Do it right the first time; it's easier than having to do it over again.

Chapter Four Creating Motivating Volunteer Positions

The single most important factor in managing an effective volunteer program is the design of the volunteer positions. Although this area is critical, Volunteer Program Managers typically pay too little attention to doing it well. An organization that has interesting and productive positions to offer will have an easy time attracting and keeping volunteers. Too many organizations, instead, provide unsatisfactory work experiences and then have an impossible time retaining volunteers. In such cases, staff may regard volunteers as unreliable. The problem of badly designed volunteer work is seldom diagnosed.

In this book we will refer to what volunteers do in a number of ways:

- position
- job
- task
- assignment

All of these may simply be taken as referring to the *work* done by the volunteer.

Consulting with Staff about Volunteer Positions

In an organization that employs paid staff, a Volunteer Program Manager should begin the process of creating volunteer positions by gaining staff involvement. To be effective, a volunteer must have the support of staff. The volunteer's work, therefore, must be something that staff want done.

The role of the Volunteer Program Manager in position development is thus one of "consulting" with staff, helping them develop volunteer positions that support the program and that volunteers want to do. During the process, the Volunteer Program Manager interviews staff to determine how they might involve volunteers. This interview does not consist of merely asking staff what positions they might have for a volunteer. That question is unlikely to provoke a creative response from staff who have had no experience working with volunteers or who have not spent much time thinking about this question.

Instead, the Volunteer Program Manager should take staff through a process (first developed by Ivan Scheier) in which staff members are encouraged to answer the following questions:

- *"What are the parts of your job that you really like to do?"*

Staff responses might include activities such as working directly with clients, doing research, or public speaking.

- *"What are the parts of your job that you dislike?"*

Responses might include activities such as compiling reports, writing the organization newsletter, or filing.

- *"What other activities or projects have you always wanted to do but never had time for?"*

Responses might include activities such as working with a new client group, investigating new sources of funding, or starting a program in a new community.

- *"What are some things you would like to see done that no one has the skills to do? (Or that we can't afford to pay someone to do?)"*

Responses might include activities such as upgrading the organization's computer capability, doing market research, or creating a new organization logo.

The answers to these questions can form the basis for defining volunteer positions that can be integrated with the staff workload and will be supported by staff. In a nutshell, if the Volunteer Program Manager can bring in a volunteer who will relieve members of the staff of the tasks they don't like doing and give staff the time to do the things they've always wanted to do, staff have a powerful incentive to make sure that the volunteer has a good experience at the organization. In addition, by involving volunteers in activities the agency cannot perform with its paid personnel (either through a lack of time or skill), we extend the effectiveness of the organization. By designing positions around the types of work staff don't like to do or lack the necessary skills to do, the Volunteer Program Manager develops volunteer work that is both "real" (i.e., it really needs to be done) and will be appreciated by the staff. As a consequence, the potential for typical staff-volunteer difficulties, such as staff forgetting to thank volunteers for their efforts, is greatly reduced.

The interview process described here can also be

used to educate staff as to the correct "shape" for a volunteer position request, as will be discussed later in this chapter. By helping the staff develop the description of the work to be done, the Volunteer Program Manager will greatly lessen the prospect of being bombarded with impossible requests for volunteers: "Someone to come in from 10-5, Monday through Friday, to do my filing."

To assist in this effort, the Volunteer Program Manager can employ a number of tools to show staff what will be possible. These tools can be used in a "menu" approach, giving staff lists of possibilities. The tools include:

- A list of the types of positions/functions that volunteers are already performing in the agency.
- A list of types of positions/functions that volunteers perform in other organizations in the community or in similar programs across the country.
- Skills/descriptions of available volunteers.

These listings will serve to provide ideas on potential positions to staff that do not have clear understanding of the potential uses of volunteers within the organization. They will serve to broaden the perspective and improve the creativity of staff in developing interesting and challenging volunteer positions.

The Circle of Staff Needs

The process of staff involvement should be a continuous one. The Volunteer Program Manager should develop a process for on-going communication with staff, either by periodic follow-up interviews or through written communication in which the process of new position development continues. One method for accomplishing this is to institute a "work wanted" section in the organization's newsletter or via a memo to all staff, in which volunteer positions are highlighted or in which the skills of new volunteers are announced. The aim of this communication is to create a demand for additional types of volunteer effort.

In essence, what is being created through this process an inventory of staff needs:

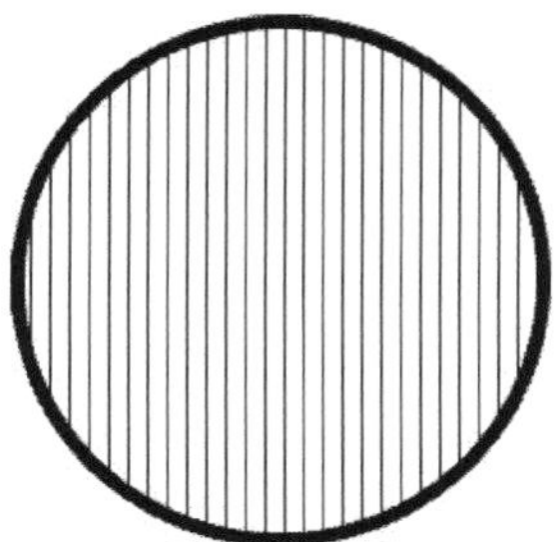

The circle represents the universe of needs and interests of the staff, formatted into a request for particular work to be done. The circle includes a request for:

- specific skills that are needed,
- the time commitment that is required,
- attitudes and other qualities that represent what the organization is looking for in a volunteer.

Within the circle are all the tasks that staff must accomplish in order to deliver current services to clients, to broaden service and clientele, or to accomplish their own internal tasks and operations. The ideas that exist within this range of work represent the possible universe of volunteer work that could be created to assist the agency.

Designing Volunteer Positions for Results

Volunteer programs are successful when volunteers are working in positions they look forward to and want to do. If we fail to give our volunteers such positions, we will be plagued by turnover, unreliability, and low morale.

When we create roles for volunteers, we tend to create them in the same way we create positions for paid people. The positions tend to be designed around the standard management practices of the non-volunteer world. Paid people, however, will usually not turn up for work if they are not paid. When designing a volunteer activity, we should look to the activities people engage in voluntarily.

Designing a position people want to do is the cornerstone of all successful volunteer programs. While paid people will do a position that is unrewarding because they are compensated for doing it, volunteers will not do so for long. This has given volunteers in general a reputation among paid people of being unreliable. On the contrary, if the volunteer does not find the position to be personally satisfying, he or she can be relied upon to quit. To attract and retain volunteers, we must deign positions they want to do.

Volunteering is a leisure time activity, as volunteer management expert Joe Lovelady once said. People engage in leisure activities for a variety of reasons, including a sense of satisfaction, challenge, reward, and accomplishment. To attract and keep volunteers, we must design their roles so that they have similar characteristics. Otherwise, people will do something else with their leisure time.

In designing volunteer positions, we might learn something from people who design games. Games are voluntary activities that are designed to be intrinsically motivating. Games are so motivating, in fact, that people will spend lots of their time and money on expensive equipment and lessons in order to get better at them, something that is rarely true of work. Games are so well designed, in fact, that people will spend lots of money to get to see other people play them. If this were true of work, we wouldn't have to worry about getting funding for our agencies—we could just sell tickets to watch our people do their work.

The point here is not that volunteering should be a game, but that it should have the same motivational qualities that games have. All games have four characteristics that work can also have but seldom does—ownership, the authority to think, responsibility for results or outcomes, and an ability to evaluate or measure what is achieved. When we design volunteer positions, therefore, it is good to try to build in these characteristics. Positions designed with these characteristics also require less supervisory effort.

- *Ownership*

The first of these factors is what we call "ownership." By ownership, we mean that the volunteer has a sense of personal responsibility for something. Their position contains something they can point to and say "This is mine." This might be a particular product or event or geographic area. In the nonprofit world, the ownership is often a volunteer's own client or project. There are many examples of volunteers having such responsibility: Mentors, big brothers and big sisters, phone workers in a crisis clinic, a companion or visitor to an elderly person, and foster grandparents are all volunteers who have one or more clients that are "theirs."

Ownership gives the volunteer something to be in charge of and hence to be proud of. Giving volunteers a project of their own, one with a clear end-point, is particularly important to today's new breed of volunteer, who are less interested in making a long-term commitment to an organization than volunteers used to be. And it is also particularly important in attracting new volunteers to an organization. A 1988 study by the J.C. Penny foundation, for example, found that 79% of US citizens who do not volunteer said that the most important incentive in getting them to volunteer would be a short-term project.

Ownership is destroyed when volunteers do only one of many activities the organization provides as part of its service to a particular person or group. In some social service agencies, for example, volunteers might do a preliminary screening of client needs, then hand the resulting paperwork over to a trained professional who would offer specific advice or determine eligibility for services. Similarly a volunteer firefighter might arrive at the scene of an accident, take the victim's vital signs, then get shoved aside by paid firefighters who do the rest of the activities related to saving the patient.

When volunteers merely do one activity in a string of activities, they can lose the intense satisfaction of helping others that drives most volunteer efforts. Although they know that somewhere down the line they have contributed to client's needs their sense of pride and ownership is diluted because all the others have had a hand in it.

Similarly, volunteers fixing up a school will tend to get more satisfaction if they do all the activities related to fixing up a particular room than if they do one activity (such as painting or washing windows) in all the rooms. The first circumstance provides them with a sense of ownership ("This is my room") whereas in the second case the sense of ownership and responsibility becomes diluted. Because their sense of pride in the work is reduced, such volunteers tend to burn out much faster than those who have full responsibility for a client or a project.

This is not to say that teamwork should be avoided in position design. Teams of people can also have ownership. In these cases, there is a sense that we have something that is "ours." In one city, for example, there is an all-volunteer program that was formed when the parks department reduced its complement of maintenance staff as a result of a budget cut. Teams of volunteers had parks of their own which they kept free of trash and graffiti. In this case, the sense of ownership was met because the team could look at "our park" and take pride in its appearance.

- *The Authority to Think*

The difference between a team and a collection of isolated individuals is that a team has the authority to plan and evaluate its work and agree on who is going to do what. This authority to think is the second key element in good position design, whether for individuals or teams. With this authority the individual or group not only does the work but can also play some part in deciding how to do it.

Many Volunteer Program Managers have a built-in resistance to allowing volunteers this authority. For one thing, the volunteer may work only a few hours per month and so have difficulty keeping up with what is going on. And for another, standard management practice holds that it is the supervisor's position to do the planning and the deciding and the employee's position to carry out whatever the supervisor thinks should be done.

Indeed, when a volunteer first comes on board, this may be the most comfortable way to proceed. As volunteers learn the position and begin to figure out what is going on, however, the fact that they are only doing what someone else decides begins to sap their motivation and dilute their feelings of pride in what they accomplish. They will tend either to resent being told what to do or to lose interest in the position. Either of these will increase the likelihood of their dropping out.

This does not mean that we should abdicate our responsibility for ensuring good results from volunteers. Obviously, we can't afford to have all our volunteers doing whatever they think is best, and without guidance. We need to make sure that they are all working toward the achievement of a coordinated and agreed set of goals. What we can do, however, is involve them in the planning and deciding process so that they do feel a sense of authority over the "how" of their position.

The process of managing all this is explained in detail in the chapter on supervising volunteers. For now, suffice it to say that in designing the position we should ask:

"How would a person who tells the volunteer what to do know what to tell him?"

Or we could ask:

"What does the volunteer's supervisor do in order to figure out what to tell the volunteer to do?"

We can then include those thinking tasks in the volunteer's position description, healing the schism between thinking and doing. In a sense, in doing this we give the volunteer back her brain.

- *Responsibility for Results*

The third critical element in developing a work structure that encourages excellence is to make sure that the volunteers are held responsible for achieving results, rather than simply for performing a set of activities or "position duties." If they are responsible for results or outcomes, they are focused on the end product of what they do, and they get the satisfaction of making progress toward a meaningful accomplishment. If, on the other hand, they are responsible only for the activities that may lead to some result, they are divorced from that satisfaction. Crime prevention volunteers in a Neighborhood Watch program, for example, will get a lot more satisfaction if they are given the responsibility for reducing burglaries, and their effectiveness is measured against this yardstick than if they see the position as the activity of knocking on doors to talk to people about planting "hostile shrubbery" under their windows.

Most position descriptions for volunteers (or for paid staff) are not defined in terms of results. Instead, they merely list a series of activities the volunteer is supposed to perform. The result is never mentioned. Most often, in fact, the responsibility for the result is fragmented, with several people all having a few activities to perform if the result is to be achieved. In fact, the responsibility is sometimes so fragmented, that the volunteer loses sight of the result. As a direct consequence of this, results are poorly and inefficiently obtained and the volunteer gets bored.

Because it can be difficult at first to grasp the concept of defining positions in terms of results, let's look at some examples. Volunteers in a drug abuse program, for example, may be told that their position is to spend three hours per week counseling a client. This is a statement of an activity to be performed. No result of the counseling has been specified, and if the volunteer doesn't achieve much, we shouldn't be surprised. The position as defined requires no particular skill, other than sitting in a room with someone for three hours. To define the result, we need to ask, "What is the outcome we want from the counseling? What do we want the volunteer to accomplish in these three hours per week?" The answer would probably be something like "Clients will be able to cope with daily life without resorting to the use of drugs. " By defining this desired result for each volunteer counselor, we offer a challenging and worthwhile accomplishment for the volunteer to be working toward.

Similarly, volunteers in a school program might be told that their position is to work with children on reading skills. When we ask only that someone "work with" the children, we are not creating any responsibility for helping the children learn. There is no challenge in the position when it is defined in this way. It is better to specify the specific skill improvements that the volunteer is responsible for helping the child achieve. The result might read something like "Bring the child's reading abilities up to grade six reading level."

When we define volunteer positions in terms of results, we help meet people's need for a sense of achievement or accomplishment. It helps them feel that their volunteer activity is valuable and worthwhile. It also helps the volunteer program operate more effectively. When people know what they are supposed to accomplish, they are more likely to do so. If we want to achieve meaningful results through our volunteers, it makes sense that we should let them know what results we expect and then hold the volunteers responsible for accomplishing them.

- *Keeping Score*

The fourth critical element in good position design is to decide how to measure whether and to what degree the results are being achieved. If we don't do this, the statement of result will fail to have any motivating value, and it will be impossible for both volunteer and supervisor to know how well the volunteer is doing.

Many Volunteer Program Managers shy away from measuring volunteer performance, thinking that doing so would discourage or demotivate them. The opposite is more likely to be the case. If people can't tell how well they are doing, if they can't tell if they are succeeding or failing, they tend to get bored with the activity. There is also no incentive to try a different course of action if you don't know that your present course isn't working.

For some positions the measure of performance is fairly obvious and easy to state. In the case of a crime prevention volunteer, for example, the number of burglaries in her area is a readily available statistical measure. We can use these statistics (provided she is responsible for the same geographic area for which statistics are being compiled) to measure the result of keeping people safe from burglaries. Every time a burglary occurs in her area, she will naturally ask "what could have been done to prevent that?" These thoughts spur her creativity, and encourage new, even more effective approaches. If the position is merely defined as talking to citizens about crime prevention, however, and there is no feedback to her on how well she is doing, there will be little likelihood that more effective approaches will be tried.

In other cases, we find the measure more difficult. In the case of the Girl Guide leader whose result is to help her girls develop self-assurance, we need to do some hard work to figure out how we are going to measure progress. We need to ask questions such as "How will we know if girls gain self-assurance? What would we see when they are and when they aren't self-assured? What questions could we ask them to determine their degree of self-confidence?"

Many Volunteer Program Managers don't want to do this much work, and so they take the easy course of holding the volunteer accountable only for performing a set of activities. By doing so, however, they deprive the volunteer of the ability to tell how well she is doing. They also deprive her of a sense of accomplishment.

Taking the time necessary to define how to measure volunteer progress toward results is management work. It is an essential position that all managers should engage in but many do not. In not doing so, we throw away a major motivator.

Many Volunteer Program Managers who do measure performance tend to measure the wrong things. They keep track of things such as hours spent or miles driven or client contacts made. These measures tend to lack any real meaning because they do not tell us whether the volunteer is accomplishing anything of value. They do not measure whether the result is being achieved.

To determine how to measure a given result, involve the volunteers who do the position. Ask them these two questions:

- "What information would tell us if you are succeeding in achieving the result?"

- "How will we collect it?"

Measuring performance makes it possible to introduce an element of competitiveness. It is possible to set targets and to encourage these targets to be surpassed, and even for the setting of records. Records are tremendously motivating. People daily do ridiculous things to break records, such as making an omelet that weighs four tons. The Guinness Book of Records lists some of these impossible achievements. If people spend time and effort to do such silly things, voluntarily, think of the productive work they might do if there were records to set for something more serious!

Volunteer Position Descriptions

Each volunteer should have a written position or role description. This position description should be jointly developed by the Volunteer Program Manager and the staff person that will supervise the volunteer. It provides a summary of the work and activities to be performed by the volunteer. It functions as an instrument that can be used in the supervision and evaluation of the volunteer.

The discipline of writing a good position description is a useful one. In some ways, position descriptions can be much more important for volunteer staff than for paid staff. Paid staff are accustomed to learning their positions by osmosis—coming to work and spending time watching what is happening and determining what they should be doing, and how they should do it. For a volunteer, this learning time period may be excessive, since ten days of on-the-position learning can easily translate into several weeks or even months for a part-time volunteer. Unless the organization is prepared for the volunteer to begin work immediately and has prepared suitable instructions, the volunteer can become discouraged right from the start. A position description that accurately represents the tasks to be undertaken and the effort that is required can serve as a method for readying the organization for the appearance of the volunteer. If you discover that either you or the staff with whom the volunteer will be working cannot put together a precise position description, it would be better to re-initiate the process of position development than to recruit a volunteer for a position that cannot be properly defined.

A position description will contain the following:

- *Title*: What the position will be called, or what position is being offered.

- *Purpose*: The result the position is to accomplish. This is the most important part of the position description.

- *Results*: If there are definable results that contribute to the overall purpose, these should be listed.

- *Suggested Activities*: Examples of what might be done to accomplish the purpose. The word "suggested" indicates that the volunteer has some authority to think, to pursue other approved activities if her supervisor agrees these might be effective in achieving the result.

- *Measures*: How we will tell if the result is being achieved.

- *Qualifications*: What skills, attitudes, and knowledge are desired, as well as any requirements requiring dress or conduct.

- *Timeframe*: Estimated number of hours, length of commitment, and flexibility in scheduling.

- *Site*: Location of work.

- *Supervision*: Relationships with staff and other volunteers, reporting requirements and supervisory relationships, as well as procedures for monitoring and dealing with problems.

- *Benefits*: Training, insurance, parking, reimbursement of expenses, child care provision, any volunteer remuneration, events to thank volunteers, etc.

An additional item to include might be the values and philosophy of the organization to which the volunteer is expected to adhere.

The precise format of the position description is not important. What is important is that all of the elements are covered and that, in particular, a well-thought-out purpose be defined for the volunteer.

An Example of a Position Description

Let's look at an example of how to write a position description incorporating the four essential principles of a well-designed position: ownership, authority to think, responsibility for results, and keeping score. In the US there is a volunteer program whose main purpose is to do household chores for handicapped and elderly people who might otherwise be institutionalized. Originally, the volunteer position description wasn't in writing. Volunteers simply were told to do whatever cleaning and home maintenance the social worker deemed necessary. The program was plagued with a high turnover rate, as volunteers often found the work more unpleasant than they had expected. In terms of our four criteria, the volunteers did have ownership – they had clients who were their own and no one else's.

But they had little control over what they did, however, as the social worker limited them to a certain list of tasks. There was no clear end result they could see. And they were measured only by whether they completed their assigned activities.

In redesigning the position, the staff member responsible for supervision and the volunteer coordinator sat down with a group of volunteers to define results and measures. At this day-long meeting, two desired outcomes were identified. The first was that clients would be able to stay in their homes so long as they had no serious medical problems that made institutionalization necessary. This result was easily measured by the number of nonmedical institutionalizations. Such a result didn't seem enough for the volunteers involved since they felt this could be easily achieved and that they still could be doing a lackluster position. They suggested that a second outcome be included, that client houses be clean. This brought up the problem of how to measure whether a house was clean, since people have different standards of acceptable cleanliness. After much discussion, the group finally decided that the client should be the one to determine if the house was clean or not. The final statement of this second result was "Clients will be satisfied with the cleanliness of their homes."

The next step was to determine how to measure this second outcome. The two key questions were asked: "What information will tell us that we are doing a good position?" and "How will we collect it?" As in most cases, the answer was implied by the desired outcome statement itself. The information required was the opinion of the client. Volunteers could get this information informally by asking the client at the end of their visit whether they were satisfied. The program also solicited the opinions of clients on a more formal basis, through a monthly survey. The results of this survey, in terms of numbers of satisfied clients, was then fed back to the volunteers.

Within the framework of what would be deemed acceptable results, the volunteer was then given the authority to do the thinking necessary to achieve them. Instead of the social worker figuring out what needed to be done, the volunteer was given the responsibility to work this out with the client. Her success in fulfilling this responsibility was measured by the degree to which she achieved the two results. Where volunteers were having difficulty achieving client satisfaction, they naturally turned to their supervisor for help and advice as to what they should do differently.

This change in the way the position was defined had a transforming effect on all concerned. The social worker was relieved of the enormous burden of determining what chores needed to be done for each client, and was able to concentrate on actually doing social work. This made her happier and, because she was able to work personally with isolated clients, it also resulted in a reduction in the number of clients who complained - because complaining was the only way they knew how to cope with their loneliness.

The volunteers got greater satisfaction from their work, as they were responsible not just for doing odious chores but for keeping their clients out of a nursing home-a much more rewarding role. They had the authority to devise ways of accomplishing this and of cleaning the homes to the clients' satisfaction. And they had clear measures of whether they were achieving their results. Because of all this, volunteer turnover was greatly reduced, dropping to a negligible level, and the volunteer program developed a statewide reputation for good client service.

In this scenario, the Volunteer Program Manager's role also changed. Instead of being the person who assigned volunteers to clients and then tried desperately to keep them interested in doing the task (by organizing recognition dinners, providing certificates of appreciation, giving motivational talks, and other time-consuming measures), she was now a resource person volunteers sought out whenever they perceived they weren't achieving their results. The amount of time she spent recruiting was greatly reduced due to much reduced volunteer turnover. And the amount of time she spent in "motivating" volunteers also dropped off, since the position itself had become more rewarding.

Here is an excerpt from the final position description:

Title: Senior Service Aide

Purpose: Clients will be satisfied with the tidiness and cleanliness of their homes.
Suggested Activities:

- Identify tasks clients can't do themselves and want done.
- Recommend tasks clients cannot do to the supervisor for approval.
- Devise ways clients can do more for themselves.
- Complete approved household chores.

Measures:

- Client response on periodic survey.
- Number of client compliments and complaints.

Qualifications: Skills in listening and the ability to communicate well with diverse populations is essential. Ability to use common household cleaning apparatus such as vacuums and sponge mops is desirable.
Timeframe: Must be able to devote four hours per week for a minimum of two months. Scheduling will be made to meet the availability of the volunteer as long as it is convenient for the client.
Site: Volunteers will work in the homes of their individual clients.
Supervision: Volunteers will report to the Senior Service supervisor in their area. Their daily work will not be closely supervised.

Benefits: Volunteers will receive training in elements of gerontology and in household cleaning as needed. While on the position, volunteers will have full liability insurance. Mileage will be reimbursed at a rate of 28 cents per mile. Other out-of-pocket expenses will also be reimbursed. A work record will be kept for each volunteer so that the position will provide them with good position references. Regular social events such as pot-lucks are held for volunteers at which they are recognized for their valuable contributions.

Negotiating And Updating

While the position description ought to be formally constructed before recruiting volunteers, it should not be considered an immutable, finished document. The reason for this is that volunteer programs only succeed when volunteers are motivated to do the position that needs to be done. To ensure this, the position description needs to adapt to meet the needs of the volunteer and the organization.

As the interviewer attempts to match the position to the needs and interests of potential volunteers, some negotiation may take place. Further negotiation should take place after the volunteer has been accepted and has begun work. As she gains more familiarity with the actual work to be done, she may make suggestions as to how the position might be modified to make it even more rewarding.

As Ivan Scheier pointed out many years ago, this is in some sense the opposite of what we do with paid staff. There we expect the person to accommodate him or herself to the position. With volunteers, we need to accommodate the position to the individual. We need to build positions volunteers *want* to do.

We can then add a second circle to the circle of staff needs discussed at the beginning of this chapter.

This is the circle of what volunteers want to do. Where there is overlap between the circles, where volunteers are doing things they want to do and that staff want done, we have the building blocks of a strong volunteer program.

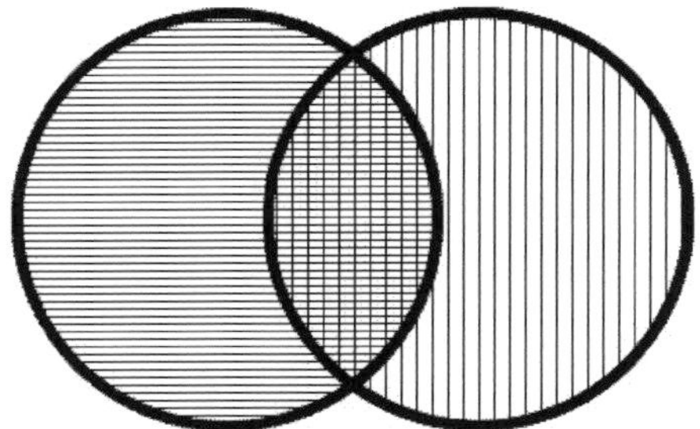

These circles represent the overlap between the needs of the organization and the motivational needs of the volunteer. The area where the two circles overlap represents the volunteer position that will benefit the organization and be suitable for the individual volunteer.

This concept will be explored and explained further in the chapter on Matching Volunteers to Work.

Chapter Five
Recruiting the Right Volunteers

Recruitment is the process of enlisting volunteers into the work of the agency. Because volunteers give their time only if they are motivated to do so, recruitment is not a process of persuading people to do something they don't want to do. Rather, recruitment should be seen as the process of showing people they can do something they already want to do.

Meeting the Needs of Potential Volunteers

In recruiting volunteers, you want to find people who are attracted by the challenge of the position and by achieving the results outlined in the volunteer position description. You might picture the process of matching two sets of needs—those of the volunteer and those of the organization. In Chapter Four you saw how good volunteer positions are created by identifying the needs and aspirations of staff. Now you will construct a circle of volunteer needs, representing those things that a volunteer might want from an agency, including such items as interesting work, flexibility, or recognition.

This circle can be constructed for each individual volunteer, because each will have a slightly different mix of needs and motivations.

The recruitment process then becomes an effort to identify and reach those volunteers whose circles of needs are congruent with what the organization needs and wants, i.e., whose motivational needs can be met by the volunteer position which the organization has to offer. It is important to remember that the recruitment process begins, and in many ways hinges upon, the creation of a good volunteer position. If you ask a person "What would it take to get you to volunteer some of your time for this agency?" the answers you get tend not to be about the recruitment technique but about the type of position you are offering. Nearly all will say something like "It would have to be an interesting position," or "It would have to be something that I felt was worthwhile," or "It should be work that allowed me to grow." Attempting to recruit volunteers without first having developed worthwhile positions to offer them is equivalent to attempting to sell a product to people who have no need for it. It can be done, but the buyer may well become unhappy later. And when volunteers are unhappy, they don't stay around long.

The recruitment process might also be pictured as a "filter." It is the procedure of identifying and separating from the entire universe of potential volunteers (the whole population of your community) those persons who best might fit the needs of the organization and its work, and of separating out those who do not.

Organizations recruiting volunteers may suffer from two very different types of recruitment problems. One problem, which is universally feared by new Volunteer Program Managers, is that of not having enough volunteers. The second problem, which is much more subtle and yet much more common, is not having enough of the "right" volunteers and, indeed, usually having too many of the "wrong" ones.

Effective recruiting consists of attracting just enough of the right volunteers.

This distinction is an important one, with significant implications for a Volunteer Program Manager. Inexperienced Volunteer Program Managers often think that it is desirable to have large numbers of potential volunteers seeking work with the agency. Unfortunately, in practice a surplus of volunteers can cause difficulties. If you advertise for volunteers for a position and have only room for two volunteers, what do you do if twenty show up? Initially, you must expend significant amounts of time in the screening and interviewing process, determining which of the volunteers should be accepted. Then you must "reject" most of the volunteers, risking the prospect of their becoming resentful. The only thing worse than having to reject these volunteers is accepting their service when you don't really have work for them to do, at which point they will really become convinced that both you and the organization are incompetent.

Recruitment, then, becomes a matter of proportion,

balancing the need for applicants with the work required in separating the qualified from the unqualified.

Planning a Volunteer Recruitment Campaign

There are five different types of volunteer recruitment processes that can be used:

- Warm body recruitment
- Targeted recruitment
- Concentric circles recruitment
- Ambient recruitment
- Brokered recruitment

Each is quite different in what it seeks to accomplish and in what it is effective in accomplishing.

Warm Body Recruitment

Warm body recruitment is effective when you are trying to recruit for a volunteer position that can be done by most people, either because no special skills are required or because almost anyone can be taught the necessary skills in a limited amount of time. Examples of volunteer positions suitable for warm body recruitment include a "Day-of" volunteer at a Special Olympics event or a worker handing out flyers at an information booth. Warm body recruitment is particularly effective when seeking large numbers of volunteers for short-term simple positions, such as those who would help at a special event, a festival or a fun run.

Methods for Warm Body Recruitment

Warm body recruitment consists of spreading the message about the potential volunteer position to as broad an audience as possible. The theory is that somewhere among this audience will be enough people who find this position attractive.

The primary methods for warm body recruitment are:

1. Distribution of organization brochures or posters advertising the need for volunteers
2. Use of public service announcements on television or radio, or newspaper publicity
3. Contacting community groups such as a neighborhood association or the Scouts that can provide the person power
4. Use of an agency website to publicize volunteer opportunities
5. Broadcast e-mails or cell phone messages

Recruitment Brochures and Posters

Another good method to reach lots of people is to distribute brochures or posters that talk about your volunteer program. The trick in these is to make them engaging enough to attract people's attention (which generally means short), but with enough information to get people to actually pay attention to the message and contact you about volunteering. Here are some examples of opening phrases that have been used in developing catchy volunteer brochures and posters:

- Do some time...as a volunteer at the jail.
- Do you stand out in a crowd?
- Finally, a plea for something other than your money.
- Helping new neighbors and future friends.
- In a Volunteer Rescue Squad, helping your neighbor is a fact of life.
- Just typical everyday heroes.
- Make a world of difference.
- Make time. Make friends. Make a difference.
- Not every wants to get involved. We want those who do.
- People helping people.
- Picture yourself as a...
- Put your heart in volunteering.
- Retirement creates a world of opportunities.
- Share the experience of a lifetime.
- The future is in your hands.
- The hero we're looking for is...you.
- Volunteering...the rent you pay for the space you take.
- Volunteers make it happen.
- Wanted: people with heart.
- You are the key to our success.

Brochures and posters are an excellent way to involve professional volunteers with advertising or marketing background. They do not, however, have to be expensively produced. One of our favorite posters is an inexpensive one produced for an RSVP program in Arkansas. The headline is "Remember when you changed the world?" with two old photographs of young adults in their military uniforms during World War II. The follow-up line is: "You still can." The poster itself is 11 x 17, and the printing is all in black and white. What is important is the message, not the media.

You can also produce inexpensive but still effective campaign materials by making use of the sentiments of your clients. A good example of this is a very small (5 by 6 inch) postcard brochure for the Washington State Capitol Museum in Olympia, WA. It says "How would you like to receive letters like this?" and shows the photograph of an actual postcard sent in by a young student who had attended a session given by a museum docent. The postcard contains a hand-done child's drawing of trees and a canoe, and says 'Thank you for telling us about the Indians. I liked the canoe.'

There are a great number of possible sites for distribution of printed information. The aim is to place brochures in locations where people are likely to pick them up and read them and where people can actually use the brochures to advise the people who come seek their advice. Possible sites include:

1. Position shops and employment counselors
2. Libraries
3. Tourist Information Centers
4. Chambers of Commerce
5. School and youth clubs
6. Church bulletin boards
7. Community centers
8. Volunteer Centers
9. Hospital waiting rooms and clinics
10. Shopping window information booths

Those programs that deliver a service within an identifiable neighborhood might best benefit from a simple "door-to-door" distribution campaign.

If you look at your brochure and notice that it contains all possible information about your agency (the "kitchen sink" approach) then it probably won't make a good recruitment brochure, but you can still make use of it as an informational adjunct during your recruitment campaign by distributing it as a handout accompanying shorter and more persuasive recruitment pitches.

Website make excellent points for distributing information, especially since they can be made interactive. For the best current example of this see www.peacecorps.gov.

Public Service Announcements
With an ad on television or radio, or a good classified ad for the local newspaper, perhaps only .01% of the audience will be interested. But if more than one million people see the ad this could result in 100 applicants.

Despite efforts to involve volunteers through the mass media, it is difficult to rely on this method to solve all of your recruitment problems. Most of the mass media recruitment done in the US is done through national organizations, working with groups such as the Ad Council. For some examples of their campaigns, go to www.adcouncil.org.

It may be difficult to describe a complicated position in the short framework of a newspaper ad or a radio or television public service announcement. If you do attempt to construct such an ad, you might wish to concentrate on "selling" the needs of your client population, since it will be simpler to describe their needs than it will be to describe the entire position. An alternative approach is to show examples of volunteers engaged in typical volunteer work, presumably having a good time or feeling good about what they are accomplishing. Other motivational needs that can usefully be mentioned include the provision of training or other support to the volunteer in preparing for the position, and the availability of flexible scheduling to make it easier for the volunteer to meet the time requirements for the position.

It is important to realize that even if ads like the above do attract a volunteer, they will not by themselves guarantee that recruitment is successful. You will still need to individually motivate the potential volunteer about the position and the work of the organization. The mass media techniques will simply serve to get you close enough to the volunteer to make an actual recruitment pitch.

Speaking to Community Groups
One of the best methods for warm body recruitment is to arrange presentations to local clubs and other groups. Examples include service organizations (Kiwanis, Rotary) church groups and student organizations. Such presentations can serve both to inform the public about what your agency does and to recruit new volunteers. In following this method of recruitment, be sure to:

1. Deliberately select those groups that you wish to speak to. There are two types who are most helpful: those groups whose membership regularly participates in helping out in the community (Rotary, service clubs, etc.), and those groups whose membership as individuals are likely to have a common interest with your cause. Schedule these types of groups first.

2. In seeking an opportunity to speak to the group, consider going through a group member. The member can serve as your authenticator to his/her peer group, paving your way to a more receptive audience with the person responsible for making the decision. They can also make it more likely that you

will be invited to speak. Many groups have a social secretary that is desperate to find good speakers.

3. Try to time your speaking to meet both the group's and your needs. Find out about other projects the group is already committed to and time your talk to coincide with their need to develop a new project. Determine how much lead time they need and make sure that your request is not too immediate for them to meet.

4. Pick your presenters carefully. Make sure the person who is speaking can explain what your organization does and exactly what is needed from the volunteers. Consider sending a volunteer who can speak forcefully about the worth of the volunteer position. Often one volunteer can more easily recruit another than can a paid person.

5. If possible, use a visual presentation (slides, pictures, etc.) to increase interest. If your presentation is boring, the group may assume that your positions will be too. (You might consider recruiting a photographer to volunteer to take such pictures.)

6. Be prepared for people to offer their services. Take along brochures, examples of positions for which they are needed, sign-up sheets, etc. If people express interest, don't leave without their names and phone numbers, and commit yourself to following up their interest. Follow up as quickly as possible.

7. Be prepared for too much success. You may need to have a back-up plan to handle the entire group wanting to volunteer together to help you, and not just a few individuals. If several group members decide to volunteer, you might want to consider ways in which they might work together as a group while performing the volunteer work.

8. Remember that at some point during your presentation you should directly and unequivocally ask the audience to volunteer. Very few people will insist on volunteering for your program without being asked to do so.

Targeted Recruitment

The second method for volunteer recruitment is called targeted recruitment. With this approach you determine the kind of person who would really like to do the position and track them down. Start by examining the motivations and backgrounds of current volunteers in the position to find out if there are any common factors. Do they all have the same type of motivation? Do they have similar backgrounds or education or experiences or occupations? Do they come from similar groups? Did they all hear about the position in the same fashion? Common factors will enable you to identify populations who seem to like the position despite its requirements, and the commonality will enable you to locate others from that population group. But remember that *who* you currently have volunteering may be determined by *how* you have recruited in the past.

Recent research studies can provide examples of this approach. A study of 4-H volunteer leaders found that 4-H volunteers who continued in their leadership roles tended to differ from their discontinuing counterparts in geographical location, number of children in the family and number of their children who had participated in 4-H. Other studies have found that individuals willing to work as volunteers in the field of mental retardation differed from non-volunteers in that they placed less emphasis on success (both social and economic) and greater emphasis on values such as equality, personal expression, and growth.

A targeted recruitment campaign involves answering a series of questions:

1. What is the job that needs to be done?

As stressed already, it is the position, the opportunity to do something that meets the volunteer's motivational needs, that is the key to attracting most volunteers. A general message, such as "Volunteers are needed at the Crisis Clinic," doesn't let anyone know what the volunteers do there. As such, the message doesn't indicate to a potential volunteer that there is anything they might find interesting.

Volunteer Program Managers who send such a general message tend to do so for one or two reasons. The first is that it is so obvious to everyone in the agency what the volunteers do that they assume the entire community is familiar with their efforts as well. If the organization does a good job of community education, this may well be so, but not all potentially interested volunteers may have gotten the message.

The second reason Volunteer Program Managers send general messages is that there are so many things volunteers do at the agency. As you will see in the next few sections, effective recruitment must be targeted to segments of the population. Different positions in an organization will appeal to different people with particular motivational needs. By targeting the particular campaign at different groups, you can stress particular positions that appeal to those groups and avoid the flabbiness of a message that mentions no attractive positions.

2. Who would want to do the job that needs to be done? This is a question that most of us don't ask, because we have been able to recruit successful volunteers from a variety of backgrounds. It is easier to recruit the right person for the position if you have answered this question, because it is easier to target the message to the needs of that particular group. When you send a message to the community in general, you often wind up speaking to no one in particular.

Ask yourself if there is a certain type of person who is being sought. Do you want someone from a particular age group? Do you want someone of a particular sex or ethnic background? Do you want someone with certain professional skills? The answers to these questions may be multiple: you may want young, old, and middle-aged people, for example. But if you have reached this conclusion in a thoughtful way (rather than merely saying, "We'll take any age group"), you can then begin to target a recruitment campaign on each of these groups, with a slightly different message to each.

The advantage of sending a slightly different message to each group is that you have a better chance of speaking directly to that group's motivational needs. You will therefore tend to get a larger percentage of people from each group to consider volunteering for your agency than you otherwise would. For example, if you identify newcomers to town as a potential group of volunteers, you might stress positions in which they can get to meet new people. Your volunteer recruiting efforts would spotlight efforts in which people work as teams. If you identify harried executives as potential volunteers, on the other hand, you might stress positions that can be done conveniently within a busy or unpredictable schedule, even at home, and which have a fixed end point.

By examining and interviewing your current volunteer population you should get a good start in developing a list of targets. But you should be careful not to assume that this list will represent all of the potential groups that might be interested in the position. Once you have developed a list of the characteristics of the volunteers who have enjoyed the position, start thinking about what other types of people are likely to have similar backgrounds or interests, and try to expand the list of potential targets before you begin analyzing how to locate and approach each potential target group.

One of the most difficult notions to accept about targeted recruitment is that somewhere in this world there are people who will want to do what will seem to you to be the strangest volunteer positions, ones that you cannot imagine anyone actually wanting to do. An article in the *Wall Street Journal* commenting on a group of volunteer professionals in New York City notes:

"The wide variety of chores is an advantage. Volunteers stand ready to give time but are not sure what positions they can handle. One young woman, for instance, explained that she started taking city children on outings but discovered 'I couldn't stand kids.' Now she hauls trash from housing-rehab sites. 'You'd be surprised,' she says, 'at the satisfaction you can get when you see a dumpster finally fill up.'"

Not your typical volunteer position, perhaps, but one that is quite satisfying to some people whose regular work doesn't give them that sense of definitive accomplishment.

Some questions that might prompt you to construct a thoughtful answer to "Who might want to do this job?" include:

- Who currently does it? What positions or occupations do they have?
- Who once did it and has now quit or retired?
- What sort of person has motivations that will be satisfied by doing this position?
- Who would like to be doing it, but is now in a position where it is not possible? Who was educated to do this, but now has a different type of position?
- Who would like to learn to do it?
- Who is now learning to do it and intends to do it more in the future? What schools or colleges teach this subject?
- Who can get someone else who is qualified to do it? Can you find a teacher or a senior practitioner in this skill who can recommend and encourage others in their field to help us?
- Who has a radically different position, such that this would be an exciting novelty?

Targeted recruitment tends to work best when you are looking for a particular type of skill, such as experience in accounting. It tends to work somewhat with psychological characteristics, but only if they are sufficiently identifiable (such as a love for children or a liking for sports) that they can be readily recognized by going beyond internal mental states into outward physical manifestations.

3. Where will you find them?
Once you have determined the type of person you are trying to recruit, you can ask "Where will you find them?" If you are after a certain type of profession, are there professional societies or clubs where such people might be found? If you are after members of a given age group or a certain ethnic group, are there places where groups of such people gather? Where do they shop? Where do they worship? Where do they go for recreational activity? Again, if you simply begin trying to recruit anyone in the general community, the answer to this question is "everywhere." This answer makes your position that much more difficult because it will be harder to focus your recruitment effort. People who are everywhere are also nowhere in particular.

The answer to the question "Where will you find them?" has a lot to do with the recruitment methods that can be used. For example, if you are trying to recruit "Yuppies" you might see about putting advertisements on grocery bags in upscale supermarkets or put flyers on the windscreens of BMWs. If you are recruiting teenagers with time on their hands, you might distribute leaflets outside schools or set up a booth at the mall. Several volunteer programs have recruited single people by advertising in singles bars. If the potential volunteers live in a particular neighborhood, you might go door-to-door (a technique often used by neighborhood and community associations).

The answer might also lead you to speak to certain groups. Such groups might be formal or informal, and your talk to them might be a prepared speech or a casual conversation. Communities are made up of circles of people: social groups, groups of employees, clubs, professional organizations, etc. In identifying who you are after and where they are to be found, you move toward identifying the circles of people you want to reach in order to present your recruitment message.

People also belong to readership, listening, and viewing groups. If you are going to use the media in your campaign, you need to select which media to use based on the profile of its audience. Any newspaper, radio station, or television station can supply you with such information.

4. How should you go about communicating with them?
As indicated above, once you have listed some locations where people can be found, the fourth step is to ask "How will you communicate your recruiting message to them?" This step is implied by the previous one, and if you have done a good job of figuring out where they can be reached, developing an appropriate message is easy.

In general, the most effective methods of recruiting a volunteer are those in which two-way communication is possible. The best form is communication from a current volunteer or board member, since they are attributed with purer motives than those of paid staff. There is always the possible subconscious suspicion that the paid person is trying to get the potential volunteer to do some of the work that the staff member does not want to do.

One of the weaknesses of having no particular target group in mind is that it is difficult to use methods that involve two-way communication with the general populace. If you are trying to recruit "members of the general community" who are "everywhere" you have to fall back on one-way communication such as direct mail, press releases, posters, public service announcements, grocery-bag messages, newspaper ads, handbills, or phone-in calls.

Such efforts do succeed in recruiting volunteers, but they are less efficient in recruiting effective, dedicated volunteers than those methods in which a potential volunteer can ask questions and where you can address the candidate's own needs and skills.

People volunteer only because they want to. Helping a person see that she can do something that she wants to do is easiest when a two-way conversation can take place. Therefore, while you should include easy and inexpensive methods of recruiting volunteers in any recruitment drive, you will be most effective if you put an emphasis on one-to-one conversations and on talking to groups small enough to get a good two-way conversation going.

Recruiting through such methods is a more labor-intensive way of going about it than a one-way communication campaign. Again, this means involving other people in the recruitment process. It means Volunteer Program Managers need to manage the recruiting effort, not do it all themselves.

5. What are the motivational needs of these people?
It is important that the recruitment message speak directly to the motivational needs of the potential volunteer. It must appeal to the reason potential volunteers want to do the position. If, for example, you are going to target newcomers to town in your recruitment campaign, you might surmise that one of their motivational needs would be to make new friends. You would then make sure that your recruitment campaign includes the information that volunteers would meet lots of friendly, interesting people while they do the valuable work you are asking of them.

In addition to doing something worthwhile, each individual has a complex of other motivations for volunteering. Some of the common ones are listed below:

- To "get out of the house"
- To get to know important people in the community
- To establish a "track record" to help get a job
- To make a transition from prison, mental illness, or other situations to the "real world"
- To "test the waters" before making a career change
- To make new friends
- To be with old friends who are already volunteering at the agency
- To gain knowledge about the problems of the community
- To maintain skills they no longer use otherwise
- To impress a present employer
- To spend "quality time" with family members by volunteering together
- To gain status
- To escape boredom
- To feel part of a group
- To express a religious or philosophical belief
- To exercise skills in a different context

When you identify your target groups, you can then guess at which of these or other needs might be most important to individuals in that group. You can then send a message that speaks directly to those needs. People might respond to messages stressing motivators as diverse as patriotism, a need to protect their families, or a need to advance their careers. Here, for example, is a very effective ad designed to recruit macho males:

"Men wanted for hazardous journey. Small wages, bitter cold, long months of complete darkness, constant danger, safe return doubtful. Honor and recognition in case of success."

This speaks effectively to a person who has a need to feel he is tough, and who has a need to test himself against very demanding physical circumstances. It was used by Scott and Shackelton for their Antarctic expedition. A similar appeal was used successfully by a Volunteer Program Manager who had been having a very difficult time trying to find people to escort children to school through gang-infested housing projects.

6. What will you say to them?
The sixth major step is to develop an effective recruitment message. Often no thought is given to this at all-you just send people out to talk about what the organization does and about the kinds of volunteer positions you want people to do. By doing this, you needlessly reduce the number of people who will respond.

An effective recruiting message has four parts, the first of which is a statement of the need. The statement of need tells the volunteer why the work he will be doing is important. Most recruiting messages seldom talk about why you want the person to do a particular position. They only talk about the activities the person will be performing. This leaves it up to the person being recruited to figure out what the need for those activities is.

- *The Need*

The need usually refers to something that exists in the community, not something that exists inside the agency. "Our senior nutrition center needs volunteers to help cook hot meals for seniors one day a week" is not the kind of statement you are referring to. The problem with such a statement is that it conjures up only the picture of sweating over a hot stove, and there are few people who are likely to be excited about doing that. Many, however, would find their interest engaged by the opportunity to do something to enhance the lives of the elderly. By including such a statement of need in the recruitment message, you show people how they can help solve a problem rather than merely undertake some activities.

Often, for volunteers involved in providing a direct service, the need will be that of the clients to be served. A few such statements of needs are listed in an abbreviated form below:

- Hospital Volunteer: "Many patients in the

hospital for long stays are lonely and depressed."

- Crisis Clinic Volunteer: "Some people in our community suffer from mental fear and anguish so intense that they do harm to themselves and to other people."

- Literacy Volunteer: "Many people from all walks of life are unable to take advantage of the full benefits of our society because they are unable to read or write."

- Girl Scout Leader: "Many girls grow up without the self-confidence and other skills to become competent, successful adults."

- Mental Health Receptionist: "Clients coming into the center are often embarrassed, confused, and uneasy."

- Museum Guide: "Many people who will visit the museum would like to know more about the exhibits. Sometimes their lack of knowledge causes them to miss a great deal of the meaning and beauty of the exhibits, and their interest in returning to the museum wanes."

- Friendly Visitor: "Some seniors live in housing developments with little or no contact with other people or the outside world. They are sometimes sick, in need of assistance, or in some instances, dying, and no one is aware of their plight."

Such statements naturally lead the potential volunteer to think "That's terrible; somebody should do something about that." Once the person is thinking this way, it is a simple step to recognizing that they could be that person. Recruiting them then becomes easy. Here is a very powerful and simple recruitment message, based on this principle:

"People are hungry. Somebody should do something about that."
Be somebody. Call [our organization].

In responding to statements of need, the volunteer is directly answering the needs that the organization itself exists to address. On the other hand, some volunteers are recruited to do things that do not directly affect the agency's main work. Some clerical types of volunteer positions, for example, exist to meet the needs of staff or of the organization more than they do the needs of clients or the community. In talking about the need in such circumstances, it is important to talk about the needs of the staff in the context of their work in meeting the needs of the community. A few examples are listed below:

- Voluntary Action Center Clerk/Typist: "When people call up wondering what they can do to help make the community a better place, staff are sometimes limited in their responses because the information we have is not filed systematically and not typed."

- Community Action Agency Bookkeeper: "In order to continue our efforts to improve the lives of the poor, we must account for our grants properly, a skill none of our staff have."

The statement of need should lead the potential volunteer naturally to the conclusion that something ought to be done about it. In one-to-one or small group situations, the recruiter can stop at this point to check to see if the potential volunteers agree that this is a need worth doing something about. Often, in such situations, the potential volunteer may stop to remark on the seriousness of the situation. Once you get a volunteer thinking that somebody should do something about the problem, recruitment is as easy as showing them that they could be somebody.

Returning to our example of the senior center, the recruiter might ask the potential volunteer if he was aware than many senior citizens in the community were unable to afford nutritionally balanced meals and were suffering from malnutrition. She might include some anecdotal evidence or some statistics, though these are often less compelling in conversation than stories about actual people. If the volunteer doesn't say anything, the recruiter might ask what she thinks about it.

- *The Position*

All this then leads naturally to the second element of an effective recruitment message, which is to show the volunteer how he or she can help solve this problem. In other words, now is the time to talk about the position description or what you want the volunteer to do. By describing these activities in the context of the need, you make your recruitment message more powerful. If you merely jump in and talk about the activities without also defining the need, some people will be able to figure out why such activities are important, but others won't. By making the assumption that people will automatically see why the work is worth doing, you needlessly screen out people who would like to give their time to a worthwhile effort but aren't able to see immediately why this position is important. Using our example, the potential volunteer might be quite eager to help out in the kitchen to help overcome the problem of malnutrition, while she may be totally uninterested in the position if it is merely described as cooking, busing dishes, or serving meals.

When talking to a potential volunteer about a position, the recruiter should attempt to help the volunteer see herself doing the work. People only do what they can picture themselves doing, so you need to make your description of the job as vivid as possible. Talk about the physical environment, the people they will meet, and all the minor details that create a full image of the situation the volunteer will encounter.

The picture you create should stress the positive elements of the position in order to encourage the person to volunteer, but it should also be honest. Although recruiting does have something in common with selling a product, you must not glamorize or misrepresent the work. If you are trying to sell the volunteer a new truck, you might exaggerate the positive aspects of the vehicle, but in recruiting you are trying to show her that she can do something she wants to do. If she volunteers under false pretenses, you will only waste a lot of time in training and trying to motivate a person who probably will not last long in the job.

In addition to painting a picture of the work to be done, you want to put the volunteer in the picture. The recruiter should always talk about what "you" will be doing, not about what "a volunteer" will do. A good technique to use in this regard is to ask the person some questions about how she would react in certain job situations. These situations should be easy and pleasant ones to handle, not questions such as "What will you do if a client throws up on you?"

The questions should also assume that the person is indeed going to volunteer. Avoid saying "If you decide to do this." Instead, ask questions such as:

- "What hours will be best for you?"
- "What appeals to you most about this work?"
- "What can you do to make the experience fun for you?"
- "Will you be able to attend our staff meetings?"

Once the potential volunteer begins making "positive" statements it will be easier to get them to commit to at least talking further about the volunteer position.

- *Fears*

For some situations, it will be desirable to address potential fears that a volunteer might have about the position. These fears might include such things as:

- A clientele that is viewed as dangerous
- A type of work at which the volunteer has little experience
- A part of town that is unfamiliar to the volunteer
- A disease that is viewed as potentially dangerous or infectious to the volunteer

The best way to deal with the issues is to be straightforward, letting the volunteer know that the organization recognizes the problem and then letting the volunteer know what steps the agency has already taken to help counter the problem. Steps could include, for example, providing extensive training for the volunteer, conducting an orientation in how to protect oneself against infection, or providing regular health checks.

Most volunteers are more afraid of the unknown than of any recognized risk. This means that potential problems are less likely to deter them from volunteering if they are addressed openly, and if the organization seems to be responsible in dealing with them.

Often the easiest way to address these fears is during a one-to-one discussion with a volunteer, but they can also be addressed in other formats, as the following shows:

Volunteer counselors needed. The Fairfax Victim Assistance Network is accepting applications from volunteers to join a dedicated team who counsel victims of domestic violence and sexual assault. Extensive training will be provided in March on counseling skills, crisis intervention, advocacy, and community resources. Persons with diverse backgrounds and life experiences are encouraged to apply. Call xxx-xxxx for information and application.

This newspaper advertisement for a volunteer actually addresses two potential fears. The first is a lack of qualification for the task of counseling, which is rebutted in the sentence that follows offering "extensive training." The other fear is that the position is only being offered to "professionals," which is countered in the next to last sentence.

- *Benefits*

In addition to talking about the need and the position, the message should also talk about how the experience will allow the volunteer to meet the motivational needs she requires from the position. This fourth part of the message, the benefits, helps people see how they can help themselves by doing activities that help the agency serve the community.

To be as effective as possible, the recruitment message needs to show the potential volunteer that whatever combination of need she has can be met by the organization. This section of the message is particularly important in recruiting volunteers for clerical or staff support positions, such as the legendary envelope stuffer. People don't volunteer to stuff envelopes because of the position or for the satisfaction of creating mountains of mail. They do it for some other reason, the most common being the pleasure of socializing with a group of other people while they do this important but not very exciting task.

If the recruitment message is presented in a one-way format, it should list some of the benefits that the Volunteer Program Manager thinks will appeal to the target group. If it is being presented in two-way format, where the recruiter has an opportunity to talk to potential volunteers about their needs, skills, and desires, the benefits can be tailored specifically to the audience.

Because each volunteer has a different combination of motivations for volunteering, the recruiter needs to know something about the potential volunteer in order to do the most effective job of encouraging her to volunteer. If the person wants to gain job experience, you should propose positions that allow her to do that, for example.

If the recruiter doesn't know the person she is trying to recruit, and if the circumstances allow, she should spend some time with the person to find out what kinds of benefits might appeal. This situation also provides the opportunity to identify some things the potential volunteer is concerned about and enjoys doing, and other clues to what it is she wants to do. This may lead to the development of new volunteer opportunities.

For example, a person who wants to help might have a hobby of photography. As the recruiter talks to the person about helping out in the kitchen (which is what the agency wants him to do), she may notice that the volunteer is only mildly interested in that particular position. When she talks about photography, however, interest perks up. She might then ask if the volunteer would be interested in using photographic skills to help the center.

If the recruiter learns what kinds of benefits are important to the volunteer, it is important that these be communicated to the Volunteer Program Manager to insure that the volunteer's needs are met. One cause of volunteer turnover is that volunteers don't get the things they volunteered to get. They volunteered to be with particular friends and got assigned to different shifts; they volunteered to get involved in a regular, soothing, non-stressful activity and were given a high-risk task; they volunteered to learn new skills and never got the chance to do anything beyond what they already know; they volunteered to impress their employer and never got a letter of thanks sent to their boss; and so on. The information obtained from effective recruiting is the same information that can be used in successful volunteer retention.

The statement of benefits in the recruitment message, like the statement of need, is often omitted by recruiters – perhaps they ascribe purer motives to volunteers or because it is so obvious to them. Leaving this out, however, needlessly reduces the number of people you can attract to assist your organization.

Stating the need, the position, the negating of fears, and the benefits are important if you are to have the best chance of recruiting as many effective people as possible.

Regardless of the types of recruitment methods you use, tell the people what the problem is (show the need); show them how they can help solve it (describe the position); alleviate their concerns (deal with fears); and tell them what they will gain (indicate the benefits) in the process. Even if the space is limited, include all these elements in your message. Here, for example, is a four-sentence recruitment message that fit on a poster:

Children are being abused. You can help by offering temporary shelter.
We'll show you how you can help these children and help yourself at the same time.
Call (phone number).

7. Who will do it?
The seventh step in preparing an effective targeted recruitment campaign is to consider "Who will do the recruiting?" This is where you decide how to get more two-way communication into the recruiting effort and who will take the responsibility for creating posters, contacting radio stations, and other forms of one-way communication.

As indicated already, the most effective people are often those who are volunteers or management committee members of the agency. In order to ensure their effectiveness, however, you need to be sure they know that they know this is their responsibility, who they are supposed to recruit, where to find those people, how they are supposed to do it, and what they are supposed to say. In short, they need to be well prepared by the volunteer coordinator to do the most effective job possible.

An often overlooked and extremely effective resource is a person who is recruited specifically to recruit other volunteers. If you are looking for volunteers from the workplace, for example, an effective first step is to recruit an employee whose volunteer position is to identify other potential volunteers within the company and recruit them for positions that they would want to do. Such a person can play this role year-round, thus providing more flexibility for other means of recruitment. Every time a need for a volunteer arises, the volunteer coordinator can put the word out through the volunteer recruiters. These people can then approach people they know who might be interested in the new opportunity to volunteer.

An effective volunteer program might have volunteer recruiters in a variety of different groups in the community at large. Such a network, once established, enables the volunteer coordinator to use the most effective form of recruitment-face-to-face contact with someone you know-in a systematic and easy way. A good way of setting up such a system is to have staff, committee members, and other volunteers think about people they know in the various community groups who might be willing to volunteer their time in this way. These people can then be brought together for a training session.

8. How will they know what to do?
The last step in preparing the recruitment effort is to train those who will be delivering the recruitment message. If you follow the principles described above, this means training everyone involved with the organization. Everybody knows potential volunteers; it's just a matter of getting them to think about asking people they know to make a commitment to solving agency needs and of equipping them to make a coherent case for doing so. In general, training should cover the participant's role in the recruitment process and provide adequate opportunity for them to role-play their presentation of the recruitment message. Ways to make sure participants learn from the training experience are covered in the chapter on training.

Combining Targeting and Warm Body Recruitment
By carefully wording your mass media communication you can actually make use of targeted recruitment in a mass appeal. Consider this elegant ad, from Washington, DC:

Interested in the arts? Volunteers know what goes on behind the scenes at the Kennedy Center. Call the Friends of the Kennedy Center.

While distributed via mass media, this ad makes use of targeted wording to appeal to a certain audience. The key words "behind the scenes" provide a strong incentive to those of artistic bent who wish either to meet and mingle with stars or to get to help with stagecraft. Contrast its effect with the following ad that utilizes exactly the same wording, but with a very different result:

My Sister's Place, a shelter for battered women and their children. Hands-on with hotline and shelter work. Behind the scenes with committee work.

By utilizing targeted recruitment techniques to identify the motivations of likely volunteers you can design a warm body campaign that will generate a greater number of qualified and interested applicants.

An excellent example of this was developed by Nancy C. Grant of the Hearing Impaired Program of the Hearing Society for the Bay Area. Here's a description:

"We have a program for multicultural inner city deaf and hard of hearing kids and their families. We do a lot of group activities aimed at improving communication and socialization skills. We couldn't do it without our volunteers, who have to be at least intermediate level signers and have some experience working with the deaf community. We especially target people who are deaf and people of color, as role models for the kids. You can imagine it's tough to find people with the skills, demographics, and

time/interest in being volunteers.
We've done a small recruitment drive this fall. I trained four members of our program Advisory Council to do 15 minute to 1 hour orientation sessions. They researched likely places to find people who might be interested in volunteering – deaf professional groups, ethnic-deaf clubs (Bay Area Asian Deaf Association, etc.) advanced (not beginner) sign language classes, universities where there are programs focusing on deaf education or rehab counseling or other deaf-related fields. At the end of the presentation, the presenter has interested folks fill out a volunteer referral form; sends the forms to me; I call them back and set up a screening interview, about half of whom actually end up becoming volunteers. It has resulted in a great crew of new volunteers (including a couple of deaf adults from Taiwan whose first language is Taiwan Sign, and who are quickly learning American Sign and English ... great role models for some of our immigrant deaf kids who have similar challenges).

Our Advisory Council members are professionals from the deaf community, parents of deaf kids, and a few are volunteers with the program as well. Most of them don't have the time or interest in doing activities with the kids, but they love the program and see the need for opportunities for the kids. They are very enthusiastic and speak from the heart about the program. They also have strong connections with the community, and are either deaf themselves or sign so well that it models the importance we put on communication."

This is exactly the kind of targeted recruitment thinking and procedure that will produce the types of volunteers you are trying to attract.

Concentric Circles Recruitment
Concentric circles recruitment is the lazy way to always have a flow of replacement volunteers applying to work at your organization. It works through the simple theory that those people who are already connected to you and your agency are the best targets for a recruitment campaign.

To visualize the theory of concentric circles, simply think of ripples in a pond when a rock is thrown in. Starting in the center of contact, the ripples spread outward.

To use the concentric circles theory, first attempt to locate a volunteer for the position by starting with the population groups who are already connected to you and then work outward. You might capitalize on the fact that most volunteers are recruited by people they already know by asking the incumbent in the position to recruit a friend of theirs to replace them. You might look among former clients or your current volunteers for a replacement. This approach will make it more likely to get a positive response, because the group of potential volunteers with whom you will be talking will already be favorably disposed toward your organization. Similar techniques are used in fundraising (donor get a donor) and in membership drives, for example for a book club (member get a member). They are simple, efficient, and cost effective.

The Gallup Survey on Volunteering continually finds that more than 50% of those volunteering do so in response to the direct request of a friend, co-worker, or acquaintance.

These results indicate one of the simple reasons for the remarkable success of concentric circles recruitment. Since it often involves face-to-face recruitment by those who already know the people whom they are approaching, one of its strengths is the personal testimony of the asking volunteer. During the conversation, the volunteer can say, either directly or indirectly, "This is a good volunteer position with a good organization. I know this because I worked there and I think it is worth your time to work there too." This is a very credible and a very persuasive argument that mass media techniques and appeals from complete strangers have a hard time equaling.

Even more direct evidence of the efficacy of concentric circles recruitment was seen in a result of the 1987 Gallup Survey: among those that have been recipients of services by a community agency, 23% volunteer; among non-recipients, only 9% volunteer. The service received need not have been given directly by the soliciting organization, but may instead be of a similar type to that received by those being asked to volunteer. One campaign to recruit volunteers for the alcoholism treatment unit in a hospital consisted of letters to members of a local Alcoholics Anonymous group. Each letter was jointly signed by the volunteer coordinator of the hospital and by a current member of the AA group (thus tapping two elements of the concentric circle concept).

These examples demonstrate that a clear strength of the concentric circles theory is that it concentrates on approaching those who may already have a good reason for helping out, either because they have received services themselves or they have seen the impact of the services on others. They have thus become convinced of the need for the services and of the ability of your agency to assist those with that need; all that remains is to demonstrate to them that they are capable of helping in meeting that need.

Ideal groups around whom to structure your concentric circles recruitment include:

- Current volunteers
- Friends and relatives of volunteers
- Clients
- Friends and relatives of clients
- "Alumni" (clients and volunteers)
- Staff
- Donors
- People in the neighborhood
- Retirees in your field or subject

In short, any population group that has already been favorably exposed to your program makes an excellent target for a concentric circles recruitment campaign. All you need to do to capitalize on this receptivity is to start a "word of mouth" recruitment campaign and a constant trickle of potential volunteers will approach your organization. Continually stress to all of these groups that they are essential to your recruitment campaign, and help them in knowing the types of volunteers for whom you are looking and the ways in which they can assist in finding and recruiting these volunteers.

Although a lot of effective person-to-person recruiting "just happens," you can make a lot more of it occur by systematically encouraging it. Everyone involved in the agency, both volunteers and staff, should understand what their recruitment responsibilities are within the framework of the overall plan. Each time a need for a new volunteer arises, the volunteer coordinator prepares a position description, and a rough statement of the need and possible benefits. This can be communicated to all staff, committee members, and current volunteers (especially those recruited for this purpose) so that they might begin looking, among the people they know, for good candidates.

If you are a new organization, you will probably not be able to take advantage of concentric circles recruitment and will have to rely on the less effective methods of mass media and targeting. In time, however, you will build up the good will among a sufficient population group to take advantage of this simplest and most efficient method of recruitment.

Ambient Recruitment

Ambient Recruitment is a method that does not work for all groups, but which is highly desirable if you are suitable for its approach.

An ambient recruitment campaign is designed for a "closed system," that is a group or people who have a high existing sense of self-identification and connectedness. Examples of possible closed systems where ambient recruitment might work include:

- a school
- a corporation
- a profession
- a church congregation
- a neighborhood
- a military base

In short, any situation where the members of the community view themselves as related to other members and view the values of the community as personally important and meaningful to themselves.

An ambient recruitment campaign seeks to create a "culture of involvement" among the members of this community, getting them to believe that volunteering is the "thing to do." This acceptance of volunteering as a value of the community then leads individual members to seek to fulfill that value by seeking to volunteer because "it's the right thing to do."

There are three steps in creating an ambient recruitment campaign.

1. Develop a philosophy of involvement

The first step in creating a culture of involvement consists in creating an official philosophy statement that explains that becoming involved is an important value of the group. Here is an example of such a statement utilized in a corporate volunteer program, the Green Giant Company:

"In two major ways the Green Giant Company recognizes and accepts its responsibility to participate substantially and responsibly in the society of which it is a part. Its first responsibility is to exhibit social responsibility in all of its own business activities. Additionally, Green Giant is also committed to acting with its expertise, personnel, influence, and financial resources to aid in solving societal problems and in improving overall life-quality, especially so in the communities where it operates.

This commitment recognizes that one of the Company's most valuable assets is its own personnel. Therefore, to carry out this commitment, Green Giant encourages its company and subsidiary employees to participate in community and civic affairs with their personal time and talents."

This statement of philosophy creates the underpinning for the cultural value. It can appear in many forms. For attorneys, for example, it appears as §6.1 of the ABA Code of Ethics. For a church group, it might be the Bible.

2. *Provide early indoctrination*

Step two in ambient recruitment is educating members of the community about the value. This is easiest done early in their membership with the group and is best done by engaging them in a discussion of the value and its meaning. This discussion can best be conducted by others who are clearly identified as fellow members of the group and works even better if these individuals are "opinion leaders" within the group. One of the best ways to continue this indoctrination process by ensuring that the community or group tells stories about volunteer activity, creating role models and legends who exemplify the cultural value. You can help this process by creating ways of recognizing individuals who carry out the value.

3. *Continually support involvement*

The final step in creating a system of ambient recruitment lies in building a support system. An effective ambient recruitment campaign gets members of the group to want to volunteer, but it does not tell them where or how to become involved. Someone must still assist them with the logistics of finding a suitable volunteer assignment and must ensure that the volunteer position is one that will be personally rewarding to the volunteer. Someone must also ensure that the volunteers enjoy and succeed at their volunteer assignments. If this does not happen, you will have recruited a highly motivated and thus highly frustrated volunteer population.

Brokered Volunteer Recruitment

It is also possible to boost your recruitment efforts by connecting with other groups whose purpose is to provide volunteers for community efforts. Possible groups with whom you can form connections include:

- Your local Volunteer Center, which acts as a clearinghouse for those seeking volunteer opportunities.
- The local Senior Corps or Retired and Senior Volunteer Program (RSVP), which places seniors in volunteer positions in other agencies.
- Local corporate volunteer programs, which may channel employees to either on-going volunteer positions or group projects.
- Youth volunteer programs in colleges and high schools, which refer students to local volunteer opportunities.
- Service groups, including clubs (Kiwanis, Rotary), fraternities and sororities, and groups such as City Cares, whose members perform community work.
- Internet sites such as Volunteer Match and Idealist.org. These sites enable you to post volunteer opportunities. They are particularly good for attracting virtual volunteers, those who provide a service from a distant location.

This type of recruitment has the advantage of not requiring a lot of effort. It has the disadvantage of possibly attracting people that are not suitable, people you will then have to reject.

The Internet is rapidly becoming an easily usable method for recruiting volunteers. Most agencies with Web sites have utilized them to describe the activities of the agency and to mention its need for volunteers. Some organizations have gone beyond this to formally incorporate mechanisms for volunteer involvement through their Web site, ranging from a simple transmission of contact information to a more formal Web-based application process. These will likely become almost universal.

In addition, Internet-based volunteer referral mechanisms are being developed in many countries. In the United States the most active of these is VolunteerMatch (www.volunteermatch.org), which has established formal relationships with many nonprofit agencies to advertise their volunteer positions. Similar efforts are underway in the United Kingdom (www. thesite.org/do-it) and Australia (www.govolunteer.com.au). In 2001, according to the Independent Sector, *"10% of those with Internet access used the Internet to search for volunteer opportunities"* This figure will likely increase as the Internet becomes an even more primary means of communication and information-gathering. The next generation of nonprofit web sites are likely to introduce interactive methods for showing potential recruits what current volunteers are doing, utilize techniques such as those pioneered by the U.S. Army at its recruitment website, www.goarmy.com.

Recruiting for Difficult Situations

Recruiting for a "controversial" cause, for a position perceived as "dangerous," or for one that is recognized as "difficult" is obviously harder than for easy positions. Recruitment can be particularly difficult when the nature of the cause or the position is likely to provoke an initial fear reaction from the potential volunteer. The following are some suggestions for trying to design a recruitment campaign for these types of volunteer positions:

1. Do advertising via local TV, radio, or newspapers so that thousands of potentially recruitable people see the message. In essence, saturate the community with your recruitment message. Some of the people you reach won't be afraid.

2. Solicit those who are acquainted with the problem area because they already work with it, or are in an industry related to it, and thus do not have the same level of fear as the general public. Be sure to remember ancillary and connected industries, such as educators who teach in subject areas that discuss the problem area. You can also solicit the families of those who work in the subject area.

3. Ask those who once worked with the problem area or those who are seeking careers related to the cause.

4. Solicit former clients, their families, and their friends and relatives. This group is less likely to be afraid, more likely to identify with your group because they have received services, and quite likely to be committed to doing something about the problem.

5. Recruit via current volunteers. Emphasize "word of mouth" communication. Their personal communication skill ("I work in this area and I know that it is both safe and rewarding.") will often overcome barriers to involvement.

6. Start with recruiting people for a non-controversial position in your agency. Develop a "two-tier" recruitment system. First recruit them for a safe and easy position, then offer them a tough assignment after they know you better.

7. Create an educational program to combat the fear. Offer seminars in the community to provide accurate information about the situation. Utilize some of your more motivated volunteers as spokespeople talking about their experiences. Recruit from those who attend the seminars.

8. Use the targeted recruitment approach, identifying people who would want to do the position. A dangerous position might appeal to certain types of people.

9. Bring people to you for some completely different reason. The London Lighthouse, for example, organizes evening concerts. This gives visitors a chance to come to your premises, perhaps feel warm about your organization, and pick up a bit of literature.

Recruiting for Diversity

The volunteer recruitment process is one way in which the agency can attempt to broaden its base of community involvement. Doing this effectively is not a simple task. Chambre suggests that an agency wishing to recruit black and hispanic volunteers should engage in efforts such as personalized approaches, establishing collaborative relationships with community groups, and arranging 'trigger events' that crystalize individual's decisions to volunteer. Latting suggests that black volunteers are more motivated by altruistic impulses than white volunteers and that recruiting attempts might best be targeted toward blacks that strongly identify with the black community and have strong feelings of social responsibility.

It is possible that agency concerns about the difficulty of minority recruitment are overstated. Carson offers data that suggests that, contrary to perceptions, blacks, for example, actually volunteer more than is thought, noting "the findings indicate that at every level of income blacks are more likely than whites to volunteer their time". Data from the 1990 Gallup Survey strongly suggests that if there is any problem with minority involvement it lies with the agency rather than the potential volunteer: *"Among the 41% of respondents who reported they were asked to volunteer in the past year, 87% volunteered; among the 57% of respondents who reported that they were not asked, only 30% volunteered. Those respondents who were least likely to be asked were blacks (26%), Hispanics (27%), persons 18-24 years of age (31%), and those with household incomes below $20,000 (26%). Among the smaller proportion of these groups who were asked, the proportion who volunteered was more than three times higher than among those who were not* *asked".* Recent Gallup Surveys on giving and volunteering have witnessed similar patterns, but with an increase in the number of minorities engaged in volunteer work (Independent Sector, 2002), which is perhaps one indication of the increased attention being given to outreach recruitment by traditional agencies.

Recent studies have suggested that those who volunteer via Internet sites may have a different demographic profile that than those attempt to volunteer via other mechanisms. A study for the GoVolunteer site in Australia found that:

- 27% speak a different language other than English
- 79% are female
- 68% were under age 34
- 40% had never volunteered before

A similar study by VolunteerMatch in the US found:

- 84% female/ 16% male
- 50% under age 30; only 32% age 40 or older
- 58% Caucasian; 11% African-American; 10% Hispanic
- 75% had not volunteered before

All of those who have examined this issue have concluded that any attempt in this area can only be effective if it is matched with overall adjustments in the agency, including examination of staff recruitment practices, changes in the composition of the agency board, re-assessment of agency priorities to diverse community populations, etc.

Some categories of volunteers, such as youth or minorities who are already uncertain about their reception by the organization, will be extremely sensitive to telltale behaviors that might "reveal" the true intent of the organization. Other populations include those with disabilities, youth, cultural minorities, emigrant populations or others outside the social and economic mainstream.

A study of youth community service programs in Los Angeles found that:

"Among the responses that indicate some fear, the students most frequently admitted the fear of making mistakes and the fear of being rejected in their service activities. Nonsectarian school students showed the greatest concern about the former and religious school students about the latter. Neither of these concerns appears unusual for adolescents who may find themselves in new or different environments."

Over half of respondents indicated some degree of fear.

In a 2003 survey the Institute for Volunteering Research in the UK uncovered the following potential barriers to volunteer involvement perceived by populations not commonly involved in volunteering:

- Lack of confidence was found to be a key barrier. It was exacerbated for individuals who had experienced exclusion in other areas of life, and when volunteering took place in unfamiliar environments.

- Delays in the recruitment process were particularly discouraging – without a prompt response it was apparent that some potential volunteers would simply walk away.

- A physically inaccessible environment created an obvious barrier, particularly for disabled people with mobility-related impairments.

They also note that solving these potential barriers is not impossible:

"By ensuring that recruitment-processes were user-friendly – minimising form filling and asking new recruits in for a chat rather than an interview, for example – some organisations had successfully made the volunteering experience seem less daunting."

Hobbs, discussing the involvement of Latino volunteers, notes that the appearance of the organization and its offices can make a difference:

"The organization's meeting and work spaces should reflect a diversity of cultures, in particular the Latino culture. This can be accomplished by such simple things as the choice of prints you hang on the wall, the artwork on your calendar, the decorative objects on tables and shelves."

While paperwork is often a barrier for populations from different languages and cultures, don't assume they are the only ones for whom it poses a problem. A study of emergency services volunteers in Western Australia suggested up to 20% of them had some form of literacy problems, with 5-7% having severe problems.

Utilizing Alternate Position Designs for Recruitment

It is also possible to enhance your recruitment effort by considering variations in volunteer position design. These variations may be considered where difficulties are encountered in finding adequate numbers of volunteers because of the complexity of the volunteer position under consideration. Included are:

1. Gang up on the position

One way to approach difficult recruitment is to make the "volunteer" not one person, but several. If the difficulty is that the position is too "large" for a single individual, then the obvious solution is to make it the responsibility of more than one person. You can approach this via two different methods:

- *Team Volunteering*

Team volunteering is the classic job-sharing approach to the situation. Make the volunteer unit a partnership, with two persons equally sharing the position, or make the position one done by a lead volunteer who is given an assistant.

The team can split up the time and work requirements. This approach is particularly useful when you are attempting to encourage a volunteer who has a particular expertise but is reluctant to volunteer because they don't feel like they have the time necessary to do all of the work. Their volunteer "aide" can provide the hands; the expert volunteer can provide the brains.

This approach can have several advantages. As Susan Chambre notes, *"Teaming up compatible volunteers builds in several key elements that enhance the success of positions performed by people who work for free: It facilitates recruitment, reduces the need for training, increases the probability of success in performing tasks since one member of the team is more experienced, and addresses the need for sociability."*

Team volunteering benefits all parties in the relationship. It will enable you to induce reluctant volunteers to attempt new challenges and enable you to convince tired volunteers to remain on a bit longer. Another potential advantage of team volunteering is that a properly constructed team may be synergistic, resulting in a whole that is stronger than the sum of its parts. Team members may individually lack skills that are compensated for by other team members, resulting in a more effective work group than any one individual worker can be.

The disadvantages of team volunteering are twofold. First, it requires careful matching of the personalities who will be involved. They must be compatible in personality, vision of the position, and work style to successfully form a team. Second, it requires greater management and supervision, particularly during its early stages when the team is attempting to work out relationships and working arrangements. If you assign volunteers to work together as a team, schedule a review session for about a month after the volunteers have been matched. Turn this session into a discussion of their working relationship, using it to determine whether they have made the transition to a smooth working unit, and using it to determine whether their personalities are suitable for a situation of shared responsibility.

While the word "team" is used to describe this type of job-sharing relationship, it is important to note that the team should not include more than two people. Job-sharing with three or more people is nearly impossible to accomplish without an extravagant amount of work. Larger groups begin to function more as committees, and the nature of that larger social interaction can result in factions and alliances.

- *Cluster Volunteering*

Recruit an entire group as the volunteer unit. The group might include an entire family, a club, or even a business. The group sub-divides the work, lessening the time burden on any single member. Start this process by recruiting one member of the group who will persuade the others to become involved, making the volunteer position their project.

Both of these approaches are substantiated by data from a J.C. Penney survey of volunteer involvement. In that study, 71% of non-volunteers said they would be attracted by a volunteer opportunity in which they could work with friends or peers, and 55% said they would be interested in an opportunity to do volunteer work with their families. By giving them these opportunities, you are essentially creating "two-fers," positions in which the volunteer can simultaneously do good and spend time with others.

A demonstration project on family volunteering conducted by VOLUNTEER: The National Center suggested the following characteristics for design of successful family volunteer positions:

- The time commitment is flexible, often beginning with one-shot or short-term positions that have the potential to grow into continuing activities
- The positions have understandable goals and logical, specific activities to be undertaken
- The positions provide something relevant for every member of the family
- The positions take advantage of the unique nature of family relationships
- The positions provide an opportunity to work with other volunteers, particularly other families

Your search for volunteer groups may lead you into some strange places. Consider, for example, Lifers Group, Inc., a volunteer club that operates out of East Jersey State Prison. The convicts have established a group that helps local agencies raise money and other resources. High school students in Philadelphia have formed a group to provide volunteer computer assistance to local organizations and other students. They call the program "Dial-a-Nerd."

Management of these "volunteer clusters" will depend upon your utilizing an existing natural leader of the group as your key supervisory mechanism. The group must enforce its own rules and will resist too much direct outside intervention. Make sure that you have worked out a way of relating to the group leader, and have that person train and direct the group.

Groups may often rotate leadership, as does "Doing Something," a volunteer group for young professionals in Washington, DC: *"Volunteers are encouraged to take the lead on a project that interests them and to coordinate the activities of the project. By rotating responsibilities, the group avoids letting one volunteer take on too much, and acts as a safeguard against burnout."*

2. Ease Them In

One of the reasons for saying "No" to a high-time or high-involvement position is that the volunteer is afraid. This fear might be based on a feeling that the volunteer won't like the position enough to devote the time and energy to it, that it isn't worth the investment required on the part of the volunteer. Sometimes volunteers also fear that they won't be able to do the position well enough and are reluctant to let the agency down.

Both of these difficulties can be dealt with by introducing the volunteer to the position gradually rather than expecting them to buy the whole package at once. Here are some ways to let the volunteer become accustomed to the more difficult position:

- *Test Driving*

Offer the potential volunteers a 30-day trial period. Tell them to try the position and see if they like it enough to keep it. This is a great approach because it allows both the volunteers to see if they like the position and the staff to see if they like the volunteer.

Schedule a review meeting when the volunteer starts the position and stress that the volunteer is under no obligation to continue the position after the test period - a "no fault" divorce clause. While you will lose some volunteers, you will gain quite a few who have had the opportunity to examine the position without pressure, learned that they liked the work, and decided that investing their time and energy was worth it.

The test drive system works quite well because most of us are accustomed to dealing with it in other parts of our lives. Would you, for example, buy a car without taking it for a drive? Would you buy a new and unfamiliar product that didn't have a money back guarantee?

The implicit promise to potential volunteers is "Try it-you'll like it!" And the reassurance is that they can honorably back away if they don't feel as though they really do like the position. At that point, however, the resourceful volunteer coordinator will try to negotiate with them about other positions with the agency. As we have stressed throughout, the goal of recruitment is not to get them to come forward but to find them a position they will stick with and enjoy.

- *Apprenticeships*

Apprenticeships work by making the volunteer an aide to the person who is currently holding the position. The volunteer then operates as an assistant at the direction of the volunteer who is presently responsible for performing that position.

Apprenticeships work exceptionally well for leadership positions or positions with large amounts of responsibility that people are reluctant to take because they don't feel totally comfortable about being able to do the work well. Examples of good positions for considering apprenticeships are chairs of committees or special events, or technical positions that require decision-making experience that the volunteer does not currently possess.

During an apprenticeship new volunteers can

learn to do the work until they are comfortable with their ability to handle it well. At the end of the apprenticeship they can be "recognized" by a promotion to being in charge, a position that they will now think they have earned and for which they will now think they are prepared.

A variation on apprenticeship is the "mentor" or "buddy" system. In these cases, the assisting experienced volunteer does not directly supervise the new volunteer but serves to provide advice as requested or needed, and often will operate as a coach to the newcomer.

4. Propinquity
This method works through obtaining volunteers for difficult positions by first recruiting them for something else instead. This might sound a bit strange if you don't understand the propinquity principle.

"Propinquity" is the process of becoming accustomed to and favorably disposed toward those things or people that you are around and used to, somewhat to the effect "familiarity breeds affection." Things, or people, or positions which seemed too large or too difficult or too frightening because they were new or strange may no longer seem quite so daunting after you've been around them for a while.

In propinquity recruitment, you attempt to recruit a person for an alternate position that is near or connected to the position for which you eventually want them to serve.

For example, if your organization were having difficulty in recruiting counselors for one-to-one work with emotionally disturbed children, you might recruit someone to assist in collecting data from the volunteers currently doing that position. Data collection is a small and simple job that is easily done, but while doing it, the volunteer is exposed to the more difficult position and can learn to understand it and how valuable it is. Through the process of propinquity, data collection volunteers are more likely to become attached to the counseling position with which they are in contact. When then asked to consider becoming counselors they are less likely to be as afraid of the position, thinking "If those guys can do it, so can I."
One way to view recruitment by propinquity is that you are simply creating a new population of "concentric circle" volunteers who will become interested in the position. Another way is to view it as the "bait and switch" approach to the problem. But any way that you view it, it works: people are much more likely to take positions that they understand and are accustomed to. In recruitment by propinquity, the position ends up speaking for itself.

Utilizing Events to Recruit Volunteers
Recruiting volunteers for a short-term event is a relatively commonplace and relatively easy practice these days. On practically any given weekend there are a variety of available volunteer activities which basic-ally require the commitment of a few hours often spent with friends, ranging from building houses to cleaning up parks to the various "a-thons" that permeate the landscape. There are even volunteer organizations that specialize in organizing these activities and targeting recruitment to those interested in short-term volunteering, such as CityCares, HandsOn Atlanta and most local Volunteer Centers).

The only problem, of course, is that operating a sustained volunteer effort off of these one-shot events is a difficult, if not impossible, task. Most organizations need volunteers who are actively involved on more than a once-a-year basis, and who are willing to come back once the fun event is over and do the hard work that really needs to be done. In particular, they need volunteers who are willing to accept responsibility and perform leadership functions.

Here are some tips for approaching this situation. We'll warn you up front that they require a planned and organized effort, and that you'll have to invest a lot of work before you earn your reward, but we think you'll find it well worth your time.

Step One: Create Attractor Events.
An attractor event is designed to engage the attentions and short-term involvement of larger numbers of volunteers. It can be organized around a clean-up (park, home, nonprofit agency), around community education (a mall show or a corporate fair), an "a-thon" fundraiser, or any other activity which meets the following requirements:

- it can involve large numbers of people in a variety of volunteer tasks and projects
- the volunteer jobs don't require any substantial training or preparation
- the work is fun and exciting and allows people to work with others
- the activity is photogenic, thus attracting media

attention

The event itself should also accomplish something worthwhile, although this isn't the primary aim. In addition, the event should allow all those who participate (volunteers and the general public) to get an introduction to the cause, clientele and operation of your agency, with a particular highlighting of the contributions made by volunteers to the work of the organization. This introduction can be provided via print, demonstrations, or whatever media seems to work in your setting. The key is that current volunteers should be a prominent part of the event.

Step Two: Operate a Scouting Process.
During the event current volunteers should be assigned to work with groups of newcomers. Part of their assignment is to manage the work to be done during the event, but another part of their assignment involves "scouting" those who are attending, looking for those who show the most interest and potential.

These scouts should be encouraged to do the following:

- establish personal contact with each of the volunteers with whom they are working
- give the newcomers a sense of "welcome" and appreciation
- get the names and addresses of those attending, so that they can be thanked afterwards
- ensure that each new volunteer gets some basic information about the agency and about its involvement of volunteers
  Particular elements to look for in volunteers with a potential for further development are:
- people having a lot of fun
- people who seem to like organizing others
- people who indicate interest in the cause
- people who seem to have some personal connection to the cause

Particular attention should be paid to locating those who are "in charge" of already-established groups of volunteers, since these are likely to be personality types who enjoy being leaders and doing additional work.

Scouts should make notes about those they think have the potential for development and a debriefing should be held following the event. The debriefing should discuss who might be receptive to further involvement, what types of volunteer work they have shown interest in, and how they will best be drawn further into the organization.

Step Three: Foster a Nurturing Process.
The process of cultivating those whose potential has been identified will vary depending upon your circumstances, but here are some possible avenues to explore:

1. If the event is a recurring one, you can increase involvement by offering additional work within the context of the event. This might include asking them to provide feedback about the event, offering them a promotion within the activity or group with whom they served in the past year, or asking them to participate in helping organize and operate the event. This invitation should be offered by the scouting volunteer who has developed a personal relationship and it should be based on being impressed with the quality of the work done by the potential volunteer.

2. The volunteer should receive some sign of promotion with the agency, such as an official title which indicates their new status, access to materials or equipment, a business card or some other items which create an official link with the organization.

3. While the volunteer is doing additional work on the event they should receive a further indoctrination about the agency and its work. This should include both information about the work of the agency and about the variety of volunteer positions that are available within it. It greatly helps, by the way, to have a wide variety of volunteer jobs available, since offering options increases your chance of resonating with the potential volunteer.

4. The types of volunteer work available should represent an ascending scale of complexity and requirements. It should include short and easy work, and then have a staircase of more difficult positions. The volunteer should be exposed to current volunteers in these positions, who are given an opportunity to talk about their work and why they enjoy it. These discussions will serve as a low-pressure recruitment effort. From time to time these current volunteers can increase the pressure by asking the potential volunteer to "help them out" on something they are working on. This work should be something that will give the potential volunteer exposure to what the volunteers are doing without requiring a big commitment.

5. The potential volunteer should also be introduced to staff and volunteers at the agency, and encouraged

to get to know them. Becoming friends with others in the organization can serve as an anchor that holds the connection of the volunteer to the agency.

6. While this exposure process is occurring, further scouting of the interests and reactions of the potential volunteer should be undertaken. This scouting should fine-tune the effort to discover the type of motivations and possible volunteer position that can be most appealing to the potential volunteer.

Potential Dangers.
As in any process, there are some easy mistakes to make. Here are some things to avoid:

• *Getting too greedy, too fast.* Offering the volunteer more than they seem to want to do can be a fatal mistake. The trick, as in fishing, is to make the volunteer want to take the bait, not to force it upon him. Remember, that unlike fishing, the volunteer can always get off the hook.

• *Relying on make-work jobs.* The early steps of this process can only succeed if the initial jobs offered to the volunteer are short-term and productive. If a volunteer thinks at any stage that their time is being wasted, you've lost the battle. All of the jobs on the "career ladder" must be meaningful ones and the volunteer must be able to stop at any point in the process and feel good about the work they are doing.

• *Having opportunities for true advancement.* The implicit offer in this process is that the volunteer can become a real leader in your organization. This is, of course, only true if your organization has upward mobility for volunteers and if the current leaders are willing to step aside as new talent emerges. If your current volunteer structure is petrified, it will be very difficult to get new blood into the system.

Identifying Potential Recruitment Appeals

All of the above methods for volunteer recruitment require that the recruiter develop a message that can explain what the agency is offering to the volunteer, and which will tap some motivational impulse of that volunteer. The possible range of volunteer motivations is very broad, encompassing practically every psychological attribute. This tends to lead organizations to develop very broad motivational appeals, believing that someone among all those potential volunteers will respond to them. It is important, however, to realize that what is needed in the development of the recruitment appeal is a slightly narrower approach, motivating potential volunteers not just to decide, in general, to volunteer, but to volunteer with this particular agency, doing this particular position.

To create this more defined appeal, the organization should develop answers to four key questions that can be communicated to potential volunteers:

1. Why should this work be done at all?
   - What is the need in the community for this work?
   - What bad things will happen if this volunteer work is not done?

2. What will the benefit be to the community or to the clientele if the work is done?
   - What will the work accomplish?
   - What changes will it make in people's lives?

3. What are some possible fears or objections concerning this work that must be overcome?
   - The type of clients?
   - The subject area?
   - The skills needed to do the work?
   - Geography?

4. What will be the personal benefit to the volunteer in doing the work?
   - Skills?
   - Experience?
   - Flexible work schedules?
   - New friends?

The appeal can then focus on communicating to the potential volunteer why the agency and its work are important, and why the potential volunteer should contribute to the accomplishment of that work. Different aspects of this message may be stressed more than others, or may be communicated differently in different recruitment drives. An appeal to young persons, for example, might stress job experience possibilities, while an appeal to previous clients of the organization may talk about the effects of the problem and the ability to help others obtain the relief that they themselves have experienced.

Creating an effective message is much more difficult than it seems, particularly when this is being done by paid employees. Quite often their own extensive knowledge of the agency and its work interferes with writing an effective appeal; in a sense they are too familiar with the subject to remember that others lack that basic knowledge. They will often forget to include the most basic of facts (numbers of persons in the community who face the problem; harmful effects of the condition) because they assume that others in the community are as familiar with the situation as they are. Their own intimate relationship with the situation makes them think that others are equally aware. This means that field-testing of recruitment appeals is quite important to make sure that the general population receives the appropriate information in a way that they can understand and relate to.

In the old days, most volunteer recruitment appeals were delivered in face-to-face meetings where you had a bit of time and space to fully describe why volunteering was a good idea. These days you're probably limited to a quick explanation, most often through a static media such as a newspaper announcement or a Web site, where space is at a premium and you need to make a good quick first impression.

Putting Your Recruitment Message into Words

Here are some tips for putting a lot of content into a short written appeal, with some examples both good and bad from the US, UK, Canada and Australia.

Catch Attention with a Good Opening

The opening of the Message must be interesting enough to entice the potential volunteer to continue reading or listening. The body of the Message must be appealing enough to interest the potential volunteer in considering the volunteer opportunity or, at least, in contacting the agency to get more information. Boring Messages are only likely to appeal to boring people.

Consider these examples:

- *Volunteers needed to sleep. NW women's shelter is recruiting for its Sunday overnight shifts. Talk, laugh, and share with the residents.*
- *Be a PhoneFriend! DC Hotline is looking for people who care about children to work as volunteers as phone friends, the afternoon phone line for children. If you want to help children who are scared, lonely or need support call 223-CALL. Training begins soon.*
- *Interested in the arts? Volunteers know what goes on behind the scenes at the Kennedy Center. Call the Friends of the Kennedy Center at 254-8700.*

The short opening line in each conveys an image that is likely to entice the reader to continue through the remainder of the message.

Present a Complete Picture

The body of the Message should present information in an order that psychologically matches how people will think about the offer:

Need:	Is there a problem?
Solution:	Can this job help solve it?
Fears:	Will I be capable of helping with it?
Benefits:	What's in it for me?
Contact::	How do I get involved?

One way to cover all this is to imagine you're directing a motion picture. Your goal is to get the prospective volunteer to "view" the movie in their head – seeing the problem you're trying to solve, the difficulties it creates and the ways that volunteers are involved. In essence you want the prospective volunteer to picture themselves as a star of the movie - the volunteer coming to the rescue.

Consider this example:

American Jewish Congress
Volunteer Corps in Israel

As war in the Persian Gulf rages on and Israel awaits the next bombing by Iraqi Scuds, many Americans are asking how they can help. In response, the American Jewish Congress has organized the AJCongress Volunteer Corps in Israel, a new program designed to serve the Israeli people who are the targets of Saddam Hussein's missiles.

Israelis have shown extraordinary courage and resilience in the face of these brutal and deadly attacks. But the anxiety and strain they live under are causing serious emotional stress among the most vulnerable – children, the elderly and the psychologically and physically handicapped.

The Israeli institutions that care for these men, women, and children are overworked and understaffed. They need help – American volunteers who will provide care and love for the innocent casualties of Iraqi brutality.

Israel's Ministry of Social Welfare has established a special program to assign volunteers from abroad where they are most required. The greatest demand is for volunteers who will serve as attendants in these institutions. Mental health professionals, nurses and physiotherapists are also needed.

All volunteers must be able to spend a minimum of two weeks in Israel and pay their own airfare. Housing and meals in Israel are provided by the institutions to which volunteers are assigned.

If you wish to serve in the AJCongress Volunteer Corps in Israel – or if you cannot volunteer but wish to support the program – please call us at 212/360-1600 or send in the coupon below.

And this example:

Office of the Public Advocate
Community Visitor
Community Visitors(CV) have a unique role in monitoring the quality of services for people who are vulnerable and living in residential services for people with a disability.

The core role of the CV is to safeguard the interests and rights of vulnerable people who have a disability and are living in eligible services. CVs do this by identifying and reporting issues and problems from the perspective of the individual resident and by referring these for resolution within the service system. CVs are responsible for performing this role by:

- *Visiting eligible services regularly, announced or unannounced and as otherwise required or requested*
- *Identifying, appraising and monitoring issues and problems from the perspective of the individual resident, keeping in mind community expectations, relevant legislative principles and service standards.*
- *Resolving identified problems through direct negotiations with the staff and management of the facility where possible.*
- *Referring on serious, persistent or unresolved issues to the Regional Convenor*
- *Participating, with the Panel Secretary, in the preparation of a report on each visit.*
- *Contributing to the development of the Annual Report through the reports made on each visit and as otherwise required.*
- *Attending training sessions convened by the CV Co-ordinating Unit as required.*
- *Attending meetings as requested by the Regional Convenor, CV Co-ordinating Unit or the Office of the Public Advocate (e.g. quarterly meetings and the Annual General* Meeting).

Each of these gives you concrete "pictures" of the kinds of thing you would be doing as a volunteer and gives you an explanation of why you would be doing them - in effect, a short movie.

As a general rule, spend more space on need than on logistics. People will first decide whether you're worth volunteering for and then decide whether they can fit you into their schedule. The need you stress may be yours, your clientele's, or a perceived need/ benefit of the volunteer.

Sometimes you can't cover the whole picture, so you selectively choose what you think your "strengths" might be. These could simply be different interests that a prospective volunteer might have. In general, there are four different types of "selling points" that might be used:

The Cause or Clientele

- *The King County Sexual Assault Center believes that all people, including children, have the right to be free to live without the fear of sexual violence. We also believe that victims of sexual abuse and their non-offending family members deserve support to alleviate the trauma of sexual abuse in their lives. Volunteer opportunities are currently available in a variety of areas and we are recruiting now for our October and January training sessions. Please call 226-5062 to help eliminate sexual violence in your community.*

- *Orphan Foundation of America: Help defend the rights of orphan children in America. Research, administration, public policy, advocacy, fundraising. Contact Father Joseph Rivers, 223-4129.*

The Solution or Accomplishment

- *Volunteers are being sought for the Auxiliary of Group Health Cooperative of Puget Sound. The Auxiliary, along with its three area councils and 14 local guilds, raises money for scholarships, medical equipment, patient aid and patient education. Over the last decade, the auxiliary has raised more than $587,000 and awarded more than 200 scholarships. The auxiliary raises money through support, two hospital gift shops, making articles for sale, and other activities. For Olympia-area information, call Paula Mittelstaedt, Olympia guild volunteer chairperson, at 491-3656.*

The Type of Work

- *Agency serving low-income youth at risk looking for photographer with equipment to volunteer taking photographs at our 1st graduation ceremony! Agency will pay for developing, etc. Help make this event a wonderful memory. Call Seattle Youth Initiative, 382-5011, ask for Patty.*

- *Cablearn cable channel 27 seeks daytime volunteers to assist with marketing, educational programming, program development and underwriting or research in educational video techniques. Good experience or background for educators interested in video. Call 545-TV27 weekdays.*

- *Put your public relations and event planning skills to work now as a volunteer for Whalefest '90! This fun and educational special event helps people learn more about whales and their marine environment. Whalefest takes place Feb. 23-25, 1990 at Pier 70. Call Whales World at 441-0629 for details.*

The Setting

- *Death Valley National Monument - This large desert valley, nearly surrounded by high mountains, contains the lowest point in the Western Hemisphere and is known as the hottest spot in North America. Here you can find spectacular wildflower displays, sand dunes, Scotty's Castle, and remnants of the gold and borax mining days. Volunteer Jobs: Opportunities that exist in the winter are involved with interpretation, campground host program, and curatorial work. Contact: Death Valley National Monument, 619/786-2331.*

Don't be Misunderstood

Recruitment messages must be easily understood. They must be intelligible and avoid jargon, unless it is included for a specific reason and will be understood by the intended reader. Messages should be examined for ease of comprehension by someone other than the author of the message. Remember: *What Can be Misunderstood, Will Be.*

Consider these embarrassing examples, crafted by experienced volunteer managers who knew exactly what they really meant to say

- *Atlanta Community Food Bank - Volunteers needed to sort donated food and make sure food is edible. 892-9822.*

- *The Travelers Aid Society needs volunteers for its service desk at Union Station. Hours are from 9:30-1:30 and 1:30-5:30, seven days a week. For more info, call 347-0101.*

If the image of a volunteer job conjured up by the first message is "food taster," then that of the second is definitely "slave."

The sad news is that an amused reader is unlikely to call up and insist that you probably don't really mean what you wrote, but is more likely to conclude volunteering for an agency that stupid probably isn't what they want to do with their time.

Test the Message

The Message should be tested on members of the target group at whom it is aimed, to make sure it is understandable to them and communicates in a way most likely to be appealing to their interests. The most common - and fatal - mistake in writing recruitment appeals is to end up with something that appeals mightily to the person who wrote it but says nothing to its intended audience.

Consider this interesting example of a message that you personally might find a bit disconcerting:

- *Seattle Mental Health Institute, a progressive community mental health center on Capitol Hill, with a $4 million budget, is seeking to fill three (3) positions on its Board of Directors. Individuals with varying backgrounds in business who are interested in a volunteer leadership position in the community are encouraged to apply. For applications, write Shobha Hathiramani, Admin. Secretary, Seattle Mental Health Institute, 1600 E. Olive St, Seattle, WA 98122.*

But when you realize that its target audience was young business executives it begins to make a bit more sense - almost like an artfully crafted Shakespearean sonnet. It "speaks the right language."

Make the Message Inviting

The whole point of a recruitment message is to make the potential volunteer contact the agency for a further discussion. This means that the message should be aimed at getting the prospective volunteer to visualize themselves successfully becoming a volunteer.

Consider this example:

Kauai Hospice
Becoming a Hospice Volunteer

Want to have more meaning in your life? Do you want to do something that is satisfying and of great service to your community? Then become a Kauai Hospice volunteer!

Volunteers are needed from the westside to service families of the terminally ill who live between Koloa and Kekeha. Becoming a hospice volunteer is similar to helping a neighbor in need.

The only qualification required is your desire to help someone in need. You don't need any medical skills; you don't even need a college degree; you don't even need to know what to say. All you need to do is sign up for our hospice volunteer training session beginning on February 17 at Kauai Veterans Memorial Hospital for an all-day session which then continues for 4 evening sessions in the following two weeks.

Another training session will be offered shortly after the westside training session for people on the eastside from Lihue to Hanalei. For more information, call Kathleen Boyle, Kauai Hospice director at 245-7277.

And contrast it with this bureaucratic nightmare:

ASAP - Asylum Seeker Assistance Project
Customer Service Officers

- *Training provided*
- *Build new friendships*
- *Learn new skills*

Tasks/Qualifications/skills required:

1. *Display good public relation skills*
2. *Basic maths skills (to give change, calculate total costs, count up money, basic record keeping)*
3. *Social conscience for people seeking asylum*
4. *Stock sorting and rotation*
5. *Pricing*
6. *Good housekeeping*
7. *General cleaning (e.g. sweeping, window cleaning, dusting)*
8. *Work well in a team*
9. *Must be reliable and punctual*

Training/supervision provided:

1. *An initial probationary period will be required in which initial on the job training will take place.*
2. *On going training will be provided on the job or through workshops as required.*
3. *Volunteers will be invited to attend seminars provided by ASAP or their sister agencies on relevant asylum seeker issues.*
4. *A team meeting will be organised on a regular basis for all volunteers to get to know each other better, catch up on what's been happening, work through any problems which may arise and review current shop policies as needed.*

Requirements:

- *Police Check*
- *Minimum time commitment of one day a week (i.e. 4 – 8 hrs on any one day)*
- *Attend training sessions as required*

All volunteers must meet the requirements of ASAP as outlined in the "Becoming A Volunteer" booklet, which will be provided on request.

One small but significant way to make a message more inviting is to give the name of a person, preferably including their first name, not just the name of the agency that is to contacted. Volunteering is a personal decision and people like to talk with other people about it.

Follow these tips and you'll be more likely to end up with a recruitment appeals that attracts precisely the kind of volunteers that you're looking for!

Persuasive Techniques in Delivering Recruitment Appeals

What follows is based on research done in fields other than volunteerism, mostly sales and marketing. It is being applied to the development of public service messages and could well be applied to requests for volunteering. We suspect that you'll see some techniques that you've either used or wondered about in what follows.

The Tactics of Persuasion

We're going to structure this discussion by considering techniques that relate to asking a person to volunteer in a face-to-face discussion:

Should I tell the whole truth, warts and all?

A fear often expressed in workshops on recruitment and interviewing is that revealing the whole truth about the volunteer situation, including the risks it entails, the real nature of the client and other obnoxious features, will simply drive the potential volunteer away. The theory being expressed is that if you let the truth sneak up on the volunteer it may be less disturbing when it finally gets there.

Alas, the opposite is true. People notice when you're leaving things out, leaving them to infer what you really think or what's really going on. When you believe that, on balance, the reasons for volunteering outweigh the reasons for not volunteering, it is better to fully explain your rationale and the logic behind it than it is to keep things disguised or uncertain. If you don't believe me, here's the conclusion of O'Keefe, after examining dozens of studies in this area:

"The observed overall effects suggest that, on the basis of

the empirical evidence to date, advocates have little to fear from being explicit about their overall standpoint. On the contrary, clearly articulating one's overall conclusion appears to dependably enhance persuasive effectiveness."

Should I use stories or statistics?
Telling example stories and citing statistics are both time-honored means to adding both credibility and vividness to appeals. Both are them seem to work, but here's a suggestion for applying them in recruitment in a way you might not have thought of.

When talking with a potential volunteer it is useful to avoid arguing with or contradicting them. So if they pose objections to your request, note if they use either a story or statistics to bolster their contention (such as "a friend of mine tried that and hated it" – using a story to suggest that volunteering would be a bad idea). To counter, try to use the opposite of the technique they are using – if they tell a story, respond with statistics, and vice versa. This will allow you to give a different viewpoint without appearing to be directly contradicting them or suggesting that they (or their friend) are mistaken. In this particular case you might simply say that "well, we track satisfaction levels of the volunteers we've placed and 94% enjoy the experience enough to re-volunteer after their initial commitment is up." You've made your point without attacking them.

FITD or DITF?
FITD and DITF are two different approaches to making requests. FITD is "foot in the door," and suggests leading with a small request that is easily granted and then following with a larger, more critical request. DITF, "door in the face," follows the opposite approach, leading with a large request that will be refused and then following with a smaller request. DITF, as you can guess, relies at least partially on guilt.

Each of these techniques seem to work, but there are some tricky aspects to consider:

- If you use FITD, then timing is crucial. You can't follow with the second request until the first one is done with. This means letting the volunteer proceed with the initial act of volunteering and then re-recruiting them as opposed to "raising the ante" during the initial interview if they say "yes" to the small volunteer assignment.

- In FITD, the second request has a better chance of success if it is phrased as a continuation of the first request as opposed to looking like an entirely different activity.

- Oddly enough, it doesn't seem to matter whether it is the same person making the second request in FITD.

- Telling the potential volunteer what others are doing raises the chance of a positive response in both FITD and DITF. This is probably due to a factor called "conforming to norm." As you introduce the request, note "this is something a lot of our potential volunteers have tried." Don't use any pressure in this technique, simply mention the fact and let it do its work. If you push you'll create resistance.

In one of the few studies that actually examined volunteering, Cantrill found that *"the use of FITD and DITF techniques allowed us to double the number of subjects who indicated a willingness to volunteer for a project."*

And That's Not All...
We can all remember seeing the ad for the Ginzu knife, along with which you received another 45 knives and gadgets. The "that's not all" technique operates by either adding value to the request (promising more stuff or benefits) or by appearing to reduce the price. So could the "that's not all" technique work in volunteer recruitment?

The answer is "maybe," but here's some tips if you try it:

- The initial request can't be so large as to be overwhelming – it cannot generate an immediate "no" mental response from the prospective volunteer.

- Watch to see if the volunteer is honestly pondering the request and, if they are, start to introduce the additional inducements. You might, for example, say, "this position can be scheduled for whenever is convenient for you," or "after 50 hours of volunteering you qualify for discounts at our gift shop."

- As a corollary to that last comment, don't deluge the volunteer with all your inducements up front. They'll tend to ignore some of them, even if you bring them up again. Part of the success of this technique relies on the progressive sequencing of the added value.

A Big Caveat

You might find some of techniques to be manipulative and they probably are. But the obvious caveat to remember here is that you would never use any of them unless you were personally convinced that saying "yes" would be a good thing for both the agency and the volunteer. This is, after all, a cardinal principle for all volunteer interviewing, selection and matching. Recruiting a volunteer is not like selling a used car – just getting the money isn't enough, since the volunteer always has the ability to get their money back by leaving. Keep these techniques for when you have an uncertain or unconfident prospective volunteer, one who doesn't know what would be good for them. If you're convinced that they really ought to become a volunteer, then these techniques may help you persuade them to do the right thing.

Beginning Your Recruitment Efforts

As this chapter indicates, there are a lot of possible ways for a volunteer program to engage in recruitment. The smart Volunteer Program Manager will pick and choose methods depending on the desired results:

- A *warm body* campaign is good for when you need a large number of volunteers for an event, or when you are just beginning a program and need to attract community attention.

- A *targeted* recruitment campaign is good for finding individuals with specific talents or interests.

- A *concentric circles* campaign is good for maintaining a steady flow of replacement volunteers.

- An *ambient* recruitment campaign creates a culture of volunteering within a group.

- A *brokered* recruitment campaign offers an easy way to reach out to individuals or groups who don't have contact with your organization.

Each type of campaign can successfully recruit volunteers; the trick is to select the campaign that will obtain the right types of volunteers with the least amount of effort. If you're just beginning within a community, then often you must rely on a warm body campaign, and then carefully sift through those who approach you. As your program matures you will find yourself making more use of targeted and concentric circles recruitment.

Each campaign, however, is dependent upon identifying possible motivational appeals that individuals might have and connecting these motivations to some volunteer opportunity that your organization has to offer.

Providing a Responsive Recruitment Process

In some ways volunteer involvement resembles any customer service relationship. Those volunteers who feel that they receive good service are likely to continue with the agency and those who do not feel as though a good relationship has been established are likely to leave. This relationship is most fragile in its early stages, and is particularly fragile when the prospective volunteer is in first contact with the organization, inquiring about the possibility of volunteering.

Most agencies pay far too little attention to making this process operate smoothly. Hobson and Malec in a study of 500 United Way-affiliated agencies in the midwest examined the experiences of prospective volunteers who phoned attempting to initiate volunteering:

- only 49.3% received an offer of assistance ("May I help you?")
- 69.3% did not receive the name of the staff person answering the phone
- 26.4% were not referred to the appropriate agency contact person
- when the contact person was not available, only 48.7% were asked for their name and phone number
- only 30% received callbacks when a message was left
- in 16.1% of the calls, prospective volunteers were not thanked for contacting the agency

This pattern makes it easy to understand why many agencies have difficulty in recruiting volunteers.

The Lasting Nature of Recruitment

Some Volunteer Program Managers make the serious mistake of assuming that recruitment stops when the potential volunteer shows up asking about a position. This is an incredibly wrong approach. The recruitment process is still in full swing during the initial interviewing of the potential volunteer (who is probably still "checking out" the agency) and it in fact continues throughout the volunteer's future relationship with the agency. Every morning that volunteers wake up they are, in fact, free to decide to stop volunteering. This means that recruitment is an on-going process, which continues as long as you need the volunteer. If you start to take the volunteer's presence for granted, your recruitment effort will ultimately fail. Volunteer retention, which we will discuss in a later chapter, is simply the continuation of the recruitment process. Successful volunteer recruitment requires that volunteers never be taken for granted.

Chapter Six
Matching Volunteers to Work

One of the most neglected areas of volunteer management training has been that of effective interviewing of volunteers. This is unfortunate, since good interviewing skills are essential to performing that most crucial of all volunteer management tasks-matching a potential volunteer with a task and a working environment that they will enjoy.

Even more unfortunate is the fact that much of the management training that does exist on interviewing deals with employment interviewing, which is a totally inappropriate approach for volunteer interviewing. The main difference is easily stated: "Volunteer interviewing consists of evaluating a person for a job, not for the job." Effective volunteer interviewing does not so much consist of examining an applicant's suitability for one job as it does evaluating the ability and desire of that applicant to fit productively in some position within the agency. Employment interviewing focuses on the question, "Who can do this job?" while volunteer interviewing should focus on the more creative questions, "Who will want to do this job?" and "What can this person contribute to accomplishing our mission?" Ivan Scheier called this "the people approach" over twenty years ago, and that phrase still exemplifies the proper attitude to the process.

Volunteer interviewing is not just a simple process of comparing candidates against a list of desired job-related characteristics; it is a much subtler process of trying to learn about the person who is being interviewed, with an ultimate intent of shaping a work situation that will be satisfying to the volunteer and to the agency.

Purposes of Volunteer Interviewing

Among other things this difference in approach means that a volunteer interview has to accomplish more than the usual job interview. There are two basic purposes:

- *Identify a "Fit"*

Finding a fit includes determining the interests and abilities of the potential volunteers, determining their suitability for particular jobs, and assessing their "rightness" for the agency, its style of operation, and its mission. "Fit" is the interpersonal matching of the needs and interests of the volunteer with the needs and interests of the agency. An examination of proper fit would include determining these items regarding the volunteer:

1. To what extent does the volunteer have both an interest in a particular job and the necessary qualifications to perform that job?

2. To what extent does the volunteer have other interests and abilities that might be used to create a different job for him or her?

3. To what extent does the volunteer have a "rightness" for working well in a particular job environment?

"Rightness," means the likelihood that the volunteer will fit comfortably into the agency's working environment. In many cases, this will be the key predictive factor for success. Rightness could involve matters of style (relaxed, frenetic), personality (neat, messy; introverted, extroverted), behavior (smoking, non-smoking), political philosophy (traditionalist, radical), or other factors that would affect how the volunteers will get along, both with the agency in general and with the particular staff group with whom each might be assigned. Very often these interpersonal relationship factors become more important than factors of technical qualification, which can be learned if the volunteer is willing to stay with the agency. Quite simply, a volunteer who is happy in their working environment will make the job happen; one who is unhappy will not try to do so.

- *Recruit*

This includes answering any questions or concerns that the potential volunteers may have and letting the volunteers know that they have the ability to make a contribution to the agency and its clientele, or that they will derive personal satisfaction from helping. It is a quite mistaken belief that the person who shows up for an interview has already decided to volunteer with the agency.

During the process of the interview, it is crucial to remember that the volunteer has not yet been recruited. At this stage each has only been "attracted" to the agency. One purpose of the screening interview is to give the volunteer the time to make a more deliberate examination of what the agency has to offer and to have a chance to "sell" the agency and its work to the volunteer. Equal time has to be given to focusing on why a particular job is important and interesting, as well as to whether the volunteer would be right for that job. Never assume that just because a volunteer has come to the interview they are already a part of the agency. If the screening interview is your first contact with the volunteer, then it is important that the volunteer feel welcomed and wanted during the interview process. We need to make sure that volunteers do not feel as though they have already been caught by an uncaring bureaucracy which is only interested in determining which square hole the each volunteer should fill.

Basic Volunteer Interviewing

Well begin by looking at the steps involved in conducting a basic volunteer interview – one in which the work to be done does not require extra effort.

Picking an Interviewer

Since the time available for assessing potential candidates for volunteer positions is relatively short, it is important to have a person conducting the interviews who is capable of making a satisfactory judgment. A number of abilities are desirable in a volunteer interviewer:

- Broad knowledge of the agency and its programs
- Personal knowledge of staff and their quirks
- Ability to relate to all types of people
- Ability to talk easily with strangers
- Ability to listen attentively both to what is and what is not said
- Ability to ask follow-up questions
- Ability to follow the agenda of the interview without appearing to dominate
- Knowledge of non-directive interview techniques
- Ability to recruit and motivate while interviewing
- Commitment to the agency and its programs
- Ability to empathize with other people
- Ability to say "no" gracefully

Volunteers often make better interviewers than paid staff. This is true for two reasons. First, they tend not to be "burned out" in interviewing because they may be involved in a lesser number. Conducting interviews is a draining process, and one that can easily be overwhelming. It is common in this situation to stop listening after a while. Second, volunteers tend to be better able to build rapport with potential volunteers, because, after all, they have something important in common (they both thought the agency was worth donating their time to).

The Interviewing Site

Since a volunteer interview requires a greater exploration of personal characteristics, site selection can be critical. Three factors are important:

- Accessibility
- A friendly atmosphere
- Privacy

The site for conducting the interviewing process will vary, but it is important during the interview that the volunteer feel a sense of privacy and comfort. Do not conduct the interview in a public place or in a shared office, since this will deter many volunteers from offering complete information about their backgrounds and their interests. None of us likes being eavesdropped on while discussing our personal lives.

Organize your own schedule so that you will not be interrupted during the interview, either by phone calls or by other staff. Besides disrupting the flow of the interview, interruptions give the impression to the volunteers that they are of lesser importance than your other work.

Remember the old adage: "You never get a second chance to make a first impression. " What the potential volunteers see and feel during the interview may shape their eventual attitude toward the agency.

Pre-Interview Preparation

The following items should be prepared and ready before the interview:

- A list of possible volunteer jobs with descriptions of work and qualifications required.
- A list of questions to be asked in relation to each job.
- An application form completed by the volunteers with background information about them and their interests.
- A set of open-ended questions to explore the motivations of the volunteer.
- Information and materials on the agency and its programs.

This preparation is vital to the success of the interview. A successful volunteer interview is quite different from simply having a pleasant conversation. As Donna Johnston of the Volunteer Centre of Great Britain noted more than ten years ago, "An interview is often defined as a conversation with a purpose; the interviewer who relies on spontaneity and impulse will often find he has had a delightful conversation but has failed to achieve his purpose. Effective interviewing relies on self-discipline in organizing and developing a conversation."

Opening the Interview
The beginning of the interview should focus on:

- Making the applicants feel welcome. Express appreciation for their coming to meet you.

- Building rapport. Explain what you would like to accomplish and how they fit into the process. Let them know that their decision about whether volunteering with you would be suitable is the intention of the discussion. Let them feel "in charge."

- Giving them background information about the agency and its work. Ask them what questions they have about the agency and its purpose and programs.

The key to beginning a successful interview is to start building rapport with the potential volunteer. It is crucial that the interview process belongs as much to the volunteer as it does to the agency. If there is a time limit for the interview, make sure that you have allocated sufficient time for the volunteer to express concerns and ask questions. The interview should be a mutual, not unilateral, information exchange process. It is a negotiation, not an interrogation. Make sure that you explain to the volunteers at the beginning of the interview that they should feel free to ask questions and express any concerns at any point during the discussion.

Offering food or a beverage is an excellent way to open a volunteer interview.

Conducting the Interview
The major portion of the interview should be devoted to the following:

- Exploration of the applicants' interests, abilities, and personal situation. Determine why the applicants are considering volunteering and what types of work environment they prefer.

- Discussion of various job possibilities. Explain the purpose and work situation of the different volunteer job opportunities available and let the applicants consider them. Use this as an opportunity to let the applicants discuss how they would approach various jobs, which will tell you more about their attitudes, their intentions and their level of interest.

- Discussion of your requirements, such as time commitments, training requirements, paperwork, and confidentiality rules. Let the volunteers know what will be expected of them.

Remember that you are still "recruiting" the volunteer at this stage so do not forget to explain why each job is important to the interests of the agency and the clientele.

Look for personality indicators that will help you match people to situations where they will be happy. This can include items such as whether they smoke, desire for individual or group work, and other preferences.

One of the important skills to possess during the interview is the ability to detect an unexpected talent in the volunteer and to begin to construct a possible volunteer role for them on the spot. This requires a good understanding of the agency and its programs. If you make use of volunteers to conduct interviews (where they are very effective in building rapport and seeing things from the viewpoint of the potential volunteer) make sure they have a good background about the agency and how its work is organized.

Here are some examples of questions that can be utilized during the interview:

Questions to get the interview started:
- "Is there anything you'd like to know before we get started?"
- "What can I tell you about our agency?"

Questions to uncover motivations:
- "Why did you decide to become a volunteer at this time?"
- "What attracted you to our agency? Is there any particular aspect of our work that most interests you?"
- "What would you like to get out of volunteering here? What will make you feel that you have been successful?"
- "What do you think is the most important thing we should be doing to help our clients and to fulfill our mission in the community?"
- "What kinds of volunteer work have you done before? What did you like best about that work?"
- "What did you like least?"

Questions to determine skills or work habits:

- "What skills do you think you have to contribute here?"
- "What do you like doing? What types of work would you rather avoid?"
- "What types of experience or training have you had in your work or other volunteering?"
- "How do you think you would go about this volunteer assignment? Where would you start and what do you think are the most important considerations?"
- "Describe a project or a work experience that you were in charge of and tell me how you went about it."
- "How do you deal with situations that don't go as you planned?"

Questions to determine "fit":

- "What have you enjoyed most or least about your previous volunteer work? About your paid employment?"
- "Describe your ideal supervisor. How do you prefer that supervisor to relate to you?"
- "Would you rather work on your own, with a group, or with a partner? Why?"
- "Are there any types of clients that you would most prefer to work with? Or that you would not feel comfortable working with?

Questions to verify or obtain more information:

- "Give me an example."
- "Tell me more."
- "Why do you think that was the case?"

While it is important to evaluate different elements for different volunteer jobs, here are some general areas to watch for while interviewing:

- Ease in answering questions about personal qualifications and background
- Ability to communicate effectively
- Level of enthusiasm and commitment
- General attitudes and emotional reactions
- Types of questions asked about the agency and the position offered
- Other interests or hobbies
- Flexibility
- Maturity and stability
- Preference for a group or individual setting for volunteer work
- Level of self-confidence
- Any sense of a hidden agenda
- Time pattern of previous work and volunteer experience
- Reasons for coming to the interview
- Preferences in type of work

Closing the Interview

The interview should be concluded by:

- Making an offer of a possible position to the volunteer, or politely explaining that you have no suitable openings for them at this time.

- Explaining what will happen next: making background or reference checks, arranging a second interview with staff, scheduling a training or signing them up for an orientation session. Explain the process, the timeframe, and what is expected of the volunteers at each stage.

- Getting the permission of the volunteer to conduct any reference or background checks.

- Responding to any questions or concerns that the volunteer might have.

Overall Interview Suggestions

Here are some overall suggestions regarding the conduct of the basic volunteer interview:

- Make sure your interview time is not interrupted. This will make the interviewer and the candidate more comfortable.

- Be an active listener. You need to understand the candidate and that requires paying very close attention both to what they are saying and what they are not saying during the interview.

- Answer any questions about the agency and its work openly and honestly. This will demonstrate your sincerity and your intelligence. You can't hide things from people who will be starting work with the agency and will, therefore, find out eventually anyway.

- Don't promise anything if you are not sure of being able to make a placement. Never promise anything that you can't deliver to the volunteer.

- Describe the volunteer position honestly. Do not hide undesirable aspects of the job in the hope that the volunteer won't mind discovering them after they've signed on.

- Evaluate people on an individual basis. Don't assume they're like anyone else that you've ever met.

Matching Volunteers to Work

Determining the correct job situation for a volunteer involves questions both of job qualifications and temperament. The volunteers must certainly be capable of doing or learning to do the job for which they are selected. But it is equally important that they "fit" into the work situation for which they are being considered. This means that volunteers must be satisfied with the job being offered, and view the job as desirable and fulfilling work. It means that the work setting (including the timing and site of the job) must also be amenable to each volunteer. And finally it means that the staff with whom each volunteer will be working must also be suitable. This last factor may ultimately be decided by some of the relatively "personal" decisions, based on issues as "small" as compatibility of personality type, style of work, or even whether one person smokes and the other doesn't.

Since it is difficult to make completely accurate decisions about such complicated areas of decision-making based on a 30-minute interview, we recommend making all beginning assignments on a trial-period basis. Let the volunteer know that the first 30 days of work will be done as a probationary period for both the volunteer and the agency. At the end of the 30 days, a second interview will be conducted in which both the agency and the volunteer will re-evaluate the assignment. During this second interview either party may request a change of assignment, based upon their additional knowledge of the situation.

This initial testing period will make it easier to induce volunteers to try out jobs about which they are uncertain and will make it more likely that any problems of mismatching will be identified early and corrected quickly.

You can sometimes get some ideas for matching volunteers to positions depending upon their basic personality framework. The sociologist David McClelland divided people into Affiliators (those who enjoy interaction with others), Achievers (those who enjoy accomplishement) and those who are Power oriented.

Here are some volunteer positions that relate to these categories:

Affiliation

- committees
- talking on the phone
- social opportunities
- mentoring
- friendly visiting
- recognition events
- collaboration
- recruiting others
- family gatherings
- welcoming new people
- listening
- relationships
- group projects
- working with clients
- outreach programs

Achievement

- gathering data or statistics
- seeing trends
- leading meetings
- documentation
- leading events
- keeping records
- technology
- skill-building tasks
- details
- keeping score
- advising professionally
- fundraising
- tracking goals and objectives

Power

- challenges
- the spotlight
- innovation
- authority positions
- teaching
- lecturing
- titles
- publicity
- leadership

Advanced Volunteer Interviewing

One of the most difficult responsibilities of any Volunteer Program Manager is attempting to evaluate the qualifications of prospective volunteers. This responsibility is particularly troublesome for those programs in which volunteers:

- will be matched one-to-one with clients in a

counseling or helping relationship;

- will be undertaking managerial or leadership duties that require autonomy and independent action; or

- will be dealing with complex issues that require a substantial training investment on the part of the agency.

In each of these situations acceptance of an inappropriate volunteer can have dire consequences.

Unfortunately the traditional method of asking interview questions does little to truly gauge the abilities of potential volunteers. Inquiries into educational or work background commonly divulge little that has immediate pertinence to either current skills or the type of situation the volunteer will encounter. Questions based upon past experience ("Tell me about a crisis situation you encountered and how you dealt with it.") are also of little immediate relevance and are usually subject to revisionist interpretations of past history and success.

Evaluating a potential volunteer is even more difficult when the type of characteristic you are attempting to determine is not a hard-core skill but is attitudinal in nature - flexibility, good judgment, ability to deal with others, creativity, cultural attitudes. Direct questions in these areas ("Do you usually display good judgment?") are simply silly.

Traditional interview situations also suffer from the drawback of measuring the applicant's skill in being interviewed more than in actually doing work of any other type. Some individuals are more comfortable in an interview situation than others, and some, quite frankly, are far better in interviews than in real life.

In short, determining the real facts of another's personality during an interview is most often left to "gut feelings" on the part of the interviewer rather than any concrete information gained during the interview itself. This is a dangerous practice, and one that this chapter will show you how to remedy.

Developing Probing Volunteer Interview Questions
Volunteer interviews commonly proceed in two quite distinct parts. The first, that of exploration, consists of asking the volunteers about their interests, in an attempt to find an area of volunteer work that they might be interested in undertaking. We have already covered this in the section above on basic volunteer interviewing. These exploratory questions should be asked even if the volunteer has come in to apply for a specific job, since they might help the interviewer identify an even more suitable placement that the volunteer wasn't initially aware of. The exploration phase of the interview is designed to give the interviewer enough perspective on the interests of the prospective volunteer to identify several potential jobs that might then be matched against the qualifications of the applicant.

This matching leads to the evaluation phase of the interview. In preparing for this part, the volunteer interviewer must first examine each job and attempt to determine the qualifications that are needed for success. These may include hard skills (such as speaking ability or knowledge of fundraising) and they may include attitudinal requirements (such as flexibility, maturity, lack of bias, ability to relate to others). This is the part where traditional short-answer questions give little help in truly determining either skills or attitudes. And this is the part where roleplay scenarios can prove extremely valuable.

Incorporating Roleplay Scenarios into the Volunteer Interview
Utilizing roleplay scenarios in the interview situation is a three-part process:

1. To make use of roleplay scenarios the interviewer must first develop a scenario situation that relates to the volunteer job to be undertaken. The simplest way to begin this process is either to think about past experiences with the job itself (identifying past difficult situations that a volunteer encountered or previous disasters) or to ask current volunteers about the types of difficult situations, problems or quandaries they have had to deal with. The problem situation should relate to several of the qualifications that have already been identified as crucial to job success.

As an example, one such scenario created for use in interviewing volunteers who were matched as mentor companions for young adults was phrased as follows:

"You are working as a mentor with a 16-year old girl. You have been together for almost a year and have developed a good and trusting working relationship. You are meeting with the girl and she turns to you and says, 'You're the only person I can look to for help. I'm pregnant and I want you to help me go about getting an abortion.' What do you say to her and how do you handle this situation?"

Note that this situation involves the ability of the volunteer to deal with a number of complex issues, some relating to judgment, some to religious beliefs, some to ethics, and also involves the ability of the volunteer to confront a touchy subject area. It is by no means a simple "yes" or "no" type of question.

After the question is asked, the prospective volunteer should be given a few minutes to think about and prepare a response.

2. You will note that the above scenario question was not introduced as a roleplay situation but was originally simply asked as a complex question. This is intentional. As volunteers start to respond to the question they will commonly say something like, "Well, I would ask her why she wanted to have the abortion and then I would..."

At the point the volunteer begins to answer, the interviewer should, without prior warning, turn the situation into a roleplay. One way to do this smoothly is to say, "Why don't we just pretend you are actually dealing with this. I'll be the 16-year old, and you can talk to me as if the situation had actually just occurred."

The interviewer should consistently stay in character and should force the applicants to also stay in character, treating the situation as a realistic one. If applicants attempt to retreat to general statements ("Well, I would smooth over the situation...") the interviewer should pressure them to speak the exact words they think they would use to accomplish this, delivered as they would speak them in real life ("Tell me what you'd say to me.")

By changing a theoretical question into a hypothetical situation, the interviewer will be able to learn much more about each volunteer. General answers are often vague; precise words give a much clearer impression of exactly what the volunteer is trying to do. And turning the situation into a roleplay will also give some clues as to whether the volunteers can not only think about the situation but also handle it. By watching their demeanor and body language during the roleplay the interviewer will learn a lot about their true level of comfort and ability.

3. The interviewer can also prepare to take the roleplay several steps further by constructing a scenario that has several levels, each with additional facets. In the example given above, interviewers were prepared with three additional "what if" alternatives to ask once the applicant had worked through the original situation:

- *"If the 16-year old revealed that the father of the baby was a member of a foster family that she had been placed with by our agency, how would you handle the situation?"*

- *"What if the person involved was 12 years old, not 16?"*

- *"If, before telling you anything, the client had asked you to keep the information totally confidential, what would you do? What if your supervisor heard about this situation and asked you whether the girl was pregnant?"*

This last question series is particularly revealing, since it places the potential volunteer in an ethical dilemma in which there is no clearly "right" answer. Ethical dilemma questions can be particularly helpful in identifying people who do think there are very simple "right" answers to complicated situations.

The interviewer can also expand the gathering of information by sometimes backing out of the role play and asking the prospective volunteers to explain the reasoning behind their answers: "What do you think is the most important objective in this situation?" or "What alternatives do you think you would have in dealing with this?" And the interviewer can even expand the roleplay into new areas. In the example given, a second layer of the scenario moved the volunteer into a meeting that included the client and her parents, to discuss the pregnancy. The volunteer was asked by the young client to participate in the discussion. Other staff members were brought in to play the parents, with instructions to initiate a conflict situation. The volunteer then had to deal with the conflict, which was partially directed at the young girl but which then shifted toward animosity from the parents directed at the volunteer.

The Benefits of Roleplay Situations

Placing potential volunteers in such a roleplay scenario is much more revealing than other types of inquiries, including even the broadest open-ended questions. In all, there are three distinct areas of advantage:

- The more fluid situation of the roleplay allows you to see how the potential volunteers think, with a view of their assumptions and reactions. This information will often be revealed without the volunteers realizing what they are showing you. This makes it more difficult for the interviewee to "guess" the correct answer.

- You can also "see" how well the volunteers actually handle the situation, not just how well they talk about it. You can thus better judge interpersonal skills and style.

- The use of the roleplay scenario does not stop at the interviewing stage. Roleplay scenarios make excellent training tools, and you might well not disqualify volunteers based on their performance but rather make notes about areas that need to be addressed during orientation or about additional skill training that will be needed before they can start work.

The best part is how easy it is to construct such scenarios. All you really have to do is remember the difficult situations that volunteers have encountered in the past. Even if the situations weren't "solvable," they will make good training tools because they are, in fact, representative of the types of real-world problems the volunteer must learn to deal with. And, who knows, you may get lucky enough to interview a prospective volunteer who can tell you how to deal with a situation you could never figure out...

Other Interviewing Considerations

Some other considerations in doing interviews are:

Face-to-Face or Over the Telephone?

Some programs are simply not in a position to conduct interviews in person. This is not a common situation, but it obviously makes the recruitment process a less personal situation, and inhibits both the ability of the agency to evaluate the volunteer and the volunteer to assess the agency. Generally speaking, it is highly desirable to conduct face-to-face interviews for job situations that have the following attributes:

- The work requires a longer time commitment and thus a higher motivational level on the part of the volunteer.

- The work entails greater responsibility or requires a capacity or skill above the ordinary.

- The position is highly sensitive because of the nature of the work or the relationship with clients.

If you are unable to conduct in-person interviews for a job that has any one of these characteristics, it is highly desirable to schedule a 30-day review with the volunteers to see how they are performing and how they are feeling.

What *Not* to do During Interviews

Avoid the following:

1. Giving advice or offering your personal opinions
2. Asking about the candidate's personal life or qualities. Avoid questions about:
   - Age
   - Race
   - National origin
   - Religion
   - Political beliefs
   - Marital status
   - Children (number, ages, status)
   - Birth control or plans for parenthood
   - Arrests or convictions
   - Sexual preference
   - Physical or mental handicaps
   - Military history
3. Formulating an opinion early in the process and screening all subsequent information through this initial opinion.
4. Making assumptions about the applicant that are not based on anything actually said or demonstrated in the interview.
5. Feeling sorry for the applicant and hearing what you wish they had said.
6. Tipping the candidate off to the right answer by body language, facial expressions, ceasing to take notes, yawning, voice inflection, or fidgeting.
7. Beginning the interview without at least one question on each of the top priority traits you are looking for.
8. Talking more than 20% of the time. You learn nothing about the applicant while you are talking.
9. Allowing interruptions to the interview.
10. Assuming that the applicant's answers to questions gives you information about the skills of the applicant. The only skill tested by interviews is the skill of answering questions.

Reference Checks

It may also be important to conduct a check of potential volunteers' credentials. This is particularly important in cases where the volunteer position requires licensing or certification or where it involves working with a clientele with diminished capacities. If you are going to check applicants' references, you

must notify them and obtain their permission. One way to do so is by having them sign a permission document, such as the one provided as a sample in Appendix Three.
Note that not all types of references would need to be checked for each volunteer, but what needs to be checked relates to a particular volunteer position.

Rejecting Potential Volunteers

The intent of volunteer interviewing is, naturally, to find a useful and enjoyable position for the interested volunteer. This, however, is not always possible. One of the key responsibilities of a volunteer interviewer is to identify those cases in which the volunteer in question should not be asked to work with the agency.

There are a number of reasons why such rejection may be necessary:

- There may be no suitable position for the volunteer within the agency.
- The volunteer may have expectations that the agency cannot meet.
- The agency and the volunteer may not have congruent philosophies.
- The volunteer refuses to agree to agency requirements (background checks, time schedules, training commitments).

In each of these cases, rejection should be automatic, and is in the best interests of the agency and the volunteer. Rejection, however, may also occur simply because the interviewer has a "gut" feeling that the person should not be accepted for the position, based on responses to questions during the interview about their skills and interests, and based on the qualifications that the interviewer knows are required for a particular type of work. Do not be unsettled when this happens, even if you cannot absolutely define why you are getting a negative feeling about the potential volunteer; go with your instincts which, after all, you have been developing for most of your life. If you're unsure, you might have another person conduct a second interview of the volunteer and compare that opinion with yours. As long as you have conducted the interview based on questions that truly explore the fitness and capability of the potential volunteer to perform the work required by a particular job then you should be comfortable with assessing that volunteer, even if you have trouble describing the nature or cause of your unease.

You might also "soften" the rejection decision by referring the potential volunteer to another agency for which you believe the person would be more suitable or by offering an alternative position within your agency. You might even, in some cases, accept the volunteer on a trial period, but you should note that this may simply be postponing the inevitable and that "firing" the volunteer down the road will be much more traumatic than not making the initial acceptance.

While "rejecting" another person who wants to help is never a pleasant feeling, try to remember that your primary obligation is to the safety and well-being of your clientele.

Liability Concerns in Screening

Rejecting volunteers has become an issue with potential legal implications in the last few years. On one hand, there are developing legal questions about the extent to which an agency can decide not to accept specific volunteers, particularly as those decisions are based upon the rejection of "classes" of individuals (sex, race, sexual preference, etc.). These questions are slowly being settled by case decisions that provide greater interpretation of the word "employee" as it relates to the various employment protection laws enacted in recent years. See, for example, Big Brothers, Inc. v. Minneapolis Commission on Civil Rights, 248 N.W. 2d 823 (1979) or Curran v. Mount Diablo Council of the Boy Scouts of America, 147 Cal. App. 3d 312, 195 Cal. Rptr. 325 (1983), appeal dismissed, 468 U.S. 1205 (1984).

Equally troubling for nonprofit agencies have been findings of legal responsibility in instances where a volunteer engages in illegal conduct such as child abuse; the agency is sued under the doctrine of negligent screening for its failure to have ascertained the risk posed by the volunteer. This has been particularly prevalent in agencies where volunteers work one-on-one with children. In this area, as well, precise legal guidelines are still being developed.

An example of the direction in which courts seem to be going is provided in Big Brother/Big Sister of Metro Atlanta v. Terrell, 359 S.E. 2d 241 (Ga. App. 1987) in which the court applies a "reasonable effort" test, noting *"There is nothing in the record to suggest that Big Brother, a non-governmental entity has access to FBI records. Nor does it appear from the record that a credit check would have revealed anything to affect Big Brother's decision whether to accept Hendrick as a volunteer. As to the other two suggestions [a psychological test and a check*

of the volunteer's lifestyle], it appears that Big Brother came as close as is practicable for a volunteer organization to meet those criteria through its application form, family history, and assessment by a case worker."
It is crucial for agencies in which volunteers are assigned to work with vulnerable clients to attempt to determine the suitability and safety of potential volunteers. This means having procedures to carefully examine volunteer applicants and ensuring that these procedures are followed with each volunteer and a record kept of findings and actions during this process.

It is also crucial, however, not to let fear overwhelm the operation of your program. While terrible when it happens, abuse by a volunteer is not particularly common. No national data is available, but files released by the Boy Scouts of America in connection with a lawsuit in San Diego indicate that from 1971 to 1991 about 1,800 scoutmasters were removed from their positions in BSA following suspicion of molestation. This number represents approximately 1 in 13,000 volunteers within BSA per year.

Involving Staff in Volunteer Interviewing

The staff with responsibility for overseeing the job the volunteer will be performing must have some involvement in the interviewing process. That involvement might take several forms:

- Assisting in writing questions and scenarios for use during the interview. This is a vital function where staff are more familiar with the demands and requirements of a particular job than the volunteer coordinator.

- Participating in the actual interview. This is not normally recommended in the initial interview. The difficulty this creates is that it limits the ability of the volunteer interviewer to negotiate with the potential volunteer about more than one job. Instead, we recommend that staff be involved in direct interviewing through conducting a second interview with potential volunteers, after preliminary ideas regarding placement have been reached.

Answering the Unasked Questions of Volunteers

Often prospective volunteers will have questions about the operation of a program or about possible requirements but will be unwilling to directly ask these questions. These questions may involve issues around: "Will I have to do that?," or "What are my options?," or similar concerns.

One way to avoid this dilemma in customer service is to anticipate questions and provide the answers without waiting for them to be asked.

As an example of this technique, here are some of the issues addressed on the website of the Indy Hospice Volunteers Program:

Requirements of Potential Volunteers

- *Completion of application*
- *Two written references on file*
- *Criminal background check*
- *Completion of volunteer training*
- *TB test or chest x-ray with negative results* **
- *Completion of OSHA requirements* **
- *Hepatitis B vaccine or a written statement declining the vaccine* **
- *Signed Confidentiality Statement form*

*** Indicates patient care volunteers only.*

A person who volunteers is trained for the area in which they chose to serve in. There are three areas with different classifications within those areas.

I. Administration Volunteer is a person who wants to volunteer but wants no direct patient contact. They may provide administrative assistance in the office setting. They may work doing paper work at the home setting. There are also volunteers who sew, knit and crochet projects during the year for patients. There are non-patient care volunteers who mow yards, shovel snow, run errands, etc. They require a three-hour orientation training class.

II. Patient Care Volunteer is a person who wants to volunteer directly with patients, whether it is in the patient's own home, primary care giver's home, assisted living home, or nursing home. They require twelve- hours orientation training.

III. Bereavement Volunteer is a person who wants to volunteer to go through the bereavement process with the patient and the family. This volunteer may start at the onset of accepting hospice services and continue out with the family thirteen months after the passing of their loved one. They require eighteen hours of orientation training.

If is easy to see how providing the volunteer with the above information helps with any doubts or concerns that the prospective volunteer might have. Providing this information in advance both serves to educate volunteers about their options and avoid unnecessary fears deterring the volunteer from making a commitment.

Unasked questions can also be addressed during the interviewing process, as noted by the Federal Emergency Management Agency (1995):

"Potential recruits may have a number of concerns about themselves and the EMS organization that they do not express. The interviewer must ensure that these "unasked questions" are addressed:

- *What do I really have to do? Can I manage it? Do I have the skill? Can I handle it emotionally?*
- *How much time will it demand? Is there enough to keep me interested? Will it put pressure on my regular job or family?*
- *What danger will I be in? What are the risks?*
- *Who benefits? Why should I do this?"*

The earlier these questions are dealt with the more likely the prospective volunteer will become involved.

Contracting

You may wish to consider initiating a process of entering into a contract with volunteers once the interviewing and matching process has been satisfactorily concluded. Contracting is not a formal legal document but is the signing by both the agency and the volunteer of a listing of the mutual commitments and intentions they are entering into. The agreement might specify the work that the volunteer is agreeing to perform, the timeframe, and the benefits and support that the agency agrees to provide the volunteer. Women in Community Services, for example, utilizes the following short agreement:

As a volunteer, I will:

- *Attend scheduled orientations and training as negotiated by the appointed Volunteer Administrator.*
- *Maintain confidentiality of sensitive information.*
- *Assume responsibility for familiarizing myself with and observing the rules and policies of this organization, including inappropriate behavior with clients, alcohol, drugs and firearms.*
- *Interact with paid/unpaid staff and clients in a courteous, cordial manner and expect the same in return.*
- *Perform duties and responsibilities according to the job description(s) to the best of my ability.*
- *Except in the direst emergency notify WICS _____ (hrs.) before my scheduled time, if I am unable to work .*
- *Present WICS in a positive manner before the General Public.*

Women in Community Services understands and agrees to the following:

- *Provide me with adequate space and supplies.*
- *Supervise and train me for my volunteer work assignment.*
- *Give me an assignment compatible with my skills and interest.*
- *Keep me informed about the organization through newsletters and other sources of information.*
- *Provide me with feedback on my performance.*
- *Treat me as a part of the team like other paid/unpaid staff.*
- *Inform me of the organization's rules and policies.*
- *Provide me with a job description that summarizes duties of the job placement and limits of responsibility.*
- *Keep accurate records of my involvement and provide references upon request.*
- *Suggest new assignments or alternate assignments as appropriate.*

The purpose of the contract (sometimes called a memorandum of agreement) is to emphasize the seriousness of both the agency and the volunteer in entering into a relationship, and is not intended to convey a sense of "legal" responsibility. Contracts work particularly well with young volunteers.

Streamlining the Intake and Matching Process

Studies of volunteers have strongly indicated that they have a desire to begin work quickly. This implies that organizations should work diligently to smooth and shorten the process for intake of volunteers, making it work as easily and as quickly as possible.

A 2002 study of motivations of Canadian volunteers found that:

"There was a clear sense that rules and screening procedures have become more onerous in recent years. Although all indicated that they understood the reasons for, and value of, police checks and other screening procedures for volunteers with access to children, sometimes the tone (the sense of being guilty until proven innocent) and length of time (months to receive word on a police check) made these processes annoying."

As a second example, consider the experience of Big Brothers/Big Sisters in the United States when they conducted an assessment of their internal processing system for volunteer applicants.

Since it matches adults with children in volunteering situations that are generally unsupervised, BB/BS has long led the field in intensive background screening of volunteer applicants. These processes include criminal background checks, multiple interviews, psychological screening, home visits and other risk management procedures.

The internal investigation, however, revealed an unfortunate consequence of these procedures - they were incredibly lengthy. An applicant might apply and then spend as long as six months waiting for the screening processes to be completed. This came as a complete surprise to prospective volunteers whose natural expectation was that they would begin volunteering relatively quickly, something they were initially eager to do.

From the standpoint of Big Brothers these screening techniques were necessary in order to ensure safe matches. It was, in fact, good management practice. From the standpoint of a potential volunteer it was another story. Their reaction was one of feeling abandoned by the organization after their initial good faith effort to help out. The result was a large hole in the retention system, occurring even before BB/BS had officially accepted the volunteers.

A critical factor in this process was that prospective volunteers weren't told in advance how long the processing might take and that for extended periods they might not learn anything from Big Brothers about how the background investigation was proceeding. They were essentially being left "in the dark."

Similar difficulties exist in other areas of management when volunteers are delayed in being matched with clients or with work. Fahey, Walker and Lennox noted the difficulty among Volunteer Ambulance Officers in Tasmania in areas where the small number of new volunteers delayed training of new recruits for months. One volunteer who was interviewed commented *"it takes typically 8-12 months for a new recruit to become trained. Most of our volunteers are now 'observers'."*

Finn Paradis and Usui discovered that turnover increased among hospice volunteers as their interest in volunteering waned if they were not immediately placed into work assignments following training. The Institute for Volunteering Research in the UK found a similar result in 2003:

"Several respondents told us they had been discouraged from volunteering because organisations took so long to respond to an initial enquiry, process an application or place the respondent once they had been recruited. Without a prompt response, many potential volunteers may walk away: they may join another organisation, or worse, they may assume that they are not wanted as volunteers and never even try again."

It is essential to make sure systems for screening work efficiently and that, if they do not, volunteers are kept informed of what is happening and why the system is taking so long. Organizations that do have complex systems for screening should develop ways for maintaining contact with prospective volunteers and ways for involving volunteers on a more limited basis (such as observers or trainees) while applications are being processed.

Final Thoughts

Good volunteer interviewing is a key trait for successful programs. It is the point at which a correct decision—one that puts the right person into the right job—will either support or undermine the nature of the volunteer/agency relationship. It is a complicated task, since occasionally even the potential volunteer will not really know what they want to do or are truly capable of doing. Successful interviewing requires skills in relating to people and the imagination to see where their skills might best be applied. In the end, however, a successful interview will create the ideal match between the agency and the volunteer because it has defined an area of mutual interest in which both parties can benefit.

Chapter Seven
Preparing Volunteers for Success

All volunteers need some level of orientation for their work with the organization. This preparation falls into two parts:

- *Orientation*, the process of preparing the volunteer for a clear relationship with the organization (sometimes known as induction); and

- *Training*, the process of preparing the volunteer to perform work for the organization.

All volunteers should know they will be required to attend an orientation and/or training session. Orientation may be distinguished from training in that it is usually more general in nature, providing information every volunteer should know. Training is designed to equip volunteers with skills and knowledge required by their specific positions.

Orientation

Even if volunteers come to the job with all the skills necessary to do the job, they will need some orientation to the organization. Orientation is the process of making volunteers feel comfortable with and understand the workings of the organization. It is designed to provide them with background and practical knowledge of the organization and to let them understand how they can contribute to the purpose of the organization. If the volunteers better understand the organization's systems, operations, and procedures, they will be able to contribute more productively.

There are three different subject areas that should be covered during the orientation process: the cause, the systems for volunteer management, and the social environment for the volunteers.

Cause Orientation

This area involves introducing the volunteers to the purpose of the organization. It should cover:

- A description of the problem or cause.
- A description of the client group.
- A description of the mission and values of the organization.
- A description of the history of the organization.
- A description of the programs and services of the organization.
- A description of other groups working in the same field, and their distinguishing characteristics from this organization.
- A description of future plans of the organization.

The presentation of these items should be a discussion rather than a dry description. The intention of this portion of the orientation is to allow the volunteer to begin to learn and adopt the basic values of the organization. Part of this will involve possible debate over the philosophy and approach the organization is taking to solve its identified community need; part may involve learning the myths and legends of the organization through hearing stories about early leaders or exemplary volunteers.

The goal of this discussion is to allow the volunteers to make an intellectual and emotional commitment to the basic purpose of the organization, to consciously decide that they believe in and are willing to work toward achieving the mission of the organization. This portion of the orientation is intended to allow the volunteers to "join the cause." It is also designed to give the volunteer sufficient background to explain the organization if ever asked to do so. Volunteers who do not have this background may give erroneous information out about the organization. This discussion will also give the Volunteer Program Manager an opportunity to learn about the philosophies of each volunteer and to determine whether these are congruent with the interests of the organization; it will allow the volunteer director to learn, for example, if a person is so motivated by a particular aspect of the cause that the volunteer might tend to go beyond organizational boundaries.

System Orientation

This portion of the orientation involves introducing the volunteers to the system of volunteer management with the organization. It would include presentation and discussion of:

- The structure and programs of the organization, with illustrations of what volunteers contribute to those programs.
- The system of volunteer involvement within the organization: policies and procedures.
- An introduction to facilities and equipment.
- A description of volunteer requirements and benefits.
- An introduction to record-keeping requirements.
- A description of timelines of organization's

activities and key events.

The simplest way to develop the agenda for this portion of the orientation session is to ask "What would I like to know about this place in order to better understand how it works?" Remember that friends will ask the volunteers about their volunteer work and about the organization. A volunteer who fully understands the organization can well serve as an effective communicator with the public about the worth of the organization, while a confused volunteer can present quite the opposite picture.

The purpose of this portion of the orientation session is to provide an organizational context for the volunteer and make them understand how they fit into the processes of the organization. This material is often presented in a factual way, with charts and descriptive handouts, followed by a question and answer period to clarify issues. It can be made more interesting by having different representatives, both paid and volunteer, describe varying aspects of the work of the organization. This part of the orientation session allows the volunteers to see how the role they will be playing relates to the work of the organization. It shows them the basic requirements of that role and how that role links to other areas of the organization.

Social Orientation

This portion of the orientation introduces the volunteers to the social community that they are being asked to join and begins to forge the personal bonds that will sustain volunteer involvement.

Included in this introduction are:

- An introduction to the leadership of the organization (who might participate in the orientation by presenting or leading part of the discussion on the mission of the organization).

- A "welcoming" by staff and current volunteers (through their participation in presenting subject areas or even as a purely social occasion).

- A description of the culture and etiquette of the organization (matters such as dress, customs, etc.)

This part of the orientation session can proceed in a variety of ways. It might be interspersed throughout the other stages of orientation, with official greeting, welcoming, and presentation serving to initiate personal contacts. It might begin right after formal acceptance of a volunteer, with the assignment of a personal mentor or companion who contacts the volunteers, meets with them informally to welcome them to the organization and introduces them to its processes, and then supports them during their early involvement. It might consist of introducing the volunteers to their future supervisors and arranging for a discussion about how they will be working together. It might consist of a welcoming party for new volunteers hosted by staff and current volunteers.

The purpose of this part of the orientation is to show the volunteers who they will be working with, and welcoming them into the social context of the organization. The goal is also to show the volunteer that they are a welcome addition to the "team."

The Importance of Orientation

The above aspects of orientation are designed to answer three basic questions for the new volunteer:

- Cause: *Why* should I be working here?
- System: *How* will I be working here?
- Social: *Where* do I fit in with everyone else?

These three questions are crucial if the volunteer is to feel comfortable. A volunteer who does not "feel" right about these three aspects of volunteering will cease to feel a part of the organization. Much of the early retention loss in some volunteer programs is due to the absence of a good orientation. Orientation should "seal the deal" between the organization and the volunteer, clearly establishing the intellectual, practical, and emotional bonds between the two.

Some organizations avoid giving an orientation because of difficulty in getting volunteers to attend. This problem can be solved by a variety of approaches. It might require altering the scheduling of orientations, placing them on weekends or during the evening. It might involve altering the format of orientations, doing them one-on-one, in small groups, or in several shorter sessions. It may require making attendance mandatory, even if that means losing some potential volunteers. Make whatever adjustments are necessary, and ensure that all new volunteers receive a proper orientation. Even volunteers participating in one-day events should receive a short orientation, focusing on the cause and a brief description of the organization. This will remind them of *why* they are engaged and open the door to further involvement. And, of course, whoever is managing the work area of volunteers at such an event should provide a "social orientation" by ensuring that volunteers get to meet and interact with other volunteers. It never hurts if food is served as well.

Perhaps the best way of understanding the importance of orientation is simply to consider its basic definition. "Orientation" is the process of learning one's direction and bearings in the world; a person without orientation is, to put it simply, "lost."

Training

Training is the process of providing volunteers with the ability to perform specific types of work.

Designing Training

Determining what training volunteers may need requires answering three questions:

- What *information* do they need to successfully perform the work?
- What *skills* do they need to successfully perform the work?
- What *attitudes* or approaches do they need to successfully perform the work?

Training to provide this information, develop these skills and engender these attitudes can be provided in three formats: formal training sessions, coaching sessions, and counseling.

Formal Training

Formal training will prepare volunteers for specific jobs. Sometimes this training can be quite lengthy, particularly when volunteers are recruited who lack the specific job skills required by the position. Crisis Lines, for example, provide many hours of training in how to deal with callers. These hours may be spread over a couple of weeks. One program for counseling delinquent children requires one evening per week of training for a year before the volunteers begin work with clients. Volunteer firefighters in the US typically attend training once a week to polish up and expand their skills for as long as they are with the fire department.

Training can be presented through lectures, readings, discussions, field trips, videos, panel discussions, demonstrations, role-playing, case studies, simulations, and more. Trainers commonly employ a variety of techniques so as to better retain the attention of the audience.

Training in Job Functions

There are two primary content areas to cover in volunteer training, regardless of the job for which the training is being provided. The first area is a description of the functions of the volunteer job to communicate to the volunteer:

1. This is what you *should* do and accomplish in your job.

2. This is what you *should not* do.

3. This is what you should *if* you encounter the following situations.

For example, a volunteer who is recruited to drive elderly clients to medical appointments might be trained as follows:

1. *Do*: be on time or notify the program coordinator at least three hours in advance if you are going to be late; help patients in and out of the car; be familiar with the city; have a roadworthy and inspected vehicle; use the recommended method of assisting patients from a wheelchair into the vehicle; follow the correct steps in folding and storing a wheelchair.

2. *Don't*: volunteer to assist clients with in-home chores; offer to take clients to other appointments on an unscheduled basis; take clients shopping; tell clients about the medical conditions of others; offer medical advice.

3. *If*: if there is a medical problem en route, go immediately to the nearest emergency room, the locations of which are marked on your map; if the client asks for your opinion of her doctor, tell the client you aren't qualified to make such a judgment.

The content of the training provides the volunteer with the collected experience (both positive and negative) that previous volunteers have acquired. The content should be developed with the assistance of staff and volunteers who are familiar with the work, and the session could be delivered by these same staff or volunteers.

A similar system can be used in training staff about volunteers. Here, for example, are the "Teacher Do's and Don'ts with School Volunteers" utilized by the Duval County School System in Florida:

Do:

- *Develop awareness about how to use volunteers*
- *Assess your needs*
- *Request volunteers for your classroom*
- *Orient volunteers to your classroom procedures*
- *Take time to know your volunteers*
- *Match the volunteer's interests and skills with needs*
- *Make volunteers feel welcome*
- *Confer often with volunteers*
- *Plan days and times to work in the classroom*
- *Be generous in offering encouragement and support*
- *Supply materials appropriate for lessons*
- *Be honest and open in talking over small problems*
- *Give volunteer proper notice of schedule changes*
- *Prepare students to work with volunteers*
- *Allow your volunteers to ask questions freely*
- *Share students' progress with the volunteers*

Don't:

- *Leave volunteers in charge of the classroom*
- *Give volunteers more than they can handle in the allotted time*
- *Expect volunteers to change their schedules without proper notice*
- *Waste volunteers' time*
- *Restrict volunteers' effectiveness by withholding appropriate information or instruction*

Training in Roles and Responsibilities

The second area might be termed a description of roles and responsibilities. It would include training that communicates to the volunteers the web of relationships in which they will be working:

1. This is with whom you will be working and this is your role in the task.

2. This is their role and how it fits into the task.

For example, this could include telling volunteers who their supervisor will be and any other staff or volunteers who will be assigned to work in concert with them. For example, a volunteer working in concert with others to serve a particular client should be introduced to those volunteers and learn what each is providing to that client and how their efforts dovetail.

Utilizing Roleplays in Training

Training is also a good opportunity for re-utilizing the roleplay scenarios questions discussed earlier in our chapter on Interviewing. These scenarios, particularly if they are based on actual problems or incidents encountered by other volunteers, can make an excellent teaching tool. They are an excellent way to engender discussion in a group setting as well, since they will give volunteers the opportunity to discuss difficult situations in depth.

Coaching

Coaching is a process of teaching or upgrading skills. It can be used in formal training sessions or in on-the-job training. It will most often be provided by the supervisor of the volunteer or a more experienced co-worker. Effective coaching follows a three-step process:

1. A demonstration of the skill to be learned or improved
2. Observation of the volunteer trying out the skill
3. Feedback and analysis

The skill can be demonstrated by anyone expert in that area. Either the person demonstrating the skill or the coach (supervisor, trainer, or volunteer program manager) should explain why the expert is doing what she is doing. The point of the demonstration is not just to allow the volunteer to see what is being done but to understand it.

To take an extremely simple example, if you were to demonstrate to a volunteer how to answer the organization's telephone, you might have the volunteer watch you answer the phone a few times. Then you might observe the volunteer answering the phone. Third, you might have the volunteer answer the phone without being observed. After each stage you would discuss the experience with the intention that the volunteer learn from it.

The EIAG Process

To increase your chances of the volunteer learning, these discussions can follow a learning model called EIAG. Although this doesn't spell anything, the four letters are the initial letters in the four major steps people go through to learn things. If you keep these steps in mind as you coach volunteers, you can make sure they get the most from the learning process.

- *Experience*

The "E" stands for experience. People learn from experiences, be they training exercises or real world events. But not always. Sometimes people have the same experience over and over again and never learn anything from it. If they are to learn from an experience, their minds go through three additional steps.

- *Identify*

The "I" is for identify. If a person is to learn from an experience, he or she has to be able to describe it. In the simple example of learning to answer the phone above, some questions you might ask at the various steps to get someone to describe the experience are:

- What did I do?
- What did you do?
- How did the other person react?
- How have things been going for you?
- What has been happening?

- *Analyze*

The third step in learning from experience is to analyze it. If a person is to learn from the identified experience, she must be able to analyze why it did. You want to get the volunteer to explore the factors in the situation that produced the experience. To continue with the example, some questions you might ask to help the volunteer analyze the steps are:

- Why did I begin by saying "Good morning?"
- What advantages are there to giving your name?
- Why did the caller get so upset with you?
- Why have things been going so well?

- *Generalize*

The "G" stands for generalize. If a person is to learn anything useful from an experience, she must be able to come up with some general rule or principle that applies beyond the specific situation to other, similar situations. Again, an effective coach relies on questions in this step. Some examples are:

- What will you do when you encounter a situation like this?
- What would you do differently if you had to do it over again?
- What would you advise someone else who is about to do this?
- What will you do to make sure things continue going so well?

An Example of EIAG

Let's see how this might work in a more complex example. As stated previously, coaching is particularly important with a volunteer who is new to a skill or concept. Imagine, for example, that you are a teacher of handicapped children and that you have a volunteer named Michael. You want Michael to help a child named Johnny learn to put his coat on and take it off. Although Michael has some experience in working with handicapped children, he has never done anything like this before. So you start by having Michael watch you work with Johnny. Afterwards, you use the EIAG technique to discuss things with Michael. Some questions you might ask include:

- What did you see me do with Johnny? (identifying)
- What problems did I encounter? (identifying)
- Why do you think these occurred? (analyzing)
- What do you think you could do to avoid such problems? (generalizing)
- What techniques seemed to work well? (identifying)
- Why did these techniques work better than others I tried? (analyzing)
- Based on what you saw, what are some things you will avoid and some things you will do when you work with Johnny? (generalizing)

Once you are confident that Michael has a grasp of what to do, you watch him carefully while he attempts to conduct the lesson. During this time, if it seems like Michael is doing something that will upset or harm Johnny in any way, you would of course interrupt and suggest a different course of action. Or you might take over the lesson again yourself. In any case, after Michael's attempts, you would again ask questions to help him learn and grown from his experience:

- How would you describe what happened? (identifying)
- Why did you put your coat on? (analyzing)
- What were the strengths of your approach? (analyzing)
- Why did Johnny throw his coat on the floor? (analyzing)
- Based on this insight, what will you do differently next time? (generalizing)

In the course of this, you may need to go back and demonstrate the skill yourself, with Michael watching. You would then go back to watching him. Eventually, when you are comfortable that Michael has mastered the skill, you would allow him to work unobserved. Nonetheless, you would continue to check on his progress from time to time, using the EIAG questions to make sure he is continuing to grow in his abilities. The checking would include direct observation by you and reports from Michael. Eventually, you would get comfortable enough to rely simply on Michael's observations.

As you begin to use the EIAG model, it is important

that the sequence of questions you use be natural. Sometimes you may have a tendency to get locked into our prepared sequence of questions while a volunteer's response might naturally bring up other questions. If you have prepared a series of identification questions, don't ask them all in a row if you get an unexpected response on the first one. It might be better to go on and analyze that response than to proceed with your other questions.

The EIAG coaching model is effective because it is a natural one. It merely makes conscious the subconscious method you employ all the time. When you employ it, you are merely making sure that your volunteers complete all the steps in the learning process instead of leaving it up to chance that they will do it on their own.

It also enables you to spot erroneous conclusions volunteers might reach from their limited experience. If Michael, for example, generalizes that "Johnny is simply incapable of learning anything," you might respond by getting him to analyze that statement: "Why do you say that?" You might give him sympathy for the difficulty of the task and encouragement to try harder. But above all you need to bring him to a different generalization based on the facts, asking questions such as:

- Is there anything else in the situation that might have caused that problem?
- What does seem to get Johnny's attention?
- Can you think of any way to use that in the lesson?
- What will you try tomorrow?

Counseling

The goal of counseling is to assist the volunteer in solving a problem or improving a behavior by getting the volunteer to acknowledge a difficulty and take responsibility for the improvement. While coaching shows volunteers how they might improve in job skills, counseling helps volunteers discover how to improve their performance.

The Counseling Process

When volunteers encounter a problem in their work or during training, they may feel that the volunteer aspect of their lives is no longer under control. When people feel a lack of control of an area, they get frustrated and their self-esteem suffers, both of which can lead to volunteer turnover. The goal of the counseling process is to restore a feeling of control in the volunteer's life by helping her find a course of action that will solve the problem.

As with coaching, the principle tool the effective manager employs in counseling is the question. The supervisor can use questions to help the volunteer do these things:

Identify the problem
- What is going wrong?
- What exactly is happening?

Identify the cause of the problem
- Why is the problem occurring?
- What is causing the problem?
- What factors in the situation are producing the problem?

Identify alternatives
- What are the alternatives you have in this situation?
- What else could you do?
- Have you considered this course of action? (making a suggestion)
- What would happen if you tried that?
- Then what would happen?

Identify a better course of action
- What are the strengths and weaknesses of each alternative?
- What can you do to solve the problem?
- Why do you think that might work?

Learn from their experiences
- What can you do differently in the future to avoid this problem?
- What would you do differently if you had it to do over again?

Providing Counseling

As indicated above, it is fine to offer suggestions when counseling, offering additional information or suggestions for courses of action that volunteers might not see. In doing so, however, you should not be telling them what to do. Your role, in counseling, is to empower them to come up with their own solutions. In doing this, you need to get them to accept ideas that originate from you by having them analyze them. The conversation might go something like this:

- "Have you considered this course of action?"

  "Oh, so that's what you want me to do?"

- "Not necessarily. Have you considered that?"

  "No."

- "What would happen if you did that?"

  "I'm not sure."

- "Do you see any risks of that approach."

  "No. I guess it might work."

- "Why do you think it would work?"

  "The clients wouldn't have to wait so long. And you would have more time to process their paperwork."

- "So what do you think?"

  "I think it sounds like a good idea."

- "Let's see how it goes."

Regardless of whether you are using formal training, coaching, or counseling, remember that the point is to make sure that volunteers learn from experience. The mix of methods that you choose may vary from volunteer to volunteer, and even will vary over the term of the volunteer's relationship with the organization.

You can determine whether the learning experience has been a successful one by asking questions of the volunteer following the training. Some useful questions include:
- What point sticks out in your mind?
- Why is that point so important?
- What did you hear that will be most useful to you?
- Why do you think so?
- How can you use this information in your volunteer job?
- What implication does this have for your ability to be successful here?

Establishing a Mentor System for New Volunteers

One excellent method of both making volunteers feel welcome and enhancing their knowledge and skill is through formally creating mentoring relationships between new and more experienced volunteers. This has been done successfully in the Master Gardener Volunteer Program with positive results on volunteer retention. Rogers comments on the success of a program in Oregon that matched mentors with newcomer volunteers - the mentors called and welcomed new volunteers to the program, reminded them of upcoming training events and spent time with them during the first training class. The mentors also work beside the newcomers during their first workdays. The results have been impressive:

"Retention of new members has been much higher since the mentor program was introduced. Before the program was introduced in 1993 approximately 50% of the new volunteers completed the class and their voluntary service commitment. Since 1993, 38 of 51 or 75% of volunteers have completed their commitments and many have gone well beyond the minimum commitment of time."

Phillips and Bradshaw report on the success of a similar effort in Florida:

"Drop-out rates for the three annual Master Gardener basic training programs prior to the Mentor program were 26%, 17% and 27% for the years 1995, 1996 and 1997, respectively. While the 1998 class in Pinellas Country was one-third smaller than the previous years, the trainee drop-out rate for the basic training program was 2%."

Mentors provide both a personal connection to the organization and the encouragement that may get a new volunteer through uncertainty.

And mentoring also applies an excellent opportunity to recognize the skills and knowledge of experienced volunteers, enabling them to model desired behaviors for the new volunteers.

Training as a Volunteer Benefit

Training might also be developed for the volunteer program because it serves as a tangible benefit that could be offered to the volunteer in addition to the training required for satisfactory job performance.

Such training could be:

- Training in ancillary skills
- Training in career/life development
- Cause-related training

The training might be developed by the organization or might consist of providing an opportunity for the volunteer to attend outside conferences or workshops. Attendance would be both an opportunity to increase knowledge and a formal recognition by the organization that the volunteer is "worth" the expense of sending him or her on the training and confidence in him or her being an effective representative of the organization.

With some volunteers, training can be a significant benefit. Young volunteers, for example, who came to volunteering as a means of gaining career experience might be offered sessions on volunteering as a step to paid employment, in resume writing, and in career planning.

You should remember that training is almost always viewed with approval by volunteers. One of the primary benefits you can provide volunteers is additional information, skills, or assistance in performing their work more productively, but you might also provide training in other areas of their lives. Do not hesitate to ask for an additional commitment or effort from volunteers in return for training, since most of them will regard it as well worth the effort. To the volunteers, your interest in them is regarded as recognition of the significance and importance of their contribution to the work of the organization.

Training may be resisted by volunteers if it begins to impose extraordinary demands on their time. This has become a problem in the volunteer firefighting community where training requires due to increased safety procedures and new equipment are sometimes onerous. It may also be resisted if it involves new techniques that require experienced volunteers to change the ways in which they have been performing their volunteer work.

Orientation and training may seem like extra efforts but they are essential in the volunteer context. Paid staff often receive neither orientation nor training; instead they learn how to fit into the organization and do their work simply by being there – more by osmosis than intent. Unfortunately this technique does not translate well into the volunteer environment - a volunteer who feels out of place and incapable of performing well will leave before they have time to accumulate knowledge by osmosis.

Remember McCurley's Rule:

> *"Nobody volunteers to be a failure."*

Chapter Eight
Supervising for Maximum Performance

Effective Volunteer Program Managers need skill in managing people for two reasons. First, they may be supervising volunteers directly. In addition, they must make sure that staff do a good job of managing the volunteers they are working with. Both of these areas demand knowledge of managing the relationship between volunteers and those they are working with and responsible to.

Being a Manager of Others

The manager's job is not to do things directly but to make sure things get done. Or, to put it another way, the manager's job is to do things that enable others to do the work. To put it still another way, a manager's job is to achieve planned results through others.

In order to succeed in this job, managers must learn to work indirectly, through other people. Most people who become Volunteer Program Managers are more used to doing things themselves, however. As we will see, the instincts that serve one well in getting work done oneself are often counterproductive when it comes to getting things done through others.

The Volunteer Program Manager faces some interesting challenges in management:

- motivating those who do not work for pay requires more skill and greater ability than is commonly the case among those who supervise paid employees

- volunteer programs may contain a much wider range of people to be managed – some programs involve volunteers as young as early teens and as old as their eighties

Creating a Motivating Environment

To succeed in managing people, our job is to make sure they are both willing and able to do the work of the agency. If they are motivated to do the work and have the skills to do it, our problems in management will be few.

The previous chapter was about making sure volunteers have the skills and knowledge necessary to do the work. In this chapter, we will concentrate on the Volunteer Program Manager's role in creating conditions that encourage volunteers to want to do the work. By building a job around the volunteer's needs for volunteering, as described previously, we begin by placing the volunteer in a job she wants to do. Further, we tap the volunteer's need for achievement by making sure there are goals to achieve, thereby providing the volunteer with a challenging responsibility that is likely to be satisfying. In this chapter we will look at tapping another need, the volunteer's need to feel in control of what she does. We do this using several techniques that empower the volunteer.

By "empowering" volunteers, we mean making them more autonomous, more capable of independent action. The wisdom of this approach is that it is easier to get good results from empowered people than from people who are dependent. We can do this by giving them authority to decide, within limits, how they will go about achieving the results for which they are responsible. In such a relationship, the manager becomes a source of help for the volunteer rather than a controller or a goad. This not only feels better for the volunteer but allows the manager to spend less time making decisions about the volunteer's work and more time to think strategically, to concentrate on grasping the opportunities that will never be seen if she is mired in the muck of day-to-day detail. It also gives her time to work with other staff of the agency on how to improve their involvement of volunteers

Levels of Control

In giving people authority over the "how" of their jobs, the danger is that there is a risk they will do the wrong things. This danger is reduced by recognizing that there are different degrees of authority volunteers can exercise in carrying out their responsibilities. The four levels of control described below define how much discretion the supervisor and the volunteer each have in deciding how each result is to be achieved.

1. The Authority for Self-assignment

Self-assignment means that the volunteer generates her own assignments. At this first level, the volunteer decides what to do, does it, and that is the end of it. A person working as a literacy tutor, for example, might meet with a client at the client's home, conduct tutoring, and go home. Next week, she repeats this routine. If the volunteer were operating at level one on the control scale, she would do this without bothering to inform the paid staff of what she had done or the progress she had made with the client.

This type of complete volunteer control rightly sends shivers of anxiety up the spine of most managers. (And many of those who have no qualms about allowing volunteers this much control should be more anxious than they are.) The supervisor has no insurance that the volunteer did the right things or indeed did anything at all. A lesser degree of control might therefore be more appropriate.

2. The Authority for Self-assignment Provided the Boss is Kept Advised of Progress

Regular progress reports are made at this second level of control. The volunteer decides what to do and does it, as at level one. But at some point (the frequency of which is determined by the supervisor) she tells her supervisor what she did. If the volunteer indeed did the wrong thing or did the right thing in the wrong way, the supervisor finds out about it and can take steps to correct mistakes. This gives the supervisor a bit more assurance that things will all work out properly in the end.

These progress reports need not be written. An informal chat between the supervisor and the volunteer is sufficient for the supervisor to be assured that things are going well.

The frequency of progress reports depends on how anxious the supervisor is about the volunteer's performance. In the above example, if the supervisor has great confidence in the volunteer, she might only check progress once a month, finding out how the tutoring had gone, what the client had learned, what problems the volunteer encountered, how she handled them, and what materials she needed. Moderate anxiety might require a report after each session. If a supervisor has high anxiety and the volunteer works at the agency, she might check mid-way through the shift as to what had been accomplished thus far. A higher degree of anxiety might warrant level three control.

3. The Authority to Recommend Self-assignment

If the supervisor is very anxious about the volunteer's performance and is worried that she is going to have to take steps to correct the situation more often than she feels is desirable, then she might want the volunteer to tell her beforehand what she intends to do. When a volunteer is operating at this third level of control, she is still the source of her own assignments. However, before she takes action her ideas must be approved by her supervisor.
When a volunteer operates at level three, the supervisor has pretty much complete assurance that the volunteer will do the right things. The supervisor has an effective veto over the volunteer's decisions.

Just as level two contains gradations of control in the form of varying frequencies of reports, level three comes in a variety of shades. In some cases, a volunteer might provide daily recommendations—"I suggest I call these people now," for example. On the other hand, the recommendation may be longer term, such as "here is my plan to raise the client's reading level." These gradations depend again on the supervisor's degree of anxiety about the volunteer's performance in pursuing particular targets.

At this third level, as with level two, volunteers should provide regular progress reports. At level three, a progress report should also contain a plan for future action.

4. No Authority for Self-assignment

If the supervisor's degree of anxiety about a volunteer's performance is extremely high, she might be tempted to allow still less control. The only step lower is essentially no control at all. At this level of control, it doesn't matter whether the volunteer sees what needs to be done. She just does what she is told.

At this level, the authority for deciding what the volunteer will do is transferred from the place where the work is actually done to the management level. The thinking required to decide how to do the task is transferred to a brain that is unconnected to the body that carries out the assignment. This is inefficient and inevitably produces more work for the manager. The more people the manager supervises, the more time she will have to spend deciding what people should be doing.

Besides taking more time, this style of management reduces the number of creative ideas you get from volunteers. Good ideas for improving services will seldom surface if the volunteer is not expected to think. As the pace of change accelerates, yesterday's practices will become increasingly obsolete. Volunteers, partly because they are not submerged in the day-to-day details of running the organization, can provide a valuable perspective on the changing environment and the innovations needed to stay relevant.

The only time you should supervise volunteers at this fourth level is when they are new to the work they do. When people first come on board, they usually don't know enough about the agency or the work they will be doing to make an informed recommendation. Usually, the volunteer knows this very well and wants to be told what to do. For this reason, short-term volunteers are appropriately managed in this way. When volunteers stick around for a while, however, you run great risks to volunteer morale if you continue to deny them the authority to think for themselves because people usually resent being controlled by someone else.

Climbing the Control Ladder

The four levels of control are a ladder for people to climb. When volunteers learn enough about the job to make an intelligent recommendation, they can be moved to level three. To do this, you simply tell them that instead of you figuring out what they should do, you would like them to do that for themselves. Instead of you telling them what to do, you want them to tell you what they think they should do.

At first, you may be glad they are at level three instead of two, because they may bring you some pretty bad recommendations. This is an opportunity to shape the thinking of each volunteer so they become more capable of independent action. If there is time to do so, tell him or her your concerns about the recommendation and have the volunteer bring you a different suggestion. For example, you might say "My concern about that activity is that it might endanger our clients. I would like you to bring me an idea that doesn't have that problem."

As the volunteers get used to this, and as they figure out the kinds of recommendations you buy and the kinds you reject, their recommendations will get better and better, meaning more like the kind of thing you would tell them to do if you had the time and inclination to do so. Eventually, you find your anxiety about their thinking drops to zero. This is a signal that it is time to move them to level two. To do this, tell them that they no longer have to clear these actions with you but are authorized to take action as they see fit. But you would, of course, like to be kept informed of their activities.

In the initial stages, you may require frequent checking. But as their reports show they are still doing the kinds of things they used to recommend, your anxiety will lessen. The checks can then become less frequent. Eventually, they may not be needed at all, and the volunteer will be at level one.

As volunteers progress up the control scale, the amount of time we have to spend managing them decreases. Level four people take the most time because we have to do all the thinking, tell them what to do, and then check their progress. Level three people take less time because they do the thinking, they tell us what they intend to do, and then we check the progress. At level two, we simply check the progress.

Of course the ultimate in time savings is level one, where we don't even have to check the progress. This level has many dangers associated with it, however. One is the volunteer may not feel that we are interested in her work and may feel devalued and drop out. Another is that she may come to feel unconnected to the program and lose the sense of belonging that is so important to so many people. And, of course, there is always the possibility that even the most trusted and proven volunteer might create a disaster that at level one strikes without warning.

Many managers see only two of these four levels of control, and they see the wrong two. For many, the only alternative to telling people what to do is to turn them loose. At level four you will reap resentment, but at level one you risk chaos. Most volunteers should work at either level three or level two on most of the results for which they are responsible.

Establishing Checkpoints

One of the most common management mistakes is failure to check progress. Unless the volunteer is at level one, the supervisor should keep track of what the volunteer has been doing. Even where the two parties have discussed in advance what was to be done, it is best to check regularly to ensure the volunteer is making progress toward the target than to wait until the end to be surprised that the result was different from what you expected.

A calendar, on which meetings or telephone conversations are scheduled is the easiest, cheapest, and one of the most effective of all management controls. By requiring regular progress reports, you gain three important advantages, not the least of which is that it lets people know that you are serious about their achievement of results. Progress reports also help avoid crises and poor quality, last minute work. This is particularly important on long-term projects where volunteers are expected to be "self-starters." Most human beings start each day asking themselves "What is the most urgent task I have to do today?" If the volunteer project is not due for six months, it is easy to put off progress today.

This will continue to happen until the due date is excruciatingly near. But if the volunteer knows she has to report progress tomorrow, she will regard the project with a greater sense of urgency today. By setting regular checkpoints, you ensure that volunteers make regular progress.

A further advantage of regular reports is that they enable the manager to spot problems in the work while there is still a chance for corrective action. If the volunteer has misunderstood your intentions, for example, you can find this out early, before she has wasted a lot effort going in the wrong direction.

A common pitfall in reporting progress happens when volunteers provide their own assessment of what they did rather than telling you what they actually did. If the volunteer says "Things went really well," this does not give the supervisor any information about what actually happened. When volunteers say things are "fine," they are saying things are going the way they pictured them going. The wise supervisor finds out if things are going the way she pictured them going.

A Case Study in Exercising Control

Let's look at three examples of the levels of control in action. For this exercise, imagine you are the Volunteer Coordinator in a Community Action Agency. You place volunteers with the various programs of the agency and supervise three others who help you out with recruitment, screening, and office work. You have recently recruited a volunteer named Frank, who is writing a grant proposal to a local community foundation to get funds that you could use to strengthen the volunteer program. Frank is new to town and is looking for a job in public relations.

1. At a meeting with your boss (the agency director), she mentions that she is concerned about the prevailing negative attitude in the community toward the agency. It is her feeling that the community regards the agency as being an ineffective body that coddles people who don't want to work. Since Frank is looking for a job in public relations, you think he might be a good person to do something about this situation. After the meeting, you ask him to write some public interest stories for release to the press which describe the good things the programs do and which spotlight clients who have gone on to play a productive role in the community.

a) What degree of control is Frank exercising?
b) What could you do to increase his control?

2. You give Frank total responsibility for the public knowing and valuing the good things community action programs do. He prepares a brief proposal, outlining two actions he could take. You aren't sure if these are good ideas or not. You tell Frank you need to think them over and put them in your briefcase to study that night at home.

a) When Frank submitted his proposal to you, what degree of control was he exercising?
b) After you told him you'd get back to him, what degree of control was he exercising?
c) What could you do to increase his control?

3. Frank hears that the state may have some funding available to support one of the agency's programs. He calls the state and finds out about it. He sends you a report, spelling out the facts. The last sentence of the report is "Do you think it's worth going after?"

a) What degree of control is Frank exercising?
b) What could you do to increase his control?

Control Quiz Discussion

In the first situation, Frank is not exercising any control over what he does. He is at level four on the control scale. This is not the worst kind of level four assignment because it is a creative task. He can decide which clients to spotlight or what words to chose, but he has exercised no authority for self-assignment; when you see him writing the stories, he is doing something that was your idea, not his.

To give him some authority for self-assignment, you first have to define the result you want from Frank. Why do you want these stories written? To change people's attitudes toward the agency? Then give him that responsibility, and let him decide how to go about doing it. At degree of control number three, the authority to recommend self-assignment, he would develop a plan for pursuing this objective; once the plan was approved, you would define how to measure progress and negotiate checkpoints for reviewing it. At degree of control number two, the plan would be assumed to be all right, and the only thing you would have to do is to define the measures and negotiate the checkpoints. At level one (probably not a wise choice if Frank had never done public relations work for you before), you would hear from Frank only if he were having difficulty achieving his result.

In situation two, you have given Frank responsibility for a result. When he brings you his ideas, he is exercising level of control number three, because he is telling you what he wants to do before he does it. But once you say you have to think this over, you have put him back to level four.

Many people find this situation difficult to understand, so let's go into it a bit more. If you are going to think the proposals over because you are unsure of them, it means you are taking the authority for thinking away from Frank. It also means that you are going to do some work on the ideas yourself.

If you are not going to do this, but if the proposals need to be thought over, who will do that thinking? Frank, of course. To keep this as efficient as possible, you can tell him what you'd like him to think about. You can tell him your concerns. If you can't figure out your concerns, tell Frank that. Try to tell him why you are unsure, what additional information you'd like to have, what points you are uneasy about. Then give him the assignment of thinking it over. Give him the assignment to gather the information, clarify the points, or explore the ramifications. Give him the assignment to do the thinking and to come back to you with a new proposal that you can approve. Then, when he begins to work on the project, all actions he takes are actions he recommended, actions he decided were the right ones (and which you approved). This means that the only way he can prove he was right is to put everything he has into making sure this works. It's his plan. He owns it. His ego is on the line (though he does have the security, at level three, that you thought it was a good idea too).

Thinking it over yourself results in your getting overworked and running the risk of getting indifferent effort and results from your volunteers and paid staff. By allowing Frank to think it over, you keep him in control of his work. You work fewer hours and get better effort and results from your people.

In situation three, Frank is almost at level two. But in the last sentence he throws it away and puts himself at level four by asking to be told what to do.

In situation two, we saw how easy it was for the boss to put an employee at level four without meaning to. In situation three we see how easy it is for employees to put themselves at level four without meaning to. In asking you to make this decision, the volunteer abdicated his authority to think and, in the process, gives an assignment to you to do the work of reading the memo, grasping its implications, maybe asking a few questions to clarify some points, and coming up with a course of action. To increase Frank's control from this abysmal level, you need to ask him to finish his work. "Frank, this is an interesting question. What is your recommendation? In order to make the decision you've asked me to make here, I need to know if you think it's worth going after and why."

This method of keeping things under control while simultaneously empowering people works only if they have clear results to achieve. Asking for a recommendation when there are no such clear results turns the authority for self-assignment into a guessing game. An employee needs responsibility before authority makes sense.

As a general guideline, give everyone the maximum amount of authority you can stand to give them. Every interaction you have with your people about their work takes time that could be spent by both of you doing other things. The higher a volunteer is on the scale, the less frequently you will have to communicate with him.

Managing by Asking Empowering Questions

To get the best results, a good manager will ask a lot of questions in interactions. Questions enable the volunteers to feel involved while leaving the questioner still very much in control.

Insecure, inexperienced supervisors think they should have all the answers. Whenever they interact with a volunteer, they feel that if they can't provide an answer to all the questions and have instant solutions for all the problems, they are failing. Such managers either make ill-considered decisions or make an excuse for a delay when presented with complex problems.

The root of this behavior is the traditional manager's concern that the volunteers should have confidence in her. By contrast, an effective manager is most concerned that volunteers have confidence in themselves.

A volunteer who depends on her supervisor for all the answers does not grow on her own. Further, since such managers often think it is their job to tell their volunteers what to do and how to do it, they tend to foster volunteer apathy and resentment. Volunteers in such circumstances tend to stagnate and decay.

Empowering questions focus people on what they can control. They begin with words such as "How can you" or "What will you do." If a person makes a mistake, for example, the manager can ask "What can you do differently next time?" or "How will you approach this kind of problem in the future?"

The process of management can be divided into sub-functions. Three of the most important are planning, empowering, and evaluating. For each function there are several key questions to ask.

Planning Questions

Planning refers to the manager's role in setting goals and making sure that the volunteer knows what to do. Planning is something managers should never do on their own; they should always involve the people who will be carrying out the plan. By involving the people who will be responsible for implementing the plan, you will give them a sense of ownership of the plan. You also make sure that the plan is based on the practical realities our volunteers face day-to-day. And you increase the likelihood that your people will pursue the plan with enthusiasm.

Some key planning questions to ask in formal, long-range planning sessions include:

- What is the purpose of our work?
- What obstacles do we face in achieving that purpose?
- What resources do we have available to help us achieve our purpose?
- What strategies can we employ to overcome our major obstacles?
- What new developments affect us?
- What are the trends?
- How can we take advantage of those developments and trends?
- If we were to start the project all over again from scratch, what would we do differently?
- What problems are looming?
- What opportunities are presenting themselves?

In groups larger than six or seven, the manager will find it easier to increase active participation by having small groups of volunteers meet to discuss these questions and then report their conclusions to the whole group. With the data generated in response to these questions, the manager brings the group to focus by using questions such as:

- Based on all this, what should we be trying to accomplish?
- What should our goals be for the forthcoming period?

In all this the manager should not play a purely facilitative role. She may have strong opinions of her own. The manager should always get the most out the group first. She should question first, suggest second, and third state her own opinion. The idea is to encourage the volunteers to take ownership of the ideas, but to stay in control and ensure that effective goals are set for the organization.

At this point, however, no one in particular has any responsibility for any specific goal. One very powerful next move is to refer to each goal and ask the question "Who will take responsibility for achieving this goal?" Again, the manager may have particular people in mind, and can certainly exercise her prerogative to assign responsibility. But where it is appropriate, asking for voluntary assumption of responsibility leads to more committed pursuit of the agency's objectives.

Other planning questions are appropriate after goals have been set and responsibility has been assigned or taken. At meetings with the responsible individual or team, these questions can be asked:

- When can you have your plan for achieving these goals to me?
- When can you have this finished?
- How will you measure your success?
- What is your timetable?

Questions can also be used to encourage volunteers to set short term goals for themselves and to maintain a sense of purpose on a daily basis. Three powerful questions in this regard include:

- What do you think you can accomplish this month?
- What can you do today to make progress toward your goals?
- What can you do today that will make the most difference?

Empowering Questions

This second group of questions can be used in counseling and coaching volunteers on job performance and motivational issues. They include:

- How do you feel about your job?
- What are your frustrations?
- Do you know what you want to achieve in your

job?
- What do you need to do your job better?
- Would you like some increased responsibility?
- Is there something you would rather do than what you do now?
- Are there other skills you would like to learn?
- Is there something you'd like to try out to see if you like doing it?

When volunteers encounter difficulties or setbacks, they tend to get discouraged and drop out. They tend to focus on what they can't control, namely their past action, and begin to feel frustrated and helpless. To avoid this, you need to keep them from focusing on what they did in the past and focus them on what they will do differently in the future. The main question you should ask about the past difficulty is:

- What can you learn from this to help you in the future?

You might want to probe a bit on this, asking questions such as:

- What is your analysis of why this problem exists?
- What alternatives do you see?
- What are the strengths and weaknesses of those alternatives?
- Is there a more productive way to look at this situation?
- If you encounter difficulties, what will you do differently?

But you quickly want to direct them to future action, to the things they can control. Questions to focus volunteers on future action include:

- What is your recommendation?
- What can you do to get back on target?
- What one small step will start to make this situation better?
- What do you wish would happen?
- What could you do to make those wishes a reality?
- How could you get closer to the desired situation than you are today?

Evaluation Questions

The third group of questions attempts to evaluate the effectiveness of the volunteer's performance. Questions that help do this include:

- How would you evaluate your performance?
- Are you on-target or off?
- What can you learn from this setback to be stronger in the future?
- Why did you do it so well?
- What are some better ways of doing what you do?

These questions ask the volunteer to evaluate her own performance and the reasons for it. They encourage the volunteer to do a self-assessment and take her own corrective action.

Questions for Yourself

Being a manager means be concerned about the ability of your people to fulfill their responsibilities to the organization and its clients. Some questions to ask yourself from time to time to make sure you are paying attention to your management responsibilities include:

- Do my volunteers know what they're supposed to accomplish?
- Do they have sufficient authority to accomplish it?
- Do I and they know if they are succeeding or not?
- Do they have the skills and knowledge necessary to succeed?
- Are things organized so that their responsibilities are clear?
- How long has it been since I gave each of them any recognition for their contributions and achievements?

If you get negative answers to the first five of these questions, it means you have probably been spending too much time doing things yourself and not enough time managing. If your volunteers don't know what they are supposed to accomplish, for example, you have some goal-setting to do. If they lack skills, you have some training to do. And so on. If your answer to the last question is more than two weeks, you should make a special effort to let volunteers know that they are appreciated.

Effective Delegation

One of the primary responsibilities of the manager is to delegate responsibility. In a volunteer management system, delegation can occur in a number of formats: Volunteer Program Manager to volunteers; agency staff to volunteers; and volunteers to volunteers.

When delegating tasks to volunteers, the following elements ought to be included :

1. Define the assignment in terms of results

Delegation is the art of giving a person the authority

to carry out a mutually agreed task. The most fundamental skill involved is defining the task. This should be phrased in terms of an outcome or something to accomplish. It should define the desired end- product, not the means of achieving it.

For example, imagine that one of the tasks on your list of things to do today is to visit an electronics fair to see if there is any new equipment your organization might profit from. Instead of telling the volunteer to go to the exhibition to see what new equipment is available, you could delegate the desired outcome of the activity. You might say something like "I would like to give you the responsibility for upgrading our equipment," or "I wonder if you would be willing to take the responsibility for improving our efficiency through the purchase of new equipment."

Delegating by telling someone to go to the electronics fair removes one task from your list of things to do. Delegating by defining the result you want to achieve also removes all the tasks related to that result from all future days' lists.

2. *Define the level of control*
The second step in delegating effectively is to define how much authority the person has in carrying out the responsibility. This involves choosing among four levels of control described earlier in this chapter. Keep as much authority for deciding how to do the work in the hands of the worker as is possible.

To continue the example above, you might say "I would like to see your plan for doing this before you get started," thereby placing the volunteer at level three. "Let's get together every Friday for a chat about your progress on this," puts the volunteer at level two.

3. *Communicate any guidelines*
If there are relevant policies, laws, or regulations that the volunteer should work within, it is important to communicate these clearly at the outset. To continue our example, the agency may have purchasing regulations that need to be adhered to, such as getting price quotations from at least three suppliers. The volunteer needs to know this before wasting a lot of time doing something that would fall outside the rules.

4. *Make resources available*
If you know of any resources that would make the job easier or that would increase the chance of success, you should mention these at the outset. Resources include people, manuals, events, institutions, and equipment that would be helpful in achieving the result. It also includes the budget, if any, for the task. At this point, you should stress that if the volunteer encounters difficulty, she must come to you for advice. When giving advice, however, it is important to make sure that you keep the authority for the work in the hands of the worker, that, if at all possible, you avoid telling the worker what to do.

In our example, you would want to tell the volunteer that the electronics fair is there. You would also refer them to any staff with expertise in this area. And above all, you would tell her how much money was available for the project. "Don't waste your time looking at anything that costs more than $1000," for example.

5. *Determine criteria for success*
The volunteer should know, at the outset, how her work will be judged. She should be involved in determining the criteria, and she should have access to the data that indicates success or failure as she attempts to fulfill the responsibility.

In our example, you might say that the organization wants a piece of equipment that will pay for itself in a year's time.

6. *Set up checkpoints*
Unless the volunteer is at level one on the control scale, she should note on her calendar when she will be expected to report progress to you. The frequency of these checkpoints depends on your anxiety about the volunteer fulfilling the particular responsibility. These should not be presented to the volunteer as an excessively formal review meeting. Rather, it is an informal chat so you can find out how things are proceeding.

When delegating consider the following thought checklist:

Planning the Assignment
I have carefully considered:

- the purpose/goal of the work
- a completion date
- required standards of performance
- parameters for the work
- degree of delegated authority
- budgetary authorization
- degree of communication/involvement with me or with others

- the fact that the assignment may be done differently than if done by me personally

Selecting the Person to Do the Assignment
I have carefully considered:

- who is most interested in doing the work
- who has the most ability to get the job done
- who has the personal contacts to get the work done amicably
- who will find the work challenging and an opportunity for advancement
- who can fit the work into their schedule with least disruption

Making the Assignment
In making the assignment, I have:

- carefully described the purpose/goal of the assignment
- explained the parameters of the work: budget, timeframe, other considerations
- explained the degree of independent authority that is being granted
- agreed on communication checkpoints
- outlined available resources: finances, additional help
- explained relationships with others who will be involved

Checking the Assignment
In following up, I have:

- informed others of the delegated authority
- set reasonable timelines and reporting schedules
- listened carefully to the opinions of the person to who the work is delegated
- allowed room for creative thinking in accomplishing the assignment
- provided follow-up support and encouragement
- remained open to the need to make changes in the delegated assignment
- intervened only if there is some absolute necessity and then with minimal interference

Maintaining Communication

It is desirable to establish a system for providing on-going supervisory support for the volunteer. There are two main elements necessary for this on-going support.

Availability

Supervisors must be available to volunteers. The volunteers must have the ability to meet with, report to, and talk with supervisors, both on a regularly scheduled basis (checkpoints) and at times of the volunteer's choosing.

If the supervisor is available to the volunteer, the volunteer will feel that her work is appreciated enough to merit the attention and time of the supervisor. Availability also encourages the volunteer to consult with the supervisor if she encounters difficulties.

Supervisors can schedule office hours during which volunteers can make appointments. Specific lunch meetings for groups of volunteers can be scheduled for open discussions. Supervisors can practice "management by walking around" so that they can be approached by volunteers. Greeting volunteers when they arrive for work and thanking them when they leave also provides the volunteer with a sense of access. The intent of all these methods is to develop a sense of open and ready communication and access.

Equal Status and Involvement

The second key element necessary to on-going supervisory support is a sense among the volunteers that they are being accorded equal status and involvement in the work of the agency.

This equal treatment includes participation in decision-making (being invited to meetings or being asked for opinions, for example) and participation in day-to-day activities of the organization (being on memo distribution lists, for example). To provide volunteers a sense of being full partners in the agency, they should be entitled to most of the same benefits that staff are entitled, such as access to training and trips, reimbursement of expenses, and proper job titles.

Perhaps the most challenging aspect of all of this is getting staff to remember volunteers' names. People often forget the name of a volunteer whom they rarely work with. When they see the volunteer, they say hello, but don't remember his or her name. One way to reduce this problem is to put pictures of volunteers and staff on a bulletin board or in a who's who directory so people can refresh their memories.

Volunteers get a sense of being second-class citizens when they perceive that they are excluded from staff activities and benefits. These exclusions are often subtle, such as reserved parking for staff but not for volunteers, or no one ever thinking to invite volunteers to staff meetings. When volunteers feel they are "less" than staff, their self-esteem suffers, and they may stop wanting to volunteer.

Perhaps the most important aspect of building a sense of equality is open and free communication. This includes adding volunteers to the newsletter mailing lists, making sure they are copied on correspondence that involves their work, or taking the time to update a volunteer on what has happened since she was last there.

Controlling by Principles

Managers need to make sure that people do the right thing in coordination with others. One way they have traditionally done this is by establishing rules. People's behavior in these organizations is governed by standard operating procedures that they are expected to memorize.

There are many instances in which standard procedures are important. In volunteer fire departments, for example, everyone needs to show up at the scene of an emergency with a clear understanding of how everyone will act together to save lives and property. In hospitals, volunteers who work with patients need to understand specifically what kinds of requests they can and can't fulfill. The same is true of other situations in which clients' lives or well-being are at stake.

The problem in many organizations, however, is that they go overboard, writing standard operating procedures for every conceivable action. In 1992, for example, the federal government's personnel manual was over 10,000 pages long. Excess rules drain the life out of an organization. They also rob the organization of the creativity of its own members, for once a standard procedure has been published, people assume there is no other way to do things. In this chapter, we offer a different approach to keeping things under control. Instead of emphasizing rules that govern people's behavior, let their behavior be governed by principles.

There are two interrelated ways of controlling through principles. One is to establish clear values. The other is to establish clear organizational policies.

Promoting Values

Underlying the purpose of the effective organization is a set of values. Much has been written lately about the importance of organizational values to a group's success. An effective group must have one set of values, otherwise members wind up working at cross-purposes. The right values, internalized by each group member, lead to lots of right actions on the part of the organization. Creating and promoting these values is the responsibility of the leader.

By values we mean a set of principles that guide people's behavior. We mean a sense of what is right and what is wrong. Examples of organizational values include the promise of help to the client at all costs, taking initiative, accepting responsibility, win-win thinking, or innovation. Here are some of the core values that drive the Boys and Girls Clubs of Canada:

- *We care about children and youth*
- *We acknowledge that a sense of self worth is fundamental to individual dignity*
- *We understand children and youth need to be heard*
- *We believe a sense of belonging is essential to healthy growth*
- *We foster cultural understanding and acceptance*
- *We are committed to volunteerism*
- *We value and practice cooperative approaches.*

Having identified these and other principles, the national organization then expects the local boys and girls club personnel to act in accordance with those values. By giving its volunteers and staff a clear sense of what is right and wrong, managers can be more comfortable with its people making decisions. If the club were approached by the boy scouts, with the idea of putting on a training for youth on self-image, for example, the decision would be guided by the principle "We value and practice cooperative approaches." If a volunteer sees two children engaged in taunting each other with ethnic slurs, his response would be guided by the value "We foster cultural understanding and acceptance." And if potential volunteers needed to have the club open at different hours in order to do their work, the decision would be guided by the principle "We are committed to volunteerism."

The difference between values and slogans is that values guide the action of each group member – they are internalized by each person. When the line between what is right and what is wrong is clear, group members know when they are stepping over the line and will refrain from doing so. It is also easier to bring someone who is behaving inappropriately back over the line when the line itself is clear.

Clear values are essential to volunteer empowerment.

Internalized values enable the manager to empower the volunteer to make decisions and maintain some insurance that the volunteer will decide to do the right thing.

Most organizations do not have clear values of this sort. If the values aren't clear, volunteers will not be sure of the best course of action. When they aren't sure, they are likely to ask their supervisor what to do, putting themselves at level four on the control scale discussed earlier. When the values are unclear, therefore, volunteers consume more management time.

All this means that the manager who wants to build a truly outstanding organization needs to go beyond the important questions of "What are we trying to achieve?" and "How will we achieve it?" to the questions of "Who are we? What do we stand for? What do we believe in? What are the characteristics of our organization? What does it mean to be one of us? What kind of person is lucky enough to work here?" These questions ought to be considered frequently by every leader, and the positive answers to these questions ought to be broadcast frequently to the employees to help create a strong sense of the group's standards and traits.

At bottom, the values of an organization should be based on the promise it is trying to keep to the people it serves. To establish organizational values, begin with the mission statement. Ask yourself "What is the promise that this mission statement implies that we are trying to keep? What is the promise that underlies our reason for existence?" For example, a child abuse agency had as its mission that every child should be free from abuse. Their answer to the question "What is the promise you are trying to keep?" was "A safe and stable home for every child." This guides the behavior of its volunteers. As they make decisions about what information to seek in advocating for the rights of a child, who to talk to, and what to recommend to juvenile authorities, they are guided by this promise.

Once the promise has been defined, the next question is to ask "What principles should guide our behavior as we attempt to keep this promise? What principles should guide us as we interact with each other and with our clients? What principles should guide our managers' interactions with their people?" The answers to these questions might include words such as "integrity," "mutual respect," and "empowerment." They might include phrases such as "We put the client's welfare above our own," or "We practice nonjudgmental listening." Moscow Charity House, for example, identified the following values to guide the behavior of its volunteers who distribute clothing and other items to low-income pensioners:

- *Honesty*
- *Openness*
- *Social Partnership*
- *Voluntary Action*
- *Respect for All People*
- *Altruism*

What Does That Mean We Do?

More important than deciding on a group of abstract principles, however, is helping people have a clear vision of what those principles mean they are supposed to do. Too often, top management develops statements of principles, announces them and assumes that they are being adhered to by the members of the organization. Because there is often a lack of communication between top management and those doing the work of the organization, these assumptions tend to go unchecked. As a consequence, there can be a great difference between what management assumes is happening and what really exists.

A volunteer fire department, for example, developed a series of five values, one of which was "We care about the citizens of our community." This was a sentiment that was hard to argue with, but it was vague to the members of the department. To make this come alive, the chief met with the volunteers one night after drill and asked, "What does this mean we do in the event of a fire?"

The first answer from the group was "We get to the scene as fast as we can and put out the fire as quickly as possible." This was something they already did, so the chief went on probing, asking them about how the principle would apply in various specific situations. One of these was "What if the citizen was present while we were fighting the fire?" After some discussion, firefighters realized it was important to keep the citizen informed of what they were doing as they fought the fire instead of ignoring him or treating him like an obstacle as they had in the past. Similarly, the group decided that if there were a child present at the scene, they should try to comfort him. As a consequence, they began to carry teddy bears on the fire engines.

After this and several similar meetings, the fire

fighters had a clear idea of what the values statements meant. They became a guide to their decision-making on the job.

Creating Values for the Volunteer Program

Although the primary responsibility for establishing shared values is that of the leader, it is best to involve as many people as possible in delineating what these values are. Using questions such as those in the previous example, the leader should guide the group in a discussion of what principles the group believes should guide its actions.

Don't let the list of values get too long. Group those that are similar into broader categories. For example, if the group comes up with characteristics such as "caring," "concerned," and "dedicated to clients," you might group them into the larger category of being service-oriented. You don't want to have your volunteers have to try to remember sixteen principles to apply in making each decision.

Once these broader values have been developed, ask the group to make a commitment to them as guiding principles. Ask "Are you willing to help build an organization that lives according to these values? Are you willing to create an excellent organization according to these criteria?"

Although it is unlikely that anyone would say "no" to such a question, some might come up with barriers that make it difficult to live up to the values. For example, if the group decides that it is important to project a positive, caring attitude toward clients, someone might point out that the burdensome, bureaucratic procedures of the organization make service slow and inconvenient for clients. Someone might say something like "It is difficult to project a caring attitude when people are frustrated by filling out the same information on twelve different forms in four different locations." Leaders welcome such objections because they point out areas in which the system can be improved. Once people see that positive changes are being made to help make the values a reality, their enthusiasm will increase. People get excited about being part of an excellent organization.

Establishing Policies

Policies can be thought of as more specific principles than values. For any particular value, the organization can establish a number of policies that implement the value. Another way to say this is that policies are to values as activities are to results.

In the chapter on designing volunteer positions, we suggested that each job in an organization have a purpose or overall goal. When we manage by policy, we manage by defining the limits on the volunteers' ability to decide what to do to achieve that goal. Basically, once the goal is established, policies are used to answer the question: "What makes me nervous about giving the volunteer free reign in deciding what to do to achieve that goal?"

Here is an example from a CASA program in Maryland. (CASA assigns volunteers to advocate for abused children in court.) In thinking about what they would worry about if volunteers did whatever they wanted to, they came up with these concerns:

- The volunteer might tell reporters about the case
- The volunteer might not see the child or might not see the child often enough
- The volunteer might offer the parents legal advice
- The volunteer might antagonize the DSS case worker
- The volunteer might take the child home
- The volunteer might become a "big brother or sister" to the child
- The volunteer might give the child things his parents can't afford
- The volunteer might make up evidence
- The volunteer might not investigate the case in a thorough enough manner to give the judge the information necessary to make an adequate determination
- The volunteer might promise the child that he or she would never be hurt again

Be specific in identifying the behavior you fear, and you have the basis of policies. For example, if you worry that a volunteer would tell confidential information to others that might get back to the people the client knows, you should institute a policy which states that all communication with clients be shared only with appropriate staff and is otherwise confidential. If you fear that a volunteer might offer unsolicited medical advice to the clients he works with, establish a policy that volunteers are not to give advice to clients.

Three other questions can also give rise to needed policies. One is "What do my volunteers ask permission to do?" When volunteers ask permission, someone makes a decision of yes or no. If you can figure out the principles that underlie that decision, you have the basis for a policy. To take a simple example, when a volunteer says, "Can I get a pen from the supply closet?" what does the supervisor consider in making that decision? One such factor might be the expense of the item being requested. Another might be the degree to which the volunteer needs the item to get the job done. Instead of making these decisions every time the volunteer asks for supplies, the supervisor could create a policy that says "Volunteers can get supplies from the supply closet when they need them without permission if the item costs less than ten dollars." Such a policy frees the supervisor from being distracted by trivial decisions. It also empowers the volunteers to act while allowing the supervisor some assurance that they will use good judgment in making their decisions.

A similar question that can help you formulate good policies is "What decisions do the volunteers bring to me to make?" Again, when a supervisor responds to such requests, he or she employs some principles in reaching the decision. Everyone will save time if the volunteers know those principles and make the decisions themselves.

A final question to ask in developing policies is "How are organizational values manifested in typical work situations?" For example, Moscow Charity House, which (among other things) distributes food to the needy, has a value of respecting the dignity of its clients. One of the ways in which this is manifested is that they do not ask clients for proof of need. This could be the basis for an explicit organizational policy that clients not be asked for proof of income or other information regarding need. In this way the program makes sure that volunteers have a clear sense of what the organization's values mean in practice.

Reinforcing Principles

Pay active attention to behavior that is in accordance with the desired values and polices. Whenever a leader observes "right" behavior, she should acknowledge it. This acknowledgment might take the form of a smile or a nod or other gesture. Or it might, given the circumstances, consist of oral, written, or symbolic praise. In order to do this, the leader must be in a position to observe the actions of the group. She should go out looking for right behavior to praise.

The leader must also make sure she knows all the facts inherent in the situation so that the praise is meaningful.

Leaders help establish values by rewarding correct behavior and acting in accordance with the values she wishes her people to exemplify. Some examples of actions we have seen leaders take to encourage certain values are described briefly below:

- At a job training center, a volunteer supervisor who placed a high value on taking initiative wrote a letter of commendation to a volunteer who put up a sign that made it easier for applicants to figure out the process of registering for training.
- A volunteer fire chief, who placed a high value on fast response to emergencies, timed responses and gave regular feedback on this to his several volunteer captains.
- A recreation leader, who put a high value on win-win thinking, refused to accept a majority decision because part of the group did not support it. She instructed them to keep communicating until they had a decision they all felt good about.

Setting Standards for Good Performance

Finally, supervision requires setting the standards for everyday performance. To accomplish this you will need to:

- Establish and inform people regarding expectations, goals, rules and procedures
- Build commitment to those standards by involving staff and volunteers in their purpose and application
- Use immediate positive reinforcement to encourage adherence to standards
- Build personal relationships so that volunteers will adhere to standards out of loyalty to you and to their colleagues
- Model what behavior you want followed and encourage other staff to model the behavior
- Refuse to accept poor performance.

Most critical of the above is ensuring that both you and other staff model the behavior which you can requiring of volunteers. If staff are seen breaking rules and behaving in ways that violate procedures of values, volunteers will emulate this behavior. Unwritten rules of conduct will invariably override written rules, especially when the unwritten rules are followed by those in seeming positions of authority.

In this chapter, we have covered some general

principles of supervision that apply to most situations. In the following two chapters we will examine some special situations that Volunteer Program Managers sometimes have to handle, looking first at situations where the volunteer must work in conditions of relative autonomy and independence and then examining variations in supervisory requirements posed by volunteers of differing backgrounds.

Chapter Nine Supervising the "Invisible" Volunteer

One of the biggest challenges in management is supervising those volunteers who work outside the normal office setting. These workers may be separated from their supervisors in a number of ways:

- assigned to a field office, which is geographically separated from the headquarters;
- in a job which requires them to work alone in a field setting, perhaps matched with a particular client; or
- working in a different timeframe from office staff, perhaps an evening or weekend assignment that doesn't overlap normal office hours.

This separation, while small in appearance, is quite significant in practice. Anyone who has ever worked in a separated environment realizes the increased potential for frustration, inefficiency, dissatisfaction and occasionally even outright revolt. Those volunteers often come to believe that the central office doesn't understand the "real problems" and those in the central offices see those in the field as not seeing the "big picture."

Dealing with Separation

The increased complexity in managing volunteers at a distance is based upon logistical and interpersonal grounds. The logistics of dealing with individuals in locations apart from our own are quite formidable. People are harder to locate when you need them; communication more often gets delayed, distorted, or goes totally awry; people don't have access to the same resources, equipment, and support.

Interpersonal problems also abound. We are accustomed to dealing with people on a face-to-face basis, so communication at distance always seems unnatural and works less perfectly. It is hard for a supervisor to trust what they can't see, so there is always doubt that workers are doing what they are supposed to. At the same time, volunteers find it difficult to take orders from a person who isn't on the front line to actually experience conditions, so it is hard to give proper credence to directives from a central office. They also often feel left "out of the loop" in decisions that affect their work.

Long distance management structures represent a vast increase in organizational complexity. Studies of more complex organizational structures have indicated that they are more likely to be subject to the following types of organizational problems:

- Tensions between the field people and the headquarters office people, with neither fully respecting the positions or needs of the other.
- Depersonalized leadership styles, with individuals relating to each other as "titles" rather than as persons.
- Fragmented understanding, with each person holding on to information and failing to share it.
- Inefficient project work and teamwork.
- Growing subservience to paperwork, and an increased feeling that the paperwork bears no relation to reality.
- Flourishing of individual agendas, as the more motivated individuals simply retreat from the organization and begin to follow their own instincts.

You may recognize a few of these characteristics in your own organization.

It is important to note that these types of difficulties are commonly caused by the structure of the more complex system, and not necessarily by the personalities involved. We are simply more accustomed to working in close proximity. We find it "natural" to adopt behavior that is based on working next to our co-workers, and we forget that working with those who are not just "down the hall" can be a quite different managerial situation than what we are used to. In many cases the structure creates problems despite the best intentions of those involved. In some cases, those same best intentions can actually worsen the situation, since some "good" management techniques that work in the normal office setting can have exactly the opposite impact in a long distance management situation.

A Volunteer Program Manager in a long-distance system must work hard to reduce this distance, and to establish a working environment that offers a sense of bonding and teamwork, better communication, and a feeling of control for all parties involved in a long distance work relationship. There are three key areas in which to concentrate efforts:

- Bonding
- Communication
- Control

Creating a Sense of Bonding

All long distance supervisory relationships work better when there is a sense of identification or 'bonding' between headquarters and field staff. Volunteers work better when they feel closely connected to the organization, when part of their identity is wrapped up in being a member of the organization. We work more effectively with those with whom we have a sense of shared experience and with those with whom we think we have a personal relationship. In the usual work situation, this feeling will often develop naturally over time; it will only happen with long-distance volunteers if you continually strive to create it:

- Strive to achieve a sense of personal contact between headquarters and the field. People are more likely to communicate with those that they know and more likely to forgive errors in communication. They are also more likely to feel comfortable being supervised by those of whom they have some personal knowledge rather than some "faceless" being from above. We are more likely to trust and work well with people when we have a sense of "who they are" and think they know us and value us enough to look after our interests as they do their own.

- The key moment in the bonding experience is when volunteers first join the organization. It is important at this point to give them a sense of welcome and inclusiveness, demonstrating that the organization truly values them and welcomes them into the group. At this early point the behavior of the volunteer and their attitudes towards others can easily be shaped by how they perceive the culture of the organization. A smart supervisor will consciously greet and welcome the new volunteer and make them feel at home, and will frequently seek out the new volunteer during initial days. Research suggests there is a 60-day "window of opportunity" in which opinions are firmly shaped regarding whether the volunteer establishes a positive or negative relationship with the organization.

- One way to get people to know each other is to bring new field people for a visit to headquarters. Frequent meetings (conferences, in-service training, workshops, trips, planning retreats) are another way to achieve this. A supervisor can get to know his or her people by visiting them in the field, but this should be mixed with attempts to get the field people into headquarters to give them a sense of relating to the larger organization.

- There are ways to assist bonding that do not require face-to-face meetings, but they are not as effective. These include electronic mail systems, telephone messaging systems, and other means of electronic communication. Publishing a telephone directory or setting up a web page with photographs is another means of getting people to see one another as human beings and not as cogs in the machine. Other ways include support groups, utilization of teams composed of people from different areas, or the swapping of assignments with other volunteers (the 'walk a mile in their shoes' approach).

- Mentors and "buddies" can also be used to establish bonds with the organization. You must be careful with this approach, however, since the bonds formed will be stronger with the individual than with the organization. If the mentor leaves or is dissatisfied with the organization, this will affect the feelings of the volunteer.

- Bonding can be strengthened through adding the personal touch to communication. Being interested and concerned in another's personal life, remembering birthdays and anniversaries, or remembering and asking about family members, are ways to show a separated volunteer that you value them as a person, not just as a worker.

- Having a common vision is another key element in bonding. People who feel they are working toward a mutual goal and who feel responsible to each other are more likely to perceive shared interests and values. This is why wide participation in strategic planning is important.

- Recognition events are great opportunities for bonding and mutual celebration. Being congratulated in front of a peer group tends to strengthen peer bonds if the recognition system is perceived as a fair and honest one.

Maintaining Communication Linkages

Supervising people who work away from your office requires proactive efforts at communication. The main danger is that people will become alienated from the organization and develop an "us versus them" attitude. Consider the following suggestions:

- People in isolated or separated settings will naturally have more communication problems than those who are gathered in one spot. The smart supervisor will simply plan for this difficulty and adjust to compensate. Generally speaking, processes will take longer, will include a greater chance of misunderstanding, and will need to be managed more carefully.

- Workers in isolated or separated settings are prone to develop fears about their degree of inclusion in the system. They will worry about whether they are being kept informed of things (both as decisions are considered and after they are made) and whether their input is sought and valued.

- Withholding information from your people creates a sense in them of having second class status. Secrets are the bricks in the walls between people. People from whom information is withheld will go to extraordinary lengths to either obtain the information or to create their own versions of what is going on.

- When decisions that affect people are being made, efforts should be undertaken to involve those people in the decision-making process. Bringing people together for interaction is the best way to accomplish this. At this stage of development, technology can supplement but not totally replace face-to-face communication. For many people, written communication is not an adequate substitute.

- The longer it takes for a decision to be made at the central office, the more left out people outside will feel. The more important the response, the longer the response time will seem. Strive to get back quickly to those in the field, if only to deliver an interim response. Remember that they can't "see" that you're doing something with their message; to them no response will seem as though they are being ignored.

- Much of communication in an office takes place by osmosis—we learn things simply because we are in the vicinity of their occurrence. A supervisor in headquarters is in a much better position to learn via osmosis than a field worker, and a smart supervisor proactively attempts to pass along as much information as possible to the field. It is better to pass more information than is needed than to give the field a sense that you are restricting their access to information.

- Good communication should be viewed as a 'web' connecting all within the system—it should function up, down, sideways and across. If you do not design your system to function this way, your workers will re-engineer it to do so, and will probably leave you out of their design.

- Claims by central office staff that it is "difficult" to communicate effectively and swiftly with geographically separated workers will never be believed by those in the field. Field staff are all connected by a highly unofficial "rumor mill" which communicates instantaneously.

- Communication and bonding strategies are often the same. One CASA program, for example, assigns each of its board members to communicate with a small group of field-placed volunteers. Each month the board member is to have some type of communication with each of their assigned volunteers, either in person via an individual or group meeting or on the phone. This gives field volunteers an opportunity to communicate (with an important "personage") and creates a sense of teamwork. It also gives the board members something "real" to do and gives them a true sense of what is happening in the organization at the work level.

- Uniformity should not be pursued as an end in itself. Use what works, which may be very different with volunteers in different situations. As a supervisor your job is to find a method of communication that works.

Using a Newsletter to Foster Communication
In a long-distance situation, one of the most important media of communication can be the agency newsletter. Although typically the newsletter is regarded as junk-mail by volunteers, it can, if created properly, help overcome many of the motivation and control problems of long-distance supervision. An effective newsletter can provide the volunteer with the following information:

- *Pride in the Program*

As mentioned previously, one CASA program includes statements from volunteers in each newsletter attesting to the reason they are proud to be part of the program. Each volunteer who reads these statements gains familiarity with other volunteers (who they may have rarely met) and can share in the pride each offers.

• *Insider Information*

The newsletter should let volunteers know everything that the agency is planning to do and even considering, including problems the agency faces. Nothing makes a volunteer feel more like a second class citizen than reading facts about the agency in the newspaper that he didn't know.

• *Who's Who*

One of the problems of working at long distance is not knowing who the agency staff members are. Volunteers typically are introduced to them at training, but may quickly forget their names. The newsletter can contain pictures and articles about the work of an agency staff person or other volunteer each week.

• *Recognition and Celebration*

The newsletter should note any accomplishments made by the agency in the past month. Volunteers who contributed can be recognized in the newsletter. The newsletter can also spotlight a volunteer each week, telling something about them and their work.

• *Keeping the Purpose alive*

The newsletter should report progress made toward the agency vision. Any small step, such as an appointment for a meeting with a funder, should be noted, so volunteers have a sense that the vision is becoming a reality.

• *Training Reinforcement*

The CASA program in Baton Rouge includes a case study in each issue. Each of these is a thorny problem volunteers might face that they were taught how to handle. Volunteers are asked how they should handle the situation and instructed to call the office if they aren't sure of the right approach.

Exerting Supervisory Control

The kind of person who works best in a long-distance relationship is a self-starter. This is a volunteer who is internally motivated rather than externally goaded, who is proactive rather than reactive, and who makes decisions instead of waiting for instructions. This volunteer takes initiative and doesn't need to rely on others to give him orders. This type of person might be referred to as having "the entrepreneurial personality."

There are two problems with such a volunteer. First, they are hard to find. The vast majority of people in our society are reactive rather than proactive. This is why many people who are placed as long-distance volunteers either wind up doing nothing at all or calling the office every fifteen minutes asking for direction.

Second, the very traits that make them desirable can also make them a Volunteer Program Manager's worst nightmare. These volunteers are totally comfortable with the freedom and responsibility but may begin to behave as though this implies complete autonomy over their work activity. They may give higher priority to their own goals than the goals of the program. They may commit their considerable energies in the name of the agency to tasks that bring the agency disrepute.

Setting Up Control Limits on Long Distance Volunteers

The challenge with these volunteers is to rein them in, to channel the energies of the entrepreneurial personality. Managing long-distance volunteers requires establishing a zone of control between these two extremes, since too much variance in either direction will impair the ability to perform effectively in a separated work unit. Some actions to control the entrepreneurial person without demotivating him include:

• *Set Priorities*

The main tension between supervisors and long-distance volunteers is between the volunteer's need to decide what he or she will do and the supervisor's need to make sure that those things are effective. To minimize the conflict, establish clear priorities to guide volunteer's daily decisions. These priorities should give volunteers a clear sense of what is important and how their time should be spent even when a supervisor is not around to give immediate instructions.

• *Establish Clear Responsibility for Results*

One problem you can face at long distance is that volunteers will stray from the focus of the program. For example, a volunteer assigned to find the facts in a case of child abuse and make recommendations to the court may begin to engage in a big brother or mentoring role with the child, taking him to the zoo, reading to him after school, buying him presents and so forth. To guard against this, set clear results for the volunteer, as described in the chapter on job design. Further, ask volunteers to recommend observable, obtainable goals each month. These goals should relate to the results they are responsible for achieving. For example, a CASA volunteer (pursuing the result of providing the judge with the information necessary to make the best placement for a child) might recommend that in the upcoming month she could compile the child's complete medical history. By agreeing on what the volunteer is trying to accomplish, the supervisor has some confidence that the volunteer is going to channel her energies in the right direction.

- *Use the Degrees of Authority*

Use the scale of control presented in the chapter on supervision to provide yourself with insurance that what volunteers do to achieve their goals is likely to be effective. Over time determine whether the volunteer is capable of working mostly on their own, whether you need to be informed as they make decisions, or whether you need to constantly approve her suggested decisions or even give her assignments. Based on this judgment, allocate your time accordingly to give more attention to those who you are less confident can work alone. Maintain bonding and communication links, but increase the volunteer's level of control to free up your own time.

Unless the volunteer is at level one on the control scale, have regularly scheduled chats to check volunteer progress toward goals. Allocate your time and attention according to your experience with each volunteer. Direct more attention to those who have shown the need for monitoring or re-direction, but do not ignore the good performers simply because they are not causing problems. If you ignore them, they may eventually cause problems just to get your attention.

- *Set Accountability*

Measure the performance of each volunteer according to the principles laid out in the chapter on job design. Make sure all volunteers get feedback on the extent to which they are achieving their results.

- *Establish Policies*

As discussed in the chapter on supervision, clear policies give the volunteer guidance in making daily decisions. By making sure all volunteers know the policies that are to guide their actions, you increase the chance that each behaves in a correct manner.

- *Communicate Values and a Common Vision*

The broadest element of control (and sometimes the most significant, since it can cover unforeseen eventualities) is to make sure that all volunteers share a common vision of what the program is attempting to accomplish and a set of common values about what is the "right" way to go about accomplishing this vision. These broad principles of proper behavior will give the volunteer a sense of what ought to be done, even in circumstances that have not before been encountered.

Dealing with Non-Entrepreneurial Volunteers

Some volunteers are not comfortable with the increased freedom and responsibility of a long-distance assignment, even though they are perfectly capable of doing the actual work and would fit in quite easily in a "normal" setting. The challenge with these non-entrepreneurial people is to get them to behave in a more self-starting manner. Here are some tips:

- *Ask for Recommended Courses of Action*

It is important that volunteers at a distance be self-assigning. Non-entrepreneurial people, however, tend to be externally motivated, meaning they are inclined to value external commands In chapter eight, you learned about four degrees of control. Those who are reluctant to self-assign should operate at level three on the control scale, meaning that you should ask them for recommended courses of action. At this level, they are unable to avoid making self-assignments.

This method requires a commitment to regular communication with the volunteer. The less likely the volunteer is to take action on his own, the more often the manager will have to communicate and ask for recommendations.

- *Check Progress Frequently*

The entrepreneurial personality is motivated by avoiding unpleasantness rather than by achieving a goal. A powerful motivator for such people is the fear of missing deadlines. Therefore, the manager should make sure that these volunteers have clear deadlines to report progress on their efforts.

- *Develop Policies*

In order to learn to make decisions on their own, non-entrepreneurial people need the safety of some approved principles to guide them. The manager needs to develop policies to perform this role. Ask yourself "What decisions do my people ask me to make?" And "What do they ask my permission to do?" After answering these questions, ask yourself "What principles do I apply in reaching these decisions?" Those principles can be communicated to your people to act as guidelines in making their own decisions.

- *Ask Questions*

The entrepreneurial personality is motivated by options; the non-entrepreneurial person prefers procedures. To develop people's ability to consider options, the manager can ask them questions such as the following:

> "What else have you thought of?"
> "How could we improve what we do?"
> "What have you done lately that's proactive?"
> "Are there other ways of achieving this goal?"

These and similar questions can spur the employee to think more creatively and to realize that the manager places a positive value on proactive thinking.

The best advice for dealing with non-entrepreneurial people is not to put them in long-distance situations to begin with. Spend more time and energy in the selection of long distance volunteers. You are looking for people whose personality will allow them to follow their own direction and maintain their own momentum. Many people are not capable of the discipline necessary to work outside the normal office setting. Effective long distance workers will need to be self motivated, well organized, and capable of dealing with problems on their own.

Supervising long-distance volunteers is much more difficult and much more uncertain than supervising volunteers who work within the same office structure. The Volunteer Program Manager working in this separated environment must accept the fact that supervision will work less perfectly, more slowly, and with greater confusion than desired.

Chapter Ten
Special Supervisory Situations

In this chapter we will discuss the following special situations that require slightly different approaches than outlined in our chapter on general supervision. These special situations include:

- The assigned volunteer
- The floating volunteer
- Volunteers on advisory committees
- Youth volunteers
- The volunteer professional
- Groups of volunteers
- Event-based volunteers
- Senior volunteers
- Staff as volunteers
- Transitional volunteers
- Volunteers from the workplace
- Alternative sentencing volunteers
- Stipended volunteers
- Government benefit volunteers
- Management volunteers
- Family volunteers

The Assigned Volunteer

An increasingly common situation involves the volunteer who is assigned to work directly with a particular member of staff rather that being under the immediate supervision of the Volunteer Program Manager.

The staff to whom the volunteer is assigned may neglect basic volunteer management functions, leaving volunteers with a feeling of being stranded without any support system. Some staff may engage in "benign neglect," appreciating whatever work they obtain from volunteers, but not viewing them as they would a paid employee doing an equivalent job. Some staff may engage in sporadic supervision of volunteers, paying close attention to specific work assignments but avoiding what they may view as "less important" aspects of supervision, such as periodic evaluations.

The key to avoiding problems with assigned volunteers is for the Volunteer Program Manager to reach a clear understanding about supervisory responsibility with those staff who are assigned volunteers. Areas of to clarify include:

- Who completes a position description for the volunteer and who periodically reviews and updates it?
- Who interviews potential candidates for the position?
- Who accepts the volunteer for the position?
- Who completes necessary paperwork and personnel forms?
- Who is responsible for on-the-job training of the volunteer?
- Who will be responsible for providing work assignments for the volunteer or for contacting the volunteer to inform him or her that no work is available on a particular day?
- Who will ensure that the volunteer is kept informed of decisions relevant to his or her work?
- Who will ensure that the volunteer has a work space and equipment?
- Who will be available to talk with the volunteer if there is a problem with work or scheduling?
- Who will evaluate the volunteer?
- Who has the authority and responsibility to correct the volunteer's behavior if there are problems, or to terminate the relationship?
- Who is responsible for the volunteer when the designated staff person is absent?

Whenever someone is assigned to supervise volunteers, the Volunteer Program Manager must make sure that they must act as the "supervisor" of the volunteer, and must provide a link to the organization and its work. This means that the staff member must accept responsibility for ensuring that the volunteer is provided with work and working conditions that enable the volunteer to both be and feel successful. More will be said about this in the chapter on volunteer-staff relationships.

The Floating Volunteer

Occasionally, volunteers may be assigned to various parts of the organization on a temporary basis, working today with one group of staff and tomorrow with another. While these volunteers will, over time, develop their own linkages with individual staff members, we recommend that the Volunteer Program Manager assume responsibility for most of the supervision of these "floating" volunteers.

Staff to whom the volunteer is temporarily assigned can provide supervision over direct job functions. They will be unable to do more than this.

To avoid problems, the Volunteer Program Manager should take responsibility for the following:

• Act as the official "greeter" to volunteers when they arrive at the organization. Receive the volunteers at the beginning of each new work assignment and escort them to their new work site to introduce them to the staff with whom they will be working.

• Ensure that there is a flow of work for the volunteer to do, and that this work is not just thrown together at the last minute. One way to encourage this is to send out reminders to staff a few days prior to the volunteer's workday, reminding them of the availability of help.

• Serve as an on-going social and communication link between the volunteer and the organization. This will mean making sure that the volunteer receives updates on organization policy and decisions relevant to their volunteer job. It might also mean creating a small social group of other floating volunteers who meet periodically to keep in touch.

• Provide on-going evaluation discussions, based on information gathered from staff with whom the volunteer has worked, and continue to strive to find volunteer assignments that will meet the volunteer's changing talents and needs.

Volunteers on Advisory Committees

One truly excellent use of volunteers is to serve on advisory groups and committees to assist the agency in reaching better decisions. Unfortunately, advisory committees are traditionally one of the biggest wastes of volunteer time. Far too many volunteer advisory committees are created first and planned second.

There are several keys to developing an effective volunteer advisory committee:

• Decide what the purpose or goal of the advisory committee will be. It might be to give input and advice to the agency, or to provide outreach and community representation, or to assist in a specific task such as fundraising. If you haven't determined the rationale for the committee in advance, it will be difficult to enable it to achieve its purpose later. Do not create an advisory committee just for the sake of having one, since you will be wasting both your time and that of the volunteers.

• Use targeted recruitment to select volunteers who have the skills you need on the committee. Try to get a mix of people who have sufficient time to devote to doing things, people with the requisite skills to assist, and people who have an interest in what the committee has been asked to do.

• The most important element in recruitment is in picking the leadership of the committee. If the committee has a chair, this person should view herself as responsible for helping generate participation from committee members, since this function cannot be entirely relegated to paid staff.

• Most committees get off to a bad start because no one provides an orientation to them. Just like other volunteers, advisory committees need to learn about the organization's cause, culture, context and conditions. To ask advisory committee volunteers to serve and make significant decisions without a good understanding of the agency is to invite trouble and bad results.

Identify a staff person who will serve as primary support for the committee. This person should be responsible for negotiating a viable working relationship between the agency and the committee. This staff job will involve support not supervision and may need to change slightly as the leadership of the advisory committee changes. The easiest way to negotiate is to have a series of quiet, low-key luncheon discussions:

- One between the outgoing and incoming chairs, to discuss what has been happening and how it has worked out.
- One between the incoming chair and the staff support person, to discuss how they will work together.
- One between the outgoing chair and the staff support person, to debrief how they worked together and then celebrate their successes.

Establishing a viable advisory group of volunteers is roughly equivalent to setting up a quasi-independent volunteer project. The more planning you do up front, the fewer problems you will have later.

Youth Volunteers

Youth volunteering is one of the fasted growing areas of volunteer involvement:

- The group Public Allies found that 72% of youth volunteered with community groups within a three-year period.
- The Close Up Foundation found that 63% of high

school students have a "great deal" of interest in volunteering.

Young people can be excellent volunteers. There are many successful upper elementary, middle-school and high-school students making meaningful contributions to community organizations. In some limited cases (trick-or-treating for UNICEF, for example) even very young children can be effective volunteers.

Upper elementary school students can be quite effective if the volunteer position is structured so they feel a sense of control and security in the work environment. This can be achieved by having the students work in small groups with an adult or high-school student that is also actively involved in the project providing training and making sure the students feel empowered to take action in the group volunteer position.

Middle school students are able to work more independently, but still require a highly structured program. This would include close supervision, clearly defined responsibilities, and a defined work environment.

When we speak of youth in this section, we will mostly be focusing on high-school age volunteers. High-school students have reached an age where they are capable of making independent decisions and are able to assume responsibility for their actions. Their role still must be clearly defined by the program, and they need to receive positive guidance and support from their supervisors and the organization.

Cooperation with the schools is most effective if the school system has a community service elective in the school curriculum. Students in a community service class volunteer in various agencies and bring their disparate experiences back to the class. The teacher can then help them analyze and learn from their experiences, and they can engage in mutual problem solving.

In varying degrees, the upper elementary, middle-school, and high-school students need to know who to look to for direction, support, and information. These elements need to be embedded in the structure of the youth volunteer program and job descriptions.

Some key, over-arching philosophical points on involving youth include:

- The youth volunteer program should be designed as a job experience, career exploration, or apprentice program, not as a social club. Volunteering should give students an opportunity to see the direct impact their volunteering has for the organization and to learn what it is like to have an engaging, rewarding, and exciting job. It should give them an opportunity to develop and experience a positive work ethic.

- Youth tend to live up or down to the expectations of adults. They are living self-fulfilling prophecies. Young volunteers must, therefore, see that what they offer to the organization is valued, respected and desired by every person representing the organization. If they begin to feel inferior, undervalued, overworked, or treated with disrespect students will become dissatisfied with their connection to the organization. Worse, damage may be done to their self-esteem, and they may gain a negative view of volunteering that lasts into adulthood?

- Adults sometimes have low expectations of youth. Adult staff may treat young volunteers in a condescending way, subtly hinting through their behavior and assignments that they don't have much faith in young people. Before you start involving youth as volunteers, staff should be encouraged to regard them as responsible partners.

- Basically, a youth program is the same as an adult program except that youth haven't had experience in a professional work environment. Youth need to be guided in a positive and supportive manner to learn the professional expectations of the organization. This guidance comes in part from an orientation session for young volunteers. It is also modeled by the professional staff as they perform their duties and responsibilities, particularly in their interaction with the youth.

- All staff must buy into the idea of utilizing youth volunteers, and no limits ought to be placed on their growth potential. If youth volunteers see themselves only as greeters or cage cleaners and not able to perform work they find interesting and meaningful, their self-esteem will go down and you will either lose them to a paying job or have to deal with a difficult volunteer.

- The basic point to remember in involving young people is that they will act responsibly if you give them responsibility. Or they will not be able to handle it and drop out of their own accord. If a 15-year-old frequently needs supplies from a locked cupboard to do her job, for example, you treat her as responsible by giving her a set of keys. This also gives her a sense of trust and empowerment. On the other hand, if the standard procedure is "Find me when you need to get into the cabinet, and I'll unlock it," the volunteer feels distrusted.

- Utilizing youth volunteers means that you are competing with their need for working for money. It is important that they recognize that you are enabling them to gain experience beyond what they might receive if they were working for a fast-food restaurant or other entry-level jobs.

- Be prepared for youth to challenge why your organization does things. Sometimes youth will react about the "stupid" way you do things. Sometimes, they are right. Do not automatically reject their challenges as youthful naiveté.

- Students will want to know why policies and procedures exist, and if you are unable to explain in a clear and positive manner the rationale for them, you may encounter passive resistance or outright defiance. This behavior is more from the desire to understand than disrespect, for if you can't tell them why they should or shouldn't do something youth will try to find out on their own or make up a reason. Negative rumors start this way. For example, if a policy states that volunteers should refrain from wearing jeans and tennis shoes to work, you may encounter some difficult situations unless you explain to the students by example and with positive reasons about the "power of dress" in a work environment.

- In designing positions for young people, follow the same principles of job design you use for adults. However, the job description for youth should be more detailed and contain more structure than is necessary for adults. Any volunteer position will no doubt contain responsibilities that are not glamorous or fun. In a sense, this prepares them for the real world because most of us enjoy parts of our jobs less than others. Try to make at least part of the job "glamorous" or "fun" to the young person. Youth can feel envelope stuffing is fulfilling if they realize the purpose of the mailing. Tell them why the mailing is important and try to make it fun. Allow them to choose music to listen to while they do the mailing. Have a friendly competition for which team can stuff the most envelopes.

- In designing jobs for youth, respect the volunteer's need to "experience the experience." Make the goals clear, but allow the job to be loose enough that youth can discover the best way to do an activity by trial and error or by observation. When young people are given this freedom to grow, they retain their enthusiasm. Youth are often in the mode of exploring options. They may want to try out a job and then switch to another. This does not necessarily indicate a lack of responsibility but rather a search for who they are and for a fit with their unique talents.

- It is important that youth volunteer training have direct relevance to the volunteer position. If the youth volunteer has signed up to provide direct contact with the public don't expect them to sit through 60 hours of instruction before the first opportunity to get in touch with the public. Structure the training so that they get some hands-on experience while the training is occurring. Pair them with a more experienced volunteer for a couple of hours for each four hours of training. This addresses their needs for immediate accomplishment and social interaction and gives them an opportunity to see what the job really is like. It can also serve as a self-screening device.

- Develop a straight-forward contract stating that by accepting a volunteer position with the organization students are agreeing to maintain high standards of conduct in their relationships with clients, visitors, staff, and fellow volunteers. Indicate that failure to live up to the program standards will result in poor evaluations, probation, and/or dismissal from the program. Note that the volunteer program is a work experience and that all scheduling, evaluation, and in most cases, disciplinary action, will be handled between the organization and the volunteers.

- One of the most powerful single things you can do to promote young people's self-esteem is to ask for and implement their ideas. In listening, you may find that a young person's ideas may be half-baked and ill-considered, and formed in ignorance of the full reality of the situation. In such a case, try to keep from telling the young person all that is wrong with an idea or rejecting it out of hand. Instead, express your concerns about the idea and encourage the youth to develop a solution that takes into account the additional information.

To maintain an environment welcoming and supporting youth involvement, it is necessary that all staff in the organization respect and listen to volunteers. Upper management and the Volunteer

Program Manager should actively and publicly provide reinforcement and recognition to staff who engage in behavior that is positive and supportive of the volunteers.

Young people frequently have many time demands, especially during the school year. Make sure you support the volunteer in trying to balance school (a full-time job), a part-time paying job, and the volunteerism. Youth need to be able to discuss their volunteer schedule with an employer and their paid work schedule with the organization. Flexibility of scheduling is of prime importance.

When you do this, however, don't devalue the volunteer program in relation to a paying job. Expect youth to keep their volunteer commitment. If you allow them always to put other things first, they will get the idea the volunteer program isn't very important. This devalues their contribution and makes them feel less important when they volunteer.

The Volunteer Professional

Another special case involves the supervision of volunteers who have professional credentials and who have greater expertise than the staff who are their supervisors. This imbalance in knowledge, experience, and sometimes even status may make it difficult for staff to feel comfortable in exercising "control" over the professional, and may make it difficult for the professional to accept close supervision.

Step one in involving professionals as volunteers is job development. A common mistake is to assume that the professionals design their own jobs, since they are the experts. While it is true that the professional can probably best determine how the work should be done, it is equally true that the other aspects of job design must be carried out with the involvement of the Volunteer Program Manager.

This includes determining the exact purpose of the job and the results that are desired. The professional will need to be told what is to be accomplished and why those results are important. Outlining these elements will serve to better motivate the professionals and to assist them in deciding how to best undertake the work. After all, the professional knows lots of "answers"; the problem lies in figuring out which ones are correct for this particular situation. The more information you can provide them about what you really need, the better they can match their knowledge to your specific concerns.

A further aspect involves setting the parameters of the job. This will include items such as desired timeframe for completion, available support system, treatment of expenses, and needs for reporting and approvals. All of these will need to be discussed and negotiated with the professional volunteers, many of whom will be accustomed to exercising virtual autonomy and independent control over their work.

While this independence on their part works well for them, you may find it uncomfortable. A common problem is that their notion of expenses may not match your capacities. A lawyer may incur several hundred dollars of quite reasonable expenses in an afternoon, and be accustomed to billing these to clients. You, on the other hand, might find that amount to be larger than the entire budget for your project...

Another common problem lies in setting out what matters require approval. If, for example, plans need to be approved by the management committee before they can be implemented, then this requirement should be explained at the start, with an explanation of the system and timeframe for this process.

And, of course, if there are restrictions that will impact the shape of the job, these should also be outlined. If a computer programmer is designing a system to enhance organization operations then any financial limitations need to be explained upfront.

In practice, more time needs to be spent on job design and negotiation with volunteer professionals than with most other categories of volunteers. Because the professionals are more likely to work independently and be self-supervising, it is imperative to have a clear initial mutual understanding of the desired results, parameters, and process of the volunteer work.

Supervision of the professional volunteer may assume some different forms. If you are working with large numbers of professionals, then it is sometimes very helpful to recruit a lead volunteer from the group, who will act as your intermediary, assuming responsibility for supervision. This peer relationship will make it easier for the leader to deal with any problem situations.

For situations in which only one professional is recruited, then sometimes a quasi-buddy system works well. One person (sometimes a member of staff and sometimes a volunteer) is appointed to "work with" the professional, operating as primary liaison with the organization. This person both monitors the progress of the work and helps the professional by retrieving information from the organization, presenting reports, etc. This informal supervision allows you to maintain some control of the situation without risking ego problems.

A common problem encountered in supervising expert professionals lies in "back seat driving". You have recruited them for their expertise: they know how to solve the problem and you don't. This means that you must trust that expertise, which is often more difficult than it sounds.

Marlene Wilson, for example, relates a wonderful story of recruiting an advertising expert to help design a new brochure for an organization. The expert was internationally acclaimed for her work, had agreed to help out, and eventually presented her suggested design. Marlene, who like most of us has her own preferences in style, started to make a few "suggestions." The expert stopped her, and asked "Why did you ask me to do this job, Marlene?" After a moment she realized that it was because he was, in fact, the expert, which meant she might well keep her opinions to herself. The brochure, unchanged, went on to win several design awards.

Volunteer professionals may, in truth, have a much better notion of how well the job is progressing than you do, and any evaluation of the work may rely on their expertise. If the contribution of the professional is to be on-going or on an annual basis, then you might want to conduct an evaluation or de-briefing session, and review the work or project much as you would a special event, concentrating on how can you do this better in the future.

Groups of Volunteers

A Volunteer Program Manager may occasionally involve as a volunteer unit a group of people, such as a club. This group will have its own identify, its own structure, and will view itself as volunteering as a group rather than as individuals. Keeping supervisory control over the actions of group volunteers can be a tricky job, as you have to keep a balance between the volunteers feeling ownership and responsibility and having your organization in control over what is done in its name. Consider the following as ways to balance the two needs:

- When events or activities are to be done by group volunteers, offer clear, simple guidelines in a step-by-step fashion. Make sure the mission of the effort is clearly outlined. If there are any restrictions or requirements that need to be explained, let people know quickly. An example of this might be any restriction on the use of the organization's name or logo or any requirement for crediting or not crediting corporate sponsorship. You don't want to wake up one morning and discover you're operating the IBM Food Bank Marathon because the group itself has gone out and secured that support in exchange for "selling" the ownership of the event.

- If the project or activity has been done before, give the group all the information you have about what was done, what worked, and what didn't.

- Be clear about the various jobs that need to be done. For complex efforts, provide sample job descriptions and indicate how the jobs interconnect and work together toward the common goal.

- Clearly outline supervisory responsibility between you, the group, and its individual members. Make sure everyone is in agreement about who is in charge of what and of whom.

- Establish reporting dates and a channel for communication between you and the group. Meet more frequently early in the relationship so you can identify any problems or confusions and be helpful.

- Get the group to appoint its own "volunteer manager" with whom you will work. This is especially important for a one-shot event, such as a weekend construction project. Work with this person to help with recruitment, on-the-job supervision, and overall management. Make sure that someone understands that he or she is in charge of overseeing the project.

- Do a walk-through with the group's leadership before the event.

- Ensure that all supplies and equipment necessary to do the work will be present and available.

- Make sure that someone is taking pictures of the event and of the group doing work so that you can present them with suitable recognition momentoes.

In delegating "chunks" of work to an outside group you are entering into a relationship with an ally or a partner, and this relationship will be somewhat different from other types of supervisory relationships. The group will probably not look at you as its supervisor but may be willing to look toward you as an advisor who will help it do its accepted workload in a fashion that will be successful. Your role is to gain trust, help define what needs to be done so that the result is "successful" for your organization, and then to give the group whatever assistance is needed.

Event-Based Volunteers

Another type of group volunteer setting is that of volunteers who come to participate in some type of short-term event. These volunteers may only be connected with the organization on the day of the event. Here are some tips for successfully involving these types of volunteers:

- Help staff to develop a plan for involving these "day-of" volunteers. Staff will typically either over- or under-estimate the numbers of volunteers that they actually need. Work with staff before the event to determine how many volunteers can be utilized and to ensure that a rough job description is available for the work to be done.

- Build an extended volunteer management system. Involve your more experienced volunteers in fulfilling the role of "volunteer volunteer directors" and let them be your assistants in providing direct supervision of volunteers in different parts of the event. They can help management sign-up, assignments, orientation, training, and direct supervision, as well as provide on-going contact for new volunteers. Staff are likely to be too busy to pay attention to these supervisory requirements.

- Use this as an opportunity to recruit from new sources of volunteers. Recruiting for one-day events is extremely easy and should be viewed as an excellent opportunity to reach out to new varieties and sources of volunteers. Key targets include corporations, service clubs (such as City Cares or the traditional ones), students (through sororities and fraternities or through community service classes in high schools), and others. A one-day volunteering experience is an excellent way to involve large numbers of people in a "test drive" of working with your organization.

- Make sure volunteers have all the equipment that they will need and that they know where it is. Proper equipment may include identification badges, forms or information sheets, tickets, machinery, etc. Nothing is more demoralizing to a motivated volunteer than to be lacking the basic equipment that is necessary to do a good job.

- Inform all volunteers who their back-up emergency resource is. All volunteers should have a clearly identified contact person who will help them in an emergency. Volunteers who "staff" an event are likely to be asked questions that are far beyond their capacity to answer. Always ensure that they know whom to refer questioners to or whom to involve in case events get beyond their control. This provides a "safety net."

- Help event volunteers feel successful and have fun. These volunteers will be evaluating your organization and deciding whether to volunteer with you again. They are likely to determine this based on whether they felt good about their participation, and the two keys for this are feeling as though they accomplished something and feeling as though they enjoyed the time they spent with you.

- If at all possible, get the names and addresses of each volunteer. This will allow you to send them a thank you recognition note and allow you to recruit them next year.

- The most important recognition item for event-based volunteering is a digital camera to commerate the event and the people working on it.

If you're not familiar with these types of volunteer events, you should quickly become so, since they appear to be a substantial growth area in volunteering. One easy way to learn about them is to go volunteer yourself in several different ones.

Senior Volunteers

Seniors represent one of our great under-tapped resources and with will become even more vital as a volunteer resource as the current population ages. A survey by Civic Ventures found that 33% of upcoming retirees list volunteering as "very important." Seniors are currently under-represented in the volunteer workforce, with the lessened representation being directly attributable to the fact that many seniors are not asked to volunteer by agencies or are asked to volunteer in ways that are demeaning.

A 2003 study by the Bureau of Labor Statistics indicates why involvement of seniors can be so valuable an asset. Here is their data on average hours of volunteering donated by different age groups:

- 40 hours 16-24 year olds
- 56 hours 25-34
- 50 hours 35-44
- 52 hours 45-54
- 60 hours 55-64
- 88 hours 65+

The success of some existing volunteer programs (RSVP, corporate retiree programs, and others) has dispelled any notion that seniors cannot contribute actively and productively.

Here are some tips about involving seniors:

- Seniors represent no more monolithic a bloc than any other segment of our population. Ultimately it will be necessary to treat them as individuals, and to negotiate for their time and talents just as one does with any other potential volunteer.

- Most seniors, particularly in the age category of 60-70 do not have health or medical conditions that would significantly restrict their ability to volunteer. With those above that age range, asking about potential restrictions is far better than assuming their existence.

- In past years many seniors were known for volunteering for social motivations. This in fact has been a hallmark of the creation of many of the all-volunteer service groups and clubs which now have many seniors among their membership. While this will still be true for many seniors, it will not be true for all and will probably diminish slightly in significance. Seniors will equally be motivated to volunteer to contribute to causes, to pass on their professional knowledge, and for all the other common reasons.

- Seniors are likely to be skilled and experienced, even though they are new to your organization. This has two implications. First, this experience can be very useful, as it will bring additional knowledge and skills to your organization. Of course, you will have to enable the senior volunteers to actually contribute their experience for it to have an effect. But, second, you will have to make sure, as with all other experienced volunteers, that they do not let their experience replace the hard-won specific knowledge that your organization has gained about the "right" way to do things.

- Seniors can be particularly useful in a number of job types. They are quite good at establishing rapport with children and teens, as many intergenerational programs have shown. They are also quite good at matching with other volunteers in an advisory or partnership arrangement, contributing their acquired wisdom and experience.

One of the particular problems now occurring with the use of senior volunteers is that staff may feel threatened by their presence. Many of the seniors now coming into the volunteer workforce possess enormous credentials, often far beyond that possessed by the staff with whom they will be working. This can be intimidating for the staff that might not wish to reveal to you the source of their discomfort. If you recruit seniors with extensive professional accomplishments, you will need to assist both the staff and the senior volunteer in negotiating their work relationship, ensuring that each is comfortable with and respectful of the contribution and level of authority of the other.

Staff as Volunteers

Almost every Volunteer Program Manager has encountered at some point the perplexing question of how to handle agency employees who wish to volunteer somewhere within the agency.

The Volunteer Program Manager who first confronts this situation, usually posed by an agency staff person who approaches them and asks (somewhat shyly) if they can "help out," often experiences a brief cognitive disorientation. After all, if staff have to be paid to do the rest of their job with the agency, it feels strange to think of them as unpaid volunteers.

If this philosophical dilemma is resolved, the Volunteer Program Manager then begins to experience an equal feeling of disequilibrium upon contemplating the logistical questions involved: can, for example, a person both volunteer and be a staff person in the same department without totally confusing everyone? Do we ask them to wear a badge marking their current status, or give them a series of hats to wear to notify others of their identity? What happens if they end up being supervised as a volunteer by someone they in turn supervise in their paid staff role?

By the time things reach the legal department, whose natural reaction is to say "no" to anything strange, the situation is in complete chaos, and the would-be volunteer is off in the corner muttering quietly "But, I was only trying to help."

It should not, however, be surprising that staff occasionally desire to volunteer, and even to volunteer within the same organization where they are employed.

Staff are, after all, human beings. Many staff members of nonprofit agencies work within their field out of a deep commitment to the clientele and cause, precisely the motivational elements that prompt volunteering. Like others, they care and want to help. Like other volunteers, staff people may see donating time to their agency as a way of further contributing to the cause, or as a way to advance their own interests, such as expressing a hobby or learning a new skill.

In fact, far more employee volunteering currently takes place than most people realize. The entire area of Employee Service and Recreation programs, in which corporate employees volunteer within their companies to operate "self help" programs in the area of wellness and sports, is one example. Another example is that of volunteering within an agency to help operate a program designed to benefit others. In the state of Washington, for example, more than 2,000 state government employees volunteer each year to operate the Combined Fund Drive that raises money to support community causes. There are even a significant number of direct client service programs in existence. One of the better known is a combined program of the US Postal Service and the postal employee unions in which mail carriers check on the well-being of seniors and shut-ins along their delivery routes, reporting addresses where mail has accumulated.

Less common are those instances where staff volunteer internally for work which is being done in the normal course of business operations of the agency. But positive examples do exist that can serve as models for staff involvement. Almost any large non-profit or governmental organization could offer numerous opportunities for staff volunteer involvement.

Legal Restrictions on Staff Volunteering

Let us first dispense with the legal questions that impinge on allowing staff to donate additional time to the same agency with whom they have a paid employment relationship.

At the federal level, the Fair Labor Standards Act, administered by the Wage and Hour Administration, is the law that governs the ability of employees of an organization to also volunteer within that same organization. The intent of the FLSA is to prevent abuse of employees, particularly those paid by the hour ("non-exempt employees").

While the issue is not directly addressed in the Act itself, a series of regulatory rulings has provided some guidance. Volunteering by employees is allowed if these criteria are met:

- There is no "coercion" or "undue pressure" on the employee to participate.
- The work done is different from that normally done by paid employees.
- The work is outside the normal business hours of the employee.

It is important to take some care in this area. The enforcement of Wage and Hours regulations is proactive, which means that claims can, and have, been brought by the Wage and Hour Administration itself. They can be brought even if the staff involved do not themselves join in the claim and can be brought even if the staff members involved disagree with the position of the Wage and Hour Administration. This means that careful records clearly demonstrating conformity with the criteria above must be maintained.

Not all organizations are subject to the federal Wage and Hour laws, but the criteria make good guidelines to follow, whether or not you are legally required to do so. You will also want to check applicable state laws and requirements.

Management Aspects of Staff Volunteer Involvement

Any complication of a managerial system is likely to cause occasional supervisory difficulties. In the case of paid staff volunteering within the same organization these supervisory difficulties fall within what is referred to as the "multiple hats" problem – an individual who is attempting to fulfill several different roles at the same time. This type of situation commonly creates:

- possible conflict between the roles, resulting in the performance of one role negatively affecting performance of the other;

- confusion over which role is being performed at what time; this confusion can afflict either the person performing the work or those around them; and

- complications to the hierarchical structure that affect communication flow and lines of authority.

Consider the following example:

Alison Smith is the Assistant Director of the Education Department of the Riparian Museum of Art. She began work in the museum as a curator of pre-historic art but over the years as opportunities arose advanced up the ranks and across departments to her present high position, where she is part of the Senior Management Team of the Museum. While she enjoys her job, she misses the opportunity to work directly with exhibits and has decided to volunteer within the Curatorial Department as a volunteer curator, assisting in the classification of new acquisitions of pre-historic art. Within this Pre-Historic Art Curatorial Unit are one unit supervisor, two other paid curators and three other volunteers.

What happens if:

1. Alison so enjoys her volunteer work that she begins to direct much of her attention to it. It is, after all, the type of work that got her into pre-historic art in the first place. This diversion bothers her supervisor, the Director of the Education Department, but since he doesn't want to directly confront Alison he instead comments to the Director of the Curatorial Department about the situation and asks that something be done. The Curatorial Director then asks the Supervisor of the Pre-Historic Art Unit why he is causing trouble by stealing staff away from other departments.

2. As Alison volunteers she gets to know the paid curators with whom she works. One of them is quite accomplished and seems perfect for an opening in the Education Department. Alison invites the curator to apply for the position, hinting that there would be a good chance of success. As it happens, the curator isn't that interested in moving away from curating, but worries about refusing such a pointed suggestion from someone so high in the Museum's executive structure. After all, he doesn't want to make an enemy either out of a co-worker or out of someone in a significant position in a department where he someday might want to work.

3. While Alison was once an accomplished curator many years have passed since she was actually involved, and the state of the art has advanced as well. Much of what Alison knows is now out of date, but Alison keeps returning to what she is accustomed to, much to the consternation of her Supervisor. Despite instructions, however, Alison keeps repeating the same mistakes, which have to be corrected by those around her. The Supervisor has tried everything, and is now at wit's end. How, after all, can he discipline someone who is three levels above him in the Museum hierarchy and who is best friends with the head of his department?

4. As Alison volunteers she concludes that her supervisor is not very accomplished and worries that he misrepresents the status of work assignments in reports. Alison has not actually seen these reports, but feels from his comments and attitude around staff that something is not right. To deal with this situation, Alison has a private talk with her friend the Director of the Curatorial Department, suggesting that something needs to be done.

Management is already difficult enough, and the more you complicate it the more likely you are to eventually get what you deserve.

Creating a System to Involve Staff as Volunteers

For those of you who are attempting to involve staff as volunteers here are some suggests that may reduce, but not eliminate, managerial problems.

1. Before accepting an employee as a volunteer, engage upper management in a discussion of the issue. If the organization decides to proceed, develop a policy which outlines the circumstances under which such volunteering is acceptable.

2. Ensure that any decision to volunteer by paid staff is entirely voluntary and without an coercion or suggestion from management. This probably means that you should avoid any organized program or project created by the agency to specifically involve staff as volunteers in which the type of work is directly connected to the normal business activity of the agency. It may also be prudent to avoid any organized internal recruitment campaign, which might be viewed as pressure from management to participate. The most suitable recruitment process, if any, would be spontaneous decisions by staff who are volunteering to tell their co-workers about what a good time they are having.

3. Compare the employee's paid position description with their proposed volunteer assignment to ensure that they are distinct in type of work, location

and timeframe. All of these factors should be as different as possible. As the volunteering continues, periodically conduct as assessment to ensure that these distinctions remain in place. It's absolute amazing how often unoffical job re-design can take place, all with the best of intentions.

4. Much greater care must also be exercised in making sure that involvement in volunteering will not negatively impact the staff person's professional work. Before allowing the staff person to submit a volunteer application, require that they consult with their work supervisor and seek approval for the volunteer work. You may also want to discuss the situation with the supervisor yourself.

The purpose of this preliminary work is to ensure that the volunteer program does not become involved in disputes between supervisors and their staff (or between labor and management) which are not really its concern and which will only harm the volunteer program. To avoid this you may want to consider a requirement that an employee's volunteer position may be temporarily suspended if it conflicts with performance of normal work duties.

It is also wise to check with the person who will be supervising the staff person in their volunteer capacity to make sure they are comfortable with this arrangement.

5. The staff person should follow all the normal enrollment procedures of the agency. This includes completing an application, being interviewed, going through orientation and training, and all other steps of volunteer involvement.

If background checks are normally conducted on volunteer applicants, they should also be conducted for the staff person, unless they have already been done by the agency's personnel department.

6. While it may seem silly to ask a staff person to participate in an orientation session about an agency where they may have worked for a number of years, this step is important for two reasons. First, it will allow the staff person to be introduced to some aspects of agency operation with which they are not familiar, such as the procedures of the volunteer program. And second, *it is important to remind the staff person that, while volunteering, they are subject to all the rules and procedures of the volunteer program.*

This last point is quite important. You will need to monitor the ability of the staff person to adapt to their new role, and to maintain that role while volunteering. This means that they must be able to keep to the status and limits of their volunteer role while interacting with staff that are assigned as their supervisors, even though in their 'work' identity they may have greater authority than those staff.

And they must also maintain their volunteer identity while working with other volunteers. Any attempt to "pull rank" or display a sense of greater knowledge or importance could be very detrimental to other volunteers.

7. It will also be important for you to keep good written records on staff that volunteer. An up-to-date position description should be maintained and time sheets of volunteer hours (recording the actual hours worked, not just the total amount) should be kept, even if you do not keep them for other volunteers. Both of these documents could become invaluable if a dispute about 'employment' status ever arises.

Special Situations to Watch Out For

Finally, the following are some special situations where you will want to take extra care or even avoid entirely.

- *Volunteering within Small Agencies*

Staff involvement works reasonably well in larger organizations because their size and complexity allows for a clear separation of work and volunteering. In smaller agencies, however, this is seldom the case. Jobs are often ill-defined, everyone does everything, and nothing can be separated.

If you encounter a staff person who wants to volunteer in a small agency, suggest that they simply add the work to their paid job description, perhaps under "other duties as assigned." Sad as it is, there are no restrictions on paid staff volunteering to work themselves to death.

- *Professional Services*

If staff whose work requires professional credentials seek to volunteer in positions where they will be utilizing those professional credentials, then some additional care must be taken. Your best bet is to try to discourage them, since it is very difficult to show a separation between their paid and volunteer work.

- *Conflicts of Interest*

Be careful about assigning staff as volunteers in departments with whom they have a "professional" relationship. This would include departments with whom they work extensively in their paid job and departments where they will have access to information which impacts on their own paid job (such as personnel information) or upon their co-workers.

- *Nepotism*

Another situation to avoid is allowing family and close relatives of staff to volunteer. The only thing more delicate than supervising the Vice President who wants to volunteer is supervising the Vice President's spouse...

- *Community Service Assignments*

While not mandatory, it may also be wise to avoid accepting volunteer applications from staff that are fulfilling community service requirements. One reason for this is that it will become difficult to maintain privacy for the employee in cases where you notify volunteer supervisors about community service volunteers. If you do accept a staff person who is fulfilling a requirement of this sort, make sure that the sentencing authority approves the placement, since there could be some dispute as to whether volunteering within one's own agency qualifies as work for the "community."

- *Organizations with Employee Unions*

In institutions with employee unions it is critical to reach an agreement with the union on the suitability of staff involvement as volunteers.

Upon first encountering this situation union representatives are likely to be as perplexed as you, and this often leads to a quick negative response. On the other hand, unions have a long history of involvement in volunteering themselves. One technique for working through the union question is to arrange a joint meeting of the requesting staff person, yourself, and a union representative to discuss this issue.

The actual "request" for union approval should come from the staff person, to avoid any semblance of management pressure.

Since the decision on this will be setting a precedent of sorts, the involvement of the union should occur whether or not the staff person involved is a member of the union or subject to collective bargaining agreements.

If the union is uncomfortable with the involvement of staff as volunteers it is probably in the best interests of the volunteer program to attempt to find a volunteer placement for the staff person in another agency. Turning volunteer utilization into an issue of contention in labor negotiations is in no one's best interest.

Transitional Volunteers

Some individuals pursue volunteering while making a "transition" in their life, either as a step from domestic into paid work, or as a means of helping overcome mental or physical difficulties. Assisting such individuals is a very worthwhile endeavor, and is one of the great fringe benefits of operating a volunteer program—being able to significantly help both the client and the volunteer at the same time. The Volunteer Center in Philadelphia has done an incredible job of nurturing some transitional volunteers within its own program, but it does so quite consciously and devotes time and attention to this effort. Working with transitional volunteer is somewhat equivalent to adding a new area of service delivery to your program.

As Volunteer Program Manager, however, one of your key duties is to ensure quality control, and this may mean being restrictive in accepting volunteers who cannot satisfactorily perform some type of service to the agency. One way to perform this duty is to add a step to your volunteer screening process in which you ask potential volunteers whether they are currently under any type of treatment which might affect their ability to perform volunteer work. This could encompass either medical or psychiatric treatment. If the response is "yes," then you may wish to ask them to have their physician review the proposed volunteer job description for its suitability.

This will protect both you and the volunteer. You are not in any position to ascertain the limits of the potential volunteer; only their physician has the knowledge to do so. If the volunteer has a limiting health condition you do not want to expose them or others to risk. If the volunteer has a limiting mental condition you do not want them to be overwhelmed with failure by their transitional step rather than experience a success on the road to recovery.

Volunteers who are making a transition back into the workforce are a much easier proposition. The best way to approach these transitional volunteers (who might be displaced housewives or teens with no prior work experience) is as if you were doing career planning with them. Ascertain what type of work they would like to get into and then help develop a volunteer job that will give them the greatest opportunity to practice skills and gain confidence. You can further assist their efforts by allowing them access to broadening experiences (such as attendance at a training session) and by maintaining records of their work experiences that can be used in letters of recommendation. Expect that they will leave you when they find paid employment, but offer them the opportunity to continue volunteering (or to return at some later date). You'll often find this to be a case of your good deed being rewarded.

Volunteers from the Workplace

The workplace is now becoming one of the great " social" institutions of our country, taking the place of clubs, the local tavern, and, for many, even religious institutions. Fortunately, many corporations and small businesses are now recognizing that, like other social institutions, they have an obligation to contribute to the well-being of the community.

In the past twenty years there has been enormous growth of business encouragement of employee involvement.

- A 2002 study by VeraWorks found that 83% of Fortune 500 companies in the US have formal company-supported employee volunteer programs.
- The 2000 National Survey of Giving, Volunteering and Participation in Canada found that 67% of volunteers received support from their employers.
- The UK MORI poll on employee volunteering found that 32% of volunteers volunteered through their place of work as opposed to on a personal basis; a Home Office study in 2003 found that 18% of employees work for an employer with an employee volunteer program; 39% of those who work for such an employer participate in the program; and the average employee donated 60.8 hours of volunteer time a year.

In general, companies may promote volunteering through a spectrum of methods. These range from simply acting as a conduit for information local volunteer opportunities up to actively participating as a full partner in providing organized teams of employees who plan and perform volunteer work.

Here are some tips about working with workplace volunteers:

- Research the company before you approach them. Most companies will be more than happy to give you full written information about what they are willing to do and what processes they utilize. Reading this information will benefit both you and them, and greatly increase your chance of getting a favorable response.

- Many companies now have designated people or departments that are in charge of helping nonprofits connect with potential employee volunteers. While it is useful to know and to utilize these connections, it should not be the only way to approach a company. If you have or can establish a personal contact with someone within the company (for example, in the PR department) there is nothing wrong with approaching them directly and asking for help.

- Some corporate employees (particularly younger ones on management tracks) may be looking at volunteering as a way to establishing credentials, making contacts, or practicing their management skills. Others may simply be attempting to do something "real" as an alternative to a boring job. Don't make assumptions—ask them what they would like to get out of volunteering and design a job that will give it to them.

  This is more difficult to do than it seems. One of your authors has a friend who is possessed of some interesting characteristics: she is an attorney, a CPA, a shrewd financial investor, compulsively energetic, and capable of making friends instantly. She once attempted to volunteer with a hospital, in a program that matched volunteers with lonely seniors for companionship. It took her three very exasperating weeks to persuade the Director of Volunteer Services that she was truly not interested in fundraising or serving on the Board of Directors, but simply wanted to "chat" with seniors (because she missed her grandfather, who had passed away).

- Many companies will expect a return on their investment, and this is particularly true of those in whom groups of employees volunteer for events. The corporation will provide extensive help, but they will also usually want some share of the good publicity generated by the event. Your job is to make sure that they get good press coverage and that they are protected from bad press coverage if something should go wrong.

- If you are involving groups of corporate volunteers for event-based projects, try to design the work so that they are together as a team. A great way to provide recognition is to have a photographer take group pictures as a remembrance of their contribution.

• If you are involving corporate volunteers as individuals in agency positions, strive to make the work challenging. The biggest complaint from corporate volunteer programs about nonprofit agencies lies in the uncreative nature of the volunteer jobs they offer. Mary Hall, the President of Weyerhaeuser, wrote: *"It's becoming harder and harder and harder to find non-profits that have developed meaningful volunteer roles. Business people don't want just to go door to door, or to serve on the banquet committee. They want to feel connected."*

Much of the growth of corporate volunteering is now working its way down to the small business community. The major difference seems to be that small businesses are much more reflective of the personal interests of their owners or operators, so it helps to have a personal connection with that individual. Workplace volunteers may also be accessed through unions (many of whom have a very strong history of volunteer service) and through professional associations.

Alternative Sentencing Volunteers

Alternative sentencing programs begin in the 1970's and have occasionally threatened to overwhelm the volunteer community. You may also find these programs referred to as "community service volunteering," although that name has been generally taken over by the national and youth service community (see the next section). Based either on pre-trial diversion or as adjuncts or alternatives to incarceration, they basically entail "sentencing" an offender to a set number of hours of "volunteer" work with a community organization. Practically every court system now utilizes these alternative sentences, operating through:

1. a program (or programs) operated from within the court system
2. a program contracted out to a community nonprofit agency (such as a Volunteer Center)
3. individual placements negotiated by defendants or their attorneys.

Here are some tips about working with alternative sentencing volunteers:

• Don't do it if you don't want do. You are under no obligation to accept alternative sentencing volunteers. Your organization will need to decide if they are willing and capable of involving alternative sentencing volunteers and if staff, volunteers and clients will be comfortable.

• Reach your own decisions about what types of offenders and what types of sentences you will be willing to accommodate. Many nonprofits will accept misdemeanors (DWI, for example), but draw the line at any type of felony. You might also decide to place limits on the number of hours of sentenced service that you will work with. A twenty-hour sentence, for example, may not be worth your while, unless you have the type of job that could be filled by new volunteers with little training (something creative, like envelope stuffing or collating, perhaps?).

• Respect the privacy of alternative sentencing volunteers. Those in your agency should know that this will be one aspect of the volunteer program, and they should know the range of offenses that may be accepted. You should not, however, broadcast particular information about any specific alternative sentencing volunteer, except on a need-to-know basis to direct supervisors.

• If you do accept alternative sentencing volunteers, recognize that you are accepting the responsibility for working with the court system to see that the imposed sentence is carried out. Make sure you know in advance what record keeping you will be required to maintain and what you should do if someone stops volunteering before their hours of service are completed.

Despite their potentially frightening aspect, many local programs operate quite productively with alternative sentencing volunteers, and some have discovered that these same volunteers may continue volunteering after their sentence has been completed. If you are uncertain about their use then find someone at your local DOVIA who is now involving them and arrange for a visit to their program.

Stipended Volunteers

With the creation of the AmeriCorps program of the Commission on National and Community Service, a large number of "volunteer" programs were created, both at the federal level and in various states, in which stipended "volunteers" (or "member" or some other name) became available to serve community agencies.

Some of these programs involve groups of volunteers who do projects, and working with them involves following the basic procedures outlined above in the section on working with groups and event-based volunteers. Other programs, however, station volunteers for extended periods with agencies. Involvement with these programs usually includes completing an application process for the service of the community service volunteer. These individuals usually fall under the jurisdiction of the Volunteer Program Manager, so we thought we would offer some suggestions about working with them:

- Although you may think of them as "volunteers," they will primarily be distinguished from other volunteers by the time element of their service. Many of their assignments are full-time, 40 hour per week periods of service, covering a year or more. This is unlike most volunteer positions, and in fact requires that you treat this individual more as "quasi-staff" than volunteer. The element of a monetary stipend is relatively unimportant.

- The longer period of service per week may make it somewhat harder to write a job description which covers all their responsibility, unless they will only be doing a job (such as tutoring a client) which is easily explained and simple in focus. Try to isolate some of the key elements of what they will be doing, and consider reconstructing the job description periodically around specific projects for which the volunteer will be responsible.

- Some of these volunteers will not be sure exactly what they would like to do when they enter service. One way to accommodate this uncertainty is to give them a series of "test drive" jobs for the first month. This will broaden their knowledge of the agency and its services and will allow them to experiment and find something to their liking.

Many student-based community service programs require participants to engage in periods of "reflection" or to maintain journals about their experiences. You will need to assist volunteers in this reflection, and you may find it to be a technique that could benefit other volunteers.

Government Benefit Volunteers

Another "growth" area for volunteering over the next ten years is likely to occur in a new area of "required" volunteering. Many jurisdictions are now beginning to impose requirements on those who wish to receive certain types of government benefits.

Examples of government benefit volunteers include:

- welfare recipients seeking to maintain benefits
- public housing inhabitants
- individuals performing community service as an alternative payment system for local taxes, fees, or fines.

If present trends continue, it is not unlikely that almost every governmental benefit program could be accompanied by some compulsory requirement for community service. The imminent result of this will be the mass infusion into volunteering of populations who have little or no experience with volunteering as we had become accustomed to thinking about it.

The philosophical backing for this approach is that those receiving public benefits should make some contribution to the public good, and that "volunteering" is an excellent way for them to do so.

This is an area which is likely to give some of those in the volunteer sector philosophical fits, since it adds yet another group (and in this case, a potentially very large group) to the category of "forced choice" volunteers.

Your best bet in this area is to treat it in a similar fashion to the alternative sentencing volunteers discussed above. Make sure that those in your agency accept what such a program represents and that you will be willing to deal with whatever record keeping requirements will exist.

Unlike the alternative sentencing volunteer, many of these government benefit volunteers may be somewhat resentful of having to volunteer to receive a benefit, particularly those that have not been so compelled before. You will need to work much harder to orient these individuals to your cause, and to convince them that what you are doing is indeed worth their contribution of time. The up-side of this situation is that you may, if you are successful, become partially responsible for helping a group in our society - those with low incomes - become involved with community social service agencies in a way in which they have traditionally not. This experience may turn them into empowered service providers rather than service recipients. You may also find that some of the observations and experiences of these volunteers will be very useful in helping your agency take a fresh look at the needs of your clients.

Here are some suggestions for working with these populations:

- *Changes in the Design of Volunteer Jobs*

The design of volunteer jobs for inexperienced volunteers who will only be with an agency for a relatively short or small period of time will require two changes. The first will be an increase in the number of "low level" volunteer jobs suitable for those with little work experience, minimal skills, and little time for extensive training. These jobs will be hard to make either interesting or rewarding.

The second change will be an increased need for and reliance upon jobs that are either shaped around projects or events, i.e., jobs that multiple volunteers can work on together and which have definite and short time frames.

The good news in all of this is that the new volunteers will alleviate one of the problem situations in volunteer job design of recent years – the difficulty in obtaining volunteers for those jobs which had to be done Monday through Friday from 9:00am to 5:00pm.

- *Changes in Volunteer Recruitment*

Those agencies that can successfully involve the new volunteer may totally eliminate any recruitment problems - there are likely to be far more new volunteers than there are agencies capable of making use of them.

There will be, however, two major changes in recruiting efforts. The first will be an increased need for targeted recruitment of volunteers for "skilled" positions (board, technical work, etc.) and for positions that require longer time commitments (mentoring, for example).

The second will be the development of what might be called "second tier" recruitment strategies, focusing on recruitment through retention and re-involvement of volunteers who have served their compulsory time and are being sought to re-volunteer with the agency of their own volition. This strategy will require great care on the part of the agency, since it can only be done if the agency invests resources and time in building commitment among new volunteers. Clearly, those programs with good volunteer management practices are most likely to be successful.

- *Changes in Screening and Matching*

Current volunteer matching practices involve learning the skills and interests of volunteers and then matching them to suitable jobs. This will become much more difficult with the new volunteers for the simple reason that many of them lack the work and life experience to know what type of job they might be either interested in or capable of. This means that interviewing of the new volunteers must expand to contain some sort of basic skills assessment process as well as an inventory of career interests around which volunteer jobs might be shaped. The skilled volunteer manager will have to operate as a career counselor, helping individuals discover their interests and talents.

- *Changes in Orientation and Training*

Many public benefit volunteers are likely to come to agencies with a total lack of knowledge about the purpose and operation of the organization. Volunteer orientation sessions will assume even greater importance, since the basic volunteer population possibly lacks both knowledge and interest in the cause for which they are to begin working. If uncorrected, this is dangerous for the agency and bodes ill for retention of the volunteer. Orientation will also need to contain sections on the basic protocols of the working environment, since for many of the new volunteers this will be their very first work experience.

Training will have to expand to include basic skills, including literacy, use of equipment and the basics of customer service and dealing with the public.

- *Changes in Volunteer Supervision*

A volunteer population which is unaccustomed to the demands of work to begin with and then coerced is likely to demand much greater attention and supervision than we are accustomed to, and is much more likely to create unintentional difficulties simply out of ignorance of what behavior or standards of conduct are expected. Coping with this will require much more focused supervision by staff or management volunteers. Smart volunteer managers will consider creating "mentor" or "buddy" systems for new volunteers, to provide one-to-one assistance in learning the new systems. At the same time, additional training will need to be done with staff that have little or no experience in working with these new populations.

- *Changes in Volunteer Recognition*

Receiving the basic organizational certificate is not likely to influence the volunteer who cares little for the organization. Neither is an annual volunteer luncheon held long after their departure.

Good volunteer recognition will need to focus around activities that are developmental in nature and thus have value for the volunteer seeking career enhancement. These could include additional training opportunities that build career or life skills. Other recognition techniques might include portable recognition of a tangible nature - books, clothing, etc. - that can be taken with the volunteer and used after their period of service.

For volunteers who come from a discrete population, such as a high school class, recognition that is given "back at the school" among their peer group will become a desirable alternative.

Remembering the Opportunities
The changes suggested above may seem challenging to you. You're probably in good company if you feel that way. I suspect that the volunteer managers of 20 years ago, faced with the influx of Short Term Volunteers, felt the same uncertainty.

Let me close with a final observation, based on the fact that we are facing an incredible opportunity. One of the little noticed side benefits of the trend toward required volunteering is that it will bring into volunteering segments of our society that traditionally have not been involved in mainstream volunteering with agencies. We have the opportunity to introduce these populations to the joys and satisfactions that successful volunteer involvement creates.

Unfortunately, we also have the opportunity, particularly with the younger population of new volunteers, of teaching them during their first experience with volunteering that volunteer work can be dull, unpleasant, and unrewarding.

Which of these happens in your agency and in your community is probably entirely up to the attitudes and skills with which you as a volunteer manager approach these new populations. It will be a learning experience for all of us.

Management Volunteers

With reductions in agency staff, volunteers are now being asked to provide increasing internal assistance to the agency, including operating as "managers" of agency programs and efforts. These "management" volunteers may even direct the efforts of other volunteers, either in discrete projects or around the office. Here are some tips about involving volunteers who will help provide management functions:

- Avoid the most common mistake in selecting management volunteers, which is simply selecting them by promoting those who are good at other jobs. Many volunteers who are quite skilled and enthusiastic about delivering direct service do not want to get involved in "administrative" work and might make the mistake of agreeing to do it simply because they don't want to disappoint you. This can be particularly a problem with those volunteers have administrative responsibilities in the paid careers and are volunteering because it gives them a sense of doing something "real" or "hands on."

- The biggest issue which must be confronted in placing volunteers in charge of other volunteers is what degree of personnel authority they will be vested with. While in theory management volunteers should have the same authority as paid managers over personnel decisions (such as hiring, firing, etc.), in practice many management volunteers have expressed personal reservations about exercising such authority. Do not be surprised if you need to negotiate this individually with each volunteer.

- A particular area of difficulty will lie with management volunteers who not only supervise volunteers, but also exercise authority over paid staff (such as support staff). This most often happens when volunteers have particular expertise that paid staff lack. You will need to exercise extreme care in helping work out potential confusion over the level of responsibility and authority which the volunteer can exercise, and in ensuring that the staff "buy in" to the exercise of this authority. Your success in this will be an excellent indication of whether volunteers are truly accepted by your agency.

- If volunteers are to act as members of the agency management team it is crucial that they be involved in all significant agency communications and decision-making processes. Volunteers who simply work with clients may be able to function without full involvement in all agency operations, but those who are representing the agency and supervising other staff need to have full general knowledge about what is happening. They need to be involved in making significant decisions, particularly in any program area that relates to their work.

The easiest place to begin utilizing management volunteers is within the volunteer program itself.

Functions such as recruitment, interviewing and training are probably performed better by volunteers and represent fruitful areas for increasing volunteer responsibility. By doing so you will not only free up some of your own time, but you will also model high-impact volunteer involvement for the rest of the agency.

Family Volunteers

Family volunteering includes the following configurations:

- a nuclear family: parents and children
- an adult with his/her senior parents
- a husband and wife
- a retired couple
- an adult guardian and child
- a non-custodial parent and child
- a single parent and child
- children and grandparents
- adult siblings
- a group unrelated by blood who is living together
- multiple children from the same family

Besides understanding the scope of "family" it is also important to understand how members of a family might engage in "volunteering." There are a variety of "shapes" that such volunteering might encompass. These include:

- Members of a family who share in the same volunteer task, working together at the same time. An example of this might be a family that provides entertainment during friendly visits together to residents at a nursing home. They might jointly put on a skit or sing.

- Members of a family who share in the same volunteer task, but who work at different times, rotating responsibility among members of the group. An example of this is a family that "adopts" a home-bound senior, with each taking responsibility for providing assistance on a different day of the week.

- Members of a family who work on different tasks, but do so at the same time or during the same event. An example of this is a family that volunteers at a local Walk-a-thon, but some members hand out T-shirts, some assist in registration, some act as officials.

- Multiple families who work together in sharing tasks or events. An example of this is a group of families who plan and manage an environmental clean-up of a park or recreation area or who host a block party.

Family volunteering is quite flexible, but the key factor distinguishing it from volunteering done by individuals is the element of sharing and working together. The maximum benefit from this family component comes from enabling families to work together on related projects, common clients, or shared tasks. This focus provides the synergistic element that makes family volunteering greater than the sum of the individual volunteers.

Developing Assignments for Family Volunteers

Developing assignments suitable for families is different from developing assignments for individual volunteers. Well-structured family volunteer assignments are likely to have different "shapes" than assignments for individuals, and this is particularly true if younger family members are present.

In considering family volunteer assignments use the following general criteria:

- activities that are active, fun, and hands-on
- activities that allow for a range of experience, talent, strength
- activities in which work can be shared
- activities that introduce families to new experiences, environments
- activities that allow families to reflect upon their feelings and learning's
- activities with flexibility in schedule and worksite
- activities with an educational component added for young children
- activities that allow interaction with other families
- activities where a direct impact can be seen

Examples of bad volunteer assignments for families:

- assignments that require all the family, all the time
- putting families with young children in an agency with young children
- assignments locked into a fixed recurring timeframe
- working with breakable objects
- dealing with confidential issues and materials
- inflexible and inhospitable worksites
- single function volunteer tasks that can't be sub-divided

Many current volunteer assignments that were designed for individuals can easily be done by families working together. This includes most assignments in which volunteers work one-on-one with clients, or community education efforts. Assignments that may seem boring in the context of an individual volunteer may appear more interesting in a family setting. Such tasks as envelope stuffing, collating, setting up rooms and others are more fun when conducted in a group setting. Families engage in conversation while performing the work, somewhat reminiscent of the old "quilting bees."

Start with assignments of a limited duration and do not place too frequent demands upon volunteers. Asking families to volunteer for four projects or events a year is a good starting point. If they enjoy the initial experiences they are likely to expand their commitment.

Recruiting Family Volunteers
Recruiting families can be easily integrated into existing volunteer recruitment efforts. Here are some very simple ways to recruit family volunteers:

- Ask prospective volunteers if they are interested in volunteering with their family
- Have a "Family Involvement Day" for current volunteers
- Prominently list family opportunities in flyers and show families volunteering
- Feature the concept of family involvement in talks to community groups
- Create a Speakers' Bureau of family members to talk about family involvement
- Ask corporate volunteer programs to expand involvement to employee families
- List family volunteering opportunities with the local Volunteer Center

Finally, involve families themselves as recruiters. Family members should be encouraged to recruit their friends and should be included when making presentations to groups. The enthusiasm and direct personal appeal of family members will do more than any statistical explanation of community needs to recruit new families

Interviewing Family Volunteers
Interviewing families is different from interviewing individuals. The difference in the volunteer interviewing process occurs in two primary ways:

1. Interview the family as a group because part of what you are attempting to discover in the interview is how the family behaves together. This will include observing the family's interaction patterns for signs of dominance, resistance, or coercion. The family volunteering assignment will be more likely to succeed if all family members are, in fact, "volunteering."

2. You must also interview members of the family as individuals, even though the interview is conducted in a group setting. The reason for doing this is to see if the types of volunteer assignments under consideration match the interests and abilities of each family member. This can be done by encouraging all family members to respond freely to questions or by asking individuals directly for a response.

Screening of families follows the same pattern as screening of individual volunteers. This means conducting appropriate criminal background checks of adults and asking both adults and children for references who can be called. In the case of children this will often be their teachers, who can provide invaluable information about maturity levels and behavior.

As with individual volunteers, every effort should be made to match volunteer assignments to the skills and interests of the volunteering family. This is more challenging when multiple individuals are involved, but is a key factor in motivating volunteers to perform tasks cheerfully and successfully.

Supervising Family Volunteers
Supervision of volunteering families takes place in a variety of formats. These will partially depend upon the type of volunteer assignment being undertaken and the location and format of the work.

Family volunteers working on long-term assignments should be integrated into the supervisory system used with individual volunteers. These should be a designated staff or volunteer supervisor whom the families report to. Follow all the normal requirements of supervision.

Here are some additional tips for supervising family volunteers:

- Strive to develop "self-supervising systems" where the families take responsibility for managing themselves. This eases the workload on you and empowers families to make decisions about what is important and how things can best be accomplished.

- Establish a clear rule that the responsible adult is in charge of their own children/youth unless specific other arrangements are made in advance with the volunteer manager.

• Individual volunteers can be used as supervisors of family units. Consider partnering experienced individual volunteers with new families. This works well for both parties.

• Pair unenthusiastic youth with enthusiastic volunteers.

• Children and teens can provide great input and information. Young does not necessarily mean "clueless."

• The amount of supervision needed in a given family volunteering situation is directly proportional to the number of children present and inversely proportional to their age.

• While it would be nice to provide child care and transportation assistance, most agencies do not. According to the Gallup Survey only 18% of agencies provide childcare to volunteering families and only 17% provide transportation assistance.

• Alert other volunteers and staff as to the presence of volunteering children.

• Families, like all groups, have their own internal dynamics and politics, and these may spill into the volunteer situation - you may end up being a mediator for something that has nothing to do with the volunteer work, or you may decide that the family needs to address its own issues away from your agency

Recognizing Family Volunteers
Providing recognition to family volunteers is one of the easiest and most rewarding parts of generating family involvement.

The family connection to volunteer involvement means that many basic volunteer recognition techniques targeted toward individuals who are affiliation-oriented will be effective. It also means that involving some family members in recognizing other family members is a highly effective technique, providing the "personal" touch that will be valued.

When working with families with young children, remember that kids love to see pictures of themselves in the newspaper and that parents are motivated by seeing their children receive recognition.

A key principle of volunteer recognition is that "stuff works." Families are perfect recipients of T-shirts, hats, temporary tattoos, snacks and other items.

Family volunteers, like all volunteers, like to see the results of their work. The impact on a single client, on a park or nature trail, or on the work done by your organization all provide recognition. Family volunteers work to "make a difference," and part of the responsibility of a volunteer manager is to design assignments for which families can feel proud of their accomplishments.

The Significance of Family Volunteering
In our opinion, family volunteering is exactly the kind of thing for which volunteer managers should be advocating, because it addresses both the needs of agencies and of society. Sociologists such as Robert Putnam have enunciated the sense of disconnection that is pervading many of the traditional social institutions in our society. As people do not connect with members of their families, so they also are failing to connect with other individuals and groups. Families constitute one of the primary building blocks of social capital within communities and their involvement, or lack of involvement, significantly affects the ability of the community to function in a congruent fashion. Family volunteering offers an elegant mechanism by which families can not only increase their degree of interaction with each other but can, in a productive fashion, learn about, connect with, and assist in the greater community.

In addition, you might consider this finding from a 2002 survey done by First Side Partners:

"Volunteers who participate with family members volunteer regularly, for more time than volunteers who do not donate their time along with family members – 45% versus 33%. They also volunteer an average of 4.3 hours per week, as compared with 2.8 hours for non-family volunteers."

Chapter Eleven
Keeping Volunteers on Track

A key role of the manager is to ensure that volunteers are performing according to the standards of the organization. We will examine this area in a variety of contexts:

- providing on-going evaluation to individual volunteers
- analyzing potential problem behavior situations
- providing positive corrective action
- why good volunteers will sometimes do wrong things
- releasing a volunteer from service
- when the volunteer is not at fault

Providing Ongoing Evaluation and Feedback

Volunteer Program Managers do not commonly look forward to the prospect of conducting an evaluation of a volunteer with great enthusiasm. Staff that work with volunteers may be even less enthusiastic. Many volunteer programs, in truth, cannot even claim to have a process for volunteer evaluation, except in a very loose sense. Evaluation, however, is not something to be avoided, especially if you realize that it can be a positive management device.

Why Evaluate Volunteers?

Rather than dreading the prospect of evaluation, the smart Volunteer Program Manager should realize two important facts:

- Most volunteers want to do the best job they can. The absence of feedback and assistance is both demeaning and disturbing to them.

- Most volunteers will "win" in assessment situations.

Failing to evaluate a volunteer sends a clear message that you don't care about the quality of the work, and that you don't care much about the volunteer. Both volunteers who know they aren't doing well and those who think they should be congratulated for good work will think less of the volunteer effort, and of you, if evaluations are not conducted.

There are two basic reasons for conducting volunteer evaluations:

1. To help the volunteers work closer to their potential.

2. To help the organization better involve volunteers.

These reasons do not include dealing with all the small performance problems that supervisors have been ignoring since the last evaluation. A periodic volunteer evaluation can help shape the overall performance of the volunteer, but it cannot and should not replace the day-to-day on-site coaching and supervising that must occur.

Setting Up the Evaluation System

There are a number of ways to develop an evaluation system. The first issue to be faced is what to call it. Here are some possibilities:

- Evaluation system
- Performance assessment system
- Work appraisal
- Progress planning session
- Feedback meeting

Clearly these have different connotations. Our suggestion is that you call the system by the same terminology as is used for paid staff, since this will send a clear message about the equal value of volunteer efforts. You should also attempt to make the volunteer evaluation process congruent, if not identical, to that utilized with staff.

Whatever system you create should contain the following elements:

- A policy on performance appraisal and review

- An initial trial period for all volunteers, before they are officially accepted and enrolled by the agency
- A system for developing and maintaining current and accurate job descriptions for each volunteer

- A periodic scheduled evaluation meeting between the volunteers and their supervisors to discuss job performance and satisfaction

- A method for reviewing commitments to change made during the evaluation meeting.

This system should be explained to each volunteer during the initial orientation session, and should be reviewed with each staff person who will be supervising volunteers.

It All Starts with the Position Description

It is impossible to conduct evaluations if you do not have accurate job descriptions for each volunteer. Remember Lynch's Law: *"Lousy position descriptions produce really lousy evaluation sessions."* Without a good job description that outlines the goals, objectives, and performance measures of the job, supervisors will not know what they are asking of the volunteers and the volunteers will not know what is expected of them. Remember McCurley's Rule of Thumb: *"If you don't know what you want from the volunteers, why should they?"*

It doesn't really matter what shape position description you follow. A paragraph is fine, as long as it tells the volunteer what they are trying to accomplish, what specific steps or work are anticipated, and how their success will be measured.

The most difficult part of this effort is getting supervisors to change the positions descriptions of volunteers as time passes. You can encourage this by having them re-write the descriptions after each evaluation session, or as part of each annual planning session (making the jobs match the new strategic efforts of the department or program).

Conducting the Evaluation Discussion

The evaluation session should be a two-way meeting. It is your chance to talk about the volunteers' performance, giving either praise or suggestions for improvement. It should also be the volunteers' opportunity to talk about how their participation can be enhanced, which might even include discussing their moving to a new volunteer position.

The easiest method of conducting the evaluation session is to follow the RAP method:

- *Review* the past.
- *Analyze* the present.
- *Plan* the future.

And here are some suggestions:

- Don't get overwhelmed by forms. We've included a sample evaluation form in the appendix but the main purpose of the session is to have a substantive conversation with the volunteer about how their volunteering can be improved, not to simply fill out forms for the filing system. The forms are helpful (and can particularly be so for your successor, who may be trying desperately to find out what went on before she got there), but they are not the major concern during the discussion.

- Start with the position description. Begin by finding out if it in fact describes what the volunteer has been doing. Take notes so you can adjust it to reflect reality. The major 'problem' with highly motivated volunteers is that they produce rapid 'scope creep' in their assignments. You don't want to discourage this, but you do want to know about it.

- Stick to the basics: job proficiency, working relationships, comparison with last review.

- Listen at least as much as you talk. Tell the volunteers this is their opportunity to evaluate the program and you want their ideas on how to make things better both for them and for other volunteers.

- Remember that the evaluation may show as much what you need to do as what the volunteer needs to do.

The Positive Side of Evaluation

Rather than thinking of evaluation as a system for dealing with problems, you ought to think of it as a means of rewarding those who are doing well. The percentage of volunteers who are troublesome is fairly small; those who are hardworking constitute the vast majority. This means that the majority of evaluation comments can be positive ones, praising the work that is being accomplished.

The evaluation session can also be diagnostic in nature, allowing you to determine how volunteers are feeling about their work. For example, volunteers who are in intensive job positions (such as providing advocacy for abused children) often get burned out. Volunteers also frequently fail to recognize such problems and fail to ask for help, since their commitment drives them to continue to work. The evaluation session can provide the astute Volunteer Program Manager with the opportunity to determine whether a good volunteer is becoming burned out, or bored, or needs to be transferred to another position. You also can find out a volunteer's readiness to be promoted to increased responsibility. The session thus becomes one of mutual evaluation, with the intent of rewarding and advancing those who have been productive.

Analyzing Problem Behavior Situations

Since volunteers are, basically speaking, normal people you will sometimes encounter difficult behaviors. We are going to examine this type of situation in some depth since it may occur for a variety of reasons.

Common Reasons for Poor Performance

Broadly speaking, poor performance results from either a lack of ability or a lack of motivation. This leads to four different types of situations:

- The volunteer is both *motivated* and *able.*
- The volunteer is *motivated* but *not able.*
- The volunteer is *able* but *not motivated.*
- The volunteer is *neither able nor motivated.*

The Motivated and Able Volunteer

If the volunteer is both motivated and able, any problems will probably be caused either by unclear performance expectations or by difficult personal relationships with paid staff (covered in the next chapter) or with other volunteers. In the former case, staff may think the expectation has been communicated clearly, but it may not have been. To take a simple example, a volunteer who is chronically late for a shift may not be aware that it matters whether he or she is exactly on time. In the second case, where the problem is interpersonal, the role of the Volunteer Program Manager is to counsel and engage in conflict negotiation or to shift the volunteer to a setting where the conflict does not exist.

The Motivated but Unskilled Volunteer

If the volunteer is motivated but not able, you can solve the problem through training, counseling or coaching, as described in chapter seven. This may involve getting staff that have the needed abilities involved in upgrading volunteer skills. Staff may not be very good at coaching and training, however, so you may need to provide some technical assistance in this area to help them transfer their knowledge and skill to the volunteer.

In some cases, staff may not have the skills themselves. This happens when you recruit a volunteer to provide a service that staff themselves lack. In this case, you may need to recruit another volunteer to serve as a mentor or coach to the volunteer who is providing the service. Imagine, for example, that a person volunteers to do some public relations work for your agency. Staff are thrilled with this, since they have no public relations expertise themselves. However, the person who volunteers to do this turns out not to be as capable in this area as you had hoped. Perhaps she is fresh out of school, and was using your agency as an opportunity to gain work experience. In this case, you might be able to recruit an experienced person from a public relations firm to give the volunteer some advice and counsel.

The Able but Unmotivated Volunteer

If the volunteer is able but not motivated, the role of the volunteer coordinator is first one of placing the volunteer in a more motivating set of circumstances. Check these points:

- Is the volunteer placed in a job he wants to do?
- Is that job designed according to the principles described in chapter four?
- Does the volunteer see the connection between his work and the mission of the organization?
- Has the volunteer received adequate recognition for the work he has done?
- Is the volunteer empowered to make decisions?

If the answer to any of these questions is "no" remedy the situation according to the principles discussed in this book. You should note that the "failure" in these cases is not that of the volunteer, but is rather a common problem in volunteer screening. Given the difficulty of fully understanding complex human needs in the short time period of a volunteer interview it is likely that either you or the volunteer will not have communicated accurately about a particular volunteer job. Rather than worrying about this, simply make sure that you check back with volunteers regularly to see how they are feeling about what they are doing and to offer them alternatives if they are not feeling good about their involvement.

The Unable and Unmotivated Volunteer

The fourth possibility is that the volunteer is neither motivated nor able to do the job that needs to be done. In such a case, you could try to find a position that will meet the volunteer's motivational needs and is more suited to his skill level. If no such position is available in your organization, you may find the easiest course to refer the volunteer to another agency where he is more appropriate. This may involve "releasimg" the volunteer, as will be discussed later in this chapter.

Regardless of the cause of the problem, the Volunteer Program Manager must insist on the volunteer meeting the organization's performance expectations. If the volunteer is not meeting those expectations, you must intercede for the good of the organization.

Determining Root Causes before Taking Action
The first thing to do when dealing with a problem volunteer is to determine what is really going on. Part of this is determining the extent of the problem situation (and, indeed, whether there really is a problem), but the more crucial element involves attempting to determine the cause of the problem.

Detecting Impending Problems
There are some common warning signs that indicate approaching problems in workers, paid or volunteer. A combination of these calls for a re-interview with the person and/or a re-examination of the job assignment to uncover what is behind the behavior. Warning signs include:

1. The quality and quantity of work begins to decline. The worker makes many mistakes.
2. The worker often comes late to assignments.
3. The volunteer simply does not show up for work or meetings.
4. There is a lack of enthusiasm.
5. Rarely, if ever, does the worker make suggestions or show initiative.
6. A normally verbal and open volunteer or employee becomes silent and closed-down.
7. The worker continues to avoid parts of their job--especially those that are more complex or disagreeable to them.
8. Workers blame others for their own errors or shortcomings.
9. They are less agreeable, affable or cooperative; they whine or complain regularly.
10. They avoid interaction with colleagues; they make sure they are unavailable for any social interaction.
11. They ignore timelines and due dates for projects.
12. Co-workers and direct supervisors complain about the worker and their performance.
13. Reports reach volunteer managers of the worker "bad-mouthing" the organization, program or key leaders.
14. They explode over insignificant instances; reactions are out of proportion to incidents.
15. They project an attitude of "nothing is right."

Finding Out What is Really Happening
Consider the demonstration of any of these behaviors a warning that something is wrong; a combination of several of these needs to be seen as symptomatic of a serious underlying problem. Take one or more of the following steps and responses:

1. Meet in private with the person. Describe what specifically has been observed and ask them if there is an underlying issue that needs to be discussed. Do not place any interpretation on the observed behavior; allow them to explain it if they will.

2. Avoid rushing to judgment of the feedback that is being given. Listen attentively, do not interrupt and allow silent spaces in the conversation that can allow them time to gather their thoughts and consider how to express themself. Encourage honest feedback through body language, attentive listening and avoidance of defensiveness.

3. Determine the real issues motivating behavior:

- Has something changed in their personal life that is forcing a shift in priorities, energy allocation, concentration, etc.? A critically ill child at home can distract a typically enthusiastic volunteer and cause many of the problem symptoms noted here.

- Are they the victims of mis-information? Do paid staff believe that they are to be replaced by a volunteer? Does the volunteer believe changes are being made without their input?

- Are they upset about a specific occurrence and thus "fighting back" by reducing their productivity?

- Have they simply burned out? Volunteers, like paid workers, can stay in a job or location beyond their energy limits. Many of them are unable to take a break because of high commitment.

4. Ask the volunteer or staff member what they see as a successful response to their issues. What would be best for them? A time-out or leave-of-absence to regain their old enthusiasm? A move to a different assignment? A full release from the perceived burden of staying?

5. Agree on a time frame for the resolution of the problem. If leaving is the chosen option, select the time frame best for the program. Allowing a disgruntled volunteer to stay for a month when the Volunteer Program Manager feels they will continue to contaminate the work climate is unwise even in the face of the volunteer's assurances that they'll be positive and productive.

When behavior becomes abnormal or negative, consider the actions as symptoms and warnings of problems about to erupt and take steps to intervene swiftly. Remember that the "problem" may be the person involved, but it might also be the situation that exists or the relationship among several persons that is the root cause.

Questions to Investigate Problem Situations

Very often, particularly in minor problem behavior, there will be no real "villain." Two people in the organization might just be not getting along, or they may even have a simple misunderstanding in which neither is really at fault. These innocent situations often create larger difficulties, however, if unaddressed. A good Volunteer Program Manager can sometimes intervene and assist the parties to look for their own solution to the situation before things get out of hand. The best process for attempting this involves talking with the parties involved on an individual basis and getting them to describe their version of the difficulty as well as what they think they could do to address the problem. Note that the solution offered here is not for the Volunteer Program Manager to act to solve the problem, but rather to encourage and assist the involved parties to identify what they themselves can do to resolve the difficulty.

The following are some good questions to use during the interview with a problem volunteer. They are grouped into examining the background of the situation (including how the problem volunteer feels about what is happening), creating possible solution options, and creating an implementation plan for helping the problem volunteer address the situation:

1. *Background Investigation*

- How are things going?
- Why do you think they are going so well?
- How could things be better?
- What problems are you having?
- Why are those problems happening?
- What factors in the situation caused the problems?
- Are the difficulties related to a single person or to most persons?
- How long has the situation been this way?
- What happened prior to this situation?
- Is there a time when this seems most likely to occur?
- Does this behavior happen with everybody or only with some people?
- What problems does this person's behavior cause?
- Why do you think the person behaves that way?
- What would a person get out of behaving that way?
- How are other staff and volunteers reacting to the behavior?
- Have you talked with the person about the behavior?
- What was the person's reaction when you talked with them?

2 *Creation of Options*

- What do you think you might do if the situation/ behavior doesn't change?
- What has been your response?
- What has been the person's reaction to your response?
- Why do you think this response didn't work?
- Are there other responses you might consider?
- How do you suppose the person will react to these?
- What are the pro's and con's of that course?
- What other options do we have?
- If you had it to do over again, what would you do differently?
- What would you advise someone else to do in this situation?
- What would you advise someone else to do to avoid this situation?

3. *Implementation*

- Of the possible options, which would best fit with your situation?
- What will you need before trying to implement the solution?
- How will this affect other volunteers and staff in your department?
- Is there a way to best communicate this change to these others?
- Are there any advantages to the way we now do things that we want to preserve?
- How will you monitor responses to this attempted solution?
- Is there anything I can do to help make your plan work?
- When can we talk about this again?

Taking Positive Corrective Action

If the volunteer does not respond to any of the approaches mentioned above, the Volunteer Program Manager can either fire the volunteer or take corrective action. If you think there is hope that the volunteer could start to perform at an acceptable level, corrective action is the best choice. This action must be taken in a positive fashion, however. By positive corrective action, we mean that the interaction with the volunteer should not do damage to the volunteer's self-esteem.

Most corrective action in organizations is destructive. If there is any improvement in performance, it comes at a cost to the individual's self-confidence and self-image. It may also produce simmering resentment. In volunteer programs, this will usually poison the atmosphere and contribute to retention problems.

In a traditional corrective action encounter, the supervisor tells the volunteer or employee what is wrong with him and often threatens the person with dire consequences if he doesn't improve. In such encounters, the supervisor often criticizes the individual's character, saying things like "You're lazy" or "You're insensitive to client needs." Or they make assumptions about the individual's attitudes or motives, with statements such as "You've got a bad attitude" or "You're trying to run the program." In such interactions, the supervisor is the accuser. Such criticism produces defensiveness and resentment. Worse, it doesn't give the individual much clue as to what they can do to improve.

To make the encounter more productive, we want to interact in a way that focuses on what the employee can do differently. Any description of past performance should focus on specific behavior, such as "You called Ms. Fleener an old bat" instead of statements about the kind of person the individual is ("You are rude") or the traits they exhibit ("You have poor manners") or their motives ("You were trying to embarrass her"). Although this may sound simple, it is not in fact the natural instinct of most people. We all have a tendency to generalize and label other people's behavior, particularly if it is negative.

The positive corrective action approach contains four basic steps. These steps place the supervisor in the role of helper rather than accuser. And they make change the responsibility of the volunteer rather than someone else.

Step One: Get the volunteer to describe the unacceptable behavior

The interaction should begin with a statement such as "How would you describe your performance (in this situation)?"

Sometimes this statement alone will clear up the performance problem. A typist, for example, frustrated her supervisor by making many errors. When asked to describe her own performance, the typist said she thought it was very good, and noted the quantity of work she produced. The supervisor then asked "How would you evaluate the accuracy of the work you do?" The typist responded "Well, sometimes I make mistakes, but when I do someone catches it and I correct it right away." It was obvious from her tone of voice, that she saw nothing wrong with this system. The supervisor realized she had never told her she expected the work to be done without error the first time. Once she clarified this, the performance problem disappeared.

On the other hand, sometimes the person will not be able (or willing) to describe the problem behavior at all. In such cases, the supervisor will have to do that for the individual. If you come to this, make sure you concentrate entirely on what the person did or did not do. Describe the behavior without judgment. Some examples include:

- "You were twenty minutes late today."
- "You were not at the meeting."
- "You interrupted both Jim and Joe before they finished speaking."
- "You made a commitment on behalf of the agency without telling us."
- "You erased all the volunteer files from the hard drive."
- "You said you were going to kill Gladys if she didn't shut up."

Step two: Divorce the behavior from the individual's self-worth

In talking to people about their unacceptable performance, we want to make sure they know that we are talking only about what they did, not who they are. If the volunteer is performing below their ability, or if their performance has tailed off, you could say something like "That's not like you" or "That's not up to your usual standards," or "Or I'm surprised," or even "You can do better than that." Say these things only if it is your true belief.

On the other hand, if the behavior is all too like them, you could say something like "I'm confused by this," or "I'm puzzled." These statements lead directly to step three.

Step Three: Say something positive about the person

The purpose of this step is to diffuse the defensiveness that is a natural result of a corrective action encounter. It is hard to get people to change when they are defending their unacceptable behavior. Here we want to praise people for a positive trait they possess. We want to validate who they are. Some examples are:

- "You care about our customers;"
- "You're a responsible worker;"
- "You're a smart person."
- "You care about the welfare of our clients."

If you can think of no positive traits the person possesses with respect to the difficult performance, you can always fall back on the statement "I believe you are capable of succeeding in this job."

Step Four: Ask the volunteer for a plan for improvement

Ask the volunteer "What should you be doing?" or "What will you do next time?" or "What can you do to fix it?" Make sure the plan they give you is clear, specific, and visualizeable. Get details. If they can't clearly picture themselves doing something different, they won't be able to improve. Listen to any excuses but insist on the performance expectation. Ask how they will make sure they meet that expectation in the future. Although the plan must be acceptable to you, it must come from the volunteer.

An Example of Positive Corrective Action

To look at how this might work in practice, let's return to the simple example of a volunteer who is chronically late for his work. Let's further assume that his job is one in which it matters that he is late, such as answering the telephone. He has been late most of the time for the last month. Today, he comes in twenty minutes late, and you decide to deal with the problem using the four steps outlined above.

You might start by saying "James, how would you describe your performance in answering the phone around here so far today?" This statement will probably elicit a statement from him acknowledging that he was late. You could then go on with "James, I'm confused by this. You usually show a high sense of responsibility in your work. What will you do to make sure you are here on time tomorrow?"

Before you finish this last sentence, James will probably interrupt with one of the fourteen brilliant excuses he made up as he was dashing toward the office. "Well you see, what happened was that I had trouble finding a parking place today. There must be some convention or something in town. I just couldn't find one anywhere."

When confronted by an excuse, you could listen to it if you like. But when he is done, come back and insist on the performance expectation. " Given that that may happen again tomorrow, what will you do to make sure you're here on time?"

You continue to do this, no matter how many excuses James throws at you. Imagine, for example that he persists and says "Oh, I'm sure it won't happen tomorrow. It never has before."

- "What happened yesterday?"

"Yesterday? Was I late yesterday too?"

- "Yes, you were ten minutes late yesterday."

"Oh. Well, yesterday there was heavy traffic on the freeway."

- "Given that there might be heavy traffic on the freeway again tomorrow, what are you going to do to make sure you're here on time?"

He may object at this point with something like "You mean it's my fault if there's traffic on the freeway or no parking?"

- "No. I'm sure that's God's fault. But given that God seems to play these little tricks on you, what are you going to do to make sure you're here on time?"

"Are you trying to say I should leave earlier?"

- "Not necessarily. I'm asking you what you think you need to do to get here on time."

"Okay, I'll leave earlier."

This may seem sufficient, victory, but remember that the volunteer's plan must be specific. Ask for details. Make sure the plan seems workable to you. "What time will you leave?"

"Oh, I don't know. I guess I'll leave at twenty to eight."

- "Is that really early enough time to get here by eight?"

"It should be."

- "What time do you leave now?"

"Ten 'til."

- "You were fifteen minutes late today, is leaving ten minutes earlier really going to do it?"

"Okay. I'll leave at twenty-five til."

Sometimes the volunteer may attempt to divert you into a discussion of someone else's performance: "Why aren't you talking to Mary? Mary was even later than I was yesterday."

In such a case, it is important to keep the volunteer's own performance as the focus of the conversation. "Mary's performance is a matter for me to discuss with Mary. What we are talking about here is your performance. I believe you have the capability to do a good job for us here. Please tell me what you will do to get here on time."

Sometimes the volunteer will attempt to minimize the performance problem. James might say, for example "Why is it such a big deal if I'm here exactly at eight or not."

In such a case, you need to explain the importance of the performance expectation. "James, your job is to answer the phone. It is important that someone do this so staff can do their interviews of clients without interruption. This morning, seven people called us between eight and eight fifteen, and you failed to answer any of them. When you are here, you do an excellent job. Can you tell me what you will do to get here on time?"

These four steps will generally improve the performance. The next two steps are supportive of the first four.

Step Five: Give praise for any improvement in performance

Say "That's more like it," or "You get better every day." But if the behavior is still unacceptable, repeat step four, asking how they will do even better the next time. As performance improves, make praise more difficult to earn.

Step Six: As performance improves, repeat step three

Praise the traits that are starting to be exhibited. Such validations will enhance the self-esteem of the volunteer and make him feel good about the work he is doing.

Sometimes, however, the behavior may continue to be unacceptable. If so, we recommend going through the first four steps again but to let him know that you must have improved performance. Make sure the employee knows you are serious. If he still performs at an unacceptable level, you should replace him with a volunteer who can do the job.

Fortunately, most of the supervisory experiences with volunteers will be pleasant, and you will be spending more time on assisting dedicated volunteers to maximize their performance. It is good, however, to be prepared for the exception, since it is one of the clear responsibilities of the Volunteer Program Manager to protect the program and the other volunteers by dealing quickly and conclusively with problem volunteers. Failing to deal with problem volunteers gives clear sign to staff and other volunteers that you are not willing to enforce quality control standards.

Not Becoming Part of the Problem Yourself

It is critical not to become a contributing part of the problem, something that is easier to do than you may think.

Managers will often avoid dealing with problem volunteers, for several reasons:

1. You may not want to admit that you have a problem volunteer because you think it reflects badly on you and your supervisory skill.

2. You don't want to confront the volunteer because you're too nice and you think that as a volunteer they should be allowed some latitude.

3. You're friends with the volunteer and don't want to appear to be criticizing them.

4. You're wrapped up in your own work and don't need any more problems to deal with.

5. You may feel sorry for the volunteer, feeling that the lack of performance is not really their fault.

Avoiding problems seldom eliminates them, and usually allows them to build into more complex and troublesome situations. Being a manager means being willing to deal with managerial problems. You can also become part of the problem by how you approach a problem situation. Here are some common ways for a manager to exacerbate a problem situation:

- *Overreacting*. Some managers explode at petty

situations, lashing out at others, especially when they are harboring some resentment for past transgressions.

- *Whining*. Some managers will spend their time complaining to others about the problem rather than directly dealing with the person involved.
- *Lecturing*. Some managers will treat offenders as though they were children, lecturing to them rather than talking with them. This technique doesn't even work very well with children.
- *Nuking*. Some managers avoid confronting problems until they unleash a massive retaliatory strike, annihilating everyone in their path.

Probably the prime sin that a manager can have is laziness, which in the case of problem volunteers often results in lax interviewing and screening processes, which allows the problem person into the volunteer program in the first place. Always remember that interviewing is the key quality control element in volunteer management.

Why Good Volunteers May Choose to Do Bad Things

John has been a volunteer with Meals on Wheels for seven years since his retirement. He came to the program out of a sense of restlessness and loneliness, but has found himself a home. He delivers meals on three days a week and has established many friendships along his accustomed route.

One day while he is delivering meals to Anne Johnson, a regular client, he stopped for a moment to ask how she is doing, since he has learned over the years that health problems due to aging have begun to afflict her. She says she is doing "fine," but that she hasn't been getting much rest because of a broken window shutter that bangs in the night wind, keeping her awake.

On his next meal delivery date, John showed up at Anne's house with his old box of tools, and proceeds to repair the shutter. Mrs. Johnson is quite pleased. John also is pleased by the results, and thereafter makes a point of looking for additional projects as he makes his rounds...

Eventually his program supervisor heard about his extra-duty activities and asked John about them, pointing out that Meals on Wheels isn't really in the home repair business. She told John that he will have to leave his toolbox at home or he will be suspended from his volunteer position. John is perplexed and disturbed. After all, he was just trying to help, wasn't he?

From a psychological standpoint, the act of volunteering is an interesting one, since it would suggest that the volunteer is acting without any self-interest, the classic altruist. In reality, however, the situation is much more complex, and as every volunteer manager knows, volunteers meet their own motivational needs through the act of volunteering. Occasionally, however, the strong urge to meet these motivational needs can conflict in strange ways with the operation of the volunteer program, causing volunteers whose behavior is otherwise good, if not exemplary, to behave in seemingly destructive ways.

Diagramming Relationships in Volunteer Programs
Let's start by drawing some diagrams of relationships in volunteer programs.

Most volunteer programs begin with a client who has problems. These problems may range from internal conditions to external situations and they may be big and complicated or small and highly defined. At any rate, they create a state of "need" in the client. We can express this state of need on the part of the client by drawing a circle that represents the entire nature of the client and then imagining that one segment of it is a location where this sub-state of need exists:

Diagram One
Circle of Client Needs

Social services agencies are created to address or solve these needs of this client. Usually the agency is not designed to solve all possible needs of the client, but is designed to address some specific issue, such as a need for hot food in the Meals on Wheels program or a need to enhance literacy in a tutoring program. In a sense the relationship that exists between the client and the agency can be diagramed by drawing a second circle overlapping the first. In this diagram there is an overlap between the "need" of the client (to solve their problem or condition; to obtain help) with the "need" of the agency (to engage in meaningful work toward achieving their mission).

Diagram Two
Overlap of Agency and Client Needs

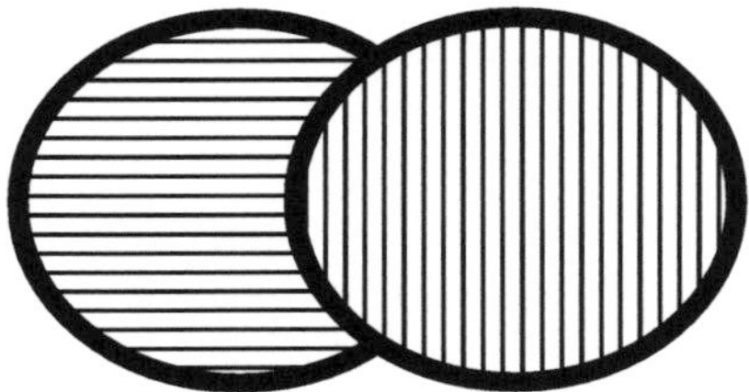

This area of overlap is what really creates the helping relationship between the two parties; it identifies the parameters within which they "need" each other.

Since social service agencies usually lack sufficient resources they often seek help in the form of volunteers. These volunteers have motivational needs of their own which tend to draw them toward particular causes or agencies and toward working on particular tasks with particular types of clients. The volunteers tend to identify with the tasks and clients and develop motivational satisfaction out of performing work to assist the agency and its clients. When you add the volunteer's needs to our already diagramed relationships, you get the following:

Diagram Three
Overlap of Volunteer, Agency and Client Needs

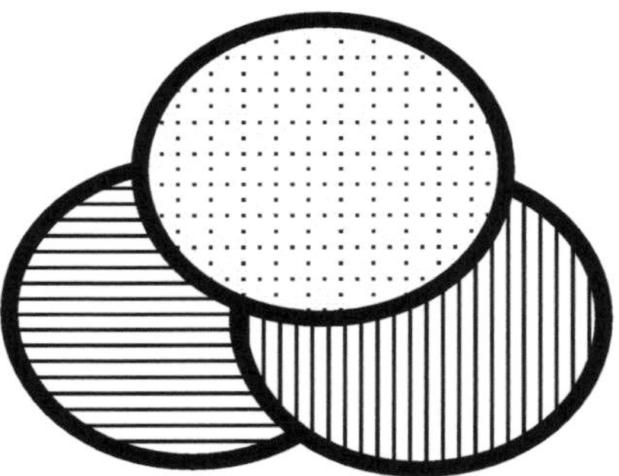

The areas of overlap actually represent the areas or ways in which complementary motivational needs are being met. The overlap between the agency and clients represents both the meeting of the client's need for assistance and the agency's need to perform work. The overlap between the volunteer and the agency represents meeting the agency's need for additional workforce with the volunteer's need for association and meaningful work. As a general rule, the larger the area of overlap the greater the meeting of motivational needs and the deeper the attraction and bonding between the various entities.

To show you how this seemingly simple system can be used to explain "bad" volunteer behavior, let's take a specific example.

The Misbehaving CASA Volunteer

One of our favorite volunteer programs is called Court Appointed Special Advocates. CASA is a program in which volunteers are recruited to serve as advocates for children who are enmeshed within the justice system, often because their parents are defendants in child abuse or neglect cases. The CASA volunteer looks after the interest of the child during the proceedings, providing an impartial representative whose sole aim is insuring that the best interests of the child are met.

The overall mission of the CASA program can be described best in the descriptive language utilized by its national organization:

A safe, permanent home isn't something a child should only dream about. Almost half a million children in the United States live in foster care, meant to be a temporary haven. They have been removed from their homes, not because they did anything wrong, but because they've been abused or neglected. It's frightening and confusing for these children to suddenly find themselves in the complex world of social workers, attorneys and judges, people who have the power to decide where they will live and whether they will go home or be freed for adoption. Sometimes, these children can spend years in foster care, waiting for those decisions to be made. With overburdened caseloads, a social worker may not have the time to give the thorough attention these children deserve. They may simply not have the time to listen. One judge had an idea to help these children find a way into safe, permanent homes more quickly. His idea was CASA -- Court Appointed Special Advocates -- trained volunteers who would be appointed by a judge to speak up for the best interests of a child. Now, there are approximately 42,400 CASA volunteers helping abused and neglected children all across the country. But 3/4 of the children who need a CASA don't have one. You can help those girls and boys have a voice in court, and a chance at a future.

CASA volunteers tend to be highly dedicated to their work, capable of dealing with both the rigors and intricacies of our legal system as well as the disturbing treatment that has been accorded their young charges. They are subject to a rigorous screening process and receive extensive training on how to approach their volunteer work successfully. CASA standards provide minimum supervisory ratio requirements to ensure that adequate staff monitoring and support is provided for all volunteers.

They are, in many ways, among the most highly qualified and committed volunteers in the country. You might expect their behavior to always reflect these qualities. CASA strives to maintain high standards. It has, in fact, a set of national program standards, one of which relates directly to volunteer management. Among its edicts is the following:

The CASA volunteer does not engage in the following activities:

- taking a child home;
- giving legal advice or therapeutic counseling;
- making placement arrangements for the child;
- giving money or expensive gifts to the child or family.

These activities are prohibited because they conflict with the need for the CASA volunteer to maintain objectivity in representing the best interests of the child. The CASA volunteer is not intended to be a companion for the child, such as in a Big Brothers program, instead they are an advocate for the best interest of the child, and they need to maintain some distance in the relationship in order to maintain and demonstrate their neutrality. Doing so is vital both to maintaining a good working relationship with the child and with maintaining credibility with judges, attorneys, social workers and others in the justice system with whom they work. Engaging in any of the prohibited activities can be grounds for discipline or even termination of the volunteer.

But if you talk with CASA volunteer managers you will find numerous examples of volunteers who are caught breaking these rules, usually through providing gifts to children or taking them within their own homes to provide a moment of safety and shelter.

Why are these good volunteers consciously doing something that they know is "wrong"?

Why Good Volunteers Will Intentionally Break Rules

To understand this phenomenon, we have to go back to our diagram of relationships.

In a well-operating volunteer/agency/client relationships there is a balancing of motivational needs and interests:

Diagram Four
Agency, Client, Volunteer Overlap

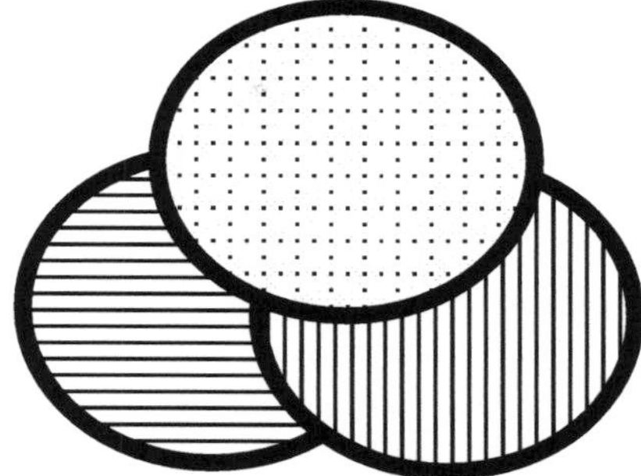

Each party actually has a relationship with two other parties, both giving and getting something from the connection. In volunteer programs that match volunteers with particular clients, however, there seems to be an inherent tendency for this overlap to begin to stray, or to become unbalanced.

The volunteer who is assigned to work with a particular client both needs to establish a relationship with that client in order to be successful. They must develop a sense of trust, liking, respect and bonding for the client, one that usually is reciprocal in nature. Volunteer and client must, in a sense, become friends.

Often the strength and attraction of this friendly bond between the volunteer and the client will grow to be quite strong over time, but in fact it can be very powerful even from the very beginning in volunteers who are highly motivated by the needs of the client group. A recent study done for CASA, for example, determined that a child involved in the CASA program would be likely to use the following descriptions about their relationship with the CASA volunteer who is assigned to them:

- "Always there for me; I wasn't alone."
- "Made me feel loved/special/important."
- "Listened to me."
- "Helped me get what I needed."

You will notice that none of these have anything to do with what a CASA volunteers actually "does," i.e., provide objective representation for the interests of the child in court. Nonetheless, these descriptions are what the child feels and, most significantly, they are also what the volunteer sees and feels from the child. And, in many cases, they are what begins to dominate the motivational framework of the volunteer - the "need" to provide as much help as possible to the child and to provide it as quickly as possible.

In a sense, CASA creates the likelihood of this occurring by the very language used in recruiting volunteers. Volunteers are not sought because of their interest in mastering the intricacies of our legal system; instead, they are recruited because of their interest in helping children - "a safe and permanent home for every child." CASA posters show pictures of appealing children, give examples of the pain and suffering they have felt, and are specifically designed to appeal to those who feel most compelled to provide help in creating happy lives for the child. The very people most likely to be highly motivated to volunteer to help the child by joining CASA are also the people who are most likely to eventually move toward assisting the child in inappropriate ways, violating the boundaries of their volunteer position.

This shift is easy to "see" if we go back to our diagrams. What has happened is that the motivational overlap has become unbalanced, with the volunteer identifying more with child than with the agency and identifying with needs of the child that do not come with the purview of these services provided by the agency:

Diagram Five
Overlap Slippage
among Agency,
Client, and
Volunteer

The fascinating thing is that those volunteers who are the most dedicated and the most committed are the ones who are most likely to move in this direction. Their own high levels of motivation are what push them to break the rules. This problem is endemic in cases where volunteers are assigned to work one-to-one with clients, but it also exists in other programs such as in crisis telephone centers where volunteers often will give advice outside the parameters of the "approved" answers or in Meals on Wheels programs where drivers suddenly start providing new and different arrays of services to the clients. To each of these volunteers what they are doing, despite being directly contrary to agency policy, seems to be absolutely the "right" thing to do.

Keeping Highly Motivated Volunteers on Track

The unfortunate thing is that while what the volunteers are doing is needed and worthy it doesn't conform to the limitations of the agency. Meals programs are not designed to do home repair. CASA volunteers are not mentors and companions. Sooner or later, straying outside the parameters of the agency only results in problems for all concerned.

So how do you restrain these powerful and natural instincts of the volunteer without destroying their motivation to continue volunteering?

Here are tactics ways we can suggest:

1. Adopt and communicate to all volunteers a "non-abandonment" policy regarding client needs that they encounter that do not fall into the normal work of the agency. Urge volunteers to bring these needs to you and let them know that you will work to find some way of meeting the needs, usually through referral to another agency. Stress to the volunteer that the agency will not intend to "abandon" the client. It is crucial to maintain open communication with the volunteers regarding these issues, and it is equally crucial to get them to know that you are on the same side as they are - each of you wants to do what it takes to help the client. If a volunteer ever gets the impression that the agency doesn't "care" about the clients they will be much more likely simply to act on their own and they will eventually be likely to stop volunteering for that agency.

2. Provide each volunteer with a clear explanation of why prohibited actions have been prohibited. Do not simply cite rules and refer to "policy." Explain why the agency has chosen not to provide some types of services. There are two generally accepted reasons: that the agency isn't capable of doing a good job in the area and that some other agency does exist to provide the help. You can also point out that in order to accomplish its specific mission the agency has had to make choices about the extent of coverage it can provide. The more volunteers connect to the "mission" of the agency the more likely they are to feel comfortable in keeping inside the boundaries of that mission and not straying.

3. Provide clear rules and procedures, with specific examples of prohibited actions, and build these into "what if" training scenarios for all volunteers. A

volunteer is most likely to stray when they meet a new situation which has not been covered in any agency discussion; the volunteer will then tend to act on their own "natural" instincts. As you encounter examples of volunteers "doing the wrong thing," collect them and use them as discussion scenarios during orientation and training. Over time this will build a set of collective wisdom about "right action" that will tend to be emulated by new volunteers. In one sense, you can intentionally create an ethic of keeping within agency boundaries, telling stories of the volunteer who "resisted temptation" and who "did the right thing."

4. Build a sense of personal connection and bonding between the agency and the volunteer that will counter-balance the relationship between the volunteer and the client. This can be done by making the volunteer feel like they are a "part" of the agency, including them in decisions, fostering their sense of identify with agency operations. It can also be done by developing personal relationships between staff and volunteers. One warning about this, however. The most common bonding occurs between the volunteer and their immediate supervisor, often the volunteer manager. A clear danger is created when this bond is severed by the departure of the staff person with whom the volunteer has bonded. In this all-too-frequent instance, the volunteer will experience a sense of loss and will often replenish their sense of connectedness by turning to the client and seeking to strengthen that relationship.

5. Develop a system of peer pressure by creating bonds among volunteers. In a sense this adds another circle to our diagram:

Diagram Six
Volunteers, Volunteer,
Agency, Client Needs Overlap

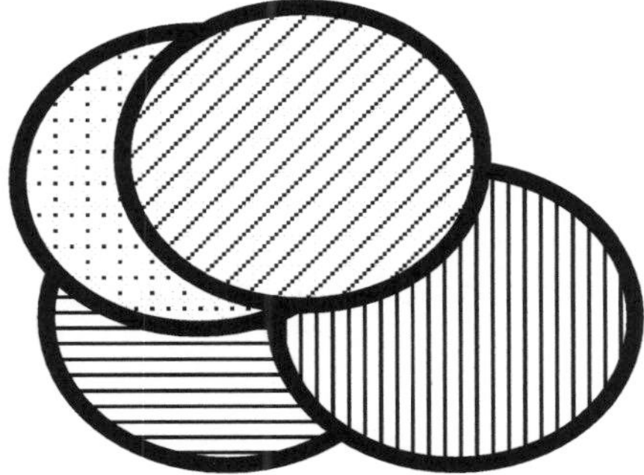

If volunteers relate to one another they will tend to reinforce good behavior patterns, because individuals will not want to "let their buddies down." Adding additional volunteers to our diagram allows us to counterbalance the altruistic needs of the volunteer which are directed to the client with the social needs of the volunteer which will be directed toward their peers.

The Good, the Bad and the Inevitable

What all this indicates is that the high motivational levels that initially cause people to volunteer have some potentially negative sides. High motivation can lead to burnout. It can also lead to disillusionment if expectations cannot be met. Each of these will result in volunteers leaving a program.

And, as discussed here, it can also lead a perfectly good volunteer to sometimes engage in behavior that is "bad" from the context of a program, but which is entirely rational from the viewpoint of the volunteer who is determined and eager to help a client they value. Volunteers have always been known for being willing to "do a little extra," and this is just one more case of where that willingness is perhaps an inherent part of the volunteer experience.

Releasing a Volunteer from Service

The steps we've outlined earlier in this chapter advocate a calmer, more rational, and more progressive approach. They view the manager as a coach and consultant to volunteers, recognizing that none of us are perfect, all of us have and cause problems occasionally, and most of us are amendable to improvement if we are approached in the right way.

This section will consider what the organization may need to do when its needs are not being met, and when the volunteer has failed to meet the expectations in performance or behavior required by the organization. We'll examine this from a variety of different perspectives, beginning with attempting to avoid having the issue becoming critical.

Alternatives to Releasing a Volunteer

It is crucial to remember that many situations that appear to warrant releasing a volunteer may actually be remediable by less stringent methods. Before contemplating releasing a volunteer, see if any of the following approaches may be more appropriate and less painful:

- *Re-supervise.*

You may have a volunteer who doesn't understand that rules have to be followed. This is a common problem with youth volunteers, some of whom automatically "test" the rules as part of their self-expression. Enforcement may end the problem.

- *Re-assign.*

Transfer the volunteer to a new position. You may, on the basis of a short interview, have mis-read their skills or inclinations. They may simply not be getting along with the staff or other volunteers with whom they are working. Try them in a new setting and see what happens.

- *Re-train.*

Send them back for a second education. Some people take longer than others to learn new techniques. Some may require a different training approach, such as one-on-one mentoring rather than classroom lectures. If the problem is lack of knowledge rather than lack of motivation, then work to provide the knowledge.

- *Re-vitalize.*

If a long-time volunteer has started to malfunction, he or she may just need a rest. This is particularly true with volunteers who have intense assignments, such as one-to-one work with troubled clients. In such cases volunteers may not realize or admit that they're burned out. Give them a sabbatical and let them re-charge. Or transfer them temporarily to something that is less emotionally draining.

- *Refer.*

Maybe they just need a whole new outlook on life, one they can only get by volunteering in an entirely different organization. Refer them to the Volunteer Center or set up an exchange program with a sister agency. Swap your volunteers for a few months and let them learn a few new tricks.

- *Retire.*

Recognize that some volunteers may no longer be able to do the work they once could and may even be a danger to themselves and to others. Give them the honor they deserve and ensure that they don't end their volunteer careers in a way they will regret. Assist them in departing with dignity before the situation becomes a crisis.

All of these alternatives are easier to implement and managerially smarter than making a decision to release a volunteer. They recognize that there are many reasons why a person may be behaving inappropriately, and that some of these reasons have answers other than dismissing that person.

We strongly urge that you consider each of these alternatives before deciding to fire any volunteer.

Establishing a Supportive Release Process

One of the recurrent nightmares of any Volunteer Program Manager is encountering a situation where they may have to consider "firing" a volunteer. For many, this prospect creates severe stress, both over the appropriateness of the action and over fear of possible legal and political consequences. Cook in a survey of Foster Grandparents Programs in 23 communities found that 82% of responding Volunteer Program Managers rated the decision to terminate a volunteer as being a "difficult or very difficult issue" for them. More than 60% of the Volunteer Program Managers reported delaying dealing with the problem and over 73% of managers did not have a termination plan or policy to guide them in the decision.

Consciously or not, many volunteer program managers are subject to what McCurley and Vineyard refer to as "Myths about Problem Volunteers:"

1. *If I ignore the problem it will go away.*
2. *No one else notices.*
3. *I can fix a dysfunctional person.*
4. *There's good in everyone...we just need to give them time to show it.*
5. *A confrontation will make things worse. They might get mad.*
6. *A confrontation will result in the volunteer leaving the program and, if they do, the program will fall apart.*
7. *If I'm a truly caring person, I can handle all the people who are problems.*
8. *Everyone wants to be fixed.*

Lee and Catagnus describe the multiple dilemmas facing the Volunteer Program Manager in a termination decision:

"Failing to act affects your reputation and the reputation of volunteers, and may put your organization at risk. Terminating the volunteer may also affect your reputation and may result in a bitter ending for a volunteer whose affiliation was valued by the organization and was, for the volunteer, a source of great pride. There are no easy answers..."

This reluctance probably occurs because most Volunteer Program Managers are very people-oriented and respect the willingness of others to help. There is particular difficulty in dealing with situations in which the decision to terminate was not because of any particular "fault" on the part of the volunteer, but is instead because of ill health or a change in program needs. Where volunteering is viewed as a benefit to the volunteer (such as in some volunteer programs for retired citizens), people have difficulty with termination because they mentally classify volunteers as "clients," and it is difficult to justify terminating a client.

One important thing to remember is that the decision to terminate the relationship between an agency and a volunteer is not a "judgment" of the volunteer or their character or any other aspect of their being. It is simply recognition that in the immediate circumstances the relationship has reached a point where it is not productive. Just as the volunteer may reach this determination and resign, so the agency can reach a similar determination, and ask the volunteer to leave. The underlying cause of the situation may, in truth, be the fault of the agency or of the volunteer. Often, however, it is the "fault" of neither – things just didn't work out. Not all volunteers can fit into all settings. Not all agencies can prove productive for all volunteers.

Getting Philosophically Ready to Release a Volunteer

The initial requirement in a system for handling volunteer termination is the decision that firing volunteers is, in the appropriate circumstances, a necessary action. There are several rationales for firing volunteers. One is that the bottom line is the ability to deliver quality service to the clients of the agency, and any barrier to that delivery is not allowable. This standard would apply to both paid and unpaid staff.

A second rationale has to do with giving meaning and value to volunteer service. By denying that there is a "right" and a "wrong" way to do a volunteer position, one conveys the impression that the volunteer work done is irrelevant and insignificant. An organization that does not care enough about the work done by volunteers to enforce quality communicates to other volunteers that the agency believes their own work to be meaningless.

The philosophical decision by an agency to fire volunteers is one that should be addressed before any need to do so arises. It should be discussed and ratified by staff and then codified as part of the overall policy statement on volunteer use and included as part of the agency's volunteer policies.

Establishing Standards for Volunteer Conduct

If behavioral issues, especially those regarding relationships between volunteers and clients, are a possibility, then the organization should establish a Code of Conduct to indicate the parameter of proper behavior.

As an example, here is the Code of Conduct for Big Brothers and Big Sisters of Canada:

- *Volunteers agree to conduct themselves in a manner consistent with their position as a positive role model to a child, and as a representative of the Agency.*

- *Volunteers will follow Agency policy and guidelines around the safety of the child as outlined in the Agency's Child Safety Program and not engage in any behaviour that may be perceived as being sexual and/or abusive with the Child or any member of the Child's family.*

- *Volunteers agree to respect the privacy and dignity of their Little/Mentee and family by not divulging confidential information without consent, except where required by law as in the case of suspected child abuse.*

- *Volunteers agree to limit their involvement in a child's life to what is deemed appropriate by the agency. Volunteers are seen as an influence, not a dominant factor, in the child's life.*

- *The adult-child relationship is based on mutual respect. Volunteers agree to treat the child in a respectful way at all times.*

- *Volunteers agree to allow their Little or Mentee to develop their friendship at their own pace.*

- *Volunteers are required to discuss problems, issues, concerns, or changes of circumstances (living situation, change of address, phone number etc) with the Agency contact person.*

- *In the event of match closure, Volunteers must be sensitive to the impact that this can have on the child, and take the necessary steps to minimize upset to the child. All matches are to be formally closed by the agency caseworker.*

Court Appointed Special Advocates utilizes the following grounds for dismissal:

Grounds for dismissal may include, but are not limited to:

- *Violation of program policies and procedures, court rules, or law*
- *Gross misconduct or insubordination*
- *Being under the influence of alcohol or drugs while performing volunteer duties*
- *Theft of property or misuse of program equipment or materials*
- *Mistreatment or inappropriate conduct toward clients, families, co-workers or cooperating agency personnel*
- *Taking action without program or court approval that endangers the child or is outside the role or powers of the program*
- *Failure to complete required initial or ongoing training*
- *Failure to accept assignments over a period of twelve months*
- *Breach of confidentiality*
- *Failure to satisfactorily perform assigned duties*
- *Conflict of interest which can not be resolved*
- *Falsification of application materials or misrepresentation of facts during the screening process*
- *Falsification of any materials included in a report to the court*
- *Failure to report significant case information to the court*
- *Criminal activities*
- *Existence of child abuse or neglect allegations*
- *Initiation of ex-parte communication with the court*

Developing a System for Making Release Decisions
If you do encounter a situation where none of the alternatives work, it is helpful to have in place a system for dealing with the problem. The system we propose is designed to help the Volunteer Program Manager in making and in justifying the decision to terminate a volunteer. Essentially, it has three parts:

1. Forewarning/notice
The first stage of the system is developing clear policies and information about the prospect of firing volunteers. To do this you need to develop the following:

- *A set of official personnel policies regarding the involvement of volunteers.*

It is especially important to have policies on probation, suspension, and termination. The policies should also outline the procedures for disciplinary action. The policies should be very similar, if not identical, to those used with paid staff.

- *A system for informing volunteers, in advance, about these policies.*

Volunteer handbooks or manuals should describe the policy and its procedures. Volunteer orientations should discuss the policies and provide examples of requirements and unacceptable behavior.

- *A mechanism for relating these policies to each volunteer position.*

This means having a position description for the volunteer that explains the requirements of the position, and has some measurable objectives for determining whether the work is being accomplished satisfactorily.

The intent of this stage is to ensure that volunteers are given adequate information regarding expectations and policies of the organization. As Cook notes: *"When the rules are not clear at the outset, enforcement may be nearly impossible."*

2. Investigation/determination
The second part of the system involves developing a process for determining whether the volunteer has broken the rules. This implies having a fair investigator take the time to examine the situation and reach a decision that something has been done wrongly. You should never terminate a volunteer "on the spot," regardless of the infraction. "Instant firing" will not allow you to determine whether there are extenuating circumstances. This is why a suspension policy is so important.

Essentially, in this part of the system the Volunteer Program Manager needs to establish a process for reviewing the performance of volunteers and recording problems. This should be done as part of the regular evaluation process for volunteers. Those volunteers whose performance is unsatisfactory are told of their deficiency, counseled on improving their work, and then re-evaluated. Failure to conform to the quality standard over time then can become grounds for termination. In cases where the unsatisfactory performance is not incremental, but is substantial in nature (inappropriate relations with a client or breach of confidentiality) then what is needed is some proof that the volunteer did in fact commit the wrongdoing. This might be testimony from other volunteers, staff, or the client.

During this part of the process, the Volunteer Program Manager also investigates whether any of the alternatives to termination would provide a more appropriate solution and determines whether the cause of the behavior may be linked to some failure in management on the part of the organization. These might include:

- Failure to provide an adequate or clear standard for behavior or performance in this area
- Failure to place the volunteer in a position for which they are suited and qualified
- Failure to provide adequate information or equipment for the volunteer to perform their work
- Failure in supervising and providing instructional feedback to the volunteer

3. Application
This final part of the system requires that the Volunteer Program Manager do a fair job of enforcing the system. It requires equal and fair application of the rules (no playing favorites), appropriate penalties (graduated to the severity of the offense) and, if possible, a review process, so that the decision does not look like a personal one.

You will note that the above three processes mirror the common personnel practices for paid staff. They are, in fact the same, as they should be, since evaluating either paid or unpaid staff should follow the same rules.

The steps above may be slightly different in various organizations. 4-H, for example, has a system of four ascending steps:

1. An official warning letter to the volunteer indicating specific information or areas that need improvement
2. Follow-up counseling along with a letter of documentation
3. Probation with explicit goals
4. Termination

The advantages of this system are two-fold. First, they assist the Volunteer Program Manager in reaching the right decision, and in feeling comfortable about making that decision. The system is fair to both the volunteer and the agency if properly followed and tends to produce "correct" answers. It also allows the Volunteer Program Manager to divert to a less drastic solution where appropriate. Second, the system helps develop a case for firing that can be used to explain the decision to others, internally and externally. A side effect of this systematic approach is that many problem volunteers decide voluntarily to resign rather than face the inevitable and seemingly inexorable conclusion of the dismissal process. Most people prefer not to sit in front of an oncoming train. This allows the volunteer to "save face," which will make it much less likely that frustration will lead to further reactions against the agency. One consequence to be avoided is an outraged former volunteer who decides to make the conflict public.

Documenting the Case for Termination
While lawsuits by volunteers against organizations for termination are rare, it is increasingly essential to make sure that you not only have a good reason for firing a volunteer, but also have the documentation to establish the validity of that reason to others. Key elements in this documentation are:

1. Records of the deficiencies in the volunteer's performance, giving as precise a description as possible of specific, observable behavior of the volunteer which violates agency rules or procedures.
2. Written records of the times you speak to the volunteer about their conduct or performance, with indications of the steps they agree to take to correct the problem and notes on the timeframe for any change in behavior.
3. Records of statements by others about the conduct or performance of the volunteers, preferably signed by the individual giving the testimony.
4. Records of the steps in the evaluation and assessment process, including warnings to the volunteer, performance agreements, formal evaluation forms, etc. Make sure that the volunteer receives copies of all memos which are directed to them, but it is not necessary to give the volunteer a copy of memorandum that you write to the personnel file or to others about their behavior.

You may discover behavior which would prompt you to dismiss a volunteer, but in reviewing their personnel file notice that all other documentation about their past behavior is either missing or else contains no criticism. In this case, you should be cautious, and take the time to see whether tough action is warranted. This is one of the occasions when new volunteer managers have been justified in cursing their predecessors, who may have left them with a problem but with no personnel file to indicate its extent or duration, or to help build a case for resolving the problem. A special section of Management Hell is reserved for those people.

Conducting the Release Meeting

Regardless of how the decision to terminate is reached, someone has to convey that decision to the volunteer. This will never be a pleasant experience, but here are some tips that may help:

• *Conduct the meeting in a private setting.*
This will preserve your dignity and that of the volunteer. The major reason for inviting witnesses is if you have serious questions about the psychological stability of the volunteer and are worried about your safety.

• *Be quick, direct, and absolute.*
Don't beat around the bush. It is embarrassing to have the volunteer show up for work the next day because they didn't get the hint. Practice the exact words you will use, and make sure they are unequivocal. Do not back down from them, even if you want to preserve your image as a "nice person."

• *Announce, don't argue.*
The purpose of the meeting is simply, and solely, to communicate to the volunteer that he is being separated from the agency. This meeting is not to re-discuss and re-argue the decision, because, if you have followed the system, all the arguments will already have been heard. You should also avoid arguing to make sure you don't put your foot in your mouth while venting your feelings. Expect the volunteer to vent, but keep quiet and do not respond, especially emotionally. Remember the old adage: "a closed mouth gathers no feet."

• *Do not attempt to counsel.*
If counseling were an option, you would not be having this meeting. Face reality; at this point you are not the friend of this former volunteer, and any attempt to appear so is misguided. Giving advice demeans the volunteer and makes it more likely that they will experience additional anger. It adds insult to injury. It also wastes your time.

• *Be prepared to end the discussion.*
You want to allow terminated volunteers some time to vent their emotions, but at some point you may need to announce that the discussion is over and that it is time for them to depart.

• *Follow-up.*
After the meeting write a letter to the volunteer reiterating the decision and informing him or her of any departure details. Make sure you also follow-up with others. Inform staff and clients of the change in status, although you do not need to inform them of the reasons behind the change. In particular, make sure that clients with a long relationship with the volunteer are informed of the new volunteer to whom they are assigned and work to foster that relationship as quickly as possible. The intent of these actions is to ensure interactions involving the terminated volunteer and the organizations or its clients are less likely to happen.

Fortunately, most of the supervisory experiences with volunteers will be pleasant, and you will be spending more time on assisting dedicated volunteers to maximize their performance. It is good, however, to be prepared for the exception, since it is one of the clear responsibilities of the Volunteer Program Manager to protect the program and the other volunteers by dealing quickly and conclusively with problem volunteers. Failing to deal with problem volunteers gives clear sign to staff and other volunteers that you are not willing to enforce quality control standards.

When the Volunteer is Not at Fault

The most difficult managerial problem in volunteer management relates to the decision as to whether or not to terminate the connection with a volunteer when the unsatisfactory performance is not the "fault" of the volunteer. In some cases this can be resolved by re-assigning the volunteer to a different position or providing additional training or support, but many volunteer programs are dealing with this situation in a more difficult scenario – the dedicated volunteer who, through age or incapacity, has reached a point where they are incapable of performing their volunteer assignment and may in fact pose a danger to themselves or others. We'll look at both of these situations.

Dealing with Changes in Volunteers Over Time

As volunteer management expert Joe Lovelady points out, motivational problems (as opposed to skill deficiencies) often stem from the volunteers' motivational needs changing over time. As Lovelady points out, "Most of us need opportunities beyond work and family to satisfy all of our motivational needs. This is the primary purpose of outside activities. In order to keep a person interested and committed to a volunteer job, it must meet the particular combination of needs that motivate a volunteer to engage in outside activities."

A person's motivational needs will vary depending on their changing life situations. Throughout life, we all find ourselves in situations about which we need more information or support in order to cope successfully. Lovelady cites these examples of life situations that may change our unmet needs:

- Puberty
- Moving to a new town
- Leaving school
- Marriage
- Pregnancy
- Child birth
- Divorce
- Unemployment
- Retirement
- Illness
- Children leaving home
- Death of a spouse

When entering each of these situations, the mix of needs that primarily motivate the volunteer to engage in outside activities may change. For example, a person whose spouse dies may experience a greater need for contact with others. She may have been happy doing a volunteer job by herself, but now may want something to do that she can do with others. On the other hand, a single volunteer with a high need for feeling part of a group, may have that need drop off when he gets engaged.

When a volunteer encounters a change in his life situation, we may need to change the volunteer's job, hours, or type of recognition. We need to be flexible about the volunteer experience so that we provide the volunteer with the "motivational paycheck" he or she finds satisfactory.

Dealing with Age-related Incapacity among Volunteers

Fraser and Gottlieb describe this phenomenon among long-term care providers in Canada, who typically have an aging pool of volunteers:

"...the staff of two different Day Programs observed that the volunteers who assist them show forgetfulness, personality quirks that interfere with their ability to relate to clients, physical frailty that precludes their ability to push a wheelchair or physically support a client with mobility problems, and excessive or inappropriate verbalization."

One staff person interviewed went on to comment "it sometimes feels like the volunteers are an extra client group."

Here are some suggestions for dealing with this type of situation:

1. First, try to determine what is really happening. Some indicators may be a clear drop in the abilities of the volunteer, increased absenteeism, health problems, reports of difficulty from other volunteers and staff, etc. Particularly with aging volunteers some conditions may be a result of changes in medication or a need for medication and can be resolved.

2. Second, determine the possible risks if the volunteer is allowed to continue in service. These include risks to clients due to a volunteer's diminished skills and a possible danger to the volunteer from inability to work safely or from personal health problems. Dangers to the volunteer themselves are quite common. Cook, in a study of RSVP volunteer programs, found that 86% of those responding indicated that health concerns of the volunteer were usually the cause of sub-standard performance, forcing the need for retirement or termination.

3. Third, determine if there are other roles that the volunteer can honorably fill. Some roles may involve utilizing the skills and historical experience that the volunteer has acquired (such as in a mentor role), others may involve transferring the volunteer to work that has fewer physical requirements. Creating an "emeritus" advisory group may allow "retired" volunteers to maintain a sense of status, connection and worthwhile releasing them from the obligations of actual service.

4. Fourth, if the decision is made that there is too much risk to the volunteer for them to continue volunteering, then seek support from peers and friends of the volunteer. They may be able to deal more directly with the situation than you can.

5. Fifth, consider ending the volunteer's relationship with the agency in a ceremonial fashion, honoring their years of service. This is particularly suitable when the volunteer has given a sustained contribution over the years; their service deserves more than dismissal. A ceremony in which they are

formally retired, with the name added to the agency "Roll of Honor" is more appropriate than termination.

6. Sometimes it helps to have in place a "retirement age" policy. This is relatively rare among volunteer programs, but if you are facing this situation you might want to consider it, especially if your organization also has a similar policy for paid staff. In the UK, 19% of voluntary organizations with volunteer programs have retirement limits for volunteers, with the upper age limit commonly being set at 70, 75, or 80. Follow-up found that organizations with retirement policies for volunteers justified them as follows:

"Organisations found it easier to have a catchall limit than to decide whether individual volunteers should continue on a case-by-case basis. Such a policy it was argued had the advantage of making it clear when the volunteer should leave without the need for interviews or assessment procedures."

As with all policies, however, make sure you are willing to enforce it in all situations before enacting it. And be aware that some organizations oppose the concept of age limits as a form of discrimination (see, for example, Volunteering England's Age Discrimination and Volunteering Campaign, www.volunteering.org.uk).

Learning from Mistakes

Problem volunteer situations, up to and including termination of a volunteer relationship are, in part, always a sign of some mistake in volunteer management, usually a result of difficulties in interviewing, placing or supervising a particular individual. As such, these incidents, while painful, provide an opportunity to examine and refine an organization's system for involving volunteers. You might want to consider the wise advice of Sarah Jane Rehnborg of the University of Texas:

"...once you have taken action and have assessed the consequences, you may also want to ask what you have learned from this situation that will reduce the likelihood of a similar situation occurring in the future."

Chapter Twelve
Making Volunteers Feel Appreciated

Retaining your volunteers is the key to success. There is no point in being good at recruitment if you cannot keep volunteers coming back. Recruitment is a solution to the problem of not having enough volunteers; retention is a way to avoid the problem altogether. This chapter looks at some aspects of retaining and recognizing volunteers. Those who wish to delve into this topic more deeply should consider looking at our book *Keeping Volunteers: A Guide to Retention*.

Volunteers choose to stop volunteering for a number of reasons. Some of these reasons are beyond the control of an organization or of the volunteer. Others are not. A 1998 study in the United States undertaken by the United Parcel Service Foundation discovered that after "conflicts with more pressing demands" (65%), poor volunteer management was the most frequent reason cited to explain why people stop volunteering:

- Charity was not well managed: 26%
- Charity did not use volunteers' time well: 23%
- Charity did not use volunteers' talents well: 18%
- Volunteers' tasks were not clearly defined: 16%
- Volunteers were not thanked: 9%

Their conclusion was straightforward:

"Poor volunteer management practices result in more lost volunteers than people losing interest because of changing personal or family needs. The best way for volunteer organizations to receive more hours of volunteer service is to be careful managers of the time already being volunteered by people of all ages and from all strata of our volunteer society."

Although not having enough time is the usual answer that volunteers will give for leaving a program, we suspect that this is often an excuse. When people really want to do something in their lives, they make the time.

A Look at Volunteer Motivation

As has been emphasized throughout this book, volunteer programs are fueled by the motivation of the volunteers and the staff of the organization. Problems of volunteer retention can usually be traced to problems of motivation.

A motivated volunteer is one who wants to do the job that needs to be done in the spirit and within the guidelines of the organization. People behave in motivated ways when the work satisfies a need of theirs. Children, for example, are motivated to open birthday presents because doing so meets a psychological need. Starting here, you correctly see that volunteer motivation comes from inside the volunteer, stemming from a set of needs that are satisfied by doing things that are found to be productive.

When you encounter volunteers who are not behaving as you would like, you may label them "unmotivated," but actually this is incorrect. So-called unmotivated people are actually just as motivated as a motivated person. Their behavior meets their motivational needs. However, for reasons you will explore in this chapter, those needs are met in counterproductive ways. They behave in the way they do because doing so is more satisfying than the behavior you would like them to choose. In other words, people behave the way they do for a particular reason.

All Behavior is Motivated

Sometimes, "unmotivated" behavior is caused by frustration. If a volunteer has a high need for achievement, for example, and he sees little to accomplish or "win" in his job, he may choose to set up a win-lose situation with those in authority. For example, a volunteer might go to the board of directors every time there was a disagreement, seeking to get the decision overturned. This so-called "unmotivated" behavior meets the volunteer's need for achievement. It provides a challenge. It creates an opportunity to win.

When we talk about motivating volunteers, we are talking about creating a volunteer experience that allows an individual to meet their motivational needs in ways that are productive for the organization and satisfying for the individual. You remove barriers to motivation by designing satisfying work experiences and create systems that allow the volunteer to meet her needs. You make sure, in other words, that volunteers receive their motivational paycheck for the valuable contributions they make to the work of our organization. This is the essence of volunteer retention.

Because each volunteer has a different combination of needs, each will do best in different working conditions. Some volunteers may be highly motivated by gaining job experience, whereas others may be highly motivated by the desire to meet new people. Still others may have a burning passion to do something to contribute to the cause. For the first type, you need to make sure that they have the opportunity to learn the skills they want to learn. The second must be placed in a work setting where they can work with others. The third needs a job that makes a meaningful contribution to the organization's mission.

This is further complicated by the fact that a volunteer's needs may change over time. For example, a volunteer may work well on an independent project. It satisfies her need to achieve something meaningful. Then her husband dies. Her need to be with others may suddenly become much more important than the need to achieve something meaningful. To satisfy this need and retain the volunteer, you might transfer her to a group project.

To Each His Own Mix

Volunteers have combinations of needs. The art of motivating volunteers lies not only in knowing how to tap a given motivator but in being able to figure out what combination of needs a particular volunteer has. One way to do that is to ask the volunteers periodically. Discuss their rating of the relative importance of the following factors:

- To gain knowledge of community problems
- To maintain skills no longer used otherwise
- To spend "quality time" with members of the family by volunteering together
- To get out of the house
- To make new friends
- To be with old friends who volunteer here
- To gain new skills
- To pay back
- To assuage guilt
- To feel useful
- To make business contacts
- To be part of a prestigious group
- To make a transition to a new life
- To fulfill a moral or religious duty
- To have fun
- To help those less fortunate
- To try out a new career
- To have fun
- To meet a challenge
- To improve the community
- To work with a certain client group
- To be in charge of something
- To be part of a group or a team
- To gain work experience to help get a job
- To meet important people in the community
- To gain status with my employer
- To get community recognition.

The mix of responses will give you a better feeling for why they want to volunteer and what you need to give them in return as their "motivational paycheck". For example, if a volunteer ranks the last three above as her highest needs, you will need to make sure she has a job which does indeed enable her to meet important people and which is highly visible in the community. To make sure that her employer is aware of her contribution, you can send a letter of commendation for her contributions.

Retaining Volunteers

The key to retaining volunteers is to make sure they are getting their particular complex of motivational needs met through their volunteer experience. Another way to say this is that if the volunteer experience makes the volunteers feel good, then they will continue to want to volunteer. When this is occurring across the volunteer program, a positive, enthusiastic climate is created which, in turn, encourages people to continue to volunteer.

An environment most likely to make a volunteer feel good is one that bolsters the volunteer's self-esteem. When the work experience boosts a person's self esteem, she feels good about her job, be it paid or volunteer work. She looks forward to going to the workplace.

Creating an Esteem-Producing Climate for Volunteers

Psychologists Harris Clemes and Reynold Bean have studied self-esteem for many years. They found that people with high self-esteem are people who simultaneously satisfy three particular motivational needs. They enjoy a sense of connectedness, a sense of uniqueness, and a sense of power.

Connectedness

When people feel connected, they feel a sense of belonging, a sense of being part of a relationship with others. In a highly mobile society, where friends and loved ones may live hundreds of miles away and the next door neighbor is sometimes a stranger, this need is often unmet, leaving people with a sense of isolation, dissatisfaction, and loneliness. The psychologist William Glasser points out that this need is often stronger even than the need to survive, in that most people who try to commit suicide do so out of loneliness.

A sense of identification with a work group can meet this need, producing healthier, happier individuals. In our seminars over the past four years, we have surveyed more than 1500 individuals who at one time in their lives felt a positive sense of connectedness. The following factors are most often mentioned as producing this:

- A common goal
- Common values
- Mutual respect
- Mutual trust
- A sense that one group member's weaknesses are made up for by another group member's strengths.

Positive feelings of connectedness can be enhanced in volunteer programs by many leadership actions, some of which have been referred to previously:

1. The Volunteer Program Manager can work with staff to make sure that there is a common purpose or goal for the team. Nothing is as fundamental to a team's effectiveness as a common sense of what they are trying to achieve together. Both staff and volunteers should see themselves as equal partners in pursuing this goal.

2. In developing jobs for volunteers (other than for one-shot volunteers whom you don't expect to retain) you should avoid setting performance standards that are too low. If the expectations are too easy to meet, people will not feel special about their participation. Volunteers should not have lower standards than paid staff.

3. The Volunteer Program Manager should insure that staff and volunteers are treated equally. Be on the lookout for inadvertent behavior that makes volunteers feel excluded. A common example is that volunteers are not invited to staff meetings, not because they are deliberately excluded but because no one thought to give them the option to attend. Such a situation can make volunteers feel like second-class citizens.

4. When working with staff to develop jobs for volunteers, the Volunteer Program Manager should make sure that volunteers (or teams of volunteers) have a sense of ownership of a client or project. Fragmentation of ownership generates blame and criticism - which is the enemy of connectedness.

5. The Volunteer Program Manager should encourage leaders to celebrate the accomplishments of volunteers in context of their contribution to the goals of the group. Recognition must be consistent so that people do not suspect favoritism. Team accomplishments can also be celebrated, giving equal credit to all team members.

People with a sense of connectedness have a sense of "we" as well as a sense of "I." The more special the "we" is, the more special the individual feels as part of the group and the greater the self-esteem that is generated. This is why it is important to have high standards for becoming a group member.

Leaders of volunteer programs should be on the look out for comments people make about the expectations they have of themselves and their co-workers. If people say things like "I'm just a volunteer," or "What do they expect for free?" it should cause alarm bells to ring. People's self-esteem drops when they regard themselves as part of a below average group. This negative sense of connectedness leads to high turnover of staff and volunteers. When they hear negative statements such as this, leaders should try to generate positive ideas for improving the situation. They might ask: "What makes you say that? What can you do to improve this situation? What kind of place would you want to work? What can you do to make this organization more like the kind of place you want it to be?"

Leaders should spread the word about positive accomplishments. They should talk about the values and standards of the organization and what it means to be part of the group.

Leaders should look for opportunities to promote interaction among group members. This is particularly important where there are few "natural" opportunities for people to share their common experiences. For example, in befriending schemes and literacy programs, volunteers will be working with the client on their own schedules. Volunteers work with little daily supervision and rarely appear in the office. Effective volunteer supervisors, knowing that "it's lonely out there," take pains to bring their people together for training, potlucks, and sharing of "war stories."

Another way to promote interaction is to involve people in the decision-making process. When each group member feels she has a say in deciding the unit's strategy, her feeling of connectedness is enhanced. In such meetings, it is important that you do not let your own biases and positions be known in advance. Group members who know what the person in authority wants will tend to support that position. If you already know the way you want to go, you might as well just tell them.

People's sense of connectedness is enhanced by engaging in new experiences together. By insisting passionately on constant improvement, leaders encourage people to try out new ways of doing things. If these are done by teams, the sense of connectedness grows.

Uniqueness

A second characteristic of people with high self-esteem is a feeling of uniqueness, a feeling that "there is no one in the world quite like me." This means that I have a sense that I am special in some way, that I have a unique combination of talents or personal qualities.

Volunteer Program Managers build feelings of uniqueness by recognizing the achievements of individual group members and by praising them for their individual qualities. They encourage individuals to express themselves and, by giving them the authority to think, explore alternative ways to achieve their results.

People's sense of uniqueness can also be enhanced by giving them challenging assignments that take advantage of their individual strengths. "This is a difficult responsibility requiring your special talents," a volunteer's supervisor might say. Such a statement, of course, should be the supervisor's sincere belief.

This need to feel unique is sometimes in conflict with a person's need to feel connected. All of us tend to make compromises in our uniqueness in order to be connected and sacrifice some connectedness in order to feel unique. Imagine, for example, a volunteer named Julie. Part of her feeling of uniqueness revolves around her image of herself as a free spirit. This manifests itself in a variety of ways, such as wearing unusual clothing and jewelry. Her organization's values, however, are quite traditional, and it is an accepted group norm to dress conservatively. Julie is faced with a choice between dressing conservatively to gain a sense of connectedness, thus sacrificing some of her uniqueness, or to continue her unique style at the risk of becoming something of an outsider to the group. Neither of these courses of action is fully satisfactory to her.

In a truly positive climate, people feel safe to be who they are. They can behave in an individual manner and yet feel supported by the group. People respect each other for their unique strengths and eccentricities. They support each other unconditionally.

Creating such a situation is often difficult. It cannot be done without lots of interaction among group members. It cannot be done without shared values and a common purpose. It may require the services of an expert facilitator to lead a retreat in which people explore their differences and gain an understanding of each person's unique point of view. It is always enhanced by leaders talking up the strengths of individual members and their contributions to the purpose of the group. It is maintained by leaders regarding as "wrong" behavior one person making fun of another or disparaging another's accomplishments or desires.

It is also enhanced by encouraging the individual development of each volunteer. Provide people with maximum training. As they learn new skills, their sense of individual competence grows. A common way to do this is to send them to conferences and workshops to keep them up to date with the latest developments in their fields.

One good idea is to have volunteers research a topic and present their findings to the others. This enhances the presenter's feelings of uniqueness—the person's special knowledge is being imparted to others—while also creating connectedness. It creates a sense that each team member can be depended on.

Power

The word power has negative connotations for many people. We have searched for a better word but have found none that includes everything Clemes and Bean mean by power. In part, power means a sense of effectiveness, a feeling that the volunteer is making a difference. This feeling is often throttled by traditional volunteer jobs. If people work in fragmented systems, doing menial tasks not connected to a final outcome, they are unlikely to feel they are making much of a difference. The self-esteem of people in such circumstances is thereby reduced.

To feel effective, volunteers need to work on things that matter. If they are engaged in support activities, for example stuffing envelopes, they should be told the purpose of the mailing and the results that are achieved from it so they can feel they are having an effect on something worthwhile.

Part of feeling effective is feeling in control of one's life. Managers often take this away from people by trying to overly control their behavior. Rather than defining results and allowing people some say in figuring out how to achieve them, managers tell people exactly what to do. When one human being attempts to control the behavior of another, the result is rarely top performance.

As explained in previous chapters, you can produce feelings of effectiveness by making volunteers responsible for results. Volunteers then have the sense of being in charge of something meaningful. You can then allow people to control their own behavior by giving them the authority to think.

The need to feel in control is often in conflict with a person's need for connectedness. People in teams sometimes yearn for more freedom of action. Their desire to influence others sometimes alienates other group members.

As Glasser points out in his book *Control Theory*, almost everyone goes through life trying to balance conflicting needs, making compromises that are never fully satisfactory. If you can create a situation in which these conflicting motivational needs are met simultaneously, you will unleash a tremendous sense of well-being in your volunteers and enthusiasm for the job.

Applying Retention Strategies to Short Term Volunteers

For many reasons, short-term volunteering is not as rewarding as long-term — it doesn't provide the emotional satisfaction of being an integral part of something. Short-term volunteering is to long-term as fast food is to a real meal: you can survive on it but you don't call it dining. Many short-termers may be engaging in sporadic volunteering as a sampling technique until they find the volunteer position that is right for them, practicing "comparison shopping."

To take advantage of this, a smart Volunteer Program Manager should develop a series of entry-level, short-term jobs that provide volunteers with the opportunity to see how they like working with the organization, its staff, and its clientele. Once volunteers are working in these "starter" jobs, the Volunteer Program Manager should work on retention, slowly grooming them for more work and ensuring that they truly enjoy the work they are doing. Volunteers are curiously rational: they won't stay in jobs that aren't enjoyable, and they will stay in those that are.

Some evidence for the effects of this phenomenon is available from studies of volunteer behavior. In the 1988 Gallup Poll on Giving and Volunteering in the United States, 14% of those volunteers who reported increasing their volunteer hours said they did so because of expanding interest and involvement in the work they were doing.

From this perspective, emphasis on volunteer retention is much more important than emphasis on recruitment. Rather than focusing on constantly bringing new volunteers into the system, with the concomitant expenditure of energy required for recruitment, screening, orientation and training, concentrate on maintenance of the existing volunteer force through retention of the incumbents. Over time, the organization will benefit from the increased experience levels of its volunteers and from the decreased costs of recruiting newcomers.

There are three different ways of "improving" volunteer jobs to make them more interesting and involving.

Give Them a Great Place to Work

The process for strengthening involvement necessarily varies from job to job and from volunteer to volunteer, but some factors are probably common to all situations. One of these is providing for the volunteer a rewarding job, one in which working facilities are satisfactory and social relationships are positive.

Some research has identified factors that might be important in this conversion process. A study of volunteer workers in three Israeli social service organizations found that organizational variables (such as adequate preparation for the task they were asked to do) and attitudinal variables (such as task achievement, relationships with other volunteers, and the nature of the work itself) were the best predictors of volunteer retention. Colony, Chen and Andrews identified "clearly defined responsibilities," "interesting work," "competence of supervisor," and "seeing results of my work" as important work factors for volunteers.

After analyzing their data, Colony, Chen and Andrews noted:

"Perhaps the single most important finding reported in this study is the relatively high importance volunteers accord situational facilities…In addition to the intrinsic and extrinsic incentives associated with volunteer work, then, it appears that individuals strongly desire conditions and organizational settings that facilitate effective and efficient volunteer work."

Roughly translated, this means that volunteers like good working conditions, just like the rest of us, and that volunteers tend to prefer jobs where the environment is friendly, supportive, and effective.

The factors that are key elements for each volunteer job will vary. A study of the Master Gardener volunteer program identified three top perceived benefits that volunteers thought essential: receiving new sources of information, obtaining new gardening knowledge, and gaining access to experts and information. Note that none of these is "altruistic." Each factor involves a benefit that the volunteer felt to be of value to herself and which was gained through volunteering and the additional training provided.

Give Them What They Don't Have

Another way of approaching the process of making a job more interesting is to look at it from the perspective of the potential volunteers. What is it, for example, that they want out of this volunteer job that they aren't getting from their current paid job?

A study of volunteers at three social service organizations tested the hypothesis that some people volunteer in order to satisfy needs that are not currently being met in their paid employment. The findings indicated that volunteers whose regular paid employment failed to satisfy their needs for psychological growth tended to be more satisfied with volunteering when it could satisfy those growth needs.

The study's conclusion was particularly intriguing: "The present study suggests that volunteers who perceive their paying jobs as relatively unfulfilling should be asked to do the more challenging work."

This would suggest that volunteer motivation could be improved by first analyzing potential volunteer's attitudes toward their current job to identify deficiencies and then structuring volunteer assignments to fill the gaps. Variables that might be examined would include whether the paid job is worthwhile, interesting, satisfying, diverse, flexible, and allowed for such factors as social interaction, expression of leadership skills, etc. Sample questions that could be used during the volunteer interview would include:

- "What do you get out of your current job?"
- "What do you not get to do sufficiently in your current job?"
- "What would your ideal job look like? "
- "What would you do in it, and what would you not do?"

The prospective volunteer would be encouraged to identify elements of a possible volunteer job that would meet motivational needs not currently being met in their life and particularly not being met in their paid work. It would then become important to make sure that the volunteer job provided this perceived need.

Give Them a Good Time

Another way of thinking about more effective retention is to develop ways to let the volunteer have more "fun."

This is not quite as strange a notion as it might seem. Henderson has suggested that one way to view volunteering is as a "leisure" activity—something which is done freely without expectation of monetary benefit. Volunteering and leisure have similar expected benefits: "People want to do something interesting, to achieve something, meet people, have fun, learn new things, be refreshed, and relax." All of these factors might be examined as aspects of volunteer jobs that could be strengthened.

Henderson suggests that the Volunteer Program Manager focus on four areas to take advantage of this relationship between leisure and volunteering:

- The self-interest and recreational expectations of volunteers that might make volunteering more appealing to people.
- Providing volunteer opportunities that will be perceived as worthy leisure.
- Utilizing the "recreational aspects" of volunteering as a technique for recruitment.
- Matching a person's leisure expectations to potential outcomes associated with a volunteer experience.

The J.C. Penney survey alluded to earlier suggests that some aspects of leisure, such as enjoying activities conducted with one's social group, may be of particular significance in tapping this aspect of motivation.

Don't Forget the Obvious

Two final comments about retention: the first is so obvious that many programs not only ignore it, they do exactly the opposite. Since volunteers are coming to the organization because they want to help, it is essential that you do everything you can to give volunteers work to do as soon as possible. Underutilization create serious retention problems, because motivated volunteers who are trying to be of assistance will feel useless if they are not actually involved in doing something. They will also lose any sense of relationship with the organization over long periods of non-involvement. In the words of Hanawi: *"There is a minimal level of activity which is necessary for volunteers to feel connected to an organization; there are individual variations in this critical level but certainly when a person's involvement falls below one or two hours a month, or when there is no continuity in the level of contact, volunteers will drift away."*

The second is equally obvious: when in doubt, ask them what they want to be doing. Part of the original volunteer interview and part of every subsequent evaluation session should consist of ascertaining what the organization might do that would meet the volunteer's motivations. This includes identifying the right job for the volunteer, but it also includes identifying what it would take for the volunteer to feel successful in the job. Questions such as: "How can we show you we care?," "What would it take to make you feel successful in this job?," "Who would you like to know about your accomplishments?," are designed to uncover possible retention and recognition strategies. It is vitally necessary to keep exploring this area because the motivational needs of volunteers will undoubtedly change over their lifetime and during the course of their relationship with the organization.

Critical Incident Points in the Volunteer Life Cycle

Most studies of volunteer motivation have concentrated on examining the factors that will influence the decision to initiate volunteering. These factors are complex, as Miller notes: *"a volunteer's involvement and satisfaction derive from a complex combination of the volunteer's personality, the nature of the volunteer activity, and the nature of the volunteer's other activities."* These studies, however, are not particularly useful in then determining what factors might influence that same volunteer's decision to *continue* volunteering with that organization. This deficiency arises because initial motivations can be quite different from subsequent attitudes and behaviors, which are based on a wide variety of factors. Paul Ilsley in his invaluable series of interviews with volunteers found that:

"Inexperienced volunteers, defined as those who have been in service for less than six months, usually can explain their reasons for volunteering without hesitation and can describe tangible ways in which they expect to be rewarded for their work... Experienced volunteers, by contrast, sometimes have difficulty explaining why they continue their work. A volunteer who had worked at a museum for fifteen years says, 'I've been here so long I can't remember why I stay.'"

This situation is further complicated by the fact that the volunteer's motivations, reactions to their volunteer work and adjustment to other life factors will tend to change over time. Each of these changes can create a re-examination by the volunteer of their commitment.

Over the length of a volunteer's relationship with an organization there will tend to occur numerous *critical incident points* at which the volunteer will review their decision to remain as a volunteer. These points seem to have some predictability, both in time of occurrence and in the content of the factors that will influence the volunteer in either leaving or staying, but are often ignored in studies of volunteer motivation. Robert Dailey, writing in 1986, noted *"researchers need to recognize there is a wide range of behaviors and attitudes that materialize and drive volunteer activity well after the decision to join and donate energy and time have been made."*

This section reviews these critical points and suggests ways for a volunteer manager to positively influence the volunteer's decision during this process of self-examination.

Initial Contact

Often the opinions of a volunteer are shaped in the very first instance of contact with an organization. Examples of this initial contact might include:

- initial call to an agency about volunteering
- first meeting or interview with volunteer manager
- orientation session

- first day on volunteer job

During each of these moments, the volunteer is forming opinions about whether the somewhat risky move they are considering (offering themselves to a strange organization) is a wise choice. At this point, any feeling of discomfort is likely to be magnified in the mind of the volunteer, and any sense that the agency is indifferent or uninterested is highly likely to result in the volunteer ending the relationship as quickly as possible. At this early and quite fragile point in the relationship, the potential volunteer is highly attuned to any signs of welcome or of rejection.

Here are some suggestions for maximizing the likelihood of a volunteer getting a positive first impression:

1. Make sure that those answering the phone for your organization know about the volunteer program and project an organized and friendly attitude to callers asking about volunteering. All of those who first meet with a potential volunteer should project a sense of welcome and appreciation. As someone once noted, "You never get a second chance to make a good first impression"

2. Make sure that you get back to those who call about volunteer opportunities as quickly as possible. There is a substantial decay factor in volunteer enthusiasm over small amounts of time, and this decay can quickly lead to a firm conclusion that the agency isn't really interested. If you're too busy to process the volunteer's request, then at a minimum, call to let them know you'll be back to them later and tell them when you will be re-contacting them.

3. When first meeting people, strive to give them a sense of understanding of the process they will be going through in applying to become a volunteer. This is especially important in these times when background checks can consume weeks. A volunteer who feels "lost" during this initial phase will quickly become lost.

4. Strive to give the new volunteer a sense of inclusion, establishing immediate social connections with staff and other volunteers. One simple way to do this is to walk them through the agency and introduce them to others, particularly those with whom they will be working.

5. Make the volunteer's first day on the job a ceremonial one, with an official greeting and thanks. This will tend to put the organizational seal of approval on the volunteer's decision.

First Month

During their first month on the job, the volunteer is learning about the position to which they have been assigned. A volunteer manager should always view this initial matching as a hopeful but occasionally incorrect experiment, commonly based on a relatively short interview in which each participant is operating with a great deal of ignorance about the other. The primary factor influencing the volunteer during this critical time is one of "job comfort," i.e., do they feel capable and interested in the work now that they are actually learning what it is really about? Reality has replaced the job description. A volunteer who discovers that the position to which they have been assigned is not one in which they feel comfortable will start to disappear.

A smart volunteer manager can easily control any danger during this period by deliberately scheduling a "review interview" about 30 days after the initial placement. This interview, arranged at the time of initial placement, is explained as an opportunity for the volunteer to really decide whether they like the job or not. The first month basically operates as a "test drive" for the volunteer to be exposed to the actual work and to determine whether they are comfortable with their ability and interest in continuing in that position.

While this creates some additional work for the volunteer manager it creates the ability to "fine-tune" placement decisions, based both on the volunteer's new knowledge about the work and the agency's new knowledge about the volunteer.

As every experienced volunteer manager knows, making a "perfect match" in placement is essential for smooth working relationships.

First Six Months

During the first six months the volunteer has an opportunity to examine and consider their developing relationship with the agency. Critical factors include:

- *Reality versus expectation.*

Does the situation in which the volunteer is now engaged meet their expectations in a positive way? Is the volunteer getting what they thought they would get out of volunteering? Is the volunteer work vastly different from what they thought or what they were told during initial orientation and training? Do the clients and work environment meet the expectations of the volunteer?

• *Job fit.*
Do the overall aspects of the task (client relations, work process, etc.) match with the volunteer's interests and abilities? Does the volunteer feel equal to the work and capable of achieving some success at it?

• *Life fit.*
Does the volunteer work and its time and logistical requirements fit comfortably into the rest of the volunteer's life, work and relationships? Is the volunteer work too demanding or too intrusive?

• *Social fit.*
Does the volunteer feel like they are becoming an accepted part of the organization's social environment? Do they feel respected and a part of the team? Are they finding friends and colleagues?

Possible solutions for helping a volunteer reach a positive conclusion during this period include:

1. Create a buddy or mentor system for new volunteers. These assigned colleagues will assume responsibility for answering any questions the volunteer has, helping them with their new roles, and introducing them to the social fabric of the organization. Experienced volunteers make excellent buddies. Note, however, that being a buddy is different from being a supervisor. The role of the buddy is primarily to help the new person become comfortable, not to manage them.

2. Assume that you (or their supervisor) will need to allocate more time for communication with new volunteers and schedule yourself accordingly. Don't assume that the volunteer will come to you; instead, create opportunities to talk with the volunteer, even if it's just a "social call."

3. Schedule a 6-month review. This is not so much an evaluation as it is a chance to talk with the volunteer in a formal way about how they are feeling and whether they are enjoying themselves. If you have assigned the volunteer to work with a staff supervisor, this review is an excellent opportunity to see how that relationship is developing.

4. Give the volunteer symbols of belonging to the organization. This can include a business card, their own voice or postal mailbox, clothing and equipment, etc. These will tend to reinforce the notion of the volunteer that they are a part of the organization.

First Anniversary/End of Initial Term or Commitment

This is one of the most serious critical incident points, because the volunteer will have fulfilled their initial commitment and now must make an affirmative decision to renew that commitment as opposed to seeking a new volunteer opportunity.

Key factors for the volunteer at this time are:

• *Bonding.*
Has the volunteer developed favorable personal relationships with others in the organization? Does the volunteer have friends among other staff and volunteers?

• *Accomplishment/Expectation.*
In reviewing their tenure, does the volunteer feel that they have accomplished what they thought they would accomplish during the job? Does the volunteer feel successful, or do they feel that they have "failed" to achieve what they wanted, either in serving the community or helping a particular client?

• *Opportunity for growth.*
In contemplating continuation of the volunteer work, does the volunteer look forward with anticipation or do they feel that the work will simply be more of the same? Does the volunteer feel that they have the opportunity for continued challenge in the job or does it appear boring?

Here are some management actions to assist a volunteer at this stage:

1. Develop a "volunteer growth plan" for each volunteer. This plan, developed with and by each volunteer, will chart out how the volunteer is feeling about their work and what might be done to re-kindle their interest if it is flagging.

2. Celebrate the volunteer's term of service, finding a way to show them what they have accomplished and how they are appreciated. Have testimonials from those with whom they have been working and examples of their accomplishments. Do not make the party seem like you're giving them the gold retirement watch; instead make the theme "Many Happy Returns."

3. Make sure the volunteer has an opportunity

to see the results of their work and of the overall work of the organization, preferably in a face-to-face encounter that conveys the real impact. A 1990 study of crisis center volunteers found a substantial difference in average volunteer tenure in centers where volunteers had opportunities for face-to-face interventions with clients over those where the volunteers had little client contact. Always remember that the ultimate impact on the client is part of a volunteer motivation, and it is difficult to feel motivated when you never know the results. Organizations that engage in outcome-based evaluations should be sure to inform volunteers about the results of these evaluations.

4. Strengthen the bonds of the volunteer to the organization by giving token items that symbolize "belonging." These can include a photo album of them working with others or mementos of past work.

5. Talk frankly to the volunteer about whether they are still enjoying their work. Many volunteers will be reluctant to tell you this, either out of a fear of seeming to let the organization down or a fear of seeming to criticize those with whom they work. Strive for an understanding with the volunteer that this discussion is not about "failure," but about "renewal," an opportunity to be even more successful in the future.

6. Be prepared with a number of different options for the volunteer that can serve to re-kindle the sense of excitement they once had. These might include a change to a new position, a "promotion" in their current position, or even a sabbatical to step aside from their volunteer work and gain a new perspective or just a feeling of re-invigoration. Volunteers can easily be "promoted" by giving them additional responsibilities such as assisting in training other volunteers, serving as mentors or resources, etc.

Longer Term

In the longer term, individual volunteers will face additional critical incident points. These are not always predictable, occurring at different times for different volunteers. Here are some of the factors that will creates these incidents:

- *Work Adjustment.*

If the volunteer's job changes in any substantial way the volunteer can experience disruption. This could include a change in the client to whom the volunteer is assigned or a change in the staff with whom the volunteer is working. It can very often include a change in the status of some other volunteer with whom there is a close attachment.

- *Life Fit.*

As the volunteer ages, their own life and needs will change. Critical change points include birth of children, change in paid work, marriage, death of spouse, retirement, etc. As Pearce noted in 1993, "Volunteers may quit because of personal changes, such as moving or returning to work or school. Since volunteering is often viewed as a peripheral activity, it may be influenced more heavily by outside events than employment is." A volunteer manager should stay attuned to how the volunteer's own life is going, since major changes in it will create critical examination of the volunteer's involvement with the agency.

Two strategies are crucial in ensuring that volunteers remain committed during these changes:

1. Giving volunteers a sense of empowerment in shaping their volunteer work. If volunteers know they can discuss their work and have the opportunity to re-design it to fit a changing situation, they are more likely to remain.

2. Making each volunteer a "true believer" in the cause of the organization. Perhaps the greatest factor in volunteer retention is the extent to which the volunteer truly believes in the work being done by the organization. Volunteers who initially join for other reasons (social factors, job experience, etc.) should be deliberately engaged in conversations about the need for the agency and its work.

A 1995 study of volunteer ombudsmen revealed that this last factor has major importance. As they noted: *"Because organizational commitment is based on volunteer attachment to organizational ideals, a volunteer program manager must take great care to communicate the organization's philosophy. It is the essential, inspiring vision that binds the program's character, social role, goals, and objectives to the volunteer's self-image."*

While the above may seem like additional work, they are designed to allow the volunteer manager to concentrate on an essential task - retaining good volunteers. It is expensive and time-consuming for an agency to always be recruiting new volunteers. To determine whether you need to pay more attention to volunteer retention you might consider keeping retention statistics on your volunteers, and, in particular, graphing the approximate timeframe of their points of departure. If you begin to see clusters of departures around the timeframes above, then improving your statistics can be a simple task.

In essence this process requires looking at your volunteers on a longitudinal basis, remembering that, like all of us, they are likely to grow and change over time. Since volunteering depends upon meeting both the needs and circumstances of the volunteer, it makes sense that volunteer management will need to adjust to changes in those needs and circumstances.

Recognizing Volunteers

Volunteers must receive a sense of appreciation and reward for their contribution. This sense can be conveyed through a number of processes, including both formal and informal recognition systems.

Formal Recognition Systems

Formal recognition systems are comprised of the awards, certificates, plaques, pins, and recognition dinners or receptions to honor volunteer achievement. Many organizations hold an annual ceremony in which individual volunteers are singled out for their achievement.

In determining whether to establish such a formal ceremony, consider the following:

- Is this being done to honor the volunteer, or so that staff can feel involved and can feel that they have shown their appreciation for volunteers?
- Is it real and not stale or mechanical?
- Does it fit? Would the volunteers feel better if you spent the money on the needs of the clients rather than on an obligatory luncheon with dubious food?
- Can you make it a sense of celebration and a builder of team identity?

Formal recognition systems are helpful mainly in satisfying the needs of the volunteer who has a need for community approval but have little impact (and occasionally have a negative impact) on volunteers whose primary focus is helping the clientele. These volunteers may very well feel more motivated and honored by a system which recognizes the achievements of "their" clients, and also recognizes the contribution that the volunteer has made towards this achievement.

Informal Recognition Practices

The most effective volunteer recognition occurs in the day-to-day interchange between the volunteer and the organization through the staff expressing sincere appreciation and thanks for the work being done by the volunteer.

This type of recognition is more powerful in part because it is much more frequent – a once-a-year dinner does not carry the same impact as 365 days of good working relationships.
Day-to-day recognition may include:

- Saying "thank you"
- Involving the volunteer in decisions that affect them
- Asking about the volunteer's family and showing an interest in their "outside" life
- Making sure that volunteers receive equal treatment to that given staff
- Sending a note of appreciation to the volunteer's family
- Allowing the volunteer to increase their skills by attending training
- Recommending the volunteer for promotion to a more responsible job
- Celebrating the volunteer's anniversary with the organization

The intention of day-to-day recognition is to convey a constant sense of appreciation and belonging to the volunteer. This sense can be better conveyed by the thousands of small interactions that compose daily life than it can be conveyed in an annual event.

Recognition can begin quite early. A card of welcome sent to a new volunteer, or a small welcome party conveys an immediate sense of appreciation.

Matching Recognition to Types of Volunteers

It is also possible to think about systems of volunteer recognition that are appropriate to particular types of volunteers:

By Motivational Orientation

One could think about recognition that was more appropriate for different basic motivational needs, as follows:

Achievement-oriented volunteers

- Ideal result of recognition is additional training or more challenging tasks.
- Subject for recognition is best linked to a very specific accomplishment

- Phrasing of recognition through "Best," "Most" awards
- Recognition decision should include "Checkpoints" or "Records"
- Awardee should be selected by co-workers

Affiliation-oriented volunteers
- Recognition should be given at group event
- Recognition should be given in presence of peers, family, other bonded groupings
- Recognition item or award should have a "Personal Touch"
- Recognition should be organizational in nature, given by the organization
- Recognition should be voted by peers
- If primary affiliative bonding is with client, not others in the organization, then the client should take part in the recognition, through a personal note of thanks or as presenter of the award

Power-oriented volunteers
- Key aspect of recognition is "Promotion," conveying greater access to authority or information
- Recognition should be commendation from "Names"
- Recognition should be announced to community at large, put in newspaper
- Recognition decision should be made by the organization's leadership

By Style of Volunteering
Recognition might also vary between long-term and short-term volunteers:

Long-term volunteer
- Recognition with and by the group
- Recognition items make use of group symbols
- Recognition entails greater power, involvement, information about the organization
- Presenter of recognition is a person in authority

Short-term volunteer
- Recognition is given in immediate work unit or social group
- Recognition is "portable;" something the volunteers can take with them when they leave—a present, photograph or other memorabilia of experience, training, etc.
- Recognition is provided via home or work—letter to employer, church, or family
- Presenter is either the immediate supervisor or the client

You should note that an "ideal" recognition system might require a mixture of different procedures in order to have something for every type of volunteer. This is not unusual and is quite appropriate. Many organizations fail to do this, with interesting results. Consider, for example, an all-too-typical organization that gives its volunteer awards only according to the amount of time donated, a "longevity" prize. If you're a short-term volunteer how do you feel about this system? Or if your busy schedule limits the time you can offer? Could you possibly ever "win" under these rules? What would this type of award suggest to you about the value that the organization places upon your own contribution of time?

Ideas for Recognition
Here are some examples of different levels of recognition activity:

Daily means of providing recognition:

- Saying "Thank you."
- Telling them they did a good job.
- Suggesting they join you for coffee.
- Asking for their opinions.
- Greeting them when they come in the morning.
- Showing interest in their personal interests.
- Smiling when you see them.
- Bragging about them to your boss (in their presence).
- Jotting small thank you notes to them.
- Having a refreshment with them after work.
- Saying something positive about their personal qualities.

Intermediate means of providing recognition:

- Taking them to lunch.
- Providing food at volunteer meetings.
- Letting them put their names on the products they produce.
- Buying the first round of beer for "the best crew of the month."
- Writing them a letter of commendation (with copies to personnel file and other appropriate people.)
- Getting a local radio station to mention them.
- Putting them on important task forces or committees.
- Giving the best parking space to the "employee of the month."
- Posting graphic displays, showing progress toward targets.
- Mentioning major contributors by name in your

status reports to upper management.

- Having them present their results to higher-ups.
- Giving permission to go to a seminar, convention, or professional meeting, if possible at the organization's expense.
- Writing articles about their performance for newsletters or newspapers.
- Having them present a training session to co-workers.
- Decorating their work area on their birthday.
- Having your boss write them a letter of thanks.
- Celebrating major accomplishments.
- Having them represent you at important meetings.
- Putting their picture on the bulletin board with news of their accomplishments.
- Cutting out articles and cartoons they might be interested in.
- Organizing informal chats with organization leadership.

Major means of providing recognition:

- Making special caps, shirts, belt buckles or lapel badges honoring the group.
- Encouraging them to write an article about some accomplishment at work.
- Giving a plaque, certificate, or trophy for being best employee, best crew, most improved results, etc.
- Offering tuition assistance.
- Buying them good equipment.
- Getting their picture in the paper for outstanding accomplishment.
- Giving additional responsibilities and a new title.
- Renting newspaper space to thank them.
- Putting up a banner celebrating a major accomplishment.
- Honoring them for years of service to the organization.
- Giving them a bigger office.
- Enlisting them in training staff and other volunteers.
- Involving them in the annual planning process.

Rules for Recognition
Whatever mix of recognition system you utilize, remember the following rules:

1. Give it or else.
The need for recognition is very important to most people. If volunteers don't get recognition for productive participation, only bad things can happen. The least of these is that they will feel unappreciated and drop out. Alternatively, they may start getting recognition from their peers (in the form of attention, laughter, camaraderie) for snide remarks and other more serious disruptive behavior.

2. Give it frequently.
The most common complaint of volunteers is that they don't get enough recognition from staff. Staff are usually surprised by this and can often cite examples in which they have given recognition to volunteers. The reason for this discrepancy of perception is that recognition has a short shelf life. Its effects start to wear off after a few days, and after several weeks of not hearing anything positive volunteers start to wonder if they are appreciated. Giving recognition once a year to a volunteer at a recognition banquet is certainly not enough.

3. Give it via a variety of methods.
One of the implications of the previous rule is that you need a variety of methods of showing appreciation to volunteers. Fortunately, there are hundreds of methods. Recognition can be categorized into four major types:

- *From a person for the work the volunteer did.*

Examples include saying "You did a great job on this" or writing a letter to that effect.

- *From a person for being part of the organization.*

Examples include birthday celebrations or personal compliments such as "I am impressed by your uniformly pleasant attitude." These have nothing to do with the volunteers' work performance but are expressions of appreciation of them as a person.

- *From the organization for work the volunteer did.*

Examples would include a plaque commemorating their work on a project or being honored as "Volunteer of the month" because of their outstanding achievements.

- *From the organization for being part of the team.*

Examples include a plaque commemorating years of service or being featured in a newsletter article that tells interesting personal facts about the volunteer but is not written due to particular job performance.

All of these types are valid. Some appeal more to some people than to others. Try to make sure that your program has a mixture of methods.

4. Give it honestly.
Don't give praise unless you mean it. If you praise

substandard performance, the praise you give to others for good work will not be valued. If a volunteer is performing poorly, you might be able to give them honest recognition for their effort or for some personality trait.

5. Give it to the person, not to the work.
This is a subtle but important distinction. If volunteers organize a fund-raising event, for example, and you praise the event without mentioning who organized it, the volunteers may feel some resentment. Make sure you connect the volunteer's name to it. It is better to say "John, Betty, and Megan did a great job of organizing this event," than to say "This event was really well-organized."

6. Give it appropriately to the achievement.
Small accomplishments should be praised with low-effort methods; large accomplishments should get something more. For example, if a volunteer tutor teaches a child to spell "cat" today, we could say " Well done!" If she writes a grant that doubles our funding, a banner lauding her accomplishments might be more appropriate.

7. Give it consistently.
If two volunteers are responsible for similar achievements, they ought to get similar recognition. If one gets her picture in the lobby and another gets an approving nod, the latter may feel resentment. This does not mean that the recognition has to be exactly the same but that it should be the result of similar effort on your part. Otherwise certain volunteers will come to be regarded as "favorites," a stigma they may grow to dread.

8. Give it on a timely basis.
Praise for work should come as soon as possible after the achievement. Don't save up your recognition for the annual banquet. If a volunteer has to wait months before hearing any word of praise, she may develop resentment for lack of praise in the meantime.

9. Give it in an individualized fashion.
Different people like different things. One might respond favorably to football tickets, another might find them useless. Some like public recognition while others find it embarrassing. In order to provide effective recognition, you need to get to know your people and what they will respond to positively.

10. Give it for what you want more of.
Too often your staff pay most attention to volunteers who are having difficulty. Unfortunately, this may result in ignoring good performers. We are not suggesting that you ignore sub-par volunteers, just that you make sure that you praise the efforts of those who are doing a good job.

If All Else Fails, Do Things Correctly

When volunteers end their service to an organization, they often will say it is because their life is very busy, that they have other commitments, that they just don't have the time. These excuses should be treated as such. They are commonly a substitute for the volunteer conveying more unpleasant facts – that the volunteer experience is unrewarding, that volunteering is too much of a hassle, or that the volunteer does not trust the organization. In fact if the volunteer experience is sufficiently compelling, people will make the time to volunteer.

The final answer to volunteer retention and recognition is quite simple – operate a well-managed program. Volunteers, like the rest of us, tend to make rational decisions about the allocation of their time; they will strive to spend it in settings where they obtain value. This value may be the social aspects, the work objectives, the situational settings, or a combination of all of these. Programs that enable volunteers to do good work, in a good setting, with good people are uniquely positioned to provide this sense of value and accomplishment, and often can do so in ways that paid work settings are not able to provide. The principles of good volunteer management described in other chapters outline the actions that can enable a volunteer program to provide this positive environment. Always remember McCurley's Law of Volunteer Retention:

"The longer a volunteer is around the more likely they are to notice when the elements of good volunteer management are not in place. The honeymoon is over."

Chapter Thirteen Building Volunteer and Staff Relationships

In a previous chapter we talked about how to handle unacceptable volunteer behavior, focusing on the ability or motivation of the volunteer. But usually, the source of "problem" volunteer behavior has more to do with the staff people that supervise them than with the volunteer. Good volunteer-staff relations are critical in all organizations, and of particular concern when you are introducing volunteering into the agency or a project.

Thinking about Volunteers from the Staff's Perspective

We will start wth an analogy. Imagine for a moment that you are a staff person who has never before worked with a computer. At a staff meeting, the director of your agency announces that she believes that computerization is the only answer to the enormous workload that your agency faces, and that she intends to obtain as much computer equipment as she can for staff, none of whom at this point is computer literate. She announces that she has just hired a Director of Computer Operations to get the organization moving on this.

Shortly after this meeting, the new Director of Computer Operations walks into your office, deposits a computer on your desk, says "Here's your new computer, hope you enjoy it!," and walks out. There is no instructional manual, no training session, you have no knowledge about how to operate the machine, and little space in your office to accommodate it.

What would you do in this situation?

Bang at the keys until something happened?

Place the computer in the corner and use it as a plant stand?

How would you feel if you were the staff person, given a possible resource that you don't fully understand and may even resent for the changes it imposes on your work style?

It may sound strange to say, but volunteers and computers have a lot in common: each resource has suffered from haphazard attempts to implement its involvement within voluntary organizations. Each resource is complicated and multi-faceted. Each requires specific skills on the part of the staff who will be working with it. And each, to be most effective, needs to be customized for the particular usage, setting, and personalities involved.

Volunteers are more complicated resources, of course, because they are people. They are more complex (they can do a greater variety of things, if involved properly), and they are less forgiving than machines. A volunteer, for example, doesn't take well to being asked to stand in the corner and serve as a plant stand until needed.

This analogy is a round-about way of explaining that staff difficulties in working with volunteers—whether those include active opposition, passive resistance, or simple inability to achieve creative usage—are probably not really the fault of any of the staff. For the most part, many staff that are being encouraged to involve volunteers are in an equivalent position to a person being given a computer and told: "Bang the keys until something happens." No matter how well meaning they are, they more are likely to become frustrated than to accomplish much. And they are very likely to damage the 'equipment.' This analogy also implies a new role for the Volunteer Program Manager.

Changes in Volunteer Involvement Patterns

Immense changes that have taken place in volunteer involvement patterns during the past few years. Thirty years ago most volunteer departments operated, for the most part, on their own. Usually a volunteer coordinator (either paid or unpaid) supervised the activities of volunteers engaged in a variety of projects or activities.

Most of the time, these volunteers were engaged in program activities that were somewhat separate from the other organizational operations. The Volunteer Program Manager was responsible for almost all recruitment, job development, and supervision of "her" volunteers.

Visually, one could represent the management relationships involved in this system as a simple, two-sided continuum:

The Volunteer Program Manager was responsible for everything that related to the volunteers. In some cases this could result in rather strange management systems where one volunteer coordinator was supposed to be in charge of hundreds or even thousands of volunteers.

As volunteer involvement has become more sophisticated, this situation has changed considerably. Volunteers have 'diffused' throughout the structure of the agency, become a more integral part of it, and sometimes assumed tasks and responsibilities that had previously been done by paid staff. As new activities were undertaken by volunteers they began to work more in partnership with staff, operating as 'aides' or members of teams, or simply as assigned workers to a staff department. They began to work regularly 'with' and 'for' other members of staff than the Volunteer Program Manager. In some cases they have been totally assigned to other staff.

This new system of volunteers working more directly with individual staff has changed the dynamics of effective volunteer management within the agency.

This new system can be represented visually as:

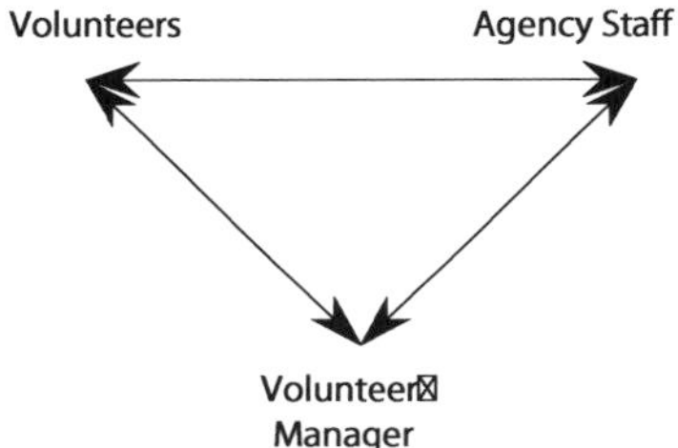

This three-sided relationship is much more complex than the two-sided continuum.

There are two major differences that this new system creates:

- A requirement that the Volunteer Program Manager view the work in a quite different fashion. As you can see from the connective lines of the triangle, the Volunteer Program Manager 'links' both to volunteers and to staff. This means that work must be done with both to be successful, not just with volunteers. It means the Volunteer Program Manager must have skills in working with staff.

- A realization that the line relationship between the staff and the volunteers is the primary line of management and supervision. If volunteers work on a day-to-day basis with staff, whether through an assignment with a single staff person, or in conjunction with several staff, then it is the quality of that management and interpersonal interaction that will determine whether the volunteer is effectively and satisfactorily involved.

The operational relationships will vary in different organizations. Generally, the larger the agency the more likely it is that volunteers will be working more directly with staff. This new style is the most effective method of achieving optimal volunteer involvement.

Think back to the computer illustration. If a staff person is provided with a computer, does the Director of Computer Operations attempt to operate the keyboard for each staff person? Obviously not; indeed, the idea is ridiculous. Why, then, should we not also expect the staff to 'operate' the volunteers with whom they work?

For volunteers to be involved effectively, each staff member must understand and be adept at volunteer management. Staff must have the capacity to comprehend the diversity of the volunteer workforce, to create imaginative and meaningful jobs for volunteers, and to lead and supervise volunteers effectively. They must become, in essence, "Managers of Volunteers."

New Roles for the Volunteer Program Manager

And, in turn, Volunteer Program Managers must realize that preparing staff for these new responsibilities may necessitate a change in their own role. For the past two decades or more, directors of volunteers have had the opportunity to attend highly sophisticated training at national, state, and local conferences. This training taught them to be experts in volunteer supervision at a time when that role was increasingly being taken on by other agency staff. Unless the Volunteer Program Manager can transfer that knowledge to staff, all of this training only makes it more frustrating to watch staff play this role badly.

One way of explaining this shift is to note the subtle but significant difference between two position titles sometimes applied to the Volunteer Program Manager:

Director of Volunteers

Director of Volunteer Services

The first, "Director of Volunteers," implies a person who "directs" volunteers. It is the person responsible for everyday management and supervision of volunteers. In our computer analogy, the equivalent phrase would be 'Computer Operator.'

The second, "Director of Volunteer Services," indicates the person who is responsible for overall operations involving volunteers, but who does not manage each individual volunteer. Instead this person enables, assists, and prepares each member of staff to make effective use of their own volunteers. In the computer analogy this would be the "Director of Computer Operations." We have used the term "Volunteer Program Manager" in this book to indicate an individual who takes responsibility for directing the overall program of volunteer involvement, not just for the individual volunteers.

Now Volunteer Program Managers must take a broader interpretation of their role, viewing themselves as being responsible for the system of volunteer involvement within the organization, which includes working closely with both volunteers and staff. The Volunteer Program Manager will then identify, recommend and implement all the organizational actions that are needed to make it possible for staff to accomplish the tasks and activities identified during the diagnosis and instructional phase.

In all of this, the Volunteer Program Manager, acting as a consultant, concentrates on working with staff, not in attempting to coerce them. The point is to persuade and empower staff to think about volunteers from the perspective of a trained "volunteer manager."

Dealing with Staff Concerns

A good Volunteer Program Manager will begin by recognizing that staff may have legitimate fears or concerns about the deployment of volunteers.

The concerns may be organizational in nature:

- a fear of diminished quality of service
- a fear that volunteers will be unreliable
- a fear of increased legal problems

The concerns may be personal in nature:

- a resentment of increased workload
- a fear of loss of a job
- a fear of having to manage volunteers without experience in doing so
- a fear of loss of control

The role of the Volunteer Program Manager is to determine the concerns of the staff and then turn these concerns into a sense of confidence among the staff that the volunteers will be a useful addition to the agency.

In general, this means imparting two feelings to staff:

- A sense of benefits greater than the difficulties or problems
- A feeling of control over the situation

Staff are more likely to be satisfied with the volunteers they will be working with if they can perceive that the return to them is greater than the effort involved, and if they believe that they will be closely involved in making decisions that affect how they are to work with the volunteers.

In dealing with staff concerns, it is wise to be aware that you may take their resistance personally. In such cases, your natural instinct may be to fight and win. This is usually disastrous. Many Volunteer Program Managers, for example, attempt to deal with staff concerns through throwing their weight around, often through seeking a top management mandate that "volunteers will be assigned to all staff."

This approach is fatal. It will leave the staff seeking revenge for what has been imposed upon them, and they will exercise this revenge upon the only available target—the volunteers.

Such a situation can also involve you in unpleasant political games. These reduce the morale of the organization. In cases where there is a lot of conflict among staff, where there is a "war zone" atmosphere, volunteer turnover will be higher. If volunteers sense tension and conflict in the agency, they will be deterred from continuing to work. Volunteer time is discretionary time, and most people prefer to spend their discretionary time in a pleasant environment.

Another natural but fatal instinct is to criticize staff for their inability to involve volunteers productively. Such criticism often leads to futile arguments; telling them five reasons why they are wrong is unlikely to persuade them to change their approach. Many of the concerns of staff will not be built entirely upon logic, and, indeed, may not even be directly related to the volunteer program. Directly confronting staff may only produce a defensiveness that will turn to hostility if you continue to push the issue.

Instead, you should attempt to work with staff in a consulting capacity, helping them to solve whatever volunteer management problem they encounter. Whereas our natural tendency is to tell them what is wrong, it is usually more effective to work with them to improve things by asking them questions. By doing so, you help staff gain a feeling of being in control of the solution.

For example, imagine you have a staff person who is experiencing turnover of volunteers assigned to him. You may be tempted to criticize his handling of the volunteers, but it is more productive to help him discover a different course of action. You might engage in a conversation that goes like this:

- *Staff person*: "These volunteers you send me just don't seem to be very reliable."
- *Volunteer Program Manager:* "Well, we certainly want to fix that problem. What do you mean by 'reliable'?"
- *Staff person*: "Well, they're not very dependable. They don't always show up."
- *Volunteer Program Manager:* "Why do you suppose that is?"
- *Staff person*: "Well, I don't know. I guess they probably have other things to do."
- *Volunteer Program Manager:* "Why would they prefer doing those other things?"
- *Staff person:* "I guess they might be more interesting or fun than coming here."
- *Volunteer Program Manager*: "Is there any way we could make their job here more interesting and fun?"
- *Staff person:* "I can't see how. It's pretty cut and dried. I guess it's pretty boring."
- *Volunteer Program Manager:* "Why is that? What makes it boring?"
- *Staff person:* "It's pretty repetitive."
- *Volunteer Program Manager*: "Could we redesign the job to make it more interesting and less repetitive?"
- *Staff person*: "That sounds like a lot of work."
- *Volunteer Program Manager:* "Would you like my help?"
- *Staff person*: "Well, if you think we can do it."

By using the consulting approach, the Volunteer Program Manager thus becomes a resource to staff, using her expertise in volunteer management to help staff involve volunteers more productively.

Using Questions to Help Staff Solve Problems

Often the consulting role begins with a problem staff are having. In assisting staff to solve problems, volunteer program managers work with them through five stages:

- to help them see the need for change
- to analyze the situation
- to generate options
- to select a solution
- to support the implementation

In each of these stages, the Volunteer Program Manager, acting as a consultant, uses questions to help the staff figure out a better way of approaching things. Below are some sample questions, to give you an idea of the kind of thing you might ask at each stage.

Awareness of need for change

- How are things working in your unit?
- What frustrations, if any, do you have in managing the volunteers?
- What sorts of frustrations, if any, do you feel with the present system?
- What keeps you from getting your work done as efficiently as you would like?
- Are there services that you receive from others that you feel could be delivered better?
- How would you describe the morale of the work group?
- What goals do you have for your unit?
- How are you doing in relation to those goals?

Analysis of the problem

- What factors in the situation contributed to the problem?
- Why do you think the problem person is behaving in this way?

- What would the person get out of behaving that way?
- Is there anyone who seems to work well with this person? What do they do?
- What have you done about the problem?
- How has that worked?
- What were the strengths of that approach? Weaknesses?
- How did people react to this approach? Why?
- Why do you think things have gone this way?
- What factors in the situation caused that to happen?
- What happened prior to the situation?
- What happened afterward?
- Is there a time when this seems most likely to occur?
- What has been your response?
- What has been the volunteer's reaction to that response?
- Why do you think he reacted that way?
- Why do you think this didn't work?

Generation of options
- What other options do we have?
- What are the pro's and con's of that course?
- What else could be done about the situation?
- What would happen if you did that?
- Then what would happen?
- If they react this way to that course of action, what else could you try?
- What other responses to the problem might you consider?
- In hindsight, what do you wish you would have done differently?
- Are there other resources that could be brought to bear on this problem?
- Have you considered this fact?
- Have you considered this course of action?
- If you had things to do over again, what would you do differently?

Selection of a solution
- Which of these options seems most likely to succeed?
- Are there any impediments to that approach working?
- What would happen if you tried this approach? Then what?
- Which of these approaches would fit best with the personalities involved?
- If you were going to advise someone else what to do, what would you tell them?
- What would you advise someone else to avoid doing?

Implementation
- What will staff need before we try this?
- How could we transfer your experience and skill to others?
- How can this new solution best be communicated to others?
- How will you monitor the staff's behavior in implementing these ideas?
- Is there a way we could find that out?
- When will you have that done?
- Is there anything I can do to help make your plan work?
- When can we talk about this again?

Dealing with Staff Resistance

As you work with staff, you may encounter resistance to the assistance you are offering. Wilson Learning Corporation identifies six sources of such resistance. For each, there are some questions that can help overcome the resistance.

Lack of Trust

The staff person who is resisting help from the Volunteer Program Manager because she isn't sure if the Volunteer Program Manager is capable of helping solve a problem or meet her needs. Some reasons for lack of trust include:

- The staff person doesn't know your personal qualities.
- The staff person feels you don't have enough influence to help.
- The staff person feels you don't know the needs of her department.
- The staff person had a bad experience with your predecessor.
- The staff person is afraid volunteers might take over paid positions.

To deal with this source of resistance, you need to reduce the personal barriers between yourself and the staff person. Questions to help overcome this source of resistance include:

- What would you like to know about me?
- What is your perception of my role?
- How did you get along with my predecessor?
- Do you see any downside to involving volunteers in your unit?
- How can we work together?

Lack of Perceived Need

Staff might resist help because they don't see the need for volunteers to work in their unit. Some reasons for not seeing the need might include:

- The problem doesn't affect the staff person in an obvious way.
- Other needs seem to be of higher priority.
- The staff person feels the agency should solve the problem by giving him more paid help.

To get staff to see the need, you might ask these questions:

- How are things going?
- How could things be better?
- Are you facing any problems?
- What are you doing now?
- How is it working?
- How would you like to see things improved?
- What do you like best about the present situation? Least?

Lack of Imagination
Staff may also resist help because they don't see any hope of a solution. Some reasons for this include:

- No one ever tried this before.
- Fear of unanticipated consequences.
- Fear of being punished for acting without approval of higher authority.

In this situation you need to get the staff person to think more creatively. Questions to help overcome this source of resistance include:

- If you were to start your unit all over again, what would you do differently?
- If you could change anything you wanted to create a more ideal situation, what would you do?
- What would you do if you had a full-time staff person assigned as your assistant?
- What are some things you would like to get done that you never have time to get around to?
- Is it possible volunteers might be able to do some of the things you wish you could do by working under your supervision?

Lack of Confidence
The staff person may also resist help because he feels the assistance you offer will not help solve the problem. Staff may have this feeling because:

- You are proposing a solution that doesn't seem likely to work.
- The staff person feels there might be better idea.
- The staff person's not sure he is capable of doing that.
- The staff person feels it is more your idea than hers.
- The staff person can't picture himself (the staff person wouldn't be comfortable) doing that.

To overcome this reason to resist help, the Volunteer Program Manager asks questions that help staff see the effectiveness of the proposed action:

- What would happen if we tried this?
- What more can you tell me about your reactions to this?
- Is there a better approach?
- How would that be better?
- Based on what you said, would it be useful if I . . .
- Do you feel that . . .
- Would you be interested in hearing about how this approach worked elsewhere?
- Shall we go ahead on this basis?
- Are there any problems you would anticipate in working with volunteers?
- Why do you think volunteers would behave that way?
- What would a volunteer get out of behaving that way?
- Is there anything you could think of that you could do to minimize the likelihood of these problems occurring?
- What do you think a volunteer would require in order to have a satisfying experience here?

Lack of Satisfaction
After the staff person has agreed to your proposed course of action, he has a new set of expectations of the relationship. Obstacles at this stage arise because:

- The staff person's not sure he made the right decision to try this.
- He is afraid others may react negatively to the course of action.
- He is afraid you my not fulfill your part of the bargain.

In this case, the Volunteer Program Manager asks questions that put her in the position of supporting the staff person:

- Other staff have felt some anxiety after deciding to use volunteers; do you?
- What can I do to support you in this?
- When and how should I keep in touch?
- How can I help?

Creating a System of Good Volunteer-Staff Relations

A good volunteer-staff relationship is helped when the organization has the following eight elements in place:

1. Overall Policy on Volunteer Involvement

The organization should have an overall policy on volunteer use, expressing why it involves volunteers. Reasons may include:

- Provide community outreach and input
- Gain additional human resources
- Cost savings
- Supplement expertise of staff
- Allow involvement of client groups
- Demonstrate community support
- Act as conduit to funders
- Provide personal touch in services to clients.

The policy should provide a clear rationale, which can be used in explaining the volunteer program to staff and to potential volunteers. It indicates to the staff that the volunteer program is not just an emergency measure dreamed up one weekend by a desperate Executive Director, but is one that fits within the overall mission of the agency. The policy should:

- Be adopted and supported by trustees and other top policy makers
- Be integrated into overall agency plans and budgets
- Encourage, but not mandate, staff involvement.

That last point is often overlooked, but is crucial. It is impossible to force staff to work effectively with volunteers. There are too many ways for staff to sabotage volunteer effort to think that staff can ever be coerced into productively involving volunteers. Even indifference of staff will quickly communicate itself to volunteers, who will equally quickly decide not to be where they are not wanted. Mandatory policies create resistance, and you will be asking for trouble if you attempt to force compliance. Plan to work through rewards for productive staff, not punishments for the recalcitrant.

A sample of such a policy on volunteers can be found in Chapter Three, Organizing a Volunteer Program.

You might also want to make sure that staff understand the need for volunteers, and understand that the volunteers are being involved to help, not hinder, staff. Here is an example of such a communication, which is included in a brochure entitled "Make Your Mark—Volunteer," which the Oregon Department of Human Resources distributes to its staff:

What's in it for me?
You can use the supervision of volunteers as experience when you are applying for promotions. By using tools such as position descriptions, training, evaluation, and feedback, you develop your own management skills. Involving volunteers in your problem solving and planning may help you gain a unique and valuable source of contributions and ideas. With the everyday workloads, it's hard to get to special projects and activities. Volunteers may be able to help you accomplish some of the things that you have had to put aside. At the same time you help yourself, you are helping volunteers reach their own goals.

Can volunteers replace paid staff?
It isn't fair to volunteers or paid staff of your organization to use volunteers to replace paid personnel. Volunteer staff can supplement and complement the work that is being done by employees. Also, volunteers can help you catch up on things that are backlogged and/or help extend some of the services that you provide.

Can I depend on volunteers to be professional?
Most volunteers have a professional attitude about their work. They take their responsibilities seriously, and uphold the policies of the agency and other requirements such as confidentiality. Identifying the assignment and carefully matching the volunteer to the job will help to eliminate future problems. Good direction from you and other staff with periodic monitoring and feedback will help the volunteer serve professionally.

Such a communication can pro-actively address staff concerns and smooth the way for a successful staff/volunteer interaction.

2. Assessment of Staff Capabilities

The more you know about your staff the better you can design a system that takes into account their individual characteristics. A very effective preliminary tool is a quick survey of staff attitudes and experience with volunteers. This should ascertain the following:

- *Previous staff experience with volunteering.*

This includes their own experience as volunteers, their previous work in an agency that used volunteers, and any previous experience in supervising volunteers.

- *Staff attitudes toward the use of volunteers.*

This would include the opinions of staff about the perceived need for volunteers, and any fears or recommendations about what jobs would be appropriate or inappropriate for volunteers. It would also include staff perceptions of what needs to happen before volunteers are brought into the agency.

3. Staff Orientation to the Volunteer Program
Staff need to learn the system for volunteer involvement within the organization. This would include educating them about the following:

- Rationale for using volunteers
- Brief history of volunteer program
- Explanation of types of volunteers and the jobs they do
- Description of the contributions of volunteers
- In-depth explanation of role of the staff in all aspects of working with volunteers

This orientation might actually be provided in different ways and at different times. Part might be given to each new staff member. Part might be given as staff begin to be involved with volunteers. It may be given either in a formal or informal setting, either in a workshop or one-on-one. It is very effective to include successful managers of volunteers and volunteers as co-presenters during these sessions.

Some information may be provided in writing, as this further example from the Oregon Department of Human Service brochure illustrates:

Can the volunteer program help clients I can't help?
Helping people is what our organizations are all about. The Volunteer Program can be a place to turn when you are unable to help a client. Sometimes volunteers will be able to meet some of the client's needs or assist you in identifying resources in the community. The Volunteer Program can make the tough part of your job just a little easier.

What happens when you make a referral?
When you make a volunteer request, the local Volunteer Program Supervisor's (VPS) response will depend on the type of request. If the help you need is available immediately, the request will be filled quickly. If the service, volunteer or resource isn't available, the Volunteer Program will try to recruit, interview and register volunteers for you, or they may help you locate and access other resources. If the request is inappropriate for volunteer involvement, the VPS will call you to discuss available alternatives. Since the Volunteer Program serves four different divisions (Adult and Family Services Division, Children's Services Division, Mental Health Division, and Senior Services Division) every effort will be made to provide equal access to the services available. Priorities for your Volunteer Program are established by a local Volunteer Program board, with representatives from each agency.

How hard can it be to find lots of volunteers?
Our Volunteer Program is competing with dozens of organizations in the recruitment of volunteers. Also, we're choosy; we want only the best. We screen all volunteer applicants to make sure they are appropriate and capable of serving our clients. Your help is important in keeping and attracting volunteers. Meaningful opportunities and positive experiences will keep present volunteers involved in our program. Also those same opportunities and experiences will help us find new volunteers. Nothing attracts like success. We welcome your help. If you would like to register as a volunteer or know of someone else who would be interested, talk to your nearest Volunteer Program. Our recruitment process is ongoing.

What does it take to get a volunteer going on a project?
Volunteers come to us with a vast range of abilities, experiences, and interests. Some may be well equipped for the jobs and others may require some training. Every volunteer you work with will need clear instructions in order to do the best job for you. The effort you spend training a volunteer and outlining clear performance expectations will make the experience positive and productive for both of you.

Also, since most volunteers have lots of other commitments, working out a mutually agreeable schedule is very important for both of you. Good planning helps ensure success for everyone, and encourages the volunteer to consider future projects that you may have.

4. Personalized Volunteer Position Creation
As discussed in the last chapter, a critical element in volunteer retention is designing positions that are interesting and rewarding enough that volunteers enjoy doing them. No recruitment campaign can compensate for boring volunteer work. This means that there needs to be a process in place for creating jobs that are meaningful to the staff who will be working with the volunteers (i.e., they really help out) and meaningful to potential volunteers. This process will work in five ways:

Linking Volunteer Roles Directly to the Agency Mission
If you can link volunteer jobs to the accomplishment

of the agency's mission, and avoid having volunteers working in peripheral areas ("nice, but not essential"), then you can better guarantee that volunteers will be spending their time on meaningful activities.

Gail Moore and Marilyn MacKenzie noted this vital need:

"If directors of volunteers want to establish credibility they must demonstrate a commitment to helping the organization (and the people that direct it - the executive director and the board) meet its objectives and achieve its mission."

To determine where within your agency volunteers can be linked to accomplishment of the mission, ask the following questions:

1. Where do we have the greatest difficulty in delivering effective services?
2. What are the biggest unmet needs of our clients?
3. Where do we have problems in reaching new populations?
4. Where are staff spending their time on work beneath their skills and capabilities?

The best time to ask these questions is either during the strategic planning process for the agency or during the initial planning phase of a new project. Each of the questions above will give you answers that could be turned into volunteer positions.

Ultimately it is desirable to have the role of volunteers directly linked to accomplishment of the agency's mission, preferably in a written statement that outlines the involvement of volunteers. Consider this example from the Volunteer Program of the Bureau of Land Management:

In the decades to come, volunteers will be woven into the fabric of BLM, playing a key role in protecting the health of the public lands and providing better service to our publics. Volunteers will be vital stewards of the public lands by serving as BLM team members, providing innovative ideas and key resources, and serving as ambassadors in their local communities.

Providing Staff with Ideas Prior to Volunteer Involvement

You might, for example, produce a guide for staff that sparks their thinking about volunteer jobs by explaining various possibilities.

You could explain the different ways in which volunteers might help:

A. Are there areas of work that staff doesn't want to do? This may be because they are not skilled in that type of work, or are too skilled for the work, or else simply have a preference to concentrate their efforts on something else.

B. Are there areas in which there is too much work for staff to do alone, and for which you might create volunteer assistants to supplement staff resources? These assistants might work directly with one member of staff or could do tasks that benefit all staff.

C. Are there areas in which you can extend services because volunteers would enable the agency to begin work that you cannot now even consider undertaking? You might also suggest the creation of volunteer jobs based on the recipients of the service. Consider the following:

- Jobs that are of direct assistance to an individual client (counseling, visiting, buddying, mentoring, etc.)
- Office administrative help.(information services, filing, messengers, etc.)
- Direct assistance to staff (research, training, computer help, etc.)
- Outreach (speakers panel, fundraising, marketing and evaluation, research, etc.)

You might also want to suggest some considerations that staff should bear in mind as they think about potential jobs:

A. The work must be meaningful and significant, both to the agency and to the clientele. The work must be needed and should be interesting to the person doing it. This means that each volunteer job must have a goal or a purpose that the volunteer can accomplish and can feel good about having achieved.

B. The volunteer ought to be able to feel some ownership and responsibility for the job. Volunteers must feel that they have some input into and control over the work they are asked to do. This will mean including the volunteer in the flow of information and decision-making within the office.

C. The work must fit a part-time situation (for a part-time volunteer). Either the work must be small enough in scope to be productively undertaken in a few hours a week, or it must be designed to be shared among a group of volunteers.

D. Volunteers must be worked with. They should be assigned to work with staff that are capable of supervising their activities in a productive fashion and of providing on-going direction, evaluation, and feedback. What arrangements will you need to make in order to ensure satisfactory supervision?

And you may want to provide some helpful hints to staff, hints that would be helpful both to them and to you:

The more flexible the timeframe of the volunteer job, the greater the likelihood that there will be someone willing to undertake it. Think about the following as different options for the job:

- Can the work be done to a totally flexible schedule at the discretion of the volunteer?
- Are there set hours during the week when the volunteer is needed?
- Could the work be done in the evenings or on weekends?
- Must the work be done on-site or at the office?

Assisting Staff in Creating Volunteer Work in Their Area of Responsibility

Staff will value volunteer positions that they see to be of direct assistance to them. Unfortunately, you, as the volunteer director, are not in a position to determine what these jobs might be. To uncover possible volunteer jobs you will need to conduct interviews with staff to determine their needs and interests. This role basically engages the volunteer director as a consultant to staff, much as computer specialists seek to specifically match applicable software and hardware to computer users.

To successfully undertake this, you will need to ask the right questions, and to ask them in the right fashion. Here are some examples of different question types that a good interviewer might use in working with staff to develop opportunities for volunteers:

Factual Questions

Factual Questions are designed to obtain objective data about the other party and their work. They are intended to give you a picture of the status of the other party, and are usually best phrased in a manner that will allow them to be answered with short, unequivocal responses. Examples include:

- "Do you do any volunteer work yourself?"
- "Have you ever worked with volunteers in the past?"
- "Are you utilizing any volunteers in your department now?"
- "How many volunteers are here now?"
- "How long have they been with you?"
- "What sort of jobs do these volunteers do?"
- "What are the major services that you deliver?"
- "What do you see as the biggest needs in your area?"
- "What kind of training should a person have to do this type of work?"
- "What resources or assistance would you need to involve volunteers in your area?"

Feeling Questions

Feeling Questions are designed to obtain subjective data on the other party's feelings, values and beliefs regarding the situation. They are intended to give you information on how the other party thinks or feels about the situation. Feeling Questions are most useful when used to follow-up a Factual Question.

Examples include:

- "How did you feel about working with volunteers then?"
- "What do you think it would take for a volunteer to enjoy working here?"
- "What do you like to do most in your job?"
- "What do you like to do least in your job?"
- Is it possible that volunteers could do some of the things you're working on if they were under your supervision?"
- "Are there jobs that you do not think it is appropriate for volunteers to do?"
- "Do you think you could train volunteers to do the job adequately?"

Third Party Questions

Third Party Questions are an indirect way to discover what the other party is thinking. They are useful because they seem less threatening than a forced direct request or question. Examples include:

- "Some people would use volunteers to do ___________. How would you feel about that."
- "One thing that other departments have tried is to __________. What would you think about that?"
- "A problem that other people sometimes have is ________. Do you think that might occur here?"
- "Has anyone else expressed any concerns about what volunteers might be doing here?"

Checking Questions
Checking Questions allow you to see how the other party feels as the discussion progresses. They also allow the other party involvement and participation in the decision-making process. Examples include:

- "How does this idea seem to you?"
- "What would happen if we did this ______?"
- "What would make this a negative experience for you?"

This process of direct interviewing of staff should be familiar to most volunteer directors, since it is precisely the kind of thing that is done in interviewing prospective volunteers about their interests and abilities.

Connecting Volunteer Positions to Wishes and Dreams
Another way to approach the development of new volunteer positions is to allow staff to dream about what they would like to do to really enhance their work. Assisting in this can be done either during direct interviewing of staff or during a planning session. It basically involves prompting staff to think about the ways they can both improve themselves and the quality of the work they are doing. The way to do this is to ask what is called a Magic Wand Question, one that allows the respondent to do a bit of daydreaming and wishful thinking.

Examples of good questions to ask to stimulate this process include:

- "What have you always wanted to do but never had enough staff?"
- "What would it be like here if you didn't have this problem or concern?"
- "What would you do if you had a full-time person assigned as your assistant?"
- "If you could design the perfect person for you to work with, what would they be like?"
- "What more would you have to do to be truly recognized for giving excellent service to your clients?"
- "What have you wanted to learn how to do better?"
- "What are some things that you would like to see done but that you never have the time to do?"

The goal of these questions is to tap into the frustrated creativity of overworked staff. This technique is also very useful in situations where staff may fear replacement of paid positions by volunteers, since it concentrates on developing new areas of activity, not re-assigning current work.

Each of the techniques above should assist you in increasing the "value" of your volunteers to the agency, resulting in the creation of positions that achieve a higher impact for the agency and more meaningful work for the volunteers.

Helping Staff Continue to Develop Innovative Jobs
The work development process is never-ending. New ideas should be continuously provided to staff. Among the ways to do this are:

- Talent advertising: disseminating information about volunteers who have recently joined the organization with particular skills or expertise.

- Success stories: highlighting examples of innovative involvement of volunteers, often best done by showing the success that staff have had in achieving some new goal or solving some problem through the involvement of volunteers

- Position upgrading: organizing scheduled evaluation sessions of volunteers to re-examine assignments and re-shape the work to take into account the growth and development of the volunteer.

5. Early Monitoring of Volunteer Placements
Those staff who are afraid of a loss of quality control will be made more comfortable if they are included in the selection and orientation process. Allow staff to help develop the criteria by which volunteers will be chosen, to participate in interviewing potential volunteers for their department, and to design and present portions of the volunteer training sessions.

Initial assignments for the volunteer can be on a trial basis. It is a bit irrational to assume that following a 30-minute interview you will know precisely where this volunteer will be most effective. It is far better to give a temporary assignment, with a review scheduled for 30 days later. During this period, the volunteer can conduct a "test drive" of the job and of the agency, and determine if it matches her needs. The staff member who works with the volunteer can see if the volunteer has the qualifications and commitment required for the job. The Volunteer Program Manager can see that the volunteer and the member of staff have those essential elements of "fit" that are essential to a mutually productive working relationship. The experience of this initial "trial period" can then be used to finalize the placement of the volunteer. If changes need to be made, it is much better to do them at this early stage than to wait until disaster strikes.

You will also need to monitor the staff providing on-the-job training for the volunteer.

6. Staff Control and Responsibility in Volunteer Management

Once staff are accustomed to the idea of supervising "their" volunteers, the majority will quickly become quite happy to accept this responsibility. The role of the Volunteer Program Manager is to teach staff how to do this correctly, particularly insofar as managing volunteers is different from managing paid staff, and to assist them in dealing with problem situations.

Be sure that you clarify the web of relationships between the volunteers, the staff, and the Volunteer Program Manager. The staff must understand whether supervision is being done by themselves or by the Volunteer Program Manager. She must understand who is in charge of what, who is responsible for what, and what should happen if things go wrong. Who, for example, is in charge of firing an unsatisfactory volunteer? The member of staff? The Volunteer Program Manager? Is it a unilateral decision or a joint one? Is there any appeal or grievance procedure?

The extent of staff involvement will vary, depending upon the particular staff member's own comfort and desire for management responsibilities. Even if the Volunteer Program Manager still supervises the volunteer, an effort should be made to make the staff feel a part of the supervisory team and to keep them informed about what is happening. You can do this by asking their advice from time to time about how the volunteer should be treated, or inquiring as to how they think their volunteers are doing at the job.

The agency might also create set standards for staff supervision of volunteers. Consider the following, from Catholic Charities of the Archdiocese of St. Paul and Minneapolis:

Minimum standards for supervisors of volunteers
We ask the volunteer supervisor to:

1. *Attend required volunteer supervisor orientation/ training.*
2. *Work with volunteer coordinator to clearly define volunteer positions which the supervisor is requesting (including duties, qualifications, and time commitment to fulfill the position). Keep volunteer coordinator informed of changes in job description.*
3. *Participate with the volunteer coordinator in the selection of volunteers for the specific position.*
4. *Provide specific on-site orientation and training for volunteers.*
5. *Assure regular contact with volunteers for whom you are responsible, and provide a minimum of annual formal evaluation session.*
6. *Communicate key information to volunteers which will affect the volunteer's performance (i.e. current operating information, changes in schedules, training, meeting dates, and changes in client status).*
7. *Assure report of volunteer's hours/impact to the volunteer coordinator.*
8. *Participate in formal and informal volunteer recognition activities.*
9. *Notify the volunteer coordinator of any problems or questions regarding a volunteer as soon as they become evident and prior to any decision to terminate.*
10. *Advise the volunteer coordinator when a volunteer terminates and/or has a change in volunteer status.*

Supervisors of volunteers exceed expectations by:

1. *Attending additional training regarding supervision.*
2. *Assisting the volunteer coordinator in recruitment of volunteers and being aware of organizational volunteer needs.*
3. *Designing and implementing the volunteer training and training materials.*
4. *Contributing to the volunteer's professional growth, including such things as resume writing, career laddering, reference letters, and special training.*
5. *Planning and implementing formal and informal recognition activities for volunteers.*
6. *Along with the volunteer coordinator, solving problems around potential issues/problems regarding volunteers and the volunteer program.*
7. *Engaging with the volunteer coordinator in the annual planning process for the volunteer program.*
8. *Participating in the divisional volunteer program by serving on a task force or advisory committee.*

You may want to consider structural ways to give staff control and responsibility over volunteer involvement. In a small way, for example, creating a "user's group" for staff who supervise volunteers can be a way to involve staff. Much as user's groups for those dealing with computers this can allow a forum for discussion of problems and triumps.

On a larger level you might consider a "staff advisory

group" who assists you in developing policies and shaping the direction of the volunteer program.

7. Feedback and Recognition.

The seventh element in a system for staff involvement is continuing to demand more volunteer help. This includes:

- Providing managerial information to staff on quantities and patterns of volunteer use.
- Showing examples of successful and innovative use of volunteers
- Implementing rewards and recognition for successful staff managers of volunteers.

Rewards for staff may range from formal recognition of their accomplishment by the agency to increased chances for promotion, and some informal recognition of their skills (represented by their inclusion in volunteer management activities, training, staff orientations, etc.).

A subtle way to get staff to recognize the importance of volunteering is to recognize volunteering that is done by staff. If you know of cases where staff have been significantly involved as volunteers in the community consider nominating them for local or national volunteer awards.

8. On-Going Relationship Building

What you are trying to create is an overall organizational climate that recognizes and respects volunteer participation. This means that true recognition should occur throughout the management process. Including volunteer use in overall evaluations of the organization's accomplishments, or evaluating staff in their proficiency in volunteer supervision, are much more meaningful indicators than certificates handed to staff on an annual basis, and staff will be well aware of the difference.

Here are some specific tips:

1. ***Support the initial decision to employ volunteers:***

- Attempt to reduce staff anxiety by indicating that the decision is under their control at all times.
- Follow-up both by telephone calls and face-to-face to discuss potential problems.
- Ask for feedback, both positive and negative.
- Introduce staff to others who involve volunteers. Build a support network.

2. ***Help manage the implementation:***

- Keep in touch, and keep staff informed on progress or lack of it.
- Assist staff with getting the decision to use volunteers approved.
- Assist staff with paperwork.
- Involve staff in recruitment, interviewing, orientation, and other aspects of volunteer involvement.
- Advise staff of key management requirements.

3. ***Deal with dissatisfaction:***

- Empathize with staff feelings.
- Respond to problems promptly.
- Continue to anticipate concerns and expectations.
- Reinforce the anticipated benefits.
- Never attempt to force continuing use of volunteers if things are not working out—withdraw the volunteers and deal with problem, then seek to reintroduce volunteers.

From time to time both staff and volunteers will use you to vent their frustrations with the other. Learn to grin and bear it, since this is a very useful part of your job and a highly valuable role for someone to play in making relationships work more effectively. It is more productive for them to be venting their frustrations on you than on one another.

4. ***Enhance the relationship:***

- Be available.
- Arrange for continual personal communication.
- Do not wait for staff to come to you - check for problems and approach them.
- Facilitate open, candid communication.
- Maintain high-quality volunteer referrals.
- Become a resource for information, help, new ideas, problem solving.
- Praise staff for good work, and inform their line manager.

Creating Senior Management Support

Senior management must not only endorse the use of volunteers in the organization but must also endorse the overall concept of a volunteer program. This applies both to the paid executives of the organization and to the volunteers on the board of directors.

Keys to Management Support

There are three elements that are essential in gaining support from senior management.

- *Understanding*

Senior management must understand the volunteer program in terms of what it aims to achieve and how it operates, including the relationship of the volunteers to the staff.

- *Information*

Senior management must understand what the volunteer program can accomplish compared with the financial and personnel costs required to run the program, and must understand that the benefits outweigh the costs.

- *Involvement*

Senior management must understand what they can and should do to assist the volunteer program.

Understanding

Obtaining a firm commitment from senior management first requires that they actually understand the nature of the volunteer program.

This requires that they themselves know why they wish to have volunteers connected with the agency. Senior management must be happy with their decision to introduce a volunteer program, and recognize that the volunteers have the ability to contribute to the success of the agency.

Their decision should be based on whatever rationale they choose to adopt, whether viewing volunteers as a source of community input or community outreach, or simply viewing volunteers as a cost-effective service delivery. The particular rationale is not as important as the fact that there is some commonly accepted rationale. If there is not one, you would be wise to lead senior staff through a planning exercise to formulate one. If you do not do this, you risk having several different, and perhaps mutually exclusive, opinions of why the volunteer program should exist, or risk the prospect that no one in senior management really understands why it does exist. It is difficult to fully support something you do not fully understand, particularly in a budget crisis.

Linked to this rationale is a second requirement, that senior management understand what needs to be done to have an effective volunteer program. They must have an understanding of the volunteer management process and the investment needed to make effective use of volunteers.

Information

Senior management support will require sufficient information to judge whether the volunteer program is successful.

This information can take a number of forms:

Patterns of volunteer use

This might consist of reports on where and how volunteers are being deployed. A report would include, for example, a department-by-department listing of how many volunteers are involved, how many hours they are contributing, and what types of jobs they are doing. The value of this type of report is that it allows senior management to identify patterns of usage, highlighting staff and departments who are doing a particularly good job of involving volunteers and those who are not.

It also shows senior management the types of work that volunteers are capable of doing.

Value of the volunteers

It is valuable to include estimates of the value to the agency of the volunteer contribution. This would include tracking a number of items:

- Value of donated volunteer time: calculating the number of volunteer hours and multiplying it by an estimated hourly wage. This estimated wage can be derived from a statistical estimate of what volunteers would otherwise earn with their time in their occupations (about $18 per hour), or by a calculated figure for each particular volunteer job (for example, a legal adviser would be valued at a much higher hourly rate than a clerical helper).

- Value of in-kind donations by volunteers: recording the value of any personal or business equipment donated by the volunteer, including use of business office space or other facilities, personal equipment, etc.

- Direct cash donations by volunteers: tracking any direct donations made by volunteers. Studies have shown that volunteers are much more likely than any other group to make a donation—although some organizations have a policy of not approaching volunteers for cash support. Another measure might be legacy pledges.

- Unreimbursed volunteer expenses: recording the expenses incurred by volunteers (mileage, phone calls, copying, etc.) for which they have not sought agency reimbursement. Some organizations have a policy of encouraging reimbursement of all volunteer expenses, but then providing a system for the redonation of such expenses back to the agency.

Information should be provided to senior management in a combination of facts (statistics, lists, etc.) and stories (anecdotes, case studies, interesting personalities, or snippets of information). This area is discussed more in Chapter Fifteen, Measuring Volunteer Program Effectiveness.

Involvement
The final element of senior management support involves telling them how and when they can be helpful to the program.
There are several functions at which an appearance by senior management is extremely valuable. These include appearing at volunteer orientations, giving out volunteer recognition items, and meeting occasionally with groups of volunteers. It also includes being generally supportive on an on-going basis.

A show of support by top management does not have to formal or time-consuming. One excellent example of top management support occurs in a hospital whose chief administrator has an hourly meeting with volunteers each Tuesday, rotating the invitees among the volunteers in various departments. Another hospital administrator memorizes names and photographs of new volunteers, and then "casually" greets them in the halls of the hospital, welcoming them on behalf of the institution. What is important in these examples is the sincerity which leadership exhibits by these small acts of connection with the volunteers.

Senior managers also have role to play in encouraging staff to value the volunteer input, to reward staff that work well with volunteers, and to convince other staff that they should work harder.

Perhaps the best encouragement that senior management can provide staff is through example. If the top management make effective use of volunteers, other staff will receive a clear message regarding the value and importance of volunteers to the organization.

Key Points

Generating conflict between staff and volunteers is not at all difficult, as this following, somewhat tongue in cheek list suggests:

How to Generate Conflict Between Paid Staff and Volunteers

- Don't involve staff in the decisions as to if and how to utilize volunteers within the agency. Everybody loves a surprise.

- Don't plan in advance the position descriptions or support and supervision systems for the volunteers. These things will work themselves out if you just give them time.

- Accept everyone who volunteers for a position, regardless of whether you think they are over-qualified or under-qualified. Quantity is everything.

- Assume that anyone who volunteers can pick up whatever skills or knowledge they need as they go along. If you do insist on training volunteers, be sure not to include the staff with whom the volunteers will be working in the design of the training.

- Assume that your staff already knows everything it needs about proper volunteer utilization. Why should they receive any better training than you did?

- Don't presume to recognize the contributions that volunteers make to the agency. After all, volunteers are simply too valuable for words.
- Don't reward staff who work well with volunteers. They are only doing their job.

- Don't let staff supervise the volunteers who work with them. As a volunteer director, you should be sure to retain all authority over 'your' volunteers.

- Try to suppress any problems that come to your attention. Listening only encourages complaints.

- In case of disputes, operate on the principle that "The Staff is Always Right." Or operate on the principle of "My Volunteers, Right or Wrong." This is no time for compromise.

To create a more motivating atmosphere, follow these general principles in planning your work with staff:

- Try to spend at least as much time working with staff as you do working directly with your volunteers. In the initial development of your program plan to spend much more time with the staff.

- If a department or project does not wish to make use of volunteers, do not attempt to force it to do so. Try to believe that if you have a winning resource, then eventually people will want to make use of it. Work first with departments that are willing to do a good job and then broaden the program from there.

• Deal with problems that arise as quickly as possible. Do not let a situation fester. And do not attempt to force people to get along. It is better for the volunteer to be transferred elsewhere than for you to try to enforce compatibility.

• Your ultimate objective is to get the staff to do the core work of volunteer management. If you can enable staff to become effective Volunteer Supervisors then you will be able to spend your time working on creative position development and troubleshooting. If you are forced to attempt to personally supervise all of the volunteers in the agency, then you will be overwhelmed by the trivial.

The willing involvement of staff is essential to the long-term success of any volunteer program. Volunteer programs cannot be done *to* staff they can only be done *with* staff.

Chapter Fourteen Risk Management

Fear of legal liability problems has become an increasing worry for volunteer program managers in the past few years. Examples of lawsuits involving volunteers in recent years include:

- Actions against volunteers and agencies for accidents in which they were involved. One 1990 lawsuit against a Boy Scout volunteer resulted in a $12.8 million judgment because of an automobile accident.

- Accusations of sexual abuse against volunteers working with children. A 1991 lawsuit in St. Paul, MN resulted in a $750,000 settlement against a neighborhood house that operated a youth camp.

- Actions based on conflict between volunteers and clients. A 1991 case in Sacramento involved a volunteer who attacked a chronic caller to a suicide prevention center. The volunteer said the client "was sucking everything out of me...he antagonized me so that I would kill him."

- Actions involving volunteers who disagreed with actions taken by the organization. A disgruntled office volunteer at a church who brought suit because the church "fired" her after she complained about its refusal to install a handrail for the handicapped at the church altar.

- Actions involving criminal behavior by volunteers. An AIDS volunteer in San Francisco who was arrested for preparing marijuana-laced brownies for AIDS patients. She was a former Volunteer of the Year at the program at which she worked.

- Actions involving public statements by volunteers about their volunteering. A volunteer who sued a local criminal justice system over his right to publicly criticize its operations, and who won based on the equal rights to free speech according paid and unpaid employees.

Although very little data exists about the actual numbers of lawsuits, two things are becoming clear:

- The likelihood of a volunteer program being involved in some incident that results in legal action is increasing; and

- The fear of such involvement is affecting the behavior of those thinking about involving themselves with programs and the behavior of those managing programs. A study in North Okanagan in Canada found that 40% of organizations thought liability concerns had made it more difficult to recruit volunteers and 11% of organizations had stopped certain types of volunteer activities out of a fear of liability.

It is important not to get carried away with liability fears about volunteer program operation. The perception of risk is much greater than the actual likelihood. Gaskin, in a 2005 study for the Institute for Volunteering Research found that 30% of volunteeer involving organizations said "Yes, definitely," when asked in their fear about liability had increased, and 31.8% said "Yes, somewhat." Then then reported that:

- 17% had volunteers stop their volunteering
- 52% had volunteer express concerns
- 22% had volunteers deterred from volunteering

A follow-up with volunteers, however, reveals a slightly different picture. Although 15% of prospective volunteers expressed concerns about possible liability from volunteering they then noted:

"However, only 2 percent said they were definitely worried and the remainder were only somewhat worried. Half said 'not really' and more than a third said 'definitely not'. Other reasons such as shortage oftime and being too busy and the fact that they keep meaning to but hadn't got around to it or didn't know how to go about it, were more important."

When asked if they had ever been involved in an incident that resulted in the organization being sued for negligence, damages or injuries, only 1% responded "yes."

The liability of operating a program with volunteers is not much different from that of operating one with paid workers. In fact, experience with volunteer insurance suggests that the two are quite comparable in terms of overall risks. The greatest likelihood of lawsuits comes from injuries caused by accidents. The greater training and experience possessed, in general, by paid staff makes them somewhat more likely to avoid accidents; on the other hand, the fact that volunteers work because they want to tends to give them a greater attention to work than that of staff who become jaded and inattentive. On balance, the two are equally "unsafe."

This chapter is designed to make general suggestions about some risk management techniques that can be useful to any volunteer program manager and that can be implemented easily. It concentrates on a process of risk management that relates to the central duty of each Volunteer Program Manager: getting capable volunteers into a job for which they are suited.

Those of you seeking more specific legal information will need to contact your organization's attorney. The specificity required in legal situations - what jurisdiction you are in, what kind of organization you are in, etc. - means that only very general rules can be provided by us. We hope, however, that this will give you the background needed to have a better conversation with your own legal staff. Remember that they are likely to be as ignorant about volunteer involvment as you are about legal issues.

A Brief Look at Volunteer Program Liability

There are three basic areas in which potential liability problems are likely to occur in volunteer programs:

1. Liability *of* the Individual Volunteer

Individuals that volunteer, just like the rest of us, are potentially liable for the consequences of their actions. There is no "halo" effect that occurs just because one is volunteering. This is true, by the way, despite the enactment in recent years of so-called "volunteer protection statutes" in all 50 states. These statutes do not eliminate liability; they simply raise the requirements for proving that a volunteer's conduct was sufficiently bad to warrant legal punishment.

Volunteers may encounter legal problems in any of three areas: criminal liability; civil liability; breach of obligation to the organization.

Under *criminal* liability, the volunteer might violate state or federal criminal statutes. This includes obvious violations (theft, assault, client abuse) as well as less obvious things (failure to report child abuse).

Under *civil* liability, the volunteer might, during performance of their volunteer work, injure another person. This injury might be physical, or financial, or psychological, or some combination of these. The injury might be caused by negligence on the part of the volunteer or through some intentional action. The volunteer might also breach contractual obligations.

Under *breach of obligation* to the organization the volunteer might violate some of the agreed rules of performance with the agency with whom they are connected. An obvious example would be a breach of confidentiality of client data.

Violations in any of these areas may make volunteers personally responsible for the consequences of their actions.

2. Liability of the Agency *to* the Volunteer

When a volunteer joins an organization as an unpaid employee, the organization assumes certain obligations to that volunteer. These fall into two general categories: protection from harm, and personnel rules.

In *protection from harm*, an organization has an obligation to not recklessly endanger its workers. Basically this means either eliminating work-related risks and dangers or else adequately alerting and preparing workers to deal with dangers. Volunteers, just like paid staff, are owed this obligation to be adequately prepared and trained for their work environment and tasks.

In *personnel procedures*, a volunteer has the right to fair treatment by the agency in hiring, firing, and other supervisory actions. This area is under rapid development at the moment, but it basically prevents the agency from taking non-job related actions against volunteers. This would prohibit discriminating against classes of individuals who wished to be volunteers, and would require acting in accordance with the series of employee rights and public accommodation laws enacted during the past 20 years—non-discrimination because of age, sex, race, disability, etc.

Failure in either of these two areas would open the agency to potential suit from its own volunteers.

3. Liability of the Agency *for* the Actions of Their Volunteers

If a person volunteering for an agency injures another, then that volunteer might be sued and the agency might be sued as well. This could occur under one of two legal approaches:

Volunteer acting within the scope of their employment duties can make the agency responsible because they are an agent of the organization, carrying out work on its behalf. The wrong-doing of a volunteer is, in essence, the wrong-doing of the agency.

Demonstrating what is within the "scope of duties" of a volunteer can more easily be done if the organization has an up-to-date position description for the volunteer and has maintained timesheets that identify when the volunteer was engaged in working on their behalf.

Volunteers who commit wrongdoing that is clearly outside the scope of their work (such as theft or child abuse) may also open the agency to suit. This is possible if the agency is itself guilty of negligent hiring, training, or supervision of the volunteer. In this case the agency may be held responsible because of its own failure to prevent the volunteer from injuring another.

In recent years the most common manifestation lawsuits against agencies for actions committed by volunteers has involved sexual misconduct involving minors participating in agency events and activities. The vast growth of these types of lawsuits – particularly in scouting, religious organizations, and sports coaching – has fueled the increasing requirement that volunteer-involving agencies perform background checks of prospective volunteers. The best information on this subject is by Linda Graff, whose works you will find in Appendix One. Any organization with children or clients with diminished capacity who are served by volunteers would do well to consult them.

These three categories are not a complete list of potential areas of volunteer program liability. Each program will have additional risks because of its particular subject area, and each program will have slightly different legal requirements because of its structure, operation, and jurisdiction.

Overview of Risk Management

Risk management is designed to allow program managers to forecast risks in advance and then to take proactive steps to deal with these identified risks in a purposeful fashion.

Basically, risk management involves working through four steps:

1. Identifying Risks

In this step, the manager brainstorms a list of possible dangers, situations, or problems that might occur incident to the operation of the program. This brainstorming is done in cooperation with others who are familiar with the program's operations and reviews both current operations and past occurrences in creating the list of risks. The intent of this process is to develop a master list of things that might go wrong in the operation of the program.

Areas to focus on include:

- Physical abilities required to perform tasks
- Attitude and maturity to perform work safely
- Worksite and equipment
- Skills required to perform work
- Nature of the clientele
- Procedures

A worksheet is provided in Appendix Three.

2. Evaluating Risks

The risks are then prioritized in terms of likelihood of occurrence and magnitude of harm. This prioritizing allows the manager to begin working with what would be the most troublesome of risks or what would be the most serious of risks.

One common way of evaluating risks has to do with the venue in which the volunteer works with the client. Here is an ascending scale of risk based on the degree of contact and the extent of exposure:

- work takes place in a highly public setting under staff supervision and volunteer has little direct client contact.

- work takes place in a normal office setting under staff supervision

- work involves direct client contact under limited staff supervision

- work allows unsupervised off-site contact between volunteer and clients.

Obviously the potential for difficulties in greater as one goes up the scale.

3. Controlling Risks

Decisions are then made about each specific risk. The basic types of possible responses are:

- *Stop the Activity*: Eliminate the risk by not engaging in the type of activity that might cause a problem. This option could include delaying the activity until adequate preparation has been made to engage in it safely.

- *Eliminate the Risk*: This would involve changing the operation of the program to reduce the likelihood of the risk occurring. This could involve changing agency procedures, paying closer attention to personnel requirements, updating equipment, etc. We will examine this operation in more detail in the next section.

- *Minimize the Harm*: This would include developing emergency procedures to deal with disasters when they do occur.

- *Transfer the Liability*: Move the consequences of the risk to some other party, via a memo of agreement, an insurance policy, or a waiver of responsibility.

4. Reviewing and Updating Risks and Procedures
As additional information is obtained about potential risks and solutions, additions and changes are made to screening, training, and supervisory techniques. The added knowledge is utilized to make the system progressively safer.

Applying Risk Management to Volunteer Management

Risk management techniques can be easily applied to volunteer management. Since volunteer management is concerned with getting qualified volunteer personnel into agency positions, it can be a crucial element in "eliminating risks," since many potential dangers are the result of an unqualified worker or a worker who was not following proper procedures.

To apply risk management planning to volunteer selection, follow these steps:

1. Identify Risks for Each Volunteer Position.
Think about what the volunteer might do wrong in performing the work. Think about accidents that might occur because of equipment use or unsafe premises. Think about who your clients are and what their special needs or limitations might be. In thinking about dangers, review past history of problem situations, and involve volunteers who have had direct experience in performing the work.

There is a tendency when performing this risk assessment to focus on volunteers who are either less motivated (and thus don't do enough of what they are supposed to) or less competent (and thus do it poorly). While this is good to consider, you might also want to think about what very highly motivated volunteers might attempt. See the discussion in Chapter Eleven on "Why Good Volunteers Choose to do Bad Things" to see why this is desirable.

2. Rewrite Volunteer Position Descriptions.
Tailor the "Qualifications" section of the position description to describe the skills, knowledge, and physical ability needed to avoid or deal with the dangers you have uncovered. This essentially involves "reversing" the identified risk to uncover the skills or characteristics necessary to avoid it.

3. Screen Potential Volunteers Based on Potential Risks.
Develop a list of items to be checked during the screening interview that will uncover volunteers who do not meet qualifications or who will need additional training. Begin collecting information that you will use during supervision and evaluation. Test potential volunteers by having them answer questions about how they would deal with potential problems that might arise in performing the volunteer position.

4. Train Volunteers in Risk Preparedness.
Develop a training program based on identified risks. Some of this can be delivered in orientations provided for all volunteers (particular requirements of the client population, for example), but some will need to be delivered as on-the-job training for particular positions. Develop "reality-based" training, examining not only how you think the work ought to go but also how, from experience, you know it might go. Your volunteers will be the first to thank you for this; your attorney will be second in line. You may lose some volunteers during this process who discover that they do not want to deal with some situations, but it is better to lose them at this point than later while they are actually attempting to perform the work.

5. Train Staff.
Make sure that staff are trained about the identified risks as well, and in particular make sure that staff are made aware of the dangers in assigning new work to volunteers who have not been adequately screened or prepared. Your biggest "hidden" danger as a Volunteer Program Manager is that "over-enthusiastic" staff will assign "over-willing" volunteers to do work they are not capable of doing.

6. Create Procedures for Risk-Based Supervision.

Develop a list of procedures, operational rules, and guidelines for problem situations. Alert staff who are supervising volunteers to potential problem behavior to watch for. Create mechanisms for continuous screening that periodically review each volunteer's qualifications for certain jobs. Be prepared to enforce your rules and procedures on volunteers who are straying a bit from the accepted path.

7. Review and Update.
Include a risk management review in your evaluation and performance assessment system. Continuously try to update and improve your risk management by maintaining a list of problem situations and using them to develop new training tools and supervisory procedures. Review each volunteer job annually to see if it has materially changed enough to require a significant updating of the job description, screening, training, or supervisory procedures.

A Case Study of Managing Risk

Suppose we were to consider a simple volunteer program that existed in order to assist homebound clients to get to medical appointments. The operation of the program consists of volunteer drivers who use their own vehicles to drive to the home of clients, pick them up, take them to doctors' offices, and then return them to home. A central office makes appointments for pickups and maintains volunteer schedules.

Identification of Risks
A quick brainstorming exercise conducted by staff and volunteer drivers might produce a list of possible risks such as the one that follows, based both on their experiences and on their imaginations:

1. Automobile accident:

a. caused by unsafe volunteer driver
b. caused by unsafe vehicle owned by volunteer driver
c. caused by collision initiated by another vehicle

2. Non-vehicle caused physical injury:

a. injury to physically-limited client while being assisted into or out of vehicle
b. injury to volunteer driver while assisting physically-limited client into or out of vehicle
c. injury to volunteer driver while loading client wheelchair into trunk of vehicle

3. Failure of driver to meet scheduled appointment:

a. driver unfamiliar with town becomes lost
b. driver has conflict and is unable to make appointment

4. Difficulty with client while in transit:

a. client has medical problem while in route
b. client makes accusation regarding improper behavior of volunteer

5. Improper activity engaged in by volunteer driver:

a. volunteer sees other needs of client, proceeds to make home visits on weekends to provide additional assistance
b. volunteer gives medical advice to clients
c. volunteer engages in conversations about other clients
d. volunteers abuse child whose is being transported

Development of Risk Management Strategies
Based on these perceived risks, the following strategies are developed:

Screening

- Check for valid driver's license.
- Ask volunteer about any physical limitations that would impact driving or providing assistance to clients.
- Gain permission to check driving record, perform background check.
- Check for and copy vehicle insurance policy; note expiration date.
- Check vehicle safety inspection; note expiration date.
- Test for physical ability to work with physically-limited clients.
- Test driving ability of volunteers.
- Get description of vehicle (s) and any limitations or special capacities, and license plate number.
- Get emergency contact number for volunteer.
- Test for suitability for job by exploring responses to sample driving problem scenarios.

Training

- Train in aiding physically-limited clients in and out of vehicle.
- Provide demonstration of wheelchair mechanics and operation.
- Work through problem-client scenarios:
  1. recommended actions if medical emergency occurs in route.

   2. reporting requirements if incident occurs with client.
- Clarify extent of volunteer role:
   1. what to do.
   2. what not to do.
   3. what to do if new situation arises.
- Provide procedures and forms for accident reporting.
- Provide tour of town and map.
- Provide 24-hour contact number for reporting scheduling problems.
- Inform volunteers about immediate reporting of change in status of driving record, vehicle, or insurance.
- Provide in-service training for volunteers regarding new policies or new potential problem situations.

Supervision

- Recruit volunteer driver back-ups to serve in emergency situations.
- Recheck driver's license, insurance, vehicle inspection at annual evaluation (or at noted expirations).
- Provide photo identification cards to volunteers so that clients may verify their status
- Ask volunteer during annual evaluation about any changes in driving status, ability.
- Deliberately schedule more qualified drivers or more suitable vehicles for difficult situations or clients; develop client screening procedures to identify special needs.
- Provide mentor-instructors to work with volunteers for first trips.
- Provide agency insurance policy to cover injuries to volunteers and clients.
- Encourage volunteers to report potential problem situations and build these into discussion sessions for volunteers to identify solutions.
- Develop process for volunteer reporting of unmet client needs and build relations with other agencies to provide client referral.
- Require escort or parent to accompany volunteers when a child is being transported

This way of thinking allows you to build preventive measures into all aspects of the volunteer program and to develop multiple approaches to combating problems. It makes it much less likely that small mistakes will slip through the cracks and turn into big disasters.

The Bottom Line

This sounds like a lot of work, and it can be. Risk management, however, is a very good way to take a hard look at your management procedures, and it is guaranteed to reduce your chance of legal involvement if done correctly. It also becomes easier the more you do it. The first time will seem like cleaning a house that hasn't been touched in years: a lot of dust has developed. You can get help from local insurance agents who specialize in risk management, and you can also make this an excellent task for mid-management volunteers who are familiar with many aspects of program operation. Just make sure that you tell them the truth about what is actually happening in your program, not just what is supposed to happen.

Ultimately the best defense to volunteer liability situations is a well-managed volunteer program – it both reduces your likelihood of being sued and provides a reasonable defense should you be sued.

Most importantly, the suggestions you see in this chapter are completely under your control - you don't have to wait for a legal opinion. They are all part of managing the volunteer program and are all things that you can decide to implement yourself. They will allow you to take responsibility and positive action to make your program the best it can be. And they will make it more likely that you never wake up one morning saying to yourself *"If only I had paid more attention to..."*

Chapter Fifteen Measuring Volunteer Program Effectiveness

One of the recurring problems of Volunteer Program Managers is demonstrating that their programs actually are of value. There are a number of ways to do this, but each requires a bit of attention and a bit of arbitrary decision-making on the part of the volunteer manager. We will discuss five different systems for determining the effectiveness of the volunteer program:

- mission-based
- output-based
- customer-based
- standards-based
- outcome-based

Mission-Based Evaluation

Mission-based evaluation examines the impact of a volunteer program by a simple standard – *to what extent do volunteers assist the organization in achieving its mission and purpose.*

Conducting a mission-based evaluation consists of examining the ways and extent to which volunteers are performing work that directly links to the established goals and objectives of the organization.

This is easy to see through an example.

Community Service Volunteers is one of the largest volunteer-involving organizations in the United Kingdom. The mission of CSV is:

"CSV creates opportunities for people to take an active part in the life of their community."

Application of mission-based evaluation would involve seeing what CSV can do through the involvement of volunteers that links to the achievement of this mission. Accordingly, CSV strategic goals for 2004-2007 include the following:

- CSV will involve 149,000 people of all ages to play an active part in the life of their communities and contribute to the effective development and delivery of public and community services across the UK in 2004/5, 160,000 in 2005/6 and 171,000 in 2006/7.
- CSV will involve more than 20,000 disadvantaged or disaffected individuals in their community each year
- CSV will develop Make a Difference Day as the single biggest day of volunteering in the UK
- CSV will 'Open Doors' for public sector volunteering
- CSV will join up our services and delivery, and will be developing geographic centres of activity across the UK to provide a wide range of volunteering, learning activities and services.

Further evaluation would examine how volunteers are directly assisting within CSV to accomplish each of these goals. Among the "results" cited by CSV in a recent year are:

- CSV involves over 130,000 volunteers every year who help to transform over a million lives – and the environment – in the UK.
- CSV harnesses the experience, time and skills of over 8,000 senior volunteers who run activities and projects for CSV and recruit other senior volunteers.

A 2004 study by the Urban Institute lists the following general types of contributions that executive directions of charities believe can be attributed to volunteers:

- Increases in the quality of services or program you provide: 66%
- cost savings to your organization: 65%
- increased public support for your programs or improved community relations: 62%
- services or levels of service you otherwise could not provide: 60%
- more detailed attention to the people you serve: 58%
- access to specialized skills possessed by volunteers: 34%

In a very real sense, mission-based evaluation looks at whether the volunteers connected to an organization are directly involved in work that ought to be done. This might sense as though it would always be the case but the grim reality is that many volunteers involve volunteers in the ways that they do simply because of history or accident, following the old consulting adage "Things are the way they are because that's the way they got to be."

Involving volunteers in non-essential activities that do not contribute to the mission is not a major sin but it is a waste of an organizational asset. In a very real sense, donated time should be treated as donated money – it should be invested in the most profitable way for the organization.

Output-Based Evaluation

In the chapter on position design, we described how to create measures of how well volunteers are achieving their results. In one sense, the effectiveness of the volunteer program can be measured by looking at the sum total of the effectiveness of the individual volunteer efforts. We would want to report, for example, how many children in tutoring program were taught how much. In this chapter, we will examine supplemental information and additional methods of measuring the value of the volunteer program. Part of this includes a simple numerical tracking of what activities are happening to what extent within the program.

Possible Output Measurements

There are a variety of possible outputs to measure.

Some of these have to do with the overall contribution of effort provided by volunteers to the agency:

- Number of volunteers involved during past year
- Number of volunteer hours
- Number of clients served
- Number of staff or departments assisted

You might also want to track these overall figures separately for each department or project, to show how volunteers are contributing differently throughout the agency.

Determining What to Measure

The ideal method for tracking involves first determining to whom you wish to present the results and then determining what item will show them what they are most interested in. Department managers, for example, may be most interested in what volunteers have given to their unit and thus will want to know overall hours contributed per department. Senior managers involved in fundraising may want to know figures that can be utilized in producing grant proposals, including items such as the composition of the volunteer population. You yourself may be most interested in the internal statistics about volunteer retention and turnover.

It is important to determine in advance what you want to track, since doing so will involve efforts both on your part and on the part of staff and volunteers. Volunteers will have to complete time sheets and both staff and volunteers will have to track volunteer assignments. Neither will be totally happy about these recordkeeping tasks, so you will want to keep the work to a minimum and make sure that the results are something that people are interested enough in that they are willing to do the work required to create the data.

Putting a Value on Volunteer Time

Most programs in the US now attempt to calculate a dollar value for their volunteers. Such a calculation has always been an acceptable one, supported by general accounting practices. The American Institute of Certified Public Accountants, in providing instructions for auditing voluntary organizations, cites three standards that must exist in order to "count" the contribution of volunteers:

1. *The services performed are a normal part of the program or supporting services and would otherwise be performed by salaried personnel.*

2. *The organization exercises control over the employment and duties of the donors of the services.*

3. *The organization has a clearly measurable basis for the amount.*

In 1993, the Financial Accounting Standards Board finally enacted a requirement that some types of volunteer services be recorded and reported in the financial records of the organization:

Contributed Services
Statement of Financial Accounting Standards No. 116
Financial Accounting Standards Board

9. Contributions of services shall be recognized if the services received (a) create or enhance non-financial assets or (b) require specialized skills, are provided by individuals possessing those skills, and would typically need to be purchased if not provided by donation. Services requiring specialized skills are provided by accountants, architects, carpenters, doctors, electricians, lawyers, nurses, plumbers, teachers, and other professionals and craftsmen. Contributed services and promises to give services that do not meet the above criteria shall not be recognized.

10. An entity that receives contributed services shall describe the programs or activities for which those services were used, including the nature and extent of contributed services received for the period and the amount recognized as revenues for the period. Entities are encouraged to disclose the fair value of contributed services received but not recognized as revenues if that is practicable.

The UK has created a system called VIVA, the Volunteer Investment and Value Audit, which examines ways of valuing volunteer time. The Knowledge Development Centre of the Canada Vounteerism Initiative has developed a similar tool called the Volunteer Value Calculator. This may be because only 7% of Canadian volunteer programs reported estimating a financial value for their volunteers in a recent study.

Regular time sheets completed by volunteers or a computerized sign-in procedure provide ways to record the number of volunteer hours. Establishing a value for these hours is a bit more difficult. There are three basic methods, each taking a slightly different approach:

- *The Minimum Wage System*

This system involves an estimate of what a volunteer would earn at a minimum if they were being paid—take the minimum wage for your state and multiply it by the number of volunteer hours. The advantage of this system is that it is difficult for anyone to argue that you are over-valuing the volunteers. The disadvantage of this method is that it provides no accurate estimate of what volunteers are really contributing and tends to demean those contributions.

- *The Imputed Wage System*

This system involves estimating what volunteers might reasonably be earning if they were being paid. To calculate this amount, assume that a volunteer is an average member of the community, and would therefore be capable of "earning" at least the average per capita income for his/her area. You can find out what this average per capita income (or, if you wish, what the average per capita wage earner makes) from your Department of Labor, either on a local or statewide basis. The national figure for volunteer contribution disseminated by the Independent Sector (see www.independentsector.org for yearly figures) is derived from a somewhat more sophisticated variation of this approach , in which the demographic and educational characteristics of volunteers are used to determine earning capacity.

- *The Equivalent Wage System*

This system attempts to establish what a volunteer would be earning if paid. The intent of the Equivalent Wage System is to produce, as nearly as possible, an accurate estimate of the prevailing salary rate for the actual type of work being done by each volunteer. The system depends upon the ability of the volunteer manager to classify correctly and track the type of work done by each volunteer.

The first step in this process is to classify the type of work to be done by the volunteer. One method for starting this classification system is to look at job definitions maintained by local labor departments and utilize their job categories and titles.

Step two is to determine the wage level for each job type. This figure may be obtained either from local labor departments or from having the personnel department of your agency provide an estimate of what salary would be paid for that type of work without your organization if you were to hire someone to perform it. If you have volunteers who are donating professional services you can establish a figure by having this provide you with a mock bill for their services.

Step three requires recording volunteer hours according to job type. This means you must keep separate hourly records for the time donated in each volunteer job category.

Step four simply involves multiplying the total hours within each job category by the wage figures for that category.

These calculations can be taken a step further. Neil Karn pointed out that valuing volunteer time by looking at comparative salaries alone ignores the fact that staff who are paid wages also receive considerable benefits, as well as vacation time. If you calculate the value of this additional compensation and add it to the hourly wage contribution of volunteers it will increase the average volunteer's contribution by about 25%, all of which would have been required if the agency were to employ paid staff instead of volunteers.

Adding in Some Other Volunteer Values

You might also consider tracking and recording some other items of value that volunteers bring. These include:

1. The direct cash contributions made by volunteers. Statistics on giving indicate that volunteers who have been solicited to give a cash donation to an organization are extremely likely to contribute. A 2003 study by AARP found that "*People age 45 and older who volunteer almost always are donors as well.*

Fully 92% of volunteers report having made a donation or donations in the past 12 months." As you recruit volunteers, you have also recruited donors, so why not take some credit for what they have given? A 2003 study by Arizona State University found that 79.6% of donor listed "because you volunteered at the organization" as a reason for giving.

2. In-kind donations by volunteers. Volunteers who are involved in projects often "contribute" far more than time. Their donations might include equipment, office space, etc. If the agency had not done the work through volunteers, the materials would have been purchased. The fact that the volunteers gave donations of both time and materials should be recognized.

3. Out-of-pocket contributions by volunteers. Many volunteers "donate" by not asking for reimbursement of expenses such as mileage, etc. These can be quite significant. Ivan Scheier estimated more than ten years ago that the average volunteer "contributed" more than $150 per year in out-of-pocket expenses. Paid staff would normally have been reimbursed for these items. The volunteers have assumed the costs, saving the agency money. The Australian Bureau of Statistics, in one of the few studies of this area, found that 43.9% of those volunteering incurred telephone costs, 43.8% incurred travel costs, 18.5% incurred postage costs, and 10.7% incurred meal costs. Reimbursement occurred in only 27.4% of cases.

Cost-Effectiveness Analysis

You can also attempt to determine some indication of the cost-effectiveness of your volunteer program by comparing the values calculated above with the costs of operating the program.

You may choose to do this in a simplistic fashion, such as comparing the budget expenditures for volunteer operations with the calculated value of volunteer contributions. This will give you a simple comparative ratio and will usually indicate a positive rate of return for the volunteer program.

A 2005 study by the National Philanthropy and Volunteer Centre in Singapore found:

"For every dollar spent on volunteers, the dollar value return of the 24 Volunteer Hosting Organisations surveyed ranges from $.77 to $139.80. The majority of the organisation's ratios are between 1:1.1 to 1:3.5."

A 2002 study of volunteers in Canadian hospitals found:

"The contribution that professionally managed volunteer programs make to hospitals is significant. Formal hospital volunteers contributed approximately 70,000 volunteers to each of the 31 hospitals studied. Estimates of the value of their time, derived from four different methods, average over $1.26 million per hospital per year against an average investment of $185,405 to staff and run a professionally managed program. This represents a cost-benefit ratio of 6.84. In other words, for every dollar that the hospitals in our study spent on professional management of volunteer resources, they derived $6.84 in value from their volunteers."

You can also, however, attempt a more significant measurement of volunteer cost-effectiveness. Jeff Brudney and Bill Duncombe have undertaken several in-depth analyses of methods of measuring volunteer effectiveness as compared to the utilization of paid workers. They have developed methods that will let the Volunteer Program Manager attempt to conduct a realistic appraisal of the use of volunteers versus paid staff in performing functions, taking into account such variables as recruitment costs, training expenditures, turnover, etc. Their formula for calculating the costs of utilizing volunteers is TCv = RTC + K C + MC where TCv is the Total Cost of Volunteers; RTC is Recruitment and Training Costs; KC is Capital Costs (equipment and facilities) and MC is Materials Cost.

The comparative equation for calculating the costs of hiring staff for comparable work is TCp = LC + KC + MC where LC = WC (Wage Cost) + FC (Fringe Benefits Cost) + RTC.

The advantage to the volunteer program during this calculation is obviously the absence of costs for wages and fringe benefits, and the usual advantage for the paid staff system during the calculation is a lessened expenditure for recruitment and training, since volunteer recruitment is more difficult than advertising for paid employment positions and since comparatively more volunteer workers will have to be recruited and trained to fill the same number of hours as provided by paid workers.

The formula does not take into account any possible differences in quality of the work provided, because that would be dependent upon both the nature of the work and the nature of the volunteer or paid staff involved.

Cautions in Measuring Results

The suggestions above will provide the volunteer

program with a set of numerical data that can be used to show overall activities and that can be tracked over time to show changes in program operation. There are two cautions about this data that you should keep in mind:

1. The data does not show overall impact in the community. It shows how much volunteers are giving, but it does not show what is happening to the community, to individual clients, or to the agency itself because of that contribution. In this respect, it is not really an indication of "volunteer effectiveness

2. The data is potentially dangerous. One troublesome aspect that some program managers have experienced is to learn after calculating a very high value for the volunteer contribution to the agency that their figure is simply too high to be accepted or believed by staff. This, by the way, is not difficult to do, particularly if you are a small agency with many volunteers.

Make sure in reaching your figures that you do not create something which will not be believed. The simplest way to ensure this is to take a low dollar value when first calculating the value of volunteer time, then explaining to staff what the figure might have been had you calculated it differently. You can also make sure that you show in the data that the contribution involved was made through the efforts of both the staff and the volunteers who were working on the project.

Measures of Importance to the Volunteer Program Manager

As the Volunteer Program Manager you might want to track some additional items related to how the volunteer program operates:

- Average length of service per volunteer
- Number of hours per volunteer per week
- Volunteers in different categories of age, race, sex, etc.
- Sources of new volunteers
- Range of jobs performed by volunteers
- Amount of volunteer turnover during the year
- Pattern of tenure among volunteers

You might want to look at the "shape" of the jobs performed by volunteers, tracking the number (and percentage) of volunteers who:

- work one-to-one with individual clients
- work directly with many clients
- work in group projects (construction, special events)
- participate in one time or once a year project or event
- assist staff (work as staff aide, little client contact)• provide technical assistance or professional skills
- perform general community-wide service (public information, speakers bureau)
- engage in fundraising (other than as a member of the board)
- serve on a board or committee work (involved with policy making)
- are all around volunteers (does a little of everything)

You might want to examine the "time patterns" of volunteers, determining how many are:

- involved only one time during the year
- involved three or four times during the year
- involved on a short-term basis (less than six months)
- involved for the long-term

You will also want to collect stories about heroic, odd, exemplary and appealing volunteer experiences. While numbers have an immediate impact, stories tend to stick in the memory.

Customer-Based Evaluation

A second method for measuring effectiveness lies in conducting customer service surveys about the volunteer program and its work. There are three primary customer groups whom you might wish to include in this effort:

- Volunteers
- Clients
- Staff
- Funders
- General public

Each of these can be surveyed to determine the extent of their relationship with the program and their levels of satisfaction with its operation. This process will create a measure of program effectiveness by ascertaining feedback from customers about their level of satisfaction with its operation and at the same time create a system for obtaining their suggestions as to how to improve the operation of the program as it effects them. There are examples of such surveys of staff and volunteers in Appendix Three.

Examples of Customer Feedback Questions
Here are some examples of feedback questions that could apply to each of your basic customer groups:

- How well do we deliver what we promise?
- How often do we do things right the first time?
- How often do we do things by when you need them?
- How quickly do we respond to your requests?
- How accessible are we when you need us?
- How helpful and polite are we?
- How well do we speak your language?
- How well do we listen to you?
- How hard do you think we try?
- How much confidence do you have in us?
- How well do we meet your special needs or requests?
- How would you rate the overall quality of our service?
- How would you compare us to other groups that you work with?
- How willing would you be to recommend us?
- How willing would you be to come back to us for further service?
- Are we doing or not doing anything that bugs you?
- What do you like best about what we do?
- How can we better serve you?
- What parts of our service are most important to you?
- How supportive do you think our staff was of your needs?
- Did we explain things to you clearly?
- Did we provide assistance in a timely manner?

Suggestions for Obtaining Customer Feedback
Here are some suggestions for obtaining feedback in a variety of formats, some formal and some informal:

- Go out and talk person-to-person with your customers. Spend some time with them. Get to know them and let them know you. Listen to them.

- Organize focus groups. Invite selected customers to come in and discuss what they like and dislike in an open forum. Invite both satisfied and dissatisfied customers.

- Ask people to respond to a customer survey, via phone or mail or on a website. Provide them with feedback on the results of the survey and what you intend to do because of it.

- Ask people face-to-face about what problems they are having, what they think should be done about the problems, what they like about your product or service, and what else they would like to see you do or provide.

- Have suggestion boxes and feedback forms easily available.

- Keep track of problems you are having, why they occur and what you have done about them.
- Thank people who tell you about problems or make suggestions. Give them the credit for helping you make things better.

Advantages of the Customer Service Approach
While this method also does not show the ultimate accomplishment of the volunteer program, it does measure the perceptions of those you are working with and those you are working to help. It provides a direct mechanism for both you and others to see whether people feel that you are doing the job the way it needs to be done. It also provides, without too much trouble, statistical information that can be compiled and measured over time to show changes in attitudes regarding the program.

Here, for example, are the results done regarding volunteer participation at the Buddhist Tzu Chi General Hospital in Taiwan:

"Of the 204 patients who participated in the survey, 88.6% felt that hospital volunteers brought them joy and hope, 73.3% felt that the more important contribution of the volunteers was their visiting and comforting, and 84.6% felt that the volunteers contributed to the quality of medical care they received."

And here is another result:

"Of the 240 nurses who participated in the survey, 50.6% felt that the visiting and comforting of patients was the volunteers' most important contribution and 92.5% felt that the volunteers had a positive impact on medical care quality."

A much fuller discussion of applying customer service principles to a volunteer program is provided in our book *Keeping Volunteers*.

Standards-Based Evaluation
A fourth method of measuring effectiveness lies in comparing it to outside standards of program operation, utilizing external standards to determine

whether the program is operating appropriately.

Some national organizations provide standards of operation for their affiliates. These standards may either suggest or require certain methods of operation. Some are connected to the overall evaluation of the local program and some concentrate on standards for volunteer involvement. You should determine whether your national group has such a set of standards.

You can also look elsewhere for overall guiding principles. Susan Ellis, for example, has produced an excellent booklet, *The Volunteer Management Audit*, which allows you to compare your program elements against some general standards of volunteer program operation. Canada, Australia and the United Kingdom have all produced versions of best practice standards for volunteer programs.

Our own recommendation is that you consider the principles of volunteer effectiveness determined by the Paradigm Project of the Points of Light Foundation. After examining the operation of numerous volunteer programs identified as "exemplary" within their communities, the Paradigm Project identified the following characteristics that tend to occur in successful volunteer programs:

Lay the Foundation through Mission and Vision

- The mission and priorities of the organization are framed in terms of the problem or issue the organization is addressing, not its short-range institutional concerns.
- There is a positive vision - clearly articulated, widely-shared and openly discussed throughout the organization - of the role of volunteers.
- Volunteers are seen as valuable human resources that can directly contribute to achievement of the organization's mission, not primarily as a means to obtaining financial or other material resources.

Combine Inspiring Leadership with Effective Management

- Leaders at all levels - policy-making, executive and middle management - work in concert to encourage and facilitate high impact volunteer involvement.
- There is a clear focal point of leadership for volunteering but the volunteer management function is well-integrated at all levels and in all parts of the organization.
- Potential barriers to volunteer involvement - liability, confidentiality, location of the organization, hours of operation, etc. - are identified and are dealt with forthrightly.

Build Understanding and Collaboration

- Paid staff are respected and are empowered to fully participate in planning, decision-making and management related to volunteer involvement.
- There is a conscious, active effort to reduce the boundaries and increase the teamwork between paid and volunteer staff.
- Success breeds success as stories of the contributions of volunteers - both historically and currently - are shared among both paid and volunteer staff.

Learn, Grow, and Change

- There is an openness to the possibility for change, an eagerness to improve performance and conscious, organized efforts to learn from and about volunteers' experience in the organization.
- There is a recognition of the value of involving, as volunteers, people from all segments of the community, including those the organization seeks to serve.

The most valuable thing about this approach is that it not only examines the elements within the volunteer program but also looks at other factors within the agency that will impact on the ultimate effectiveness of the volunteer program. The Points of Light Foundation has a number of assessment manuals that will help you implement this analysis and show you ways of improving the performance of your program, as well as ways of involving staff and volunteers in the process of looking at the volunteer program.

Outcome-Based Evaluation

Outcome-based evaluation asks a seemingly simple question: *"To what extent do the activities conducted by the program actually achieve their goals."*

In most cases this translate into a very basic inquiry: "Has the condition of the client improved?"

Outcome-based evaluation tracks a program logic model:

Inputs that lead to *Activities* that create *Outputs* that foster *Outcomes*

This obviously can be quite complex and those wishing to consider outcome-based evaluation should consider professional assistance. United Way of America has done extensive work in assisting its member organizations to develop methods for outcome-based evaluation. In Canada the Voluntary Sector Evaluation Research Project is doing similar work.

We'll make four observations about outcome-based evaluation:

1. Outcome evaluation tends to be very expensive in terms of thought, time and money. It can be very complicated to track precisely what is happening to clients.

2. Outcome evaluation is especially difficult in cases where the outcome itself is fuzzy (particularly if attitudes as well as behaviors are involved) and where other groups are working with the same client on similar issues.

3. Measuring long-term changes in attitude, behavior or status is an especially complex and expensive undertaking.

4. Outcome evaluation, when it works, is *really* good. It impresses clients, funders, prospective volunteers and everyone else. Here, for example, are results of an intensive study of Big Brothers/Big Sisters done by Public Private Ventures:

"Taken together, the results presented here show that having a Big Brother or Big Sister offers tangible benefits for youth. At the conclusion of the 18-month study period, we found that Little Brothers and Little Sisters were less likely to have started using drugs or alcohol, felt more competent about doing schoolwork, attended school more, got better grades, and ad better relationships with their parents and peers than they would have had they not participated in the program."

And here is the result of a 1996 study of volunteers in the National Health Service in the UK:

"Research shows that involving volunteers in General Practice reduces drug consumption by 30%, hospital appointments by 35% and hugely improves the quality of life of the doctors."

During the lifetime of a volunteer program each of these evaluation methods might well be utilized, depending upon the resources available and the demands of management and funders. Each method assists the Volunteer Program Manager in determining whether the work of volunteers, and of the volunteer management staff, is effective.

Chapter Sixteen Enhancing the Status of the Volunteer Program

To make the most difference, a Volunteer Program Manager and the volunteer program itself must have influence in the larger organization. In order to have influence, paid staff of the organization must place a high value on the volunteer program. If they are to place a high value on the volunteer program, staff must place a high value on the things volunteers do. Agencies will respect Volunteer Program Managers only to the extent that they also respect volunteers. They may like you personally, but they will only value you to the extent that volunteers make a significant contribution to the agency.

In too many agencies, staff pay lip service to the value of volunteers, but their actions say otherwise. Although they find the work of the volunteers to be useful, they too often do not value it as highly as the work of paid people.

This lack of value is reflected in the low salaries of those in the field. In agencies that have both a Volunteer Program Manager and a development officer (someone in charge of raising money), the development officer is usually paid far more. Both are responsible for raising resources to help their agency, but the development officer is often the highest paid management person in the agency (excepting the executive director) and the Volunteer Program Manager is often the lowest. The reason is that the things agencies buy with money—including the efforts of staff and consultants—are perceived as being more valuable than the things volunteers do.

The respect given the volunteer program will probably hinge on two things: the respect accorded volunteers and the respect accorded the volunteer director.

Ensuring Respect for Volunteers

In order for the Volunteer Program Manager to gain influence, staff must respect and value the contributions of volunteers. A theme of this book has been to upgrade the volunteer program, to make it more mission-critical in the life of the agency. As the Volunteer Program Manager begins to engage volunteers in high-impact ways, staff will start to think about volunteers in new ways.

An example comes from a hospital volunteer program. For decades, volunteers had done the usual things, such as transporting patients from one place to another, acting as a runner in the pharmacy, or providing information to visitors. The administration of the hospital talked about how "we couldn't stay open without volunteers," but in truth people never thought of volunteers as doing things that were as important as the things staff did.

One day the director of volunteers met with the purchasing manager of the hospital. With her she brought the purchasing manager of a large defense contractor who had agreed to volunteer his expertise to help the hospital. She had arranged the meeting by telling the purchasing manager that she had found a volunteer who might be helpful in purchasing. The purchasing manager was skeptical about this, but agreed to the meeting. At the meeting, the volunteer asked the purchasing manager three questions about the purchasing system of the hospital. The purchasing manager was embarrassed to admit he did not know the answers to any of the questions and was smart enough to see that he ought to know them.

To make a long story short, the volunteer helped to revamp the entire purchasing system of the hospital, saving it thousands of dollars each year. As the purchasing manager told his peers about this, they began to see volunteers in a different light and were receptive to talking to the director of volunteers about new roles for volunteers in their departments. The status of the volunteer department is now so high in this hospital that the director of volunteers recently served as acting director of the hospital for two months.

To gain increased status for the volunteer program, Volunteer Program Managers must act as leaders. They must make positive change in the way people view volunteers. To do this, they should follow the planning suggestions in the second and fourth chapters of this book, connecting the work of volunteers to the mission in both traditional and non-traditional ways. As more volunteers engage in new mission-critical activities, more staff will view them in new ways.

Making the Case for the Volunteer Program

One of the more difficult tasks faced by some volunteer managers is convincing their own organization of the value of volunteers and the need to put adequate organizational resources into the operation of the volunteer program.

This case can best be made by being able to demonstrate how volunteers have helped within the organization - utilizing statistics, examples and stories - but it's also nice to be able to quote studies and research.

Accordingly, we've sifted through about 1,000 research papers, studies, surveys and analyses of volunteer involvement and put together a set of The Good Stuff - the best and most pithy statements of what volunteers have to offer to an organization and what the organization needs to provide in order to effectively involve volunteers.

In the interests of conserving space we've just provided the author, title and date of the publications, but a lot of them are available for download from the Internet, so if you're interested do a quick search using the title and you too can read about 5000 pages of supporting documentation.

What Volunteers Have to Offer
Here are some of the findings regarding how volunteers make a contribution:

1. Giving New Hampshire, *Charitable Giving and Volunteering in New Hampshire*, 2003

"There is a strong relationship between giving and volunteering among New Hampshire residents. People who volunteer their time also give their money to charitable causes. Average giving is four times as high among those who volunteer as among those who do not…Those volunteers who volunteer most frequently – weekly or every other week – give 33% on average more than volunteers as a whole – or $1951."

2. Gianni Zappala and Tracy Burrell, *The Giving of Time and Money: An Analysis of Donor Behavior among Volunteers*, July 2002

"The most recent voluntary work survey conducted by the Australian Bureau of Statistics in 2000 showed that while almost three-quarters (74%) of people aged 18 and over made a personal donation of money to an organisation, volunteers had a higher donation rate (84%) than non-volunteers (70%)."

3. Center for Nonprofit Leadership, Arizona State University, *2003 Survey on Arizona Giving and Volunteering*

Reason for giving to a particular organization: 79.6%, "because you volunteered at the organization."

4. Statistics Canada, *2000 Survey on Giving, Volunteering and Participation*

"In 2000, approximately 67% of volunteers were employed and many received support from their employers for their volunteer activities. As in 1997, the most common type of support reported by volunteers was the approved use of their employer's facilities and equipment (28%)."

5. Silicon Valley Foundation, *The Culture of Giving and Volunteerism in Silicon Valley*, 1997

Despite the relative newness of many Silicon Valley companies, they appear to have a clear interest in supporting employee giving and volunteerism:

- *56% match employee contributions to charity.*
- *38% offered matching gifts programs for volunteering employees.*
- *38% offered release time for volunteering.*

6. The Consulting Network, *Practices in Corporate Employee Volunteer Programs*, December 2002

"The practice of offering cash grants to organizations where employees volunteer continues to grow, from 45 companies in 1997 to 64 companies in 2002...Fifty-one of the companies with a matching program indicate they contribute dollars for individual or team volunteer projects."

7. Canada West Foundation, *Making a Difference: Volunteers and Non-Profits*, March 1999

"In addition to assisting non-profits with service delivery, fundraising, and administrative tasks, volunteers are a visible manifestation of community involvement in an organization and a strong indication of the 'civic' qualities associated with non-profits such as the generation of social trust and social exchange…A similar point was made by the director of a well-established multi-service agency: 'volunteers are potential ambassadors of the organization and can develop the positive profile the organization wants in the community."

8. Canadian Centre for Philanthropy, *The Benefits of Volunteering*, 2000

"64% of volunteers reported an increase in their knowledge about such issues as health, women, politics, or the environment.

9. Lions Clubs International, *2004 Lions Clubs International Volunteerism Survey Results*

"The majority (57%) of respondents believe that volunteering has helped their career by enhancing their networking and skill-building opportunities, and 13% report finding a job/career change as a result of volunteering. For volunteers ages 18-24, volunteering offers significant career and social opportunities. Among this group, 87% believe that volunteering has helped their career, with 34% reporting they found a job or changed careers as a result of volunteering."

10. Femida Handy and Narasimhan Srinivasan, *Ontario Hospital Volunteers: How Hospital CEOs Perceive Their Contributions, 2004*

"CEOs were asked to identify the volunteer activities that enhance patient care. The most frequently mentioned, by 72% of CEOs, were activities that provide patients with human contact. The next most frequently mentioned (17%) was interacting with families and providing information. Less frequently mentioned, although still valued, were labour-intensive activities, such as helping with the mail or running the reception desk (7%), and activities that enhance the hospital's links with the community (3%). When asked to identify volunteer activities that provide the most support to staff, CEOs mentioned patient contact most frequently (52%). Next most frequently mentioned (29%) was providing assistance with hospital services (e.g., helping with the mail, running the reception desk). Less frequently mentioned were activities relating to family contact (15%) and enhancing the hospital's links with the community."

11. Grantmaker Forum on Community and National Service, *The Cost of a Volunteer*, March 2003

"Consider how the value of volunteers accrues. First, the act of volunteering is an expression of commitment to the community, and that has value to the nation. Second, the benefit or the services provided by volunteers may differ in fundamental ways from services offered by professional staff since the motivation to serve may be different. In some cases, a unique benefit is derived when the volunteer has more in common with the person being served (age, race, economic background or experience) than does the professional staff. Third, volunteers expand the base of community support for the nonprofit organization that sponsors them by making the work of the nonprofit transparent to the community - by bringing the community in, so to speak. In doing this, volunteers provide organizations with word-of-mouth publicity and have the potential to cultivate a broader base of supporters for the agency and its mission. And, of course, in addition to these benefits, volunteers expand organizations' capacity to deliver services to clients and communities in need."

What It Takes to Generate a Return from Involving Volunteers

And here are findings of what organizations need to do in order to make effective use of volunteers:

1. Volunteer Development England, *Volunteering Infrastructure: Shaping the Future*, December 2003

"...volunteer management is the most frequently overlooked building block in a volunteer involving organisation's internal infrastructure...Whilst volunteering is freely given, it is not cost free - volunteering requires an effectively resourced and professionally run infrastructure to sustain and develop it."

2. Sarah Jane Rehnborg, Catherine Fallon and Benjamin Hinerfeld, *Investing in Volunteerism: The Impact of Service Initiatives in Selected Texas State Agencies*, August 2002

"A strong relationship appears to exist between staffing levels and effective volunteer management practices. Programs and agencies with staff positions dedicated to volunteer management demonstrate more attention to the tasks associated with effective management."

3. Canadian Centre for Philanthropy, *Survey of Managers of Volunteer Resources*, May 2003

"Respondents who devote a greater proportion of their time to volunteer management activities...are more likely to report that the number of volunteers working for them has increased over the past three years."

4. Jean Grossman and Kathryn Furano, *Making the Most of Volunteers*, July 2002

"Based on our studies of programs that use volunteers in major ways (mentoring programs, service programs and community-based initiatives), we have concluded that three areas are vitally important to their success: screening, training, and ongoing management and support."

5. Grantmaker Forum on Community and National Service, *The Cost of a Volunteer*, March 2003

"In order to accommodate more volunteers, program managers say they need more organizational capacity - more professional staff, more funding, more infrastructure. Of the nine programs that stated they do in fact need more volunteers, their needs are specific in terms of scheduling and skills. The key issue is having the capacity to incorporate volunteer labor effectively so that neither the

organization nor the volunteer is wasting time."

6. Urban Institute, *Volunteer Management Capacity in America's Charities and Congregations*, February 2004

"The percentage of time a paid staff volunteer coordinator devotes to volunteer management is positively related to the capacity of organizations to take on additional volunteers. The best prepared and most effective volunteer programs are those with paid staff members who dedicate a substantial portion of their time to management of volunteers. This study demonstrated that, as staff time spent on volunteer management increased, adoption of volunteer management practices increased as well. Moreover, investments in volunteer management and benefits derived from volunteers feed on each other, with investments bringing benefits and these benefits justify greater investments."

7. Mark Hager and Jeffrey Brudney, *Volunteer Management Practices and Retention of Volunteers*, Urban Institute, June 2004

"Adoption of volunteer management practices can help organizations to retain volunteers, but charities interested in retaining volunteers should not stop there. They should also allocate sufficient funds to support volunteer involvement, cultivate an organizational climate that is welcoming to volunteers, give their volunteers an experience worth sharing, and enlist volunteers in recruiting other volunteers one-on-one. Charities that want to retain these essential human resources should adopt relevant volunteer management practices and invest in the infrastructure, culture and volunteer experience that will keep volunteers coming back."

8. Kimberly Spring and Robert Grimm, *Volunteer Management in America's Religious Organizations*, Urban Institute, June 2004

"The presence of a paid volunteer coordinator significantly impacts the extent to which congregations adopt management practices. Of congregations with a paid volunteer coordinator, 62 percent have implemented management practices to a moderately high degree, compared to 34 percent of congregations with a volunteer who coordinates other volunteers and just 19 percent of congregations without any volunteer coordinator. Similarly, the lack of a paid volunteer coordinator in charities with a religious mission has a substantial negative impact on the adoption of management practices.

Playing a Personal Leadership Role and Wielding Power

In order to play a leadership role in making this shift in the way volunteers are viewed, the Volunteer Program Manager must have the ability to influence others. This means having some personal power.

By personal power we mean the ability to influence others through force of who you are (in contrast to influencing people through force of the position you hold). You might think that this means being charismatic, but people with personal power can be out-going or introverted, energetic or low-key.

You might also think that personal power is something that people are born with or develop as children. On the contrary, it is something that can be developed.

Five major sources of personal power include:

- The power that stems from a director of volunteers' reputation in her field
- The director of volunteers' technical ability
- The director of volunteers' clarity of personal objectives
- The value the followers place on their relationship with the director of volunteers
- The optimism that stems from the director of volunteers' self-confidence and self-esteem.

Although discussed separately below, these five elements are closely related. The common thread that binds them together is that others admire these personal aspects of the leader. Leaders embody the aspirations and dreams of the followers. They are the kind of people the followers want to become.

Reputation Power

One aspect of personal power is the volunteer leader's professional reputation. If the leader has developed a reputation in her field, others will confer upon her a certain respect. Leaders gain this sort of power by networking with others beyond the organization. They are active in professional organizations, attend professional conventions, and chair professional societies.

In most American communities there are local, state, regional and national opportunities for such involvement. In many communities, there is an association of Directors of Volunteers in Agencies (often called a DOVIA). Attending training sessions, networking with others, and perhaps serving as a volunteer officer will help build your reputation. There are also major national conferences of the field in general that afford opportunities to establish relationships beyond your region. The same is true if there are national conferences within your field, such as the ASDVS or Special Olympics conferences.

Another way for Volunteer Program Managers to enhance their personal power is by creating new approaches within their fields or keep up with those who are. A leader may build a reputation by disseminating word of her successes to her colleagues by such means as writing articles for professional journals or by serving as a speaker or member of a panel discussion at conferences. Performing workshops at your local DOVIA meetings can be a springboard to speaking at regional or even national conferences.

A good and cheap way to network nationally with others in the field is through on line computer listservs. A selection of some of the major volunteer manager listservs is provided in Appendix Three, but there are many others for specific areas.

Reputation power does not necessarily have to do with the leader's technical competence. In one non-profit organization we work with, a leader was the last person anyone would turn to for help in solving a technical problem, but she still managed to have a great deal of influence due to her national reputation in her field. This reputation was built by her willingness to devote time to building the national, professional organization she was associated with. This, in turn, led to her becoming president of an advisory board for a federal agency that granted money to organizations like hers. Her opinion on a grant application to this organization would guarantee its success or failure. As a consequence, she had great influence in her field and was respected in her organization.

By being actively involved in this way you can increase your status in your field. By gaining office in your local DOVIA or other professional group, you let the staff of your agency know that volunteer management is a profession and that you are a leader in that profession. This will enhance your credibility when it comes to making change within your agency.

Reputation power is also built by managers within an organization by being proactive. Reactive people, who work only on that which is required, do things that are expected and hence are unremarkable. Reputations in an agency are not built by meeting other people's deadlines. Proactive people are people who go beyond the normal expectation of their job requirements and so get noticed. When they succeed at improving the services of the organization or the way in which those services are delivered, they build a reputation.

Positive reputations are built from positive achievements, from being "the one who" made something happen. "She's the one who developed that program. He's the one who got a volunteer to automate our procedures. She's the one who managed to get us a receptionist so we can have some uninterrupted time." These are the kinds of things said of budding leaders.

Ability Power

Closely related to reputation power is the influence a leader derives from having skills or knowledge that can be relied upon. If she is an expert in a certain area, this will give her influence over those who have less expertise. When others need and want information the leader has, they see the leader as someone who can help them succeed in their work. When they need and want skills the leader has, they see the leader as someone who can help them grow in their abilities.

To develop this kind of power, you should be concerned with ever improving your skills. Leaders with this kind of influence are always trying to gain new knowledge they can employ. They further their education by reading, attending seminars, and enrolling in college courses. They apply this knowledge in their own jobs and can be relied upon by others to help them with problems. Such a leader is therefore the person people naturally turn to for help and advice.

Sometimes people in leadership positions stagnate and cease to keep up with either their technical field or with new developments in management. Gradually, the skills of such people become outmoded. Their information is no longer up-to-date. They have lost this source of influence. In order to keep it, you must keep growing. Leaders are sources of information and skill only if they never stop learning.

There are many books published in the field of volunteerism each year, most of which can be seen at www.energizeinc.com or www.jtcinc.ca.

In addition to knowledge in one particular field, influential leaders often enhance their creativity and value as a resource to others by keeping abreast of many fields. This enables them to approach problems with a broader perspective and to generate new solutions and new ways of thinking about the organization. Subscribe to journals from related professions and read books about the latest developments in other fields. This is particularly true of reading books on management. You might, for example, subscribe to the Harvard Business Review, even though the articles in it are almost always directed toward the world of competitive business. Even though such information may have little direct application, the leader may find new constructs or different perspectives that stimulate her creative thinking. Reading an article on industrial re-engineering, for example, might start you to thinking about "re-engineering the volunteer program" in your agency. Such "break-through" ideas are frequently impressive to volunteers and staff and enhance their confidence that you are leading them in an effective direction.

Direction Power

Perhaps the most common source of personal power that leaders exert is the influence that derives from the leader being a goal-directed person. A person who has no particular goals in life or who is tentative about her belief in them is likely to spend a lot of time changing direction and spinning her wheels. Such a person is not likely to inspire much confidence in others. People tend to respond positively to someone with a clear sense of direction and with a strongly internalized purpose. In order to lead, one must have a firm sense of identity and a burning desire to accomplish a purpose.

The ability to influence others thus starts with an ability to influence oneself. It begins with quiet self-assessment of where one wants to go and what impact one wants to make. It begins with setting clear goals that burn within you and fuel your desire to succeed.

The source of a leader's desire is a clear vision of what she wants to accomplish in all areas of her life. One major difference between leaders who succeed and those who fail is that the goals leaders have are ones they can be passionate about. Leaders tend to love what they do. They have a passion for the purposes of their lives.

If you don't like your chosen field, you are unlikely to inspire others to pursue their goals with passion. Both you and they will proceed in a lackadaisical manner. Effective leaders of volunteer programs have a passion for the mission of their organizations and a passionate belief that volunteers can make the agency much more effective in accomplishing that mission.

It is surprising how many people seek to succeed in a profession they don't really like, that they barely endure. Without a love for what you do, it is difficult to exhibit the determination, persistence, and commitment that influential people display. Without these qualities, people tend to give up in the face of adversity, and the road to a high-impact volunteer program is often filled with frustrations and setbacks.

Leaders succeed because they keep trying when they encounter setbacks. As long as you are still trying, you have not yet failed. Giving up is thus the only way to fail. If you are determined enough, it is impossible to fail at whatever you set your mind to.

Influence from the Relationship

A fourth source of personal power comes from the value the staff and volunteers place on the relationship they have with the Volunteer Program Manager. She can enhance this source of personal power by trying to make each interaction with other people a positive one. When interacting with your volunteers or other staff, never criticize. When someone does something wrong, tell them what to do next time rather than dwelling on past mistakes. Find the good in people and praise it.

Positive statements about another person's qualities are called validations. They differ from recognition in that recognition is for a particular act while a validation is for being a certain kind of person. In giving recognition, the leader says, "you did a good job on this." In validating, the leader says "I am impressed by your abilities." Through validating, leaders make people feel good.

Leaders build relationship power by making people feel welcome, valued, and cared about. Show interest in your people. Ask them questions about what they are interested in. Try always to greet them before they greet you. Listen to their ideas, even if your initial reaction is negative. Call them by name. Compliment them. Remember their birthdays. Share the credit with them. People will only care about their relationship with you if you show them that you care about them.

You can also gain significant power simply by being helpful to others. You might do this in their work setting, passing on information about upcoming events (workshops, conferences, etc.) that you know would be of interest to them, or giving them copies of articles that you have read. You can also do this directly by conducting the job development interviews discussed in Chapter Four, and consciously striving to find volunteers who can make a substantial impact on the work that the staff person is doing.

Communication Power
People follow leaders readily when the leader articulates a message the follower wants to hear. Throughout history, people have influenced groups by communicating powerfully a belief the group already holds. Patrick Henry, for example, inspired a nation with his "liberty or death" speech by articulating in a compelling way a yearning for freedom that the majority already believed.

In organizations, this means that leaders must listen to their people. They must learn their dreams and aspirations. They find out what people would like their work to mean to them. They then communicate the purpose of the organization to people in a compelling and powerful way. By helping the organization build a positive vision of the role of volunteers in accomplishing the agency mission, leaders keep people connected to a purpose.

Optimism Power
Perhaps the most important element of personal power is optimism. Leaders inspire confidence. And having a pessimistic outlook does not inspire much confidence.

Effective leaders of volunteers are optimistic. Leaders focus on the future, a better future. They must be optimists, keeping hope alive in those around them. The self-talk of leaders with respect to fortune and misfortune is therefore very important, because it is difficult to keep others up if you are not optimistic yourself. Also, in times of stress, our self-talk tends to be voiced to others. Saying something pessimistic like "We never should have tried this" is not likely to build the confidence of others.

By remaining focused on the future, you inspire confidence in those around you. It is essential that leaders ask themselves these kinds of empowering questions because it is important for the leader to stay "up," to set an example of enthusiastic optimism. The others will feel more confidence in themselves if they know the leader is confident in herself. It is also more pleasant to be around a leader who is in a good mood, who feels in control of her life, thus enhancing the power the leader derives from the relationship she has with her people.

Effective leaders are motivators. They keep others enthused and thinking positively. In tough times for the organization, people look to the leader for cues as to how to respond. If the leader is depressed and dwelling on the pessimistic side of the picture, the others will too. On the other hand, if the leader is confident and optimistic, people will continue to put out their best efforts. This is therefore a self-fulfilling attitude.

One of the most important characteristics a leader can develop is the ability to be optimistic, to stay "up," even in the face of adversity. Of course it is difficult to maintain a positive, cheery mood all the time. In addition to organizational difficulties, the leader will no doubt also face personal adversity from time to time. Below are some keys to staying up when the world around you rocks on its foundation.

- *Self-Talk*

In the face of setbacks, it is easy to get down on yourself, to blame yourself, to castigate yourself for not performing well enough. In order to gain the confidence of others, it is important to have confidence in yourself. This is difficult, if you are belittling yourself.

For example, when he makes a mistake, a pessimist will say things like "I'm so stupid," a statement which does damage to his future confidence. Optimists, on the other hand, would make a less global statement as to the cause of the misfortune, limiting the damage. They might think "I forgot to backup that file on the computer," or "I had trouble concentrating today."

Optimists will then let themselves off the hook, thinking something like "that's not like me." This prepares us for a more positive next thought, such as "How can I do better in the future?"

The difference between these two styles of internal reaction is the primary reason that some succeed and some do not.

- *Mental Images*

When you feel negative emotions, they are inevitably accompanied by negative mental images, pictures of frustrating or unsuccessful events. These mental images are often vivid enough to provoke the same physiological responses (a rise in blood pressure, for example) they would if they were really happening. They also provoke negative emotional states. We can control what we think. If you can create pictures of success rather than failure in your mind, your emotional state will improve.

In a setback, it is important not to replay the situation continually in your mind. Instead, focus on the future. Imagine a better situation, and begin planning how to create it.

• *Focus On Goals*

Low emotional ebbs happen rarely to people who are focused on long-term goals, and when they do happen they tend to last for a relatively short period of time. It is easier to see adversity as a temporary setback that will be overcome tomorrow, if you focus on your goals.

It is important, however, that your goals be exciting to you, otherwise they will not contribute to your optimistic outlook.

• *Focus On Learning*

Leaders are in the business of making constant improvements in the way things work. As such, they are in the business of promoting learning. They encourage people to take reasonable risks and to strive for goals without certainty of success. They react to setbacks and "failure" by asking for learning rather than with blame and recrimination.

In his books and articles, management guru Tom Peters frequently stresses the importance of fast failures, of getting to the failure quickly so we can learn from it and go on wiser than before. Equally as important as learning from failure, however, is learning from success. A success unlearned from is a success that does not strengthen the leader or her people.

• *Persistence*

What would you attempt if you knew it was impossible to fail? Remember that you never fail until you quit. Abraham Lincoln, for example, never succeeded in anything he tried until he ran for President. Had he never run for that office, had he quit politics after he lost his Senate race to Stephen Douglas, for example, he would have been judged a failure. Most people who succeed do so after persisting in the face of setbacks.

The ability to persist is tied directly to doing what you love and to the degree of optimism you possess. As Martin Seligman found in his study of pessimism, those with a negative view of the future tend to give up when they encounter a situation in which they lose control.

To use an analogy, if you think of your brain as a computer, you are stuck with the computer you have. You can't trade your nerve cells in for a different batch. But you are not stuck with the software you have acquired along the way. You are not stuck with the habits of thought and emotion you have adopted to respond to life. All of us have the ability to reprogram the software of our images by using the power of vivid imagining. All of us have the potential to possess the positive personal qualities we desire and to achieve the things that people with such qualities achieve. Most of us, however, do not take control of our lives in this way. Most of us become what we become by accident. Don't live by accident. Live on purpose.

The Language of Leadership

The power of leaders stems in part from the language they use. Leaders' formal and informal conversations and writings tend to have these characteristics:

• *Positive*

Volunteer Program Managers must also communicate in a positive fashion. One of the most common management mistakes is communicating in negatives. We tell volunteers what not to do instead of what they should be doing. We tell them what they can't do instead of what they can. We tell them we don't know the answer instead of directing them to someone who can. Consider the difference in impact between these two statements:

"You can't take a break until ten o'clock."

"You can take a break at ten o'clock."

The facts of the matter described in these two cases are exactly the same. But one is a restrictive, negative, demotivating statement. The other, by focusing on what the volunteer can do, is more positive; it grants permission. By habitually making positive statements, the effective manager contributes to a positive climate.

We have been struck by how hard it is for people to do this. It seems that almost everyone habitually describes situations with negative language instead of positives, especially when some form of bad news has to be delivered.

Leaders accent the positive when they talk about things. Instead of telling people what they can't do, they tell them what they can do. Instead of telling someone they can't have what they want, they tell them what their options are. Instead of telling someone they're in the wrong place, they tell them what the right place is. Instead of telling someone what they should have done, they tell them what the right thing to do is. These are very subtle but powerful differences.

• *Descriptive*

Leaders are non-judgmental and non-blaming. They steer clear of asserting negative assumptions and generalizations about people. When behavior is inappropriate and must be described to be corrected, they simply report what the person did without judging. Rather than making statements about the person's attitudes, motives or personality traits, they describe exactly what the person did.

• *Optimistic*

Leaders focus people on a positive future. Although they give praise to people for their accomplishments, their primary focus is on building a better situation. When things are going badly, leaders focus people on what they can control. Rather than dwelling on past mistakes, leaders ask "What have you learned from this?" and "What will you do next time?"

• *Validative*

Leaders praise people for their positive qualities as well as for their accomplishments. Instead of dwelling on people's faults, they praise their strengths. They say things like "I admire your persistence," or "You sure are smart." They "find the good and praise it," and in so doing, their interactions bolster the self-image of others. When someone makes a mistake, leaders use words such as "That's not like you" to divorce the person's sense of self-worth from that one behavior.

• *Empowering*

Leaders communicate options to people. They stress focusing on what individuals and groups can control and give people maximum authority to take action. They encourage proactive efforts. When they give people assignments, they delegate real power and use words such as "I'd like to put you in charge of this," or "Would you be willing to take the responsibility for this?"

• *Inclusive*

Leaders are includers. They invite participation. One of their primary tools is the question. By saying things such as "How will we solve this problem?" or "Would you be willing to join us for this discussion?" they make people feel they are equal members of the group.

Being Proactive

The most effective way leaders build positive reputations is by making things happen. As opposed to those who merely muddle along, successful Volunteer Program Managers do not merely react to the demands of outside forces. They do not wait to be goaded to action by others. They cause things to happen. This is the foundation of success—rather than responding to things that come up, living life with a purpose.

Another way to say this is that to be successful you must be proactive. Proactive is the opposite of reactive. Instead of spending your life mired in the demands of others, you must take action of your own volition. By doing so you will have an effect on events and gain control of your life.

The vast majority of people in our society are reactive, and this makes their success impossible. Reactive people work only on that which is urgent, meaning that someone else will be upset if they do not get it done by a certain time. Anything that is not urgent is put off until it is urgent, a habit that leads to paralyzing procrastination. Things that will never be urgent are never pursued.

Building Your Own Success

To be effective, we must work on things according to their importance, according to the difference they will make. It is only in this way that we can build success. No one builds a monument to you in Washington DC that says "She met other people's deadlines" at the bottom. To succeed, you have to make things happen on your own volition and let the hordes of reactive people start reacting to you.

For example, an activity director in a nursing home had a volunteer "friendly visitor" who called upon some of the residents who had no family members close by. This volunteer was particularly popular because she brought her two-year-old with her. All the residents were enthralled by the child. This got the activity director to begin to think about the possibility of adding a day-care center to their facility and creating cross-generational activities.

She suggested the idea to the nursing home director who made modestly favorable statements. But no action ensued. The activity director then sought out an architect that she knew through a service club she belonged to. The architect volunteered to do a rough sketch of the addition and create a cost estimate. This was regarded with greater interest by the executive director. But still no action ensued. The activity director then got a friend of hers who ran a day-care center, to volunteer to do a cost projection on the profitability of such an addition. This time the executive director was impressed enough to take the idea to the board.

None of this was part of the activity director's job description. She did these things because she was bent on making a positive difference in the lives of the residents. She was committed enough to the idea that she persisted in the face of inaction by her boss. By persisting and by involving high-impact volunteers, she contributed something of great value to the nursing home This enhanced her reputation and the status of her program in the facility.

Most people are too immersed in the daily details of their jobs to make the time to do something like this. They respond only to that which is urgent. If something is not urgent, they put it off until it is urgent. This habit produces the anxiety of procrastination. And it produces the stress of constantly responding to other people's demands. It is the habit of a person who will at best muddle through in life but will never make anything happen.

In the stress of responding to the demands of outside forces, we tend to lose sight of our purpose. The distinction between what will make a difference and what will not begins to blur. And eventually the only distinction between one activity and another is the due date. It is impossible for you to be an effective, successful person in this situation.

Because of this habit, anything that is not urgent will be put off until "someday," a day that never occurs on a calendar. This habit is one that leaves people, at the end of life, wishing they had had the time to get to some of those ideas they had. Or it leads them to rage in jealous disappointment when someone else does what they have only dreamed of doing for years.

Success, then, requires two characteristics, the capacity to have a dream or a vision of a positive difference you want to make and the capacity to devote time to making things happen that will realize that vision. We urge you to make this effort, because what you can provide to your agency is a worthy endeavor. We hope you will remember the following piece of wisdom:

"A volunteer is a terrible thing to waste...so is a Volunteer Program Manager."

Chapter Seventeen
Some Final Suggestions

Finding an Overall Approach
In tackling the work outlined in the previous chapters, it is essential to employ a coherent philosophical approach. Our suggestion for this approach would have you concentrate on two theories, which we think will make success more probable:

Start Small, and Grow with Success
Do not expect to accomplish everything at once, and do not try to do so. Operating a volunteer program is a delicate and complicated task, made so in part by the fact that the more successful you are at some things (such as recruitment), then the more work you will create for yourself. It is better to begin with little things and then grow a bit at a time than to become over-extended and create bad feelings with unsuccessful volunteer placements. Happy staff and happy volunteers will become your best salespeople for the program, but you have to make sure everyone is truly happy.

One way to start small is to begin with an ad hoc effort, a program intended to make use of volunteers to accomplish just one thing. This will allow you to test the use of volunteers and identify the strengths and weaknesses that the organization brings to involving volunteers.

Rely on Persuasion, Not Coercion
Do not try to force volunteers on the organization or on any member of staff. The use of volunteers will help an organization, but only if a positive approach is adopted. Rely on the persuasion that is created by competence and success—when staff realize that some departments are gaining benefits through the use of volunteers, they will eventually decide to seek the same advantages for themselves. Have confidence in the value of volunteers, and be willing to let staff come to you, rather than feeling compelled to beg them. Never be foolish enough to believe that you can coerce anyone into using volunteers. A well-operated small volunteer program is much more valuable than an ineffective and unhappy large one.

Do not be afraid to make staff "earn" the right to have volunteers assigned to them. This will help to convince staff that volunteers are not a "free" resource, and will demonstrate that the organization considers volunteers too valuable to be distributed to those who are not willing to involve them effectively.

The Geometry of Volunteer Involvement
As you think about operating the volunteer program, try to keep in mind the simple geometric shapes:

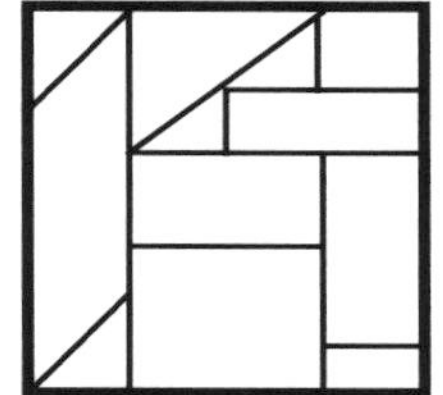

The Puzzle Square representing the work that the organization needs done.

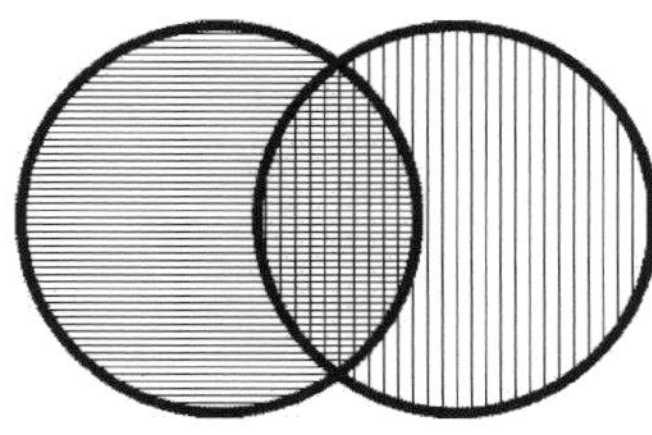

The Overlapping Circles representing the commonly met needs of the organization and the volunteers.

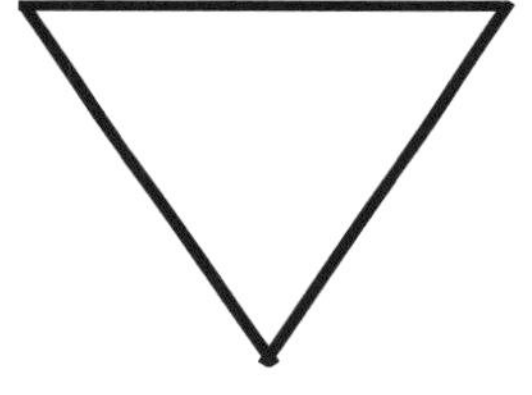

The Triangle representing the web of relationships among the Volunteer Program Manager, the volunteers, and staff.

If you can construct a volunteer program that embodies these three shapes, you will have created an effective mechanism for using volunteer resources.

Positioning Yourself for the Future
And what should you do to continue to expand, change, learn and grow? We suggest that the following will be key elements for the future:

Get Diverse
For much of their history, volunteer programs were opportunities for people of common interests to come together. Quite often these people were of common backgrounds, which easily explained why they had common interests to work on. The future of volunteerism, however, is rapidly moving toward a very different direction, that of diversity, and is manifesting itself in two specific areas:

Diversity of Volunteer Positions

The successful program of the future will be the program that offers the greatest variety of volunteer jobs. This variety will occur in a number of ways: variety in time commitment, variety in scope and difficulty of the work, and variety in the type of work to be done. We are entering a world in which people expect choices, and volunteers are becoming less and less amenable to a "take it or leave it" approach. A volunteer program with only one type of volunteer opportunity is a lot like a store that only sells one product in one size and one color - some people will love it, but a lot of people won't be interested at all.

Attracting the volunteer of the future is a competitive task, and that competition will become easier as you have more possibilities to offer. For the Volunteer Program Manager this means making jobs flexible enough in terms of different "sizes" (short-term, long-term, evenings, weekends, etc.), and different "shapes" (at the office, at home, with my family, working with youth, etc.) In the words of Frank Wylie of California State University: *"Volunteer jobs, for the most part, haven't changed. Staff is still recruiting by the numbers...asking professional women to come in and do menial clerical jobs. It's a wonder that we still have as many volunteers as we do, especially as we have never recruited men or young people well...It is we who have not learned to recruit and utilize the modern volunteer effectively."*

Diversity of Volunteers

Volunteer management is the management of people, and as the American population becomes more diverse, volunteer programs need to follow. One of the most useful pieces of information from the Gallup Surveys on Giving and Volunteering is the simple statistic that people are more than three times as likely to volunteer when asked than when they are not. Among the 44% of respondents who reported that they were asked to volunteer during the past year, 86% volunteered; among the 55% who were not asked, only 24% volunteered. Those least likely to be asked to volunteer were Blacks, Hispanics, youth, seniors, and those with low-incomes, but among the small populations of these groups who were asked, the proportion who volunteered was nearly four times higher than the proportion of those who were not asked. The significance of all this is quite simple: if you can reach people and directly ask them to volunteer for you, they are likely to do so. They are even more likely to do so if they feel some link or connection with the asker, such as being friends, neighbors, or co-workers.

Programs that are not diverse find it increasingly hard to recruit for the simple reason that they quickly use up the pool of potential volunteers to whom they are "linked." Picture this: if my program is made up of three volunteers, all from similar backgrounds, then it is very likely that they have a lot of friends in common. If they are from different backgrounds, then it is very likely that they have a much wider total pool of potential "links" because they will be drawing from different sets of acquaintances. The bigger and more diverse your pool of volunteers, the wider the "net" you can cast to recruit new people. And this positive impact of diversity on recruitment actually has a cumulative effect - the more people from new backgrounds you bring in, the easier it is to bring in additional people linked to other new backgrounds. Smart Volunteer Program Managers will start widening their pool of volunteers as quickly as possible.

Get Connected

The smart Volunteer Program Manager also needs to build support from the wider community of volunteer-utilizing agencies, communicating with other Volunteer Program Managers and sharing information and resources. Admiral Hyman Rickover expressed this need best: *"All of us must become better informed. It is necessary for us to learn from others' mistakes. You will not live long enough to make them all yourself."* Volunteer Program Managers who are not involved with a local DOVIA or a member of a national volunteer organization, such as the Points of Light Foundation, is choosing to ignore the wisdom of others, making their jobs and their lives a lot harder.

Volunteer Program Managers also need to build better connections within their own organization. The primary "problem" in volunteer involvement right now does not lie in finding new volunteers, it lies in enabling those who are already involved to accomplish productive work. In the past ten years volunteer jobs have shifted to within agencies, placing volunteers more in contact and working relationships with agency staff. In many agencies, the primary coordinator or supervisor of volunteers is not the Volunteer Program Manager, but the staff person with whom the volunteer works with on a day-to-day basis. Most of these staff have little or no experience in working with volunteers.

This is a pretty silly situation. The primary worry of Volunteer Program Managers should at this point be "staff competence," the ability of staff to handle the highly technical resources that volunteers represent.

This need increases dramatically as we draw from volunteer professionals who expect to be treated in a professional manner. Smart Volunteer Program Managers need to spend a little less time with their volunteers and a lot more time and energy enabling staff to make creative use of those volunteers.

Get Used to Change

One of the key learning experiences for the future is the realization that nothing should be taken as a given. Volunteer programs have experienced more changes in the past ten years than in the previous fifty. We have invented entirely new types of "volunteers" – national service participants, corporate employee teams, alternative sentencing programs – and we have developed entirely new areas of service for volunteers. But the likely reality is that the next ten years will witness and require even greater change to accommodate what is happening in society. The smart Volunteer Program Manager will continually need to take a fresh look at how things are done. One of the probable shifts that will occur in well-managed programs is an increased reliance on new technologies. Within ten years practically every volunteer program will rely on volunteer management software to keep track of volunteers, record hours and availability, and produce reports. Other programs will make use of electronic information systems to communicate with existing volunteers and to recruit new ones. If you're from a generation that doesn't view computers as a comfortable way of operating, you need to realize that the children of today are growing up with computers, and that means that the adults of tomorrow will view them as the natural way to do things.

Even smarter Volunteer Program Managers will constantly re-examine and re-evaluate everything they are doing, aiming not just for efficiency, but also for correctness. Remember the words of Peter Drucker, "There is nothing so useless as doing efficiently that which should not be done at all." The trick for the future is not just in doing things correctly, it also lies in allocating scarce management time towards doing the right things. And that requires being a smart leader, not just an administrator. The reality of volunteer management is that what works today will probably not work as well tomorrow, and within twenty years may be absolutely the wrong thing to do. Volunteer management is actually a process, not a particular structure or thing. The role of the Volunteer Program Manager will be to scrutinize every aspect of program operation and ask, "How do we need to adjust this so that it will work?" The focus needs to be on reaching the goal and achieving the mission rather than preserving the way things are done. The future will merely require making changes even faster and more often than we have done in the last ten years.

Perhaps the most exciting thing about the future is that it is bound to be different, more different than we do know and probably more different than we could know. This guarantees that volunteer management will continue to be a creative art, requiring imagination and daring and courage. And it guarantees that practitioners will always have a fresh approach and attitude toward their work, since much of it will always be new to them. In the words of Fresco's Discovery: "If you knew what you were doing, you'd probably be bored." The future holds a lot of possibilities for volunteer involvement, but it is safe to predict that boredom is not one of them. As Pogo says, "We are confronted by insurmountable opportunities."

Starting Work as a Volunteer Program Manager

Volunteer management involves working with people and, as such, effective volunteer management requires adjusting to changes in the ways that people operate. The system of managing volunteers that worked quite efficiently 30 years ago is no longer appropriate to a population that has itself undergone significant alterations. You will need to examine the existing volunteer involvement system within your agency to see if it needs to change to fit new realities of volunteering.

Among the changes in management which we know are required are:

- *Alterations in position design*: making changes in the styles of jobs so that they better fit short-term involvement while leaving room for growth and ensuring that all jobs have a significant impact on the agency mission. Right now, the quality of available volunteers far outstrips the general quality of most volunteer jobs. It is very difficult to persuade people to volunteer for bad jobs and it is even harder to persuade them to keep doing so.

- *Proactive recruitment*: Most agencies do not seriously plan and implement their recruitment campaigns, mostly because they have never had to. Unfortunately, the pool of reliable volunteers that agencies have utilized is disappearing and the replacement group is in a "Show Me" mood. This is particularly true when the agency is attempting to recruit types of volunteers who have no previous experience with the agency and have no particular reason to believe that it is truly interested in developing a relationship with them.

• *A true concern for involving volunteers:* This means ensuring that volunteer jobs contribute significantly to the mission of the agency. It also means paying attention to the changing needs of volunteers over the entire cycle of their relationship with the organization.

• *Real support from the agency:* Agencies have traditionally treated volunteers like they were some magical breed of elves, capable of mysteriously accomplishing tasks with no real support system. The new volunteer workforce expects to receive all the training, supplies, and back-up it needs, and to receive it without asking. And they also expect a flexible approach from the agency that will adjust support and requirements based upon the needs of the volunteer.

• *Staff proficiency*: Perhaps the most important requirement for the future will be an upgraded capacity on the part of agency staff to handle both volunteers in general, and volunteers from diverse backgrounds in particular, with more skill than every before. Agency staff will be the volunteer coordinators of the future, and they will need to know how to effectively interact and manage volunteers. Staff that currently have no background in or training on working with volunteers will need to learn how to use a resource that thinks for itself.

The next 20 years will witness a re-invention and re-application of all of the basic principles of volunteer management, applying them to a new world and to new organizational resources and needs.

This development will not occur without leadership, and the primary person for accomplishing this change successfully will be the manager of volunteer resources within the agency. The change will not happen automatically and it will not happen accidentally.

You might choose to accept three guiding principles or truths in evaluating this need for guided change:

1. *Basically, volunteers are just like real people – they won't go where they aren't wanted and they won't stay where they aren't appreciated.*
2. *Basically, staff are just like real people – they'll get frustrated by what they don't understand.*
3. *Basically, agencies are just like real people – they'll learn faster with a little help.*

Volunteer Program Managers are in a unique position to argue for, plan for, and train for the alterations in agency operation that will be necessary for receptivity of new audiences, whether they be clients, paid staff, or volunteers. They will make the difference in whether agencies struggle with diminishing resources against overwhelming odds or whether agencies are truly able to involve volunteers effectively enough to mobilize all the resources of the community.

The Golden Rule

Finally, remember the "Golden Rule" of volunteer management:

"Their niceness will let you recruit a volunteer, but only your competence will let you keep them..."

Appendix One

Further Reading

What follows is a short listing of references on volunteer management. A much larger listing, current as of December 2002 is available in Steve McCurley's *The Volunteerism Bibliography* available at no charge from www.energizeinc.com. Updated listings of additional works available via the Internet are available in the quarterly "Along the Web" section of the *e-Volunteerism* journal, www.e-volunteerism.com.

For those of you who would simply like a core list of books likely to be on the shelves of most Volunteer Program Managers, we'll recommend the following:

- Ellis, Susan, *From the Top Down: The Executive's Role in Volunteer Program Success* (Philadelphia: Energize, Inc.) 1996
- Ellis, Susan, *The Volunteer Management Audit*, (Philadelphia: Energize, Inc.) 2003.
- Graff, Linda, Graff, Linda, *Better Safe.. Risk Management in Volunteer Programs and Community Service* (Dundas: Linda Graff and Associates) 2003.
- Hager, Mark and Jeffrey Brudney, *Balancing Act: The Challenges and Benefits of Volunteers*, Urban Institute, December 2004.
- Lasby, David, *The Volunteer Spirit: Motivations and Barriers*, (Toronto: Canadian Centre for Philanthropy) 2004.
- McClintock, Norah, *Understanding Canadian Volunteers: Using the National Survey of Giving, Volunteering and Participating to Build Your Volunteer Program*, (Ontario: Canadian Centre for Philanthropy) 2004.
- McCurley, Steve and Rick Lynch, *Keeping Volunteers: A Guide to Retention*, (Olympia: Fat Cat Press) 2005.

What follows is a listing of some, but not all, of the resources used in this book.

1. Active Community Unit, *Giving time, Getting Involved*, Home Office Communication Directorate, UK, 1999.
2. Active Community Unit, *Volunteering: a Code of Good Practice* (London: Home Office).
3. Affat, Danny, "Involving Black and Minority Ethnic Volunteers," National Centre for Volunteering, ww.diversitychallenge.org/affat.htm.
4. Aitken, Allen, "Identifying Key Issues Affecting the Retention of Emergency Service Volunteers," *Australian Journal of Emergency Management*, Winter 2000, www.ema.gov.au/5virtuallibrary/pdfs/vol15no2/aitken.pdf
5. American Association of Retired Persons, *Study of Older Hispanics: Needs, Volunteerism, Language Preferences, and Media Use* (Washington: AARP) 1994.
6. American Association of Retired Persons, *Volunteerism: A Survey of New York Members*, (Washington: AARP) January 2002.
7. American Cancer Society, Points of Light Foundation, and National Health Council, *Assessing the Volunteer Paradigm: A Report on Volunteerism among the Nation's Voluntary Health Agencies* (Washington: Points of Light Foundation) 1996.
8. Australian Bureau of Statistics, Voluntary Work, Australia, June 2001, www.abs.gov.au/ausstats.
9. Badgett, M and N. Cunningham, *Creating Communities: Giving and Volunteering by Gay, Lesbian, Bisexual and Transgender People* (New York: Working Group on Funding Lesbian and Gay Issues) 1998.
10. Bowen, Paddy and A-J. McKechnie, *Family Volunteering: A Discussion Paper*, (Ottawa: Volunteer Canada) 2002.
11. Bowgett, Kate, *Homeless People and Volunteering*, OSW-Off the Streets and Into Work, May 2005.
12. Brown, E. and Zahrly, J. "Commitment and Tenure of Highly Skilled Volunteers: Management Issues in a Nonprofit Agency," Working Paper No. 12. San Francisco: Institute for Nonprofit Organization Management, University of

San Francisco, February 1990.

13. Brown, Eleanor, "Assessing the Value of Volunteer Activity in the United States," Hudson Institute, www.hudson.org/ncpcr/report/brown.html.

14. Brown, Kathleen, "Thoughts on the Supervision of Volunteers," *Voluntary Action Leadership*, Spring 1984.

15. Brudney, J. and Duncombe, W. "An Economic Evaluation of Paid, Volunteer, and Mixed Staffing Options for Public Services," *Public Administration Review*, 1992.

16. Brudney, J. *Fostering Volunteer Programs in the Public Sector* (San Francisco: Jossey-Bass) 1990.

17. Brudney, Jeffrey and J. Edward Kellough, "Volunteers in State Government: Involvement, Management, and Benefits," *Nonprofit and Voluntary Sector Quarterly*, March 2000.

18. Brudney, Jeffrey and S. Schmahl, *Volunteer Administration: A Survey of the Profession*, (Richmond: Association for Volunteer Administration) 2001.

19. Bureau of Labor Statistics, *Volunteering in the United States 2005*, (Washington: Dept of Labor).

20. Campbell, Katherine Noyes and Susan Ellis, *The (Help!) I Don't Have Enough Time Guide to Volunteer Management* (Philadelphia: Energize) 1995.

21. Canadian Centre for Philanthropy, *The Giving and Volunteering of Seniors* (Toronto: CCP) 2002.

22. Carson, Emmett, "The Charitable Activities of Black Americans: a Portrait of Self-Help," *The Review of Black Political Economy*, Winter 1987.

23. Center for Corporate Citizenship at Boston College and Volunteers of America, *Expanding the Boundaries of Corporate Volunteerism: Retirees as a Valuable Resource*, June 2005.

24. Clark, Sherry, *You Cannot be Serious! A Guide to Involving Volunteers with Mental Health Problems*, National Centre for Volunteering, 2003.

25. Clary, E. Gil, Mark Snyder and Arthur Stukas, "Volunteers' Motivations: Findings from a National Survey," *Nonprofit and Voluntary Sector Quarterly*, December 1996.

26. Clary, E.G, Mark Snyder, Robert Ridge, John Copeland, Arthur Stukas, Julie Haugen and Peter Miene, "Understanding and Assessing the Motivations of Volunteers: A Functional Approach," *Journal of Personality and Social Psychology*, June 1998.

27. Cnaan, R. A., & Cascio, T., "Performance and Commitment: Issues in Management of Volunteers in Human Service Organizations," *Journal of Social Service Research*, 1998, 24 (3/4).

28. Cnaan, Ram and Robin Goldberg-Glen, "Comparison of Volunteers in Public and Nonprofit Service Agencies," *Nonprofit and Voluntary Sector Quarterly*, Winter 1990.

29. Cnaan, Ram and Robin Goldberg-Glen, "Measuring Motivation to Volunteer in Human Services," *Journal of Applied Behavioral Science*, September 1991.

30. Cnaan, Ram, Femida Handy and Margaret Wadsworth, "Defining Who is A Volunteer: Conceptual and Empirical Considerations," *Nonprofit and Voluntary Sector Quarterly*, September 1996.

31. Colomy, P., Chen, H. and Andrews, G., "Situational Facilities and Volunteer Work," *Journal of Volunteer Administration*, Winter 1987-88.

32. Community Service Volunteers, *About Time: Understanding the Motivation to Volunteer*, (London: Community Service Volunteers) 2000.

33. Community Service Volunteers, *Hidden Volunteers: Evaluating the Extent and Impact of Unrecognised Volunteering in the UK*, (London: Community Service Volunteers) January 2000.

34. Community Service Volunteers, *The State of the Volunteering Nation*, (London: Community Service Volunteers) April 2002.

35. Community Service Volunteers, *Volunteers with Disabilities: Who's Helping Whom?* www.csv-rsvp.org.uk/Report6s.pdf

36. Cook, Ann, "Retiring the Volunteer: Facing Reality when Service is No Longer Possible," *Journal of Volunteer Administration*, Summer 1992.

37. Corporation for National and Community Service, *Youth Helping America: Building Active Citizens – The Role of Social Institutions in Teen Volunteering* (Washington: CNCS) November 2005.

38. Ellis, Jennifer, *Best Practices in Volunteer Management: An Action Planning Guide for Small and Rural Nonprofit Organizations*, (Toronto: Volunteer Canada) 2005.

39. Ellis, S. and Noyes, K. *By the People: A History of Americans as Volunteers*, (Philadelphia: Energize, Inc.) 2005.

40. Ellis, Susan & Cravens, Jayne, 2000, *The virtual volunteering guidebook: how to apply the principles of real-world volunteer management to online service*, Impact Online, USA

41. Ellis, Susan and Katherine Noyes, *Proof Positive: Developing Significant Recordkeeping Systems* (Philadelphia: Energize Inc.) 1990, revised edition.

42. Ellis, Susan and Steve McCurley, "Protection or Paranoia: The Realities of Volunteer Liability," *Journal of Volunteer Administration*, Spring 1998.

43. Ellis, Susan and Steve McCurley, "Thinking the Unthinkable: Are We Using the Wrong Model for Volunteer Work?," e-Volunteerism, Vol. 3(3), 2003.

44. Ellis, Susan, *From the Top Down: The Executive Role in Volunteer Program Success* (Philadelphia: Energize, Inc.) 1996.

45. Ellis, Susan, *The Board's Role in Effective Volunteer Involvement* (Philadelphia: Energize Inc.) 1995.

46. Ellis, Susan, *The Volunteer Recruitment (and Membership Development Book* (Philadelphia: Energize Books) 3rd edition, 2002.

47. Ellis, Susan, *Volunteer Management Audit* (Philadelphia: Enegize) 2002.

48. Environics Research Group, *Survey of Managers of Volunteer Resources*, May 2003.

49. Esmond, Judy and Patrick Dunlop, *Developing the Volunteer Motivation Inventory to Assess the Underlying Motivational Drives of Volunteers in Western Australia*, CLAN WA, 2004.

50. Esmond, Judy, "The Untapped Potential of Australian University Students," *Australian Journal*

51. Esmond, Judy, *Boomnet: Capturing the Baby Boomer Volunteers*, (Perth: Department of the Premier and the Cabinet) December 2001, www.dpc.wa.gov.au/volunteer/boom.pdf

52. Esmond, Judy, *From 'Boomnet' to 'Boomnot,' Part Two of a Research Project on Baby Boomers and Volunteering*, Department for Community Development, Government of Western Australia, May 2002.

53. Eystad, Melissa, *Measuring the Difference Volunteers Make: A Guide to Outcome Evaluation for Volunteer Program Managers* (St Paul: Minnesota Department of Human Services) 1997.

54. Fahey Christine and Judi Walker, *Asking Volunteers: The Development of Strategies to Improve Recruitment, Retention, Training and Support of Volunteer Ambulance Officers*, (University Department of Public Health, University of Tasmania) 2001.

55. Family Matters Project, *Family Friendly Volunteering: A Guide for Agencies*, (Washington: Points of Light Foundation) 1999.

56. Fischer, Lucy Rose and Kay Schaffer, Older Volunteers: A Guide to Research and Practice (Newbury Park: Sage Publications) 1993.

57. Fleishman-Hillard Research, *Managing Volunteers: A Report from United Parcel Service*, 1998.

58. Gaskin, Katherine, *A Choice Blend: What Volunteers Want from Organisations and Management*, (London: Institute for Volunteering Research) April 2003.

59. Gaskin, Katherine, *Getting a Grip – Risk, Risk Management and Volunteering – A Review of the Literature*, National Centre for Volunteering, October 2005.

60. Gidron, B., "Predictors of Retention and Turnover among Service Volunteer Workers," *Journal of Social Science Research*, Fall 1984.

61. Gidron, Benjamin, "Sources of Job Satisfaction among Service Volunteers," *Journal of Voluntary Action Research*, Jan/March 1983.

62. Goss, Kristin, "Volunteering and the Long Civic Generation," Nonprofit and Voluntary Sector Quarterly, December 1999.

63. Goulborne, Michele and Don Embuldeniya, *Assigning Economic Value to Volunteer Activity: Eight Tools for Efficient Program Management*, Canadian Center for Philanthropy, 2002.

64. Graff, Linda, "Considering the Many Aspects of Volunteer/Union Relations,"

Voluntary Action Leadership, Summer 1984.

65. Graff, Linda, "Making the Case for Risk Management in Volunteer Programs," *Journal of Volunteer Administration*, Vol. 20, no 2, 2002.

66. Graff, Linda, "The Role of Volunteers During a Strike," *Journal of Volunteer Administration*, Summer 1984.

67. Graff, Linda, *Best of All: The Quick Reference Guide to Effective Volunteer Involvement*, (Otobicoke: Linda Graff and Associates) 2005.

68. Graff, Linda, *Beyond Police Checks: The Definitive Volunteer and Employee Screening Guidebook*, (Dundas, Ontario: Graff and Associates) 1999.

69. Graff, Linda, *By Definition: Policies for Volunteer Programs* (Otobicoke: Linda Graff and Associates) 1997, 2nd Edition.

70. Graff, Linda, *Better Safe..Risk Management in Volunteer Programs and Community Service* (Dundas: Linda Graff and Associates) 2003.

71. Hager, Mark and Jeffrey Brudney, *Balancing Act: The Challenges and Benefits of Volunteers*, Urban Institute, December 2004.

72. Hager, Mark and Jeffrey Brudney, *Volunteer Management Practices and Retention of Volunteers*, (Washington: Urban Institute) 2004.

73. Hall, Michael, A-J. McKechnie, Katie Davidman and Fleur Leslie, *An Environmental Scan on Volunteering and Improving Volunteering* (Toronto: Canadian Centre for Philanthropy) 2001.

74. Hall, Michael, Larry McKeown, and Karen Roberts, *Caring Canadians, Involved Canadians: Highlights of the 2000 National Survey of Giving, Volunteering and Participating*, Ontario: Canadian Centre for Philanthropy, August 2001.

75. Handy, Femida and Narasimhan Srinivasan, *Costs and Contributions of Professional Volunteer Management: Lessons from Ontario Hospitals*, Canadian Centre for Philanthropy, 2003.

76. Handy, Femida, Robert Mound, Lisa=Marie Vaccaro, and Karin Prochazka, *Promising Practices for Volunteer Administration in Hospitals*, Canadian Centre for Philanthropy, 2004.

77. Hobson, Charles and Kathryn Malec, "Initial Telephone Contact of Prospective Volunteers with Nonprofits: An Operational Definition of Quality and Norms for 500 Agencies," Journal of Volunteer Administration, Summer/Fall 1999.

78. Hustinx, Lesley, "Individualism and New Styles of Youth Volunteering: An Empirical Exploration," *Voluntary Action*, Spring 2001.

79. Ilsley, Paul, *Enhancing the Volunteer Experience* (San Francisco: Jossey-Bass) 1990.

80. Imagine, Volunteer Canada, and the Calgary Workplace Volunteer Council, *Engaging Employees in the Community: How to Establish Employer Supported Volunteerism in Your Community* (Toronto: Canadian Centre for Philanthropy) February 2002.

81. Independent Sector, *America's Family Volunteers*, (Washington: Independent Sector) 2001. www.independentsector.org/PDFs/FamilyVols.pdf

82. Independent Sector, *America's Informal Volunteers* (Washington: Independent Sector) 2001, www.independentsector.org/PDFs/InformalVols.pdf

83. Independent Sector, *America's Religious Congregation: Measuring Their Contribution to Society* (Washington: Independent Sector? 2000.

84. Independent Sector, *America's Senior Volunteers* Washington: Independent Sector) www.independentsector.org/PDFs/SeniorVolun.pdf

85. Independent Sector, *America's Teenage Volunteers*, (Washington: Independent Sector) 2000, www.independentsector.org/programs/research/teenvolun1.pdf

86. Independent Sector, *Giving and Volunteering in the United States, 2001* (Washington: Independent Sector) 2002.

87. Institute for Volunteering Research, *1997 National Survey of Volunteering in the UK*, www.ivr.org.uk.natinalsurvey.htm.

88. Institute for Volunteering Research, *Public sector support for volunteering: an audit*, (London: Institute for Volunteer Research) 1999, www.ivr.org.uk/audit.htm

89. Institute for Volunteering Research, *Volunteering for All? Exploring the Link between Volunteering and Social Exclusion*, 2003, http://www.ivr.org.uk/socialexclusion/index.htm

90. Institute for Volunteering Research,

Volunteering in the NHS: A Report of a Survey, www.ivr.org.uk/nhs.htm.

91. Institute for Volunteering Research, *Volunteers in the Cultural Sector* (London: The Council for Museums, Archives and Libraries) March 2002.

92. Lake Snell Perry & Associates, *Short-Term Impacts, Long-Term Opportunities: The Political and Civic Engagement of Young Adults in America*, Washington, Center for Information and Research in Civic Learning and Engagement, March 2002.

93. Lasby, David, *The Volunteer Spirit: Motivations and Barriers*, (Toronto: Canadian Centre for Philanthropy) 2004.

94. Lee, Jarene Francis and Julia Catagnus, *What We Learned (the Hard Way) about Supervising Volunteers* (Philadelphia: Energize Inc) 1998.

95. Lynch, Richard, "Volunteer Retention and Feelings of Connection," e-Volunteerism, July/Sept 2002.

96. Lynch, Rick, *Laying the Foundation with Mission and Vision: Creating a Strategic Volunteer Program* (Washington: Points of Light Foundation) 1996.

97. Macduff, Nancy, *Episodic Volunteering: Building the Short-Term Volunteer Program.* (Walla Walla, Wash.: MBA Associates) 1991

98. McClintock, Norah, *Understanding Canadian Volunteers: Using the National Survey of Giving, Volunteering and Participating to Build Your Volunteer Program*, (Ontario: Canadian Centre for Philanthropy) 2004.

99. McCurley, Steve and Rick Lynch, *Keeping Volunteers: A Guide to Retention*, (Olympia: Fat Cat Press) 2005.

100. McCurley, Steve and Sue Vineyard, *101 Ideas for Volunteer Programs*, (Downers Grove: Heritage Arts) 1986.

101. McCurley, Steve and Sue Vineyard, *Best Practices for Volunteer Programs*, (Downers Grove: Heritage Arts) 2001.

102. McCurley, Steve and Sue Vineyard, *Handling Problem Volunteers* (Downers Grove: Heritage Arts) 1998.

103. McCurley, Steve and Sue Vineyard, *Measuring Up: Assessment Tools for Volunteer Programs*, (Downers Grove: Heritage Arts) 1997.

104. McCurley, Steve and Susan Ellis, "Mandated Service - The Future of Volunteering," *e-Volunteerism*, July/Sept 2002.

105. McCurley, Steve, "A User's Guide to Online Volunteer Recruitment Sites," *e-Volunteerism*, Winter 2001.

106. McCurley, Steve, "Recruiting and Retaining Volunteers," in *The Jossey-Bass Handbook of Nonprofit Leadership and Management*, Robert Herman, ed., (San Francisco: Jossey Bass) 2004.

107. McFarland, Betsy, *Volunteer Management for Animal Care Organizations*, Humane Society of the United States, 2005.

108. McKeown, Larry, David McIver, Jason Moreton and Anita Rotondo, *Giving and Volunteering: The Role of Religion* (Toronto: Canadian Centre for Philanthropy) 2004.

109. Mook, Laurie and Jack Quarter, *Estimating and Reporting the Value of Volunteer Contributions* (Toronto: Canadian Centre for Philanthropy) 2004.

110. Mook, Laurie and Jack Quarter, *How to Assign a Monetary Value to Volunteer Contributions* (Toronto: Canadian Centre for Philanthropy) 2004.

111. Murray, Vic and Yvonne Harrison, *The Impact of Information and Communications Technology on Volunteer Management*, (Toronto: Canadian Centre for Philanthropy) 2002.

112. Murray, Vic and Yvonne Harrison, *Virtual Volunteering: Current Status and Future Prospects*, (Toronto: Canadian Centre for Philanthropy) 2002.

113. Musick, Marc, John Wilson and William Bynum, "Race and Formal Volunteering: The Differential Effects of Class and Religion," *Social Forces*, Vol. 78, no 4, 2000.

114. National Centre for Volunteering, *Employee Volunteering: The Guide* (London: National Centre for Volunteering).

115. National Centre for Volunteering, *From Barriers to Bridges: A Guide for Volunteer-Involving Organisations* (London: National Centre for Volunteering, 2001.

116. National Centre for Volunteering, *Get It Right from the Start: Volunteer Policies – the Key to Diverse Volunteer Involvement*, (London: National Centre for Volunteering) 2002.

117. National Centre for Volunteering, *Safe*

Involvement of Volunteers with Vulnerable Clients, www.volunteering.org.uk/sheets.htm.

118. New Zealand Federation of Voluntary Welfare Organisations, *Counting for Something: Value Added by Voluntary Agencies*, September 2004.

119. nfpSynergy, *The 21st Century Volunteer: A Report on the Changing Face of Volunteering in the 21st Century*, November 2005.

120. Noble, Joy, Louise Rogers and Andy Fryar, *Volunteer Management: An Essential Guide*, 2nd Edition (Adelaide: Volunteering SA, Inc) 2003.

121. Pearce, Jone, *The Organizational Behavior of Unpaid Workers* (New York: Routleadge, Chapman & Hall) 1993.

122. Penner, Louis, "Dispositional and Organizational Influences on Sustained Volunteerism: An Interactionist Perspective," *Journal of Social Issues*, Fall 2002.

123. Phillips, Susan, Brian Little and Laura Goodine, *Caregiving Volunteers: A Coming Crisis?* (Toronto: Canadian Centre for Philanthropy) 2002.

124. Phillips, Susan, Brian Little and Laura Goodine, *Recruiting, Retaining and Rewarding Volunteers: What Volunteers Have to Say* (Toronto: Canadian Centre for Philanthropy) 2002

125. Points of Light Foundation, Assessing the Volunteer Paradigm: A Report on Volunteerism among the Nation's Health Agencies (Washington: Points of Light Foundation) 1996.

126. Princeton Survey Research Associates, The Do Something Inc. Young People's Community Involvement Survey, (Princeton: PSRA) June 1998.

127. Quarter, Jack, Laurie Mook and Betty Jane Richmond, *What Volunteers Contribute: Calculating and Communicating Value Added* (Toronto: Canadian Centre for Philanthropy) 2002.

128. Reed, Paul and L. Kevin Selbee, *Distinguishing Characteristics of Active Volunteers in Canada*, (Ottawa: Statistics Canada) 2000.

129. Rehnborg, Sarah Jane and Katy Fallon, *Environmental Scan of Volunteerism in Texas*, (Austin: LBJ School of Public Affairs, University of Texas) August 2001.

130. Rising Tide Co-operative Ltd., *Attracting and Keeping Youth Volunteers: Creating a Governance Culture that Nurtures and Values Youth*, (Toronto: Imagine Canada) 2005.

131. Rog, Evelina, Mark Pancer and Mark Baetz, *Corporate Volunteer Programs: Maximizing Employee Motivation and Minimizing Barriers to Program Participation* (Toronto: Canadian Centre for Philanthropy) 2003.

132. Ruddle, H. and Mulvihill, R. *Reaching out: Charitable Giving and Volunteering in the Republic of Ireland - 1997/98 Survey* National College of Ireland, 1999.

133. Russell Commission, A National Framework for Youth Action and Engagement, Report of the Russell Commission, March 2005, http://www.russellcommission.org.

134. Scheier, Ivan, *Building Staff/Volunteer Relations* (Philadelphia: Energize Books) 1993.

135. Scheier, Ivan, *Building Work that Satisfies: Volunteers and the Window of Work* (Santa Fe, NM: Center for Creative Community)1988.

136. Scheier, Ivan, *Exploding the Big Banquet Theory of Volunteer Recognition: An Incendiary Analysis* (Santa Fe, NM: Center for Creative Community) 1988.

137. Scheier, Ivan, *Exploring Volunteer Space*, (Santa Fe, NM: Center for Creative Community)1980.

138. Scheier, Ivan, *When Everyone's a Volunteer: The Effective Functioning of All-Volunteer Groups* (Philadelphia: Energize, Inc.), 1992.

139. Schmidl, Barry, *Simple Solutions: How NGOs Can Eliminate Barriers to Volunteering by People with Disabilities*, (Toronto: Imagine Canada) 2005.

140. Selbee, Kevin and Paul Reed, "Patterns of Volunteering over the Life Cycle," *Canadian Social Trends*, Summer 2001.

141. Shresta, Bandana and Chris Cihlar, *Volunteering in Under-Resourced Rural Communities*, Points of Light Foundation, 2004.

142. Silver, Nora, *At the Heart: The New Volunteer Challenge to Community Agencies*, (Pleasanton: Valley Volunteer Center) 1988.

143. Silver, Nora, *Positioning the Profession: Communicating the Power of Results for Volunteer Leadership Professionals*

(Richmond: Association for Volunteer Administration) 1999.

144. Singh, Mar, Dvora Levin and John Forde, *Engaging Retired Leaders as Volunteers*, (Toronto: Imagine Canada) 2005.

145. Social Planning and Research Council of British Columbia, *What Motivates Low-Income Volunteers?* (Toronto: Imagine Canada) 2005.

146. Sport England, *Sports Volunteering In England in 2002: A Summary Report*, (London: Sport England) 2003.

147. Sundeen, Richard and Sally Raskoff, "Points of Entry and Obstacles: Teenagers' Access to Volunteer Activities," *Nonprofit Management and Leadership*, Winter 2000.

148. The Smith Family, *Possible Futures: Changes, Volunteering and the Not-for-Profit Sector in Australia*, 2005.

149. Tremper, Charles and Gwynne Kostin, *No Surprises: Controlling Risks in Volunteer Programs* (Washington, DC: Nonprofit Risk Management Center) 1993.

150. Tremper, Charles, and Jeffrey Kahn, *Managing Legal Liability and Insurance for Corporate Volunteer Programs* (Washington, DC: Nonprofit Risk Management Center) 1992.

151. Tremper, Charles, Anna Seidman and Suzanne Tufts, *Managing Volunteers Within the Law* (Washington, DC: Nonprofit Risk Management Center) 1994.

152. Tremper, Charles, *Legal Barriers to Volunteer Service* (Washington, DC: Nonprofit Risk Management Center) 1994.

153. Tschirhart, Mary, Debra Mesch, James Perry, Theodore Miller and Geunjoo Lee, "Stipended Volunteers: Their Goals, Experiences, Satisfaction and Likelihood of Future Service," *Nonprofit and Voluntary Sector Quarterly*, September 2001.

154. Urban Institute, *Volunteer Management Capacity in America's Charities and Congregations: A Briefing Report*, 2004.

155. Vineyard, Sue, and Steve McCurley, eds., *Managing Volunteer Diversity*, (Downers Grove: Heritage Arts) 1989.

156. Vineyard, Sue, and Steve McCurley, *101 More Ideas for Volunteer Programs* (Downers Grove: Heritage Arts) 1995.

157. Volunteer Canada, *A Guide to Volunteer Program Management Resources*, (Ottawa: Volunteer Canada) 2001.

158. Volunteer Canada, *A Matter of Design: Job Design Theory and Application to the Voluntary Sector*, (Ottawa: Volunteer Canada) 2001.

159. Volunteer Canada, *Volunteer Connections: New Strategies for Involving Youth* (Ottawa: Volunteer Canada) 2001.

160. Volunteer Canada, *Volunteer Connections: The Benefits and Challenges of Employer-Supported Volunteerism*, (Ottawa: Volunteer Canada) 2001.

161. Volunteer Canada, *Volunteering…A Booming Trend: Experience Personal Fulfillment and Satisfaction Later in Life through Volunteering* (Ottawa: Volunteer Canada) 2000.

162. Volunteer Development Scotland, *Engaging Volunteers: A Good Practice Guide* (Stirling: VDS) 1995.

163. Volunteer Development Scotland, *Framework for Volunteering: Policy and Procedures on Volunteers in Voluntary Organisations* (Stirling: VDS) 1998.

164. Volunteer Development Scotland, *Volunteering and Disability: Experiences and Perceptions of Volunteering from Disabled People and Organisations*, September 2005.

165. Wilson, Carla, *The Changing Face of Social Service Volunteering: A Literature Review*, Ministry of Social Development, Wellington, December 2001

166. Wilson, J., and M. Musick. "Attachment to Volunteering." *Sociological Forum* 14(2):243-72. . 1999.

167. Wilson, John and Marc Musick, "Work and Volunteering: the Long Arm of the Job," *Social Forces*, Vol. 76, 1997.

168. Wilson, John, "Volunteering," *Annual Review of Sociology*, 2000.

169. Wilson, John, and Marc Musick, "Who Cares? Toward an Integrated Theory of Volunteer Work." *American Sociological Review* Vol. 62, 1997.

170. Zappala Gianni and Tracy Burrell, Why are Some Volunteers More Committed than Others? A Socio-Psychological Approach to Volunteer Commitment in Community Services, Working Paper No. 5, Research and Social Policy Team, The Smith Family, November 2001, http://www.smithfamily.com.au.

171. Zappala Gianni, Ben Parker and Vanessa Green, *The 'New Face' of Volunteering in Social Enterprises: The Smith Family Experience*, Background Paper No 2, Research and Advocacy Team, The Smith Family, April 2001, http://www.smithfamily.com.au.

172. Zappala, G. (2000) *How Many People Volunteer in Australia and Why Do They Do It?* Research and Advocacy Briefing Paper No. 4, Research and Advocacy Team, The Smith Family, New South Wales.

173. Zappala, G., B. Parker and V. Green (2001) *The "New Face" of Volunteering in Social Enterprises*: The Smith Family Experience, Background Paper No. 2, Research and Advocacy Team, The Smith Family, New South Wales.

174. Zappala, Gianni and Tracy Burrell, *The Giving of Time and Money: An Analysis of Donor Behavior among Volunteers*, Working Paper No. 7, Research and Social Policy Team, The Smith Family, July 2002, http://www.smithfamily.com.au.

175. Zarinpoush, Fataneh, Cathy Barr and Jason Moreton, *Volunteer Managers: A Portrait of the Profession*, (Toronto: Imagine Canada) 2004.

Appendix Two
Internet Resources

National Organizations
The following are some of the internet sites which contain material useful for volunteer programs.

Australia
1. Volunteering Australia
   www.volunteeringaustralia.org
2. Volunteering Western Australia
   www.volunteer.org.au/index.htm
3. Volunteering New South Wales
   www.volunteering.com.au
4. Volunteering Queensland
   www.volunteeringqueensland.org.au/index.html
5. Volunteering SA
   www.volunteeringsa.org.au

Canada
1. Volunteer Canada
   www.volunteer.ca/volunteer/index.html
2. National Survey on Giving, Volunteering and Participating
   www.nsgvp.org
3. Voluntary Sector Roundtable
   www.vsr-trsb.net/main-e.html
4. Canadian Administrators of Volunteer Resources
   www.cavr.org
5. Canadian Business for Social Responsibility
   www.cbsr.bc.ca

Central & South America
1. Centro Nacional de Voluntariado, Bolivia
   www.cebofil.org
2. Programa Voluntarios, Brazil
   www.programavoluntarios.org.br
3. Corporacion Colombiana de Trabajo Voluntario, Columbia
   www.ccong.org.co/cctv.html
4. Centro Mexicano para la Filantropia
   www.cemefi.org
5. Voluntar, Chile
   www.chilevoluntario.cl/orgs/voluntar.htm
6. Voluntariado en Uruguay
   www.icd.org.uy/filantropia/voluntariado.html
7. Centro de Estudos do Terceiro Setor, Brazil
   www.fgvsp.br/cets
8. Asociaciion Mexicana de Voluntarios
   amevac@prodigy.net.mx

Europe
1. European Volunteer Centre
   www.cev.be
2. Volunteer Resource Centre, Ireland
   www.volunteeringireland.com
3. Association pour le Volontariat a l'acte Gratuity en Europe, France
   www.ave-europe.org/home.html
4. Association pour le Volontariat, Belgium
   www.enter.org/volontariat/assvol.htm
5. Foundazione Italiana per il Volontariato, Italy
   www.fivol.it
6. Centro Nazionale per il Volontariato, Italy
   cnv.cpr.it
7. Volonteurope
   www.newnet.org.uk/epcsv.htm
8. Center for Frivilligt Socialt Arbejde, Denmark
   www.frivsocarb.dk/english/index0.html
9. Centre National du Volontariat, France
   www.globenet.org/CNV
10. Institut de Recherche et d'Information sur le Volontariat, France
    www.iriv.net
11. Association pour L'etude et al Promotion de l'action Benevole, Switzerland
    www.benevolat.ch
12. Nederlandse Organisaties Vrijwilligerswerk, Netherlands
    www.volunteer.nl

13 Federacio Catalana de Voluntariat Social, Spain
   www.federacio.es.org

14 Euro-Volunteer Information Pool
   www.euro-volunteer.org

15. Corporate Social Responsibility, Europe
    www.csreurope.org

16 Danish Committee on Volunteer Effort
   www.frivsocarb.dk/English

17. Forum For Frivilligt Socialt Arbete, Sweden
    www.socialforum.a.se

United Kingdom
1. Volunteering England
   www.volunteering.org.uk
2. Institute for Volunteering Research
   www.ivr.org.uk
3. Volunteer Development Scotland
   www.vds.org.uk
4. Wales Council for Voluntary Action
   www.wcva.org.uk
5. Active Community Unit, Home Office,
   www.homeoffice.gov.uk/new_index
   index_volunteering.htm
6. Millennium Volunteers
   www.millenniumvolunteers.gov.uk
7. Scottish Association of Volunteers Managers
   www.savm.org.uk

8. National Volunteer Managers Forum
www.volunteering.org.uk/volunteering/nvmf
9. Association for Research in the Voluntary and Community Sector
www.charitynet.org/arvac/index.html
10. Business in the Community
www.bitc.org.uk
11. Community Service Volunteers
www.csv.org.uk

United States
1. International Association of Justice Volunteerism
www.justicevolunteers.org
2. Independent Sector
www.independentsector.org
3. Points of Light Foundation
www.pointsoflight.org
4. American Society of Directors of Volunteer Services
www.asdvs.org
5. Corporation for National Service
www.cns.gov
6. Association for Research on Nonprofit Organizations and Voluntary Action
www.arnova.org
7. National Association of Partners in Education
www.napehq.org
8. National Mentoring Partnership
www.mentoring,org
9. National Center for Charitable Statistics
nccs.urban.org
10 Energize, Inc
www.energizeinc.com
11. National Association of Retired and Senior Volunteer Program Directors
www.narsvpd.org
12. Independent Sector
www.independentsector.org
14. National Association of Volunteer Programs in 13 Government
www.naco.org/affils/navplg
14. Opera Volunteers International
www.operavol.org
15. Volunteers in Prevention, Probation and Prisons, Inc.
comnet.org/vip
16. Virtual Volunteering Project
www.serviceleader.org

Internet Chat Groups
There are a number of major chat groups tailored to managers of volunteer programs. Each is free.

1. CyberVPM
www.avaintl.org/networks/cybervpm.html

2. UKVPMs
groups.yahoo.com/group/UKVPMs

3. OZVPMs
groups.yahoo.com/group/ozvpm

4. GOV-VPM
www.pointsoflight.org/government/gov-join.html

Volunteer Management Software Programs
These are some of the volunteer management software programs. Most have demo software available from their web site.

1. DVS Manager, Volunteer Equation Express, Corporate Citizen Volunteer, Student Citizen Volunteer
RUR Group (US)
www.rur.nxt.net

2. INVOLVE, Computerised Volunteer Audit System
National Centre for Volunteering (UK)
www.volunteering.org.uk/involve.htm

3. Qmember
QED Software Solutions (Canada)
www.dynamicthinking.com/qmember.htm

4. RE: Volunteer
Blackbaud (US)
www.blackbaud.com

5. ROVIR
Creative Software Solutions (US)
www.rovirinfo.com

6. RSVP Reporter, Volunteer Reporter Professional
Volunteer Software (US)
www.volsoft.com/demo.htm

7. Samaritan Coordinator, Samaritan Recruiter, Samaritan eCoordinator
Samaritan Software (US)
www.samaritan.com

8. TDS Volunteer File
Performance Masters Inc. (US)
www.tdsvfp.com

9. V-Base

do-it.org.uk (UK)
www.do-it.org.uk/do-it/vbase.html

10. VICTA
InfoServe Systems (US)
www.victasystem.com

11. Vol-Track
SP Extreme (US)
www.spextreme.com/voltrack

12. VolCentre
Original Software Limited (US, Canada, New Zealand, Australia, UK)
www.original-software.com/products/volcentre

13. VolStar
Granite Consulting (Canada)
www.volstar.com

14. VolTrak 3.0
ClarenceSoftware, Ltd (UK)
www.bhs.com/downloads/file.asp?id=5414

15. Volunteer Coordination System
Opal Computing (US)
www.opalcomputing.com/vcs.html

16. Volunteer Coordinator, HospiceAid, Festival Events
Affirmative Communications (Canada)
www.volunteercoordinator.com
www.hospiceaid.com/volmanage.asp
www.festivalevents.com/

17. Volunteer Info Tracker
Salmon Falls Software (US)
members.aol.com/infotraker/volunter.htm

18. Volunteer Information System
Provelle (US)
polyt.home.mindspring.com/polyt/provelle.htm

19. Volunteer Manager
Dynamic Design and Development (US)
www.CIBIXsolutions.com

20. Volunteer Module GiftMaker Pro
Campagne Associates Ltd (US)
www.campagne.com/VOL.html

21. Volunteer Works
Red Ridge Software (US)
www.redridge.com

22. Volunteer/Client Scheduling Database, Volunteer Activity Scheduler
Selston Investments (Canada)
www.selston.ca

23. VolWare 2.0
Organizational Software Inc. (US)
www.orgsoftware.com

Volunteer Books, Products andRecognition Items

1. Energize, Inc
800-395-9800
www.energizeinc.com

2. VolunCHEER
408-792-3456
www.voluncheer.com

3. Volunteer Marketplace, Points of Light Foundation
800-272-8306
www.pointsoflight.org/volunteermarketplace.cfm

4. Positive Promotions
800-635-2666
www.positivepromotions.com

5. The Thanks Company
888-875-0903
www.thankscompany.com

6. Volunteer Appreciation
877-369-4109
www.volunteer-appreciation.com

7. Volunteer Canada
800-670-0401
www.volunteer.ca

8. Volunteer Calgary
800-200-2207
www.volunteercalgary.ab.ca

9. VolunteerGifts.com
561-487-5684
www.VolunteerGifts.com

10. JTC, Inc
www.jtcinc.ca

Volunteer Management Periodicals

1. Australian Journal on Volunteering
   Volunteer Centre of South Australia Inc.
   www.volunteer.org.au/vrn/journal.htm

2. Canadian Journal of Volunteer Resource Management
   www.cavr.org

3. e-Volunteerism: An Electronic Journal for the Volunteerism Community
   Susan Ellis and Steve McCurley
   www.e-volunteerism.com

4. Leadership
   Points of Light Foundation.
   www.pointsoflight.org

5. Nonprofit and Voluntary Sector Quarterly
   ARNOVA
   www.arnova.org

6. Nonprofit Management and Leadership
   Mandel Center for Nonprofit Organizations
   Jossey-Bass Publishers
   www.josseybass.com

7. Voluntary Action
   Institute for Volunteering Research
   www.ivr.org.uk

8. The Volunteer Management Report
   Stevenson Consultants
   www.stevensoninc.com

9. Volunteer Management Review
   Nan Hawthorne, Charity Channel
   charitychannel.com/resources/volunteer_management_review

10. Volunteer Today
    Nancy Macduff
    www.volunteertoday.com

11. VOLUNTEERING
    The National Centre for Volunteering
    www.volunteering.org.uk

Volunteer Recruitment Websites

1. Action without Borders (global)
   www.idealist.org

2. Do-It (UK)
   www.thesite.org/do-it/

3. Go Volunteer (Australia)
   www.govolunteer.com.au

4. The Interchange (Canada)
   www.web.net/~interchg

5. ServeNet (US)
   www.servenet.org

6. Volunteer Hub (US)
   www.volunteerhub.com

7. Volunteer Match (US)
   www.volunteermatch.org

8. Volunteer Opportunities Exchange (Canada)
   www.voe-reb.org/welcome.jhtml

9. Volunteer Solutions (US)
   www.volunteersolutions.org

Appendix Three
Sample Forms and Worksheets

Staff Assessment Survey on Volunteer Involvement

As part of our organizational plan to utilize volunteer assistance, we would like you to complete the following questionnaire. This survey assesses our readiness to utilize volunteers and to determine what we need to do to ensure continued delivery of high quality service to our clientele. All of the information collected will be kept confidential.

I. Your Previous Experience with Volunteers

1. Have you previously worked in an agency that utilized volunteers?

❑ Yes ❑ No ❑ Don't Know

2. Have you previously supervised any volunteers?

❑ Yes ❑ No ❑ Don't Know

3. Do you do any volunteer work yourself?

❑ Yes ❑ No ❑ Once did, but not anymore

II. Your Assessment of Volunteer Involvement

1. What is your overall assessment of utilizing volunteers in our agency at this time?

❑ Very desirable ❑ Somewhat desirable ❑ Uncertain
❑ Not desirable at this time ❑ Would never be appropriate

2. What is your overall assessment of our current readiness to utilize volunteers?

❑ Very ready ❑ Somewhat ready ❑ Uncertain ❑ Not ready

3. Are there any areas or types of work for which you think volunteers are particularly needed and suited?

4. Are there any areas of work that you think volunteers should not do in our agency?

5. What issues or concerns would you like to see addressed before we involve volunteers?

6. What type of training or assistance would you like to receive before you are asked to work with volunteers?

7. Are there any other comments or suggestions you would like to express about the involvement of volunteers in our agency?

Creating Strategic Volunteer Jobs Worksheet

1. What is the problem your organization is trying to solve or the need in the community it is trying to meet? Solving this problem is your agency mission. Use your own words to write a brief description of that problems and its effects:

2. What are the factors that contribute to that problem? What are the obstacles you face in accomplishing your mission?

3. What are the best strategies for overcoming these obstacles? These strategies form the basis of your strategic goals.

4. What are the actions necessary to carry out these strategies? This is your strategic plan.

5. What actions do paid staff lack the time or skill to do? These are your high-impact volunteer opportunities.

Sample Staff Request for Volunteer Assistance

Date of Request: Department:

Staff Contact: Phone:

Brief Description of the Work to be Performed:
(Give both the goal of the job and examples of activities to be performed)

Number of Volunteers Sought for This Position:

Qualifications Sought:
(Include both skills and attributes needed to perform the work and any items that might disqualify an applicant)

Worksite:

Timeframe:

Hours Preferred: ❑ Flexible to availability of volunteer ❑ Needed:

Length of Commitment Sought:

❑ Open-ended ❑ Minimum of :

❑ One-time situation (give date and time):

When do you want this work to start?

❑ Upon availability ❑ Start:

Sample Volunteer Position Description

Title/Position:

Goal of Position:

Sample Activities:

1.

2.

3.

4.

Timeframe:

Length of commitment:

Estimated total hours:

Scheduling:

- ❑ At discretion of volunteer
- ❑ Needed:

Worksite:

Qualifications Sought:

1.

2.

3.

Benefits:

1.

2.

Staff Contact:

Targeted Recruitment Planning Worksheet

Volunteer Position:____

1. What are the skills/attitudes needed to do this work?
(I.e., if we draw a picture of the type of person who could do this work and would ***enjoy*** *doing it, what would they look like? Cover age, sex, hobbies, possible occupations, related interests, and whatever else better illustrates the picture.)*

1. ____
2. ____
3. ____
4. ____
5. ____

2. Based on this picture, where can we find these types of people?
(Think about work setting, educational background, leisure time organizations and activities, publications they might read, parts of town in which they are likely to live, etc.)

1. ____
2. ____
3. ____
4. ____
5. ____

3. What motivations of this person can we appeal to in our recruitment effort?
(Self-help, job enhancement, socialization, learning new skills, career exploration, leadership testing, giving back to the community, keeping productively involved, meeting new people, etc.)

1. ____
2. ____
3. ____
4. ____
5. ____

Volunteer Recruitment Message Worksheet

1. Why should this work be done at all? What is the need in the community for this work? What bad things will happen if this work is not done? Use both statistics and examples to illustrate the harm or problem area.

2. What will the benefit be to the community or to the client if the work is done? What will the work accomplish? What changes will it make in their lives? What will the volunteer be able to accomplish if they accept the job?

3. What are some possible fears or objections concerning this work which must be overcome? The type of clients? The subject area? The skills needed to do the work? Geography? Liability?

4. What will be the personal benefit to the volunteer in doing the work? Skills? Experience? Flexible work schedules? Parking? New Friends?

Sample Volunteer Application Form

Name:

Address:

City: State: Zip:

Phone: (Home) (Office) E-mail:

Contact in emergency: Phone:

I. Skills and Interests

1. Education background:

2. Current occupation:

3. Hobbies, skills, interests:

4. Previous volunteer experience:

II. Preferences in Volunteering

1. Is there a particular type of volunteer work in which you are interested? (Please check all that apply.)

- ❑ Working one-on-one with a single client
- ❑ Doing public speaking, fundraising, etc.
- ❑ Working directly with a staff person as an assistant
- ❑ Providing service to several clients
- ❑ Helping around the office in general administrative duties
- ❑ Doing research, training or an individual project
- ❑ Working on group projects
- ❑ Other:
- ❑ No preference

2. Is there a person or group with whom you are particularly interested in working? (Check all that apply.)

❑ No preference	❑ Adults	❑ Seniors
❑ Teens	❑ Children	❑ People with Disabilities
❑ Agency Staff	❑ Males	❑ Females
❑ Animals	❑ Other:	

3. Are there any groups with which you would not feel comfortable working?

❑ No ❑ Yes:

III. Availability

1. At what times are you interested in volunteering?

❑ Am flexible	❑ Prefer weekdays	❑ Prefer evenings
❑ Prefer weekends	❑ Prefer days	❑ Other:

2. Do you have a geographic preference as to where you do volunteer work?

❑ No ❑ Yes:

3. Do you have access to an automobile you can use for volunteer work?

❑ Yes ❑ No

IV. Background Verification

1. Have you been convicted of a criminal offense?

❑ Yes ❑ No

2. Have you ever been charged with neglect, abuse, or assault?

❑ Yes ❑ No

3. Has your driver's license ever been suspended or revoked in any state?

❑ Yes ❑ No

4. Do you use illegal drugs?

❑ Yes ❑ No

5. Do you have any physical limitations or are you under any course of treatment which might limit your ability to perform certain types of work?

❑ Yes ❑ No

6. Please list two non-family references whom we might contact:

a. Phone:
b. Phone:

7. How did you hear about us?

❑ Saw job description ❑ Saw advertisement ❑ Volunteer Center ❑ Website
❑ From client of agency ❑ Referred by friend ❑ From agency/school
❑ Other:

Sample Volunteer Interview Record

Interviewer: Date:

Name of Volunteer: Phone:

I. Review of Enrollment Form

Review and clarify information on Volunteer Application Form. Correct any misinformation on form and place other comments below.

II. Non-Directive Interview Questions

1. What attracted you to our agency? Is there any aspect of our work that most motivates you to seek to volunteer here?

2. What would you like to get out of volunteering here? What would make you feel like you've been successful?

3. What have you enjoyed most about your previous volunteer work? About previous paid employment?

4. Describe your ideal supervisor. What sort of supervisory style do you prefer to work under?

5. Would you rather work on your own, with a group, or with a partner? Why?

6. What skills do you feel you have to contribute?

7. What can I tell you about our agency?

III. Match with Volunteer Positions

Discuss potential volunteer positions and check match of interests, qualifications, and availability.

1.

2.

3.

To be completed after interview

IV. Interviewer Assessment

Appearance:

- ❑ Poised, neat ❑ Acceptable ❑ Unkempt

Reactions to Questions:

- ❑ Helpful, interested, volunteered information ❑ Answers questions
- ❑ Evasive ❑ Confused

Disposition:

- ❑ Outgoing, pleasant, confident ❑ Reserved
- ❑ Withdrawn, moody ❑ Suspicious, antagonistic

Interpersonal Skills:

- ❑ Adept at dealing with others ❑ Relatively at ease with others
- ❑ Uncomfortable

Physical Restrictions:

V. Recommended Action

❑ Consider for following positions:

1.

2.

❑ Schedule for second interview with

❑ Hold in reserve for position of:

1.

2.

❑ Investigate further:

❑ Refer to:

❑ Not suitable for agency at this time

Volunteer Interviewing Scenarios Worksheet

1. Think about past problems which your volunteers have encountered, Select one which has some of the following characteristics:

- worries you and might occur again
- has no clear "right" answer
- a volunteer might be likely to rush to their own "right" answer to the problem
- a volunteer might have difficulty in dealing with the subject matter
- a volunteer might have difficulty in dealing with the interpersonal relations involved in the situation

2. Use the space below to describe this situation. Briefly outline:

    - main facts and characters
    - basic "dilemma"
    - key elements
    - "wrong" responses

3. Use the space below to develop this situation into an interviewing scenario:

    - description of basic setting to be given to volunteer
    - characters involved
    - key questions
    - secondary twists and complexities

Sample Physician Referral Clearance Form

Name of Patient:

Volunteer Work Under Consideration:

Agency:

The above named individual is currently or has just been under my treatment or care. Based upon my examination of the volunteer work description provided for the positions for which this person is being considered, it is my professional opinion that the condition for which they are receiving treatment or care will not prevent or limit their safe and satisfactory performance of the described work activities.

I agree to notify the agency cited above if the capacity of the patient while under my treatment or care alters in any way that might materially change my evaluation of their suitability to perform the described volunteer work.

Signed Date

Sample Permission to Perform Background Check

I hereby allow [name of agency] to perform a check of my background, including

- ❑ criminal record
- ❑ driving record
- ❑ past employment/volunteer history
- ❑ finances
- ❑ educational/professional status
- ❑ personal references
- ❑ physician or therapist

and other persons or sources as appropriate for the volunteer work in which I have expressed an interest.

I understand that I do not have to agree to this background check, but that refusal to do so may exclude me from consideration for some types of volunteer work.

I understand that information collected during this background check will be limited to that appropriate to determining my suitability for particular types of volunteer work and that all such information collected during the check will be kept confidential.

I hereby also extend my permission to those individuals or organizations contacted for the purpose of this background check to give their full and honest evaluation of my suitability of the described volunteer work and such other information as they deem appropriate.

Signed   Date

Sample Parental Consent Form

In order for your child to become a volunteer with us, we need your consent and your involvement in helping them have a productive experience. Please read and sign this parental consent form if you would like us to continue our process of considering your child as a possible volunteer. Please call the Volunteer Department if you have any questions, would like further information, or would just like to discuss this with someone.

Name of agency:

Name of prospective youth volunteer:

1. Description of anticipated volunteer work:

2. Anticipated number of hours per week and schedule for volunteer work:

3. Expected duration of volunteer work:

4. Anticipated location of volunteer work:

I understand that my child named above wishes to be considered for volunteer work and I hereby give my permission for them to serve in that capacity, if accepted by the agency. I understand that they will be provided with orientation and training necessary for the safe and responsible performance of their duties and that they will be expected to meet all the requirements of the position, including regular attendance and adherence to agency policies and procedures. I understand that they will not receive monetary compensation for the services contributed.

Name:

Nature of relationship to volunteer:

Date:

Sample Telephone Reference Check Form

Date:

Name of Volunteer Applicant:

Name of Reference:

Telephone:

I. Introductory Comments

Briefly cover the following in requesting that the references consent to a discussion of the applicant:

- Your name
- Name of agency
- Applicant requested that we call you to verify some information about possible volunteer position
- Applicant has given permission for them to provide full and honest information
- Conversation will probably take about 10 minutes and can be conducted at their convenience
- Information given will be kept confidential

II. Reference Check Questions

1. How long and in what capacity have you known the applicant?

2. How would you describe the applicant? What three words would you use if you were giving a thumbnail sketch?

3. Describe how the applicant gets along with people in general.

4. How would you describe the applicant's ability to get along with (client group)?

5. What would you describe as the primary positive skills or traits of the applicant?

6. What would you describe as negative traits or areas of weakness?

7. How comfortable would you be in having the applicant work for you on an important project?

8. Are you aware of any financial difficulties, drug abuse problems or history of criminal conduct on the part of the applicant?

9. The position that the applicant is being considered for is. What do you think the applicant would be good at and not so good at in performing that type of work?

10. Is there anything else you can tell us that might help us reach a good decision?

Name of Reference Checker:

Sample Agency/Volunteer Agreement

This agreement is intended to indicate the seriousness which with we treat our volunteers. The intent of the agreement is to assure you both of our deep appreciation for your services and to indicate our commitment to do the very best we can to make your volunteer experience here a productive and rewarding one.

I. Agency

We, (agency) , agree to accept the services of (volunteer) beginning (date)

and we commit to the following:

1. To provide adequate information, training, and assistance for the volunteer to be able to meet the responsibilities of their position.

2. To ensure diligent supervisory aid to the volunteer and to provide feedback on their performance.

3. To respect the skills, dignity, and individual needs of the volunteer, and to do our best to adjust to these individual requirements.

4. To be receptive to any comments from the volunteer regarding ways in which we might mutually better accomplish our respective tasks.

5. To treat the volunteer as an equal partner with agency staff, jointly responsible for accomplishment of the agency mission.

II. Volunteer

I, , agree to serve as a volunteer and commit to the following:

1. To perform my volunteer duties to the best of my ability.

2. To adhere to agency rules and procedures, including recordkeeping requirements and confidentiality of agency and client information.

3. To meet time and duty commitment, or to provide adequate notice so that alternate arrangements can be made.

4. To act at all times as a member of the team responsible for accomplishing the mission of the agency.

III. Agreed to:

Volunteer: Agency Representative:

Date: Date:

Sample Volunteer Code of Ethics

As a volunteer I realize that I am subject to a code of ethics similar to that which binds the professionals in the organization in which I will participate. In agreeing to serve, I assume certain responsibilities and expect to account for what I do in terms of what I these professional expectations. I will honor the goals, rules and regulations of the program. I will keep confidential matters confidential.

I interpret volunteering to mean that I have been accepted as a "partner-in-service" and I expect to do my work according to the highest standards, as the paid staff members expect to do their work.

I promise to take to my work an attitude of open mindedness, to be willing to be trained for it according to the standards and practices of the organization, and to bring to my work my full interest and attention. I believe my attitude toward volunteer work should be professional. I believe that I have an obligation to my work, to those who direct it, to my colleagues, to those for whom it is done, and to the public.

Being eager to contribute all that I can to the goals of this program, I accept this code of ethics, to be followed carefully and cheerfully.

____________________________ _______________

Volunteer signature Date

Sample Volunteer Personnel Record

Name:

Address:

Telephone: (Home) (Office) (Cell)

E-Mail Address:

Spouse's Name: Phone:

Children:

In case of emergency, notify: Phone:

Health or physical information:

1. Period during which volunteer worked with agency:

   Beginning date:

   Ending date:

2. Types of volunteer positions held:

   a.

   b.

   c.

   d.

   e.

3. Comments and other pertinent information:

Volunteer Training Design Worksheet

1. Who are the individuals/positions/groups to receive training? What are their previous levels of involvement with this subject or with the requirements of this job?

2. What information, experience, and attitudes do we wish each to have at the ending of the training?

A. *Information* may include knowledge of the project and the system, knowledge about the position or the recipients of the service, "how-to's" related to the position's functions or specific skills:

B. *Experience* may include practice at being someone (such as through role-playing or role discussion) or practice at doing something (such as constructing a tentative plan of action or operating equipment).

C. *Attitudes* may include a clear sense of purpose and direction, a sense of their ability to do the work well, or the motivation to do the job correctly and according to established procedures.

3. In what order does the above material need to be presented in order to be useful and understandable?

4. What are the available formats for delivery of training?

A. Self-study

- ❑ Videotape
- ❑ Book/manual
- ❑ Magazine/newsletter
- ❑ Computer

B. One-to-one assistance

- ❑ Telephone technical assistance
- ❑ Mentor/buddy system
- ❑ Assigned staff/volunteer coach
- ❑ Apprenticeship

C. Training event/workshop

- ❑ Lecture
- ❑ Exercise
- ❑ Role play
- ❑ Group discussion
- ❑ Case study
- ❑ Worksheet development

5. What format best matches each of the informational, experiential, and attitudinal needs that have been identified?

a. Format:

b. Format:

c. Format:

d. Format:

e. Format:

f. Format:

g. Format:

6. Who should be involved in designing and delivering each component of the training? Consider the desirability of "insiders" versus "neutrals," needed facilitative skills, technical knowledge and experience, and ability to build credibility or to forge relationships.

7. Who else needs to be involved or informed to make this training work in the real world?

❑ Supervisors

❑ Co-workers

❑ Clients

❑ Other:

Sample Volunteer Expense Report

This form is to be utilized to record those expenses you incur while volunteering for us for which you wish to be reimbursed. The types of expenses for which we provide reimbursement are:

1.

2.

3.

4.

Date	Type of Expenditure	Amount

These represent an accurate account of my expenses. Receipts are attached for appropriate items.

Volunteer: Date:

Approved for reimbursement:

Staff: Date:

Charge to Account #:

Risk Identification Worksheet

Use this worksheet to brainstorm possible areas of risk related to a volunteer position. Consider possible risks or problems that might arise in each of the categories below:

Physical Ability:

1.
2.
3.
4.
5.
6.

Skills:

1.
2.
3.
4.
5.
6.

Attitude, Maturity:

1.
2.
3.
4
5.
6.

Equipment Use:

1.
1.
2.
3.
4.
5.
6.

Worksite:

1.
2.
3.
4.
5.
6.

Clientele:

1.
2.
3.
4.
5.
6.

Failure to Follow Procedures:

1.

2.

3.

4.

Risk Management Planning Worksheet

Volunteer Position:

Identified Major Risks of this Position:

1.

2.

3.

4.

5.

6.

Special Measures to be Undertaken in Screening Volunteers for Position:

1.

2.

3.

4.

Special Measures to be Undertaken in Training Volunteers for Position:

1.

2.

3.

4.

5.

Special Measures to be Undertaken in Supervision of Volunteers in Position:

1.

2.

3.

4.

Staff Assessment Survey on Volunteer Involvement

This form is to allow you to provide feedback regarding our utilization of volunteers. Please answer all questions as completely as possible. Do not sign the survey unless you wish to. All responses will be kept confidential.

1. Are volunteers involved in your area of direct responsibility or in your department?

    ❑ Yes ❑ No ❑ Don't know

2. Are the volunteers with our agency adequately trained for their responsibilities?

    ❑ Yes ❑ No ❑ Don't know

3. How would you describe the utilization of volunteers in our agency by other staff?

    ❑ Well utilized ❑ Generally well utilized, but some poor use
    ❑ Generally not well utilized ❑ Don't know

4. Do you think our staff has received adequate training in how to work with volunteers?

    ❑ Yes ❑ No ❑ Don't know

5. What else should be done to help our staff work better with volunteers?

6. How would you describe the reaction of our clients to the volunteers?

    ❑ Favorable ❑ Mixed ❑ Unfavorable ❑ Don't know

7. What benefits do you think we have gained from the utilization of volunteers?

8. What problems have we created with the use of volunteers?

9. How has your own workload changed as a result of our utilizing volunteers?

    ❑ Lessened ❑ Remained the same ❑ Increased
    ❑ Changed in type of work done

10. How would you describe the assistance you have received from the volunteer management department?

    ❑ Helpful ❑ Not helpful ❑ Haven't made use of help

11. Use the space below to make any comments regarding our involvement of volunteers, any additions you would like to make to your answers above, or any suggestions you have about how we might make better use of volunteers.

Volunteer Assessment Survey of the Volunteer Program

As part of our continued effort to improve our volunteer program, we would like your responses to the following questions. All responses will be kept completely confidential. Do not sign the survey unless you wish to.

1. How long have you been volunteering with us?

2. To what extent do you think that volunteers are well accepted by the staff at our agency?

❑ Well accepted ❑ Generally well accepted, but some exceptions
❑ Not well accepted ❑ Generally not well accepted, but some exceptions

3. To what extent do you think volunteers are involved in decisions that will affect their volunteer work?

❑ Well involved ❑ Sometimes involved ❑ Not well involved

4. To what extent do you think volunteers are accepted and welcomed by clients?

❑ Well accepted ❑ Mixed reception ❑ Not well accepted

5. To what extent do you think volunteers feel comfortable with the assignments they are given?

❑ Comfortable ❑ Not comfortable ❑ Don't know

6. Do you feel that volunteers receive sufficient orientation about our agency before they begin work?

❑ Yes ❑ No ❑ Don't know

7. Do you feel that volunteers receive enough training to carry out their assignments?

❑ Yes ❑ No ❑ Don't know

8. In your experience, does your volunteer job match the position description you were given?

❑ Yes ❑ No ❑ Not given job description

9. Do you find your volunteer work to be interesting, challenging, and rewarding?

❑ Yes ❑ Somewhat ❑ No

10. Do you think that volunteers are provided with sufficient feedback by those they work with?

❑ Yes ❑ No ❑ Somewhat ❑ Don't know

11. Do you think volunteers have sufficient opportunity to advance in responsibility in this agency?

❑ Yes ❑ No ❑ Don't know

12. Can you think of any new areas or new jobs in which volunteers might be of help to our agency?

13. Can you suggest any ways that we might use to recruit new volunteers?

14. What's the best experience you've had while volunteering for us?

15. What's the worst experience?

16. If you could make three changes in our volunteer program, what would they be?

    1.

    2.

    3.

17. Overall, how would you rate our volunteer program? (Please circle. 1 = Terrible; 7 = Great)

    1 2 3 4 5 6 7

18. Use the space below to make any other comments regarding our utilization of volunteers, or any additions you would like to make to any of your answers above.

Sample Volunteer Position Feedback and Evaluation Form

Name of Volunteer: Period covered:

Position: Date of evaluation:

1. Position Goals:

	Not Met		Satisfactory		Superior
1.	1	2	3	4	5
2.	1	2	3	4	5
3.	1	2	3	4	5
4.	1	2	3	4	5
5.	1	2	3	4	5

2. Work Relationships:

	Needs Improvement	*Satisfactory*			*Excellent*
a. Relations with other volunteers	1	2	3	4	5
b. Relations with staff	1	2	3	4	5
c. Relations with clients	1	2	3	4	5
d. Meeting commitments on hours and task deadlines	1	2	3	4	5
e. Initiative	1	2	3	4	5
f. Flexibility	1	2	3	4	5

3. Comments by supervisor regarding above areas:

4. Comments by volunteer regarding above areas:

5. Most significant achievement during period of evaluation:

6. Major area in which improvement, change, or further training would be desirable, with description of suggested course of action:

7. Overall, how does the volunteer feel about remaining in this position? What change in nature of responsibilities or procedures would improve the ability of the volunteer to contribute to the agency?

8. What are the major goals for the volunteer to accomplish in their position between now and the next evaluation period?

1.

2.

3.

4.

5.

9. Scheduled date of next evaluation:

Signatures:

Supervisor: Date:

Volunteer (Optional): Date:

Sample Volunteer Discharge Record

Name of volunteer:

Position of volunteer:

Name of supervisor:

1. Nature of difficulty regarding volunteer (check all that apply):

- ❑ Providing false or misleading information on application
- ❑ Absenteeism
- ❑ Tardiness
- ❑ Insubordination
- ❑ Physically or mentally unable to work
- ❑ Failure to follow agency policies and procedures
- ❑ Intoxication or drug use
- ❑ Inability to work with staff, clients or other volunteers
- ❑ Failure to meet work performance standards
- ❑ Breach of confidentiality
- ❑ Other:

2. Explain and give examples of behavior in areas checked above:

3. Give dates and nature of relevant warnings and attempts to get volunteer to correct behavior:

4. Date volunteer was discharged:

5. Person conducting discharge session:

6. Written notice of discharge of volunteer provided to:

❑ Volunteer ❑ Appropriate Staff ❑ Appropriate clients ❑ Other:

Please attach copies of appropriate records and materials related to discharge.

Sample Exit Interview Questionnaire

We are always striving to improve the performance of our volunteer involvement system. As one of our volunteers, we would appreciate your help in identifying areas in which we might do better. Please be as complete and honest as you can in answering the following questions - all of the information collected will be kept strictly confidential, but it will be utilized to ensure that others who volunteer will receive the best possible treatment.

1. Approximately how long did you volunteer with us?

2. In general, what type of volunteer work did you do with us?

3. Why are you leaving? (Please check all that apply.)

❑ Job accomplished ❑ Moving to new location ❑ Need a change

❑ Didn't like work I was given ❑ Didn't feel welcome ❑ Didn't feel well utilized

❑ Other time commitments ❑ Other:

4. What did you like best about volunteering with us?

5. What suggestions would you make for changes or improvements in our volunteer effort?

6. Overall, how would you rate your experience in volunteering with us?

Terrible		*Average*		*Great*
1	2	3	4	5

Thanks for your help in completing this form and during your volunteering with us. We appreciate the help you've given us in trying to assist our clients and our community.

Appendix Four
Sample Volunteer Management Policies

This sample set of policies on volunteer management includes many of the ideas for good volunteer involvement expressed in this book. Not every item will be appropriate for every organization, nor will the specific policy items suggested necessarily conform to how the organization wishes to work with its volunteers. The sample policies are included more as a structure to help you construct your own policy on volunteer management which matches your views and needs, and which is appropriate to the size of your organization and the ways in which you involve volunteers. To construct such a policy you may remove or amend any item, or even add further items not included here.

If you only have the time to do a quick job on policy development and would like to make use of the samples that follow, be our guest, but be careful because some items have options of construction included in [brackets] to indicate that an alternative course of policy-making is possible in that item.

1. The Volunteer Program

1.1 Overall policy on use of volunteers
The achievement of the goals of this organization is best served by the active participation of citizens of the community. To this end, the organization accepts and encourages the involvement of volunteers at all levels in the organization and within all appropriate programs and activities. All staff are encouraged to assist in the creation of meaningful and productive roles in which volunteers might serve and to assist in recruitment of volunteers from the community.

1.2 Purpose of the volunteer policy
The purpose of the policy is to provide overall guidance and direction to staff and volunteers engaged in volunteer involvement and management efforts. The policy is intended for internal management guidance only, and does not constitute, either implicitly or explicitly, a binding contractual or personnel agreement. The organization reserves the exclusive right to change any aspect of the policy at any time and to expect adherence to the changed policy. Alterations to or exceptions from these policies may only be granted by the Volunteer Program Manager, and must be obtained in advance and in writing. Policies and procedures not specifically covered in these policies shall be determined by the Volunteer Program Manager.

1.3 Scope of the volunteer policy
Unless specifically stated, the policy applies to all non-elected volunteers in all programs and projects undertaken by or on behalf of the organization, and to all departments and sites of operation of the organization.

1.4 Role of the volunteer management department
The productive use of volunteers requires a planned and organized effort. The function of the volunteer management department is to provide a central coordinating point for effective volunteer involvement within the organization, and to direct and assist staff and volunteer efforts jointly to provide more productive services. The department shall also bear responsibility for maintaining liaison with other volunteer programs in the community and assisting in community-wide efforts to recognize and promote volunteering. The Volunteer Program Manager shall bear primary responsibility for planning for effective volunteer deployment, for assisting staff in identifying productive and creative volunteer roles, for recruiting suitable volunteers, and for tracking and evaluating the contribution of volunteers to the organization.

1.5 Definition of 'volunteer'
A "volunteer" is anyone who without compensation or expectation of compensation beyond reimbursement of expenses incurred in the course of his or her volunteer duties performs a task at the direction of and on behalf of the organization. A "volunteer" must be officially accepted and enrolled by the organization prior

to performance of the task. Unless specifically stated, volunteers shall not be considered as "employees" of the organization.

1.6 Special case volunteers
The organization also accepts as volunteers those participating in student community service activities, student intern projects, alternative sentencing programs, employee volunteering programs, and other volunteer referral programs. In each of these cases, however, a special agreement must be in effect with the agency, school, company, or program from which the special case volunteers originate and must identify responsibility for management and care of the volunteers.

1.7 Group volunteers
Special arrangements will be undertaken when members of a group or an organization volunteer their time as a group effort. These arrangements will include changes in normal orientation, training, screening and recordkeeping requirements as determined necessary by the Volunteer Program Manager.

1.8 Employees as volunteers
The organization accepts [does not accept] the services of its own staff as volunteers. This service is accepted provided that the volunteer service is provided totally without any coercive nature, involves work which is outside the scope of normal staff duties, and is provided outside usual working hours. Family members of staff are [are not] allowed to volunteer with the organization. When family members are enrolled as volunteers, they will not be placed under the direct supervision or within the same department as other members of their family who are employees.

1.9 Friends, relatives, clients and family members as volunteers
Friends, relatives, and family members of staff and volunteers are encouraged to volunteer. All individuals will go through the standard volunteer application procedures.

1.10 Clients and relatives as volunteers
Clients of the organization may be accepted as volunteers, where such service does not constitute an obstruction to or conflict with provision of services to the client or to others. Relatives of clients may also serve as volunteers, but will not be placed in a position of direct service or relationship to members of their family who are receiving services.

1.11 Service at the discretion of the organization
The organization accepts the service of all volunteers with the understanding that such service is at the sole discretion of the organization. Volunteers agree that the organization may at any time, for whatever reason, decide to terminate the volunteer's relationship with the organization or to make changes in the nature of their volunteer assignment.

A volunteer may at any time, for whatever reason, decide to sever the volunteer's relationship with the organization. Notice of such a decision should be communicated as soon as possible to the volunteer's supervisor.

1.12 Volunteer rights and responsibilities
Volunteers are viewed as a valuable resource to this organization, its staff, and its clients. Volunteers shall be extended the right to be given meaningful assignments, the right to be treated as equal co-workers, the right to effective supervision, the right to full involvement and participation, and the right to recognition for work done. In return, volunteers shall agree to actively perform their duties to the best of their abilities and to remain loyal to the values, goals and procedures of the organization.

1.13 Scope of volunteer involvement
Volunteers may be involved in all programs and activities of the organization, and serve at all levels of skill and decision-making. Volunteers should not, however, be used to displace any paid employees from their positions.

2. Volunteer Management Procedures

2.1 Maintenance of records
A system of records will be maintained on each volunteer, including dates of service, positions held, duties performed, evaluation of work, and awards received. Volunteers and appropriate staff shall be responsible for submitting all appropriate records and information to the volunteer management department in a timely and accurate fashion.

Volunteer personnel records shall be accorded the same confidentiality as staff personnel records.

2.2 Two hat policy
Members of the organization's board are [are not] accepted as direct service volunteers with the organization.

2.3 Conflict of interest
No person who has a conflict of interest with any activity or program of the organization, whether personal, philosophical, or financial shall be accepted or serve as a volunteer.

2.4 Representation of the organization
Prior to any action or statement that might significantly affect or obligate the organization, volunteers should seek prior consultation and approval from appropriate staff. These actions may include, but are not limited to, public statements to the press, lobbying efforts with other organizations, collaborations or joint initiatives, or any agreements involving contractual or other financial obligations. Volunteers are authorized to act as representatives of the organization as specifically indicated within their job descriptions and only to the extent of such written specifications.

2.5 Confidentiality
Volunteers are responsible for maintaining the confidentiality of all proprietary or privileged information to which they are exposed while serving as a volunteer, whether this information involves a single member of staff, volunteer, client, or other person or involves the overall business of the organization.

Failure to maintain confidentiality may result in termination of the volunteer's relationship with the organization or other corrective action.

2.6 Worksite
An appropriate worksite shall be established prior to the enrollment of any volunteer. This worksite shall contain necessary facilities, equipment, and space to enable the volunteer to effectively and comfortably perform his or her duties. Worksites and equipment provided to volunteers shall be comparable to that of paid staff performing similar duties.

2.7 Dress code
As representatives of the organization, volunteers, like staff, are responsible for presenting a good image to clients and to the community. Volunteers shall dress appropriately for the conditions and performance of their duties.

2.8 Timesheets
Individual volunteers are responsible for the accurate completion and timely submission of timesheets.

3. Volunteer Recruitment and Selection

3.1 Position descriptions
Volunteers benefit from a clear, complete, and current description of the duties and responsibilities of the position that they are expected to fill. Prior to any volunteer assignment or recruitment effort, a position description must be developed for each volunteer post. This will be given to each accepted volunteer and used in subsequent management and evaluation efforts. Position descriptions should be reviewed and updated at

least every two years, or whenever the work involved in the position changes substantially.

All position descriptions shall include a description of the purpose and duties of the position, a designated supervisor and worksite, a timeframe for the performance of the job, a listing of job qualifications, and a description of job benefits. The volunteer management department is available to assist staff in the development of volunteer assignments and position descriptions.

3.2 Staff requests for volunteers
Requests for volunteers shall be submitted in writing by interested staff, complete with a draft position description and a requested timeframe. All parties should understand that the recruitment of volunteers is enhanced by creative and interesting jobs and by advance notice. The volunteer management department reserves the right to refuse to recruit or place any volunteers until staff are prepared to make effective use of the volunteer resource.

3.3 Recruitment
Volunteers shall be recruited by the organization on a pro-active basis, with the intent of broadening and expanding the volunteer involvement of the community. Volunteers shall be recruited without regard to gender, disability, age, race or other condition. The sole qualification for volunteer recruitment shall be suitability to perform a task on behalf of the organization. Volunteers may be recruited either through an interest in specific functions or through a general interest in volunteering which will later be matched with a specific function. No final acceptance of a volunteer shall take place without a specific written volunteer position description for that volunteer.

3.4 Recruitment of minors
Volunteers who have not reached the age of majority must have the written consent of a parent or legal guardian prior to volunteering. The volunteer responsibilities assigned to a minor should be performed in a non-hazardous environment and should comply with all appropriate requirements of child labor laws.

3.5 Interviewing
Prior to being assigned or appointed to a position, all volunteers will be interviewed to ascertain their suitability for and interest in that position. The interview should determine the qualifications of the volunteer, their commitment to fulfill the requirements of the position, and should answer any questions that the volunteer might have about the position. Interviews may be conducted either in person or by other means.

3.6 Availability of suitable volunteer positions
In cases where the interview does not uncover a suitable position or placement for a volunteer, the appropriate course of action is to recommend that the volunteer seek placement elsewhere.

3.7 Health screening
In cases where volunteers will be working with clients with health difficulties, a health screening procedure may be required prior to confirming the volunteer assignment. In addition, if there are physical requirements necessary for performance of a volunteer task, a screening or testing procedure may be required to ascertain the ability of the volunteer to safely perform that task.

3.8 Criminal records check
As appropriate for the protection of clients, volunteers in certain assignments may be asked to submit to a background criminal record check. Volunteers who do not agree to the background check may be refused assignment.

3.9 Placement with at-risk clients
Where volunteers are to be placed in direct contact with at-risk clients, additional screening procedures may be instituted. These procedures may include reference checks, direct background investigation, criminal investigation, etc. Volunteers who refuse permission for conduct of these checks will not be accepted for placement with clients.

3.10 Certificate of ability
Any potential volunteer who indicates that they are under the care of a doctor for either physical or psychological treatment may be asked to present a certificate from the doctor or medical supervisor as to their ability to satisfactorily and safely perform their volunteer duties. Volunteers under a course of treatment that might affect their volunteer work will not be accepted without written verification of suitability from their doctor. Any volunteer who, after acceptance and assignment by the organization, enters a course of treatment that might adversely impact upon the performance of their volunteer duties should consult with the Volunteer Program Manager.

3.11 Falsification of Information
Falsification of information, including material omission or misrepresentation, on a volunteer application is grounds for immediate dismissal.

3.12 Placement
In placing a volunteer in a position, attention shall be paid to the interests and capabilities of the volunteer and to the requirements of the volunteer position. No placement shall be made unless the requirements of both the volunteer and the supervising staff can be met: no volunteer should be assigned to a "make-work" position and no position should be given to an unqualified or uninterested volunteer.

3.13 Term of work agreement
Volunteers may be asked to sign an agreement as to a designated term of work. This agreement will normally be required of positions for which extensive training is required or positions that involve matching of volunteers with individual clients in one-to-one relationships.

3.14 Staff participation in interviewing and placement
Wherever possible, staff that will be working with the volunteer should participate in the design and conduct of the placement interview. Final assignment of a potential volunteer should not take place without the approval of appropriate staff with whom the volunteer will be working.

3.15 Acceptance and appointment
Service as a volunteer with the organization shall begin with an official notice of acceptance or appointment to a volunteer position. Such notice may only be given by an authorized representative of the organization. This will normally be the Volunteer Program Manager. No volunteer shall begin performance of any position until they have been officially accepted for that position and have completed all necessary screening and paperwork. At the time of final acceptance, each volunteer shall complete all necessary enrollment paperwork and shall receive a copy of their job description and agreement of service with the organization.

3.16 Timing of acceptance
Potential volunteers should be informed of the outcome of their application as expeditiously as possible, preferably within one week. Volunteers should be informed of a projected timeline for determination of their application at the time of their initial interview and updated if processing takes longer than expected. Following acceptance, volunteers should be enabled to begin work as soon as practically possible.

3.17 Probationary period
All volunteer placements shall initially be done on a trial period of 30 days. At the end of this period a second interview with the volunteer shall be conducted, at which point either the volunteer or staff may request a re-assignment of the volunteer to a different position or may determine the unsuitability of the volunteer for a position within the organization. This is a mutual opportunity for assessment of the initial placement.

3.18 Re-assignment
Volunteers who are at any time re-assigned to a new position shall be interviewed for that position and shall receive all appropriate orientation and training for that position before they begin work. In addition, any screening procedures appropriate for that specific position must be completed, even if the volunteer has already been working with the organization.

3.19 Professional services
Volunteers shall not perform professional services for which certification or a license is required unless currently certified or licensed to do so. A copy of such certificate or license will be maintained by the volunteer management department. The volunteer is responsible for providing a current copy of the certificate or license upon its renewal or re-issue. The volunteer is responsible for immediately informing the volunteer management department if such certification or licensing shall cease to be in effect.

3.20 Length of service
All volunteer positions shall have a set term of duration. It is highly recommended that this term shall not be longer than one-year, with an option for renewal at the discretion of both parties. All volunteer assignments shall end at the conclusion of their set term, without expectation or requirement of re-assignment of that position to the incumbent.

Volunteers are neither expected nor required to continue their involvement with the organization at the end of their set term, although in most cases they are welcome to do so. They may instead seek a different volunteer assignment within the organization or with another organization, or may retire from volunteer service.

3.21 Leave of absence
At the discretion of the supervisor, leaves of absence may be granted to volunteers. This leave of absence will not alter or extend the previously agreed upon ending date of the volunteer's term of service.

4. Volunteer Training and Development

4.1 Orientation
All volunteers will receive a general orientation on the nature and purpose of the organization, an orientation on the nature and operation of the program or activity for which they are recruited, and a specific orientation on the purposes and requirements of the position that they are accepting.

4.2 On-the-job training
Volunteers will receive specific on-the-job training to provide them with the information and skills necessary to perform their volunteer assignment. The timing and methods for delivery of such training should be appropriate to the complexity and demands of the position and the capabilities of the volunteer.

4.3 Staff involvement in orientation and training
Staff members with responsibility for delivery of services should have an active role in the design and delivery of both orientation and training of volunteers. Staff who will be in a supervisory capacity to volunteers shall have primary responsibility for design and delivery of on-the-job training to those volunteers assigned to them.

4.4 Volunteer involvement in orientation and training
Experienced volunteers should be included in the design and delivery of volunteer orientation and training.

4.5 Continuing education
Just as with staff, volunteers should attempt to improve their levels of skill during their terms of service. Additional training and educational opportunities will be made available to volunteers during their connection with the organization where deemed appropriate. This continuing education may include both additional information on performance of their current volunteer assignment as well as more general information, and might be provided either by the organization or by assisting the volunteer to participate in educational programs provided by other groups.

4.6 Conference attendance
Volunteers are authorized to attend conferences and meetings that are relevant to their volunteer assignments, including those run by the organization and those run by other organizations. Prior approval from the volunteer's supervisor should be obtained before attending any conference or meeting if attendance will

interfere with the volunteer's work schedule or if reimbursement of expenses is sought.

4.7 Risk management
Volunteers will be informed of any hazardous aspects, materials, equipment, processes or persons that they may encounter while performing volunteer work and will be trained and equipped in methods to deal with all identified risks.

5. Volunteer Supervision and Evaluation

5.1 Requirement of a supervisor
Each volunteer who is accepted to a position with the organization must have a clearly identified supervisor who is responsible for direct management of that volunteer. This supervisor shall be responsible for day-to-day management and guidance of the work of the volunteer, and shall be available to the volunteer for consultation and assistance. The supervisor will have primary responsibility for developing suitable assignments for the volunteer, for involving the volunteer in the communication flow of the agency, and for providing feedback to the volunteer regarding their work. Staff assigned supervisory responsibility for volunteers shall have this responsibility delineated in their job descriptions.

5.2 Volunteers as volunteer supervisors
A volunteer may act as a supervisor of other volunteers, provided that the supervising volunteer is under the direct supervision of a paid member of staff.

5.3 Volunteer-staff relationships
Volunteers and paid staff are considered to be partners in implementing the mission and programs of the organization, with each having an equal but complementary role to play. It is essential to the proper operation of this relationship that each partner understands and respects the needs and abilities of the other.

5.4 Acceptance of volunteers by staff
Since individual staff are in a better position to determine the requirements of their work and their own abilities, no volunteer will be assigned to work with a member of staff without the consent of that person. Since volunteers are considered a valuable resource in performing the organization's work, staff should consider creative ways in which volunteers might be of service to the organization and to consult with the volunteer management department if they feel in need of assistance or additional training. Assignment of volunteers to programs will be at the discretion of the Volunteer Program Manager.

5.5 Volunteer management training for members of staff
An orientation on working with volunteers will be provided to all staff. In-service training on effective volunteer deployment and use will be provided to those staff highly involved in volunteer management.

5.6 Volunteer involvement in staff evaluation
Examination of their effective use of volunteers may be a component in the evaluation of staff performance where that member of staff is working with volunteers. In such cases, supervisors should ask for the input and participation of those volunteers in evaluating staff performance.

5.7 Staff involvement in volunteer evaluation
Affected staff should be involved in any evaluation and in deciding all work assignments of volunteers with whom they are working.

5.8 Evaluation of volunteer/staff teams
Where volunteers and staff are working together in teams they will be evaluated both on their individual performance and on their ability to develop a strong and effective working relationship as a team.

5.9 Lines of communication
Volunteers are entitled to all necessary information pertinent to the performance of their work assignments.

Accordingly, volunteers should be included in and have access to all appropriate information, memos, materials, meetings, and client records relevant to the work assignments. To facilitate the receipt of this information on a timely basis, volunteers should be included on all relevant distribution schedules and should be given a method for receipt of information circulated in their absence. Primary responsibility for ensuring that the volunteer receives such information will rest with the direct supervisor of the volunteer.

Lines of communication should operate in both directions, and should exist both formally and informally. Volunteers should be consulted regarding all decisions that would substantially affect the performance of their duties.

5.10 Absenteeism

Volunteers are expected to perform their duties on a regular scheduled and punctual basis. When expecting to be absent from a scheduled duty, volunteers should inform their staff supervisor as far in advance as possible so that alternative arrangements may be made. Continual absenteeism will result in a review of the volunteer's work assignment or term of service.

5.11 Substitution

Volunteers may be encouraged to find a substitute for any future absences that could be filled by another volunteer. Such substitution should only be taken following consultation with a supervisor, and care should be taken to find a substitute who is qualified for the position. Substitutes may only be recruited from those who are currently enrolled as volunteers with the organization.

5.12 Standards of performance

Standards of performance shall be established for each volunteer position. These standards should list the work to be done in that position, measurable indicators of whether the work was accomplished to the required standards, and appropriate timeframes for accomplishment of the work. Creation of these standards will be a joint function of staff and the volunteer assigned to the position, and a copy of the standards should be provided to the volunteer along with a copy of their job description at the beginning of their assignment.

5.13 Refusal of assignments

Volunteers have the right to refuse any tasks or work, especially where they go beyond those that are outlined in their volunteer position description. It is the responsibility of staff not to make unreasonable demands on volunteers.

5.14 Harassment

A respectful work environment is essential to the wellbeing of both paid and unpaid employees. Harassment of an applicant, employee, volunteer or program participant on the basis of race, religion, color, national origin, ancestry, mental or physical disability, medical condition, political activity, marital status, sexual preference, sex or age will not be tolerated. Harassment includes: verbal harassment, physical harassment, visual forms of harassment, and sexual harassment. All volunteers should speak to their staff supervisor immediately if they are made to feel uncomfortable through any behaviors or comments of participants, staff or other volunteers.

5.15 Alcohol and drugs

All volunteers should report to work fit to perform their responsibilities. The use or possession of alcohol or illegal drugs is strictly prohibited. No volunteer may use, possess, transfer, distribute, manufacture, or sell alcohol or any illegal drug while on the organization's property, while on duty, or while operating a vehicle that is owned by the organization.

Any volunteer who reports for service under the influence of illegal drugs is subject to immediate termination. Any volunteer who reports for service while impaired by the use of alcohol, over-the counter medications, prescription drugs, or other controlled substance is also subject to immediate termination.

5.16 Acceptance of gifts and gratuities
Volunteers are discouraged from accepting gifts, donation or gratuities from participants, clients or members of the community. All such items should be reported immediately to the Volunteer Program Manager.

5.17 Evaluations
Volunteers shall receive periodic evaluation to review their work. The evaluation session will review the performance of the volunteer, suggest any changes in work style, seek suggestions from the volunteer on means of enhancing the volunteer's relationship with the organization, convey appreciation to the volunteer, and ascertain the continued interest of the volunteer in serving in that position. Evaluations should include both an examination of the volunteer's performance of his or her responsibilities and a discussion of any suggestions that the volunteer may have concerning the position or project with which the volunteer is connected.

The evaluation session is an opportunity for both the volunteer and the organization to examine and improve their relationship and effectiveness.

5.18 Written basis for evaluation
The position description and standards of performance for a volunteer position should form the basis of an evaluation. A written record should be kept of each evaluation session.

5.19 Staff responsibility for evaluation
It shall be the responsibility of each member of staff in a supervisory relationship with a volunteer to schedule and perform periodic evaluation and to maintain records of the evaluation.

5.20 Corrective action
In appropriate situations, corrective action may be taken following an evaluation. Examples of corrective action include the requirement for additional training, re-assignment of the volunteer to a new position, suspension of the volunteer, or dismissal from volunteer service.

5.21 Dismissal of a volunteer
Volunteers who do not adhere to the rules and procedures of the organization or who fail satisfactorily to perform a volunteer assignment may be subject to dismissal. No volunteer will be terminated until the volunteer has had an opportunity to discuss the reasons for possible dismissal with supervisory staff. Prior to dismissal of a volunteer, any affected member of staff should seek the consultation and assistance of the Volunteer Program Manager.

5.22 Reasons for dismissal
Possible grounds for dismissal may include, but are not limited to, the following: gross misconduct or insubordination, being under the influence of alcohol or drugs, theft of property or misuse of organization equipment or materials, abuse or mistreatment of clients or co-workers, failure to abide by organization policies and procedures, failure to meet physical or mental standards of performance, and failure satisfactorily to perform assigned duties.

5.23 Injuries
Volunteers should immediately report any injuries sustained while volunteering to their immediate supervisor.

5.24 Concerns and grievances
Decisions involving corrective action of a volunteer may be reviewed for appropriateness. If corrective action is taken, the affected volunteer shall be informed of the procedures for expressing their concern or grievance.

5.25 Notice of departure or re-assignment of a volunteer
In the event that a volunteer departs from the organization, whether voluntarily or involuntarily, or is re-assigned to a new position, it shall be the responsibility of the volunteer management department to inform

those affected staff and clients that the volunteer is no longer assigned to work with them. In cases of dismissal for good reason, this notification should be given in writing and should clearly indicate that any further contact with the volunteer must be outside the scope of any relationship with the organization.

5.26 Resignation
Volunteers may resign from their volunteer service with the organization at any time. It is requested that volunteers who intend to resign provide advance notice of their departure and a reason for their decision.

5.27 Exit interviews
Exit interviews, where possible, should be conducted with volunteers who are leaving their positions. The interview should ascertain why the volunteer is leaving the position, suggestions the volunteer may have to improving the position, and the possibility of involving the volunteer in some other capacity with the organization in the future.

5.28 Communication with the volunteer management department
Staff supervising volunteers are responsible for maintaining regular communication with the volunteer management department on the status of the volunteers they are supervising, and are responsible for the timely provision of all necessary paperwork to the department. The department should be informed immediately of any substantial change in the work or status of a volunteer and should be consulted in advance before any corrective action is taken.

5.29 Evaluation of the organization's volunteer usage
The volunteer management department shall conduct an annual evaluation of the use of volunteers by the organization. This evaluation will include information gathered from volunteers, staff, and clients.

6. Volunteer Support and Recognition

6.1 Reimbursement of expenses
Volunteers may be eligible for reimbursement of reasonable expenses incurred while undertaking business for the organization. The volunteer management department shall distribute information to all volunteers regarding specific reimbursable items. Prior approval must be sought for any major expenditure.

6.2 Access to organization property and materials
As appropriate, volunteers shall have access to property of the organization and those materials necessary to fulfill their duties, and shall receive training in the operation of any equipment. Property and materials shall be used only when directly required for the volunteer task. This policy includes [does not include] access to and use of organization vehicles.

6.3 Insurance
Liability and accident insurance is [is not] provided for all volunteers engaged in the organization's business. [Volunteers are encouraged to consult with their own insurance agents regarding the extension of their personal insurance to include community volunteer work. Specific information regarding such insurance is available from the volunteer management department.]

6.4 Recognition
An annual volunteer recognition event will be conducted to highlight and reward the contribution of volunteers to the organization. Volunteers will be consulted and involved in order to develop an appropriate format for the event.

6.5 Informal recognition
All staff and volunteers responsible for volunteer supervision are encouraged to undertake methods of recognition of volunteer service on a regular basis throughout the year. These methods of informal recognition should range from simple "Thank You's" to a concerted effort to include volunteers as full participants in decision making and implementation for projects which involve the volunteer.

6.6 Volunteer career paths

Volunteers are encouraged to develop their skills while serving with the organization, and are to be assisted through promotion to new volunteer jobs to assume additional and greater responsibilities. If so desired by the volunteer, the organization will assist the volunteer in maintaining appropriate records of volunteer experience that will assist the volunteer in future career opportunities, both paid and volunteer.

6.7 Staff recognition

The volunteer management department shall design recognition systems for staff that work effectively with volunteers, and shall consult with volunteers and staff supervisors to identify appropriate staff to receive such awards.

About the Authors

Steve McCurley

Steve McCurley is an internationally-known trainer and speaker in the field of effective volunteer involvement. He is currently a principal in VM Systems, a management consulting firm specializing in helping organizations improve their utilization of volunteers.

He has served as a consultant on volunteer program development to the American Association of Retired Persons, the National Association of Partners in Education, the US Tennis Association, Special Olympics International, the National Park Service, the Points of Light Foundation and other groups. He is the co-editor with Susan Ellis of the *e-Volunteerism* on-line journal. He is one of the founding faculty of the Institute on Advanced Volunteer Management, held in the United Kingdom each year. He has been involved in most of the innovations in volunteering over the past twenty years, including workplace volunteering, online and family volunteering, and the development of the Volunteer Center network.

He has trained over 500,000 managers of volunteer efforts. He is the author of 15 books and more than 150 articles on volunteer involvement, including the bestselling basic text, *Volunteer Management*.

On the international front, Steve has done work in Canada, Ireland, Germany, the United Kingdom, the Caribbean, Australia and South America. His works on volunteer involvement have been translated into Spanish, Portuguese, Russian, Ukrainian, Hebrew, Chinese and Korean, among other languages.

Steve can be reached at shm12@aol.com.

Rick Lynch

Richard Lynch is a Seattle-based management consultant with a variety of clients in the United States, Canada, England and Russia. He is the President of Lynch Associates, a consulting firm whose mission is to help organizations create work environments which foster commitment and excitement and positive self-esteem.

Each year, Rick speaks at approximately 150 workshops, conventions, and conferences in North America and Europe on topics related to personal growth and management effectiveness. He is the author of the books *Precision Management* and Getting Out of Your Own Way and of a monograph called "Developing Your Leadership Potential." *Lead*, his book on leadership, was published by Jossey-Bass in January 1993.

Before starting his own firm in 1977, Rick worked for five years as a project director and senior trainer for three management consulting firms in New York and Washington, DC. He holds a master's degree from the University of Iowa.

Rick's experience in the field of volunteer management includes work as a volunteer coordinator and as the training director for the Washington State Office of Voluntary Action, where he set up a unique system of delivering management training to volunteer directors through a network of volunteer training organizers. He has served on the boards of directors of a number of non-profit organizations, including a volunteer center, a retired senior volunteer program, a United Way, and national and local literacy programs. He has been a featured speaker on volunteer management at national, international, and state conferences since 1979.

At various times during his career, Rick has served as a reading teacher, a bass player in a blues band, and Chief of a volunteer fire department.

Rick can be reached at rdsl@aol.com.

Volunteer Management:

Mobilizing all the Resources of the Community

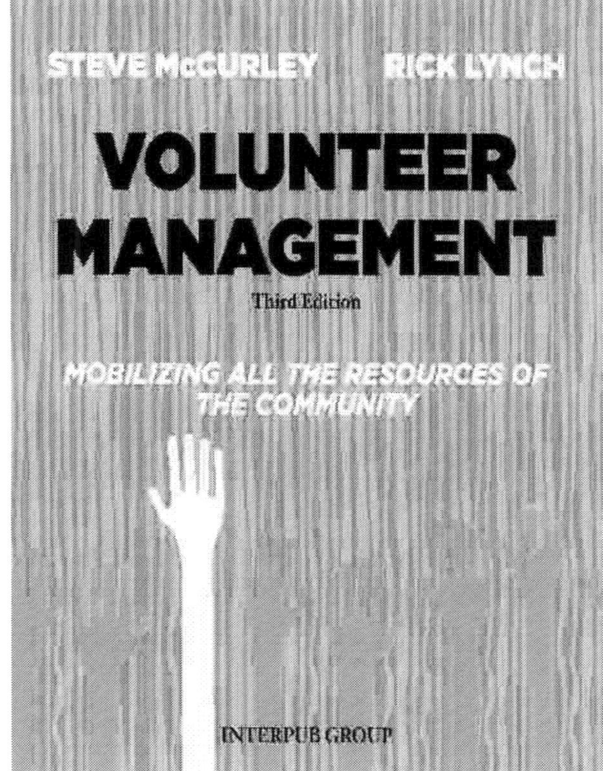

By Steve McCurley and Rick Lynch

THIRD EDITION

Over 100,000 IN USE WORLDWIDE.

Acclaimed as "the Bible of the Volunteer Management field", and used in colleges and universities worldwide in Non-Profit, Volunteer, and Public Administration programs. This is 'the' textbook on the subject; the authors are widely regarded as the "go to" people on all aspects of Volunteer Management.

You can also find this amazing resource on the desks of tens of thousands of Volunteer Managers in organizations large and small all over North America!

This comprehensive text not only instructs, but offers hands on solutions. Answers all the questions: how to involve volunteers in agencies, how to supervise, how to deal with problem volunteers, and much more. Over 150 *more* pages than the last edition! This edition includes eighteen chapters and over *100* pages of Appendices with dozens of reproducible checklists and assessment tools.

UPDATED AND EXPANDED: Packed with information for you and your organization.

- How to structure your volunteer program, complete with ple forms and policies
- How to recruit the right volunteers for even the most difficult assignments
- How to keep volunteers on track and what to do when this fails
- and much more

JTC-VM3 Volunteer Management-*Third* Edition, Softcover, 8 ½ x 11, 425 pages $49.

ISBN: 978-1-895271-63-8

Keeping Volunteers: A Guide to Retention

By Steve McCurley & Rick Lynch

From the bestselling authors of Volunteer Management, leaders in the Volunteer Management field. Here is a detailed manual packed full of critical information on the subject of retaining volunteers. Explains how the volunteer manager can shift resources from recruitment to retention, while understanding what motivates volunteers to stay involved. Have you wondered what creates that sense of fulfillment in a volunteer? Here are coping strategies and most importantly how to recognize and prevent volunteer burnout.

Keeping Volunteers is simply the most thoroughly researched and tested, comprehensive book on retaining volunteers, from the experts who can tell you how to get that job done.

.PARTIAL TABLE OF CONTENTS

JTC-KV1 Keeping Volunteers, Paperback, 8½ x 11, 103 pages **$30.**
ISBN: 978-1-895271-38-6

NON PROFIT BOARDS 'Solutions Series'

Our Comprehensive, Eleven Workbook 'Solutions' Series for Non-Profit Boards

This highly recommended Series meets the needs of Boards of Directors and Officers.

Step by step solutions show how to implement day to day, and broader management, issues, in light of 'Federal' rules and regulations.

From basic recordkeeping, to creating effective policies... Each book in this series includes charts, checklists, numerous examples, recommendations, and plenty of places to insert your own notes, and ideas. Here's an excellent way to have customized workbooks for current and new Board members every year.

- V **Board Responsibilities**
- V **Boards & Fund Raising**
- V **Evaluation Responsibilities of Boards**
- V **Financial Responsibilities of Boards**
- V **Meetings**
- V **Orientation for Boards**
- V **Policy Development**
- V **Risk Management for Boards**
- V **The Role of the Executive Director**
- V **The Role of the President**
- V **Selection & Recruitment of Board Members**

JTC-SSUS-01 "Solutions" Series, *U.S. Edition* $159. (Regularly $219. ***Save $60.***)
JTC-SSCA-01 "Solutions" Series, *Canadian Edition* $159. (Regularly $219. ***Save $60.***)

Titles are available individually for $19.95 each, US or Canadian Editions.

Stand Out When You Stand Up:

An A to Z Guide to Powerful Presentations

By Barbara Busey

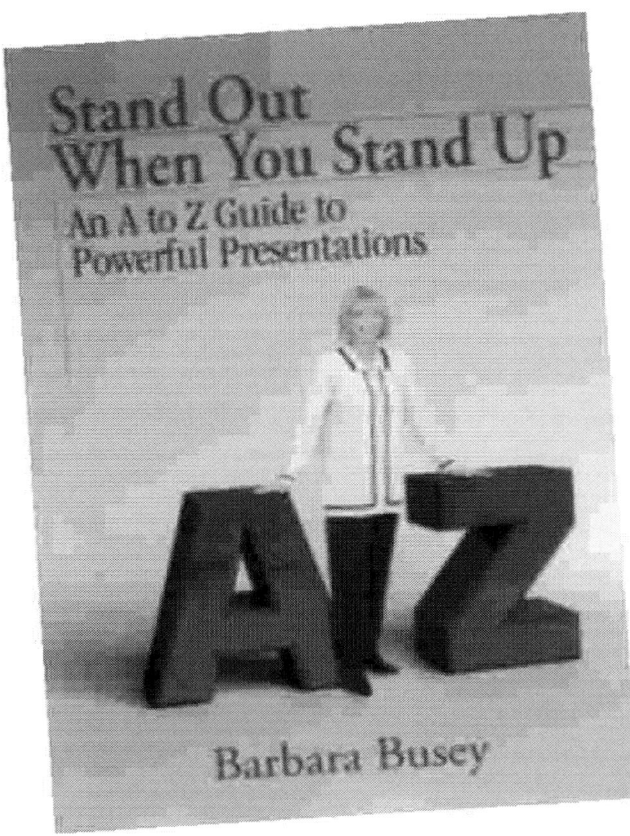

Here's how to add pizzazz to your presentations!

In an easy to use **A** to **Z** format, here are dozens of techniques and tips to make yours the presentation they remember. Consider how often, working in the Non-Profit arena, you need to speak to a group... from Board presentations, to donor and grant presentations... from giving a talk to staff or volunteers, to a speech to the local Chamber of Commerce. Presentation skills are critical if you are to succeed, and quite honestly, on the other hand, nothing is more daunting than the idea of getting up in front of others to speak.

Twenty year professional speaker and motivational trainer Barbara Busey shows you how to not only survive speaking engagements, but thrive on making them! Use these simp ll points to advance your career by being the "go to" person for making presentations and speeches on behalf of your group.

In this hands-on, powerful handbook, you'll learn:

- è **How to minimize anxiety** before and while you speak
- è **The three components** necessary to be a believable speaker
- è **The seven keys** to more dynamic delivery
- è **How to rise above** the challenges presented by a difficult audience
- è **Guidelines for using PowerPoint** and other computer aids

IPG-SOSU1 Stand Out When You Stand Up, 5 ½ x 8 ½, 162 pages...... $17.95